P9-CEV-967

The Unified Modeling Language User Guide

SECOND EDITION

The Addison-Wesley Object Technology Series

Grady Booch, Ivar Jacobson, and James Rumbaugh, Series Editors

For more information, check out the series web site at www.awprofessional.com/otseries.

Ahmed/Umrysh, *Developing Enterprise Java Applications with J2EE™ and UML*

Arlow/Neustadt, *Enterprise Patterns and MDA: Building Better Software with Archetype Patterns and UML*

Arlow/Neustadt, *UML and the Unified Process: Practical Object-Oriented Analysis and Design*

Armour/Miller, *Advanced Use Case Modeling: Software Systems*

Bellin/Simone, *The CRC Card Book*

Bergström/Råberg, *Adopting the Rational Unified Process: Success with the RUP*

Binder, *Testing Object-Oriented Systems: Models, Patterns, and Tools*

Bittner/Spence, *Use Case Modeling*

Booch, *Object Solutions: Managing the Object-Oriented Project*

Booch, *Object-Oriented Analysis and Design with Applications, 2E*

Booch/Bryan, *Software Engineering with ADA, 3E*

Booch/Rumbaugh/Jacobson, *The Unified Modeling Language User Guide*

Box/Brown/Ewald/Sells, *Effective COM: 50 Ways to Improve Your COM and MTS-based Applications*

Carlson, *Modeling XML Applications with UML: Practical e-Business Applications*

Collins, *Designing Object-Oriented User Interfaces*

Conallen, *Building Web Applications with UML, 2E*

D'Souza/Wills, *Objects, Components, and Frameworks with UML: The Catalysis(SM) Approach*

Douglass, *Doing Hard Time: Developing Real-Time Systems with UML, Objects, Frameworks, and Patterns*

Douglass, *Real-Time Design Patterns: Robust Scalable Architecture for Real-Time Systems*

Douglass, *Real Time UML, 3E: Advances in The UML for Real-Time Systems*

Eeles/Houston/Kozaczynski, *Building J2EE™ Applications with the Rational Unified Process*

Fontoura/Pree/Rumpe, *The UML Profile for Framework Architectures*

Fowler, *Analysis Patterns: Reusable Object Models*

Fowler et al., *Refactoring: Improving the Design of Existing Code*

Fowler, *UML Distilled, 3E: A Brief Guide to the Standard Object Modeling Language*

Gomaa, *Designing Concurrent, Distributed, and Real-Time Applications with UML*

Gomaa, *Designing Software Product Lines with UML*

Graham, *Object-Oriented Methods, 3E: Principles and Practice*

Heinckiens, *Building Scalable Database Applications: Object-Oriented Design, Architectures, and Implementations*

Hofmeister/Nord/Dilip, *Applied Software Architecture*

Jacobson/Booch/Rumbaugh, *The Unified Software Development Process*

Jordan, *C++ Object Databases: Programming with the ODMG Standard*

Kleppe/Warmer/Bast, *MDA Explained: The Model Driven Architecture™: Practice and Promise*

Kroll/Kruchten, *The Rational Unified Process Made Easy: A Practitioner's Guide to the RUP*

Kruchten, *The Rational Unified Process, 3E: An Introduction*

Lau, *The Art of Objects: Object-Oriented Design and Architecture*

Leffingwell/Widrig, *Managing Software Requirements, 2E: A Use Case Approach*

Manassis, *Practical Software Engineering: Analysis and Design for the .NET Platform*

Marshall, *Enterprise Modeling with UML: Designing Successful Software through Business Analysis*

McGregor/Sykes, *A Practical Guide to Testing Object-Oriented Software*

Mellor/Balcer, *Executable UML: A Foundation for Model-Driven Architecture*

Mellor et al., *MDA Distilled: Principles of Model-Driven Architecture*

Naiburg/Maksimchuk, *UML for Database Design*

Oestereich, *Developing Software with UML, 2E: Object-Oriented Analysis and Design in Practice*

Page-Jones, *Fundamentals of Object-Oriented Design in UML*

Pohl, *Object-Oriented Programming Using C++, 2E*

Pollice et al. *Software Development for Small Teams: A RUP-Centric Approach*

Quatrani, *Visual Modeling with Rational Rose 2002 and UML*

Rector/Sells, *ATL Internals*

Reed, *Developing Applications with Visual Basic and UML*

Rosenberg/Scott, *Applying Use Case Driven Object Modeling with UML: An Annotated e-Commerce Example*

Rosenberg/Scott, *Use Case Driven Object Modeling with UML: A Practical Approach*

Royce, *Software Project Management: A Unified Framework*

Rumbaugh/Jacobson/Booch, *The Unified Modeling Language Reference Manual*

Schneider/Winters, *Applying Use Cases, 2E: A Practical Guide*

Smith/Williams, *Performance Solutions: A Practical Guide to Creating Responsive, Scalable Software*

Stevens/Pooley, *Using UML, Updated Edition: Software Engineering with Objects and Components*

Unhelkar, *Process Quality Assurance for UML-Based Projects*

van Harmelen, *Object Modeling and User Interface Design: Designing Interactive Systems*

Wake, *Refactoring Workbook*

Warmer/Kleppe, *The Object Constraint Language, 2E: Getting Your Models Ready for MDA*

White, *Software Configuration Management Strategies and Rational ClearCase®: A Practical Introduction*

The Component Software Series

Clemens Szyperski, Series Editor

For more information, check out the series web site at www.awprofessional.com/csseries.

Allen, *Realizing eBusiness with Components*

Apperly et al., *Service- and Component-based Development: Using the Select Perspective™ and UML*

Atkinson et al., *Component-Based Product Line Engineering with UML*

Cheesman/Daniels, *UML Components: A Simple Process for Specifying Component-Based Software*

Szyperski, *Component Software, 2E: Beyond Object-Oriented Programming*

Whitehead, *Component-Based Development: Principles and Planning for Business Systems*

The Unified Modeling Language User Guide

SECOND EDITION

Grady Booch
James Rumbaugh
Ivar Jacobson

Addison-Wesley

Upper Saddle River, NJ • Boston • Indianapolis • San Francisco
New York • Toronto • Montreal • London • Munich • Paris • Madrid
Capetown • Sydney • Tokyo • Singapore • Mexico City

The publisher offers excellent discounts on this book when ordered in quantity for bulk purchases or special sales, which may include electronic versions and/or custom covers and content particular to your business, training goals, marketing focus, and branding interests. For more information, please contact:

U.S. Corporate and Government Sales
(800) 382-3419
corpsales@pearsontechgroup.com

For sales outside the U.S., please contact:

International Sales
international@pearsoned.com

Visit us on the Web: www.awprofessional.com

Library of Congress Cataloging-in-Publication Data
Booch, Grady.
The unified modeling language user guide / Grady Booch, James Rumbaugh, Ivar Jacobson.—2nd ed.
p. cm.
Includes index.
ISBN 0-321-26797-4 (hardcover : alk. paper)
1. Computer software—Development. 2. UML (Computer science) I. Rumbaugh, James. II. Jacobson, Ivar. III. Title.
QA76.76.D47B655 2005
005.1'7—dc22

200505678

The illustrations on pages 1, 207, and 349 are from *A Visual Dictionary of Architecture,* Francis Ching, ©1997 by Van Nostrand Reinhold. Adapted by permission of John Wiley & Sons, Inc. The illustrations on pages 45, 115, 285, and 431 are from *Architecture: Form, Space, and Order, Second Edition,* Francis Ching, ©1996 by Van Nostrand Reinhold. Adapted by permission of John Wiley & Sons, Inc.

ISBN 0-321-26797-4
Text printed in the United States on recycled paper at Courier in Westford, Massachusetts.
First printing, May 2005

To my loving wife, Jan, and my goddaughter, Elyse, both of whom make me whole.

—Grady Booch

CONTENTS

PREFACE

The Unified Modeling Language (UML) is a graphical language for visualizing, specifying, constructing, and documenting the artifacts of a software-intensive system. The UML gives you a standard way to write a system's blueprints, covering conceptual things such as business processes and system functions, as well as concrete things such as classes written in a specific programming language, database schemas, and reusable software components.

This book teaches you how to use the UML effectively.

This book covers UML version 2.0.

Goals

In this book, you will

- Learn what the UML is, what it is not, and why the UML is relevant to the process of developing software-intensive systems.
- Master the vocabulary, rules, and idioms of the UML and, in general, learn how to "speak" the language effectively.
- Understand how to apply the UML to solve a number of common modeling problems.

The user guide provides a reference to the use of specific UML features. However, it is not intended to be a comprehensive reference manual for the UML; that is the focus of another book, *The Unified Modeling Language Reference Manual, Second Edition* (Rumbaugh, Jacobson, Booch, Addison-Wesley, 2005).

The user guide describes a development process for use with the UML. However, it is not intended to provide a complete reference to that process; that is the focus of yet another book, *The Unified Software Development Process* (Jacobson, Booch, Rumbaugh, Addison-Wesley, 1999).

Finally, this book provides hints and tips for using the UML to solve a number of common modeling problems, but it does not teach you how to model. This is similar to a user guide for a programming language that teaches you how to use the language but does not teach you how to program.

Audience

The UML is applicable to anyone involved in the production, deployment, and maintenance of software. The user guide is primarily directed to members of the development team who create UML models. However, it is also suitable to those who read them, working together to understand, build, test, and release a software-intensive system. Although this encompasses almost every role in a software development organization, the user guide is especially relevant to analysts and end users (who specify the required structure and behavior of a system), architects (who design systems that satisfy those requirements), developers (who turn those architectures into executable code), quality assurance personnel (who verify and validate the system's structure and behavior), librarians (who create and catalogue components), and project and program managers (who generally wrestle with chaos, provide leadership and direction, and orchestrate the resources necessary to deliver a successful system).

The user guide assumes a basic knowledge of object-oriented concepts. Experience in an object-oriented programming language or method is helpful but not required.

How to Use This Book

For the developer approaching the UML for the first time, the user guide is best read linearly. You should pay particular attention to Chapter 2, which presents a conceptual model of the UML. All chapters are structured so that each builds upon the content of the previous one, thus forming a linear progression.

For the experienced developer seeking answers to common modeling problems using the UML, this book can be read in any order. You should pay particular attention to the common modeling problems presented in each chapter.

Organization and Special Features

The user guide is organized into seven parts:

- Part 1 Getting Started
- Part 2 Basic Structural Modeling
- Part 3 Advanced Structural Modeling
- Part 4 Basic Behavioral Modeling
- Part 5 Advanced Behavioral Modeling
- Part 6 Architectural Modeling
- Part 7 Wrapping Up

The user guide contains two appendices: a summary of the UML notation and a summary of the Rational Unified Process. A glossary of common terms is also provided. An index follows.

Each chapter addresses the use of a specific UML feature, and most are organized into the following four sections:

1. Getting Started
2. Terms and Concepts
3. Common Modeling Techniques
4. Hints and Tips

The third section introduces and then solves a set of common modeling problems. To make it easy for you to browse the guide in search of these use cases for the UML, each problem is identified by a distinct heading, as in the following example.

Modeling Architectural Patterns

Each chapter begins with a summary of the features it covers, as in the following example.

In this chapter

- Active objects, processes, and threads
- Modeling multiple flows of control
- Modeling interprocess communication
- Building thread-safe abstractions

Similarly, parenthetical comments and general guidance are set apart as notes, as in the following example.

Note: Abstract operations map to what C++ calls pure virtual operations; leaf operations in the UML map to C++ nonvirtual operations.

Components are discussed in Chapter 25.

The UML is semantically rich. Therefore, a presentation about one feature may naturally involve another. In such cases, cross references are provided in the left margin, as on this page.

Blue highlights are used in figures to indicate explanations about a model, as opposed to the model itself, which is always shown in black. Code is distinguished by displaying it in a monospace font, as in `this example`.

Acknowledgement. The authors wish to thank Bruce Douglass, Per Krol, and Joaquin Miller for their assistance in reviewing the manuscript of the second edition.

A Brief History of the UML

The first object-oriented language is generally acknowledged to be Simula-67, developed by Dahl and Nygaard in Norway in 1967. This language never had a large following, but its concepts were a major inspiration for later languages. Smalltalk became widely available in the early 1980s, followed by other object-oriented languages such as Objective C, C++, and Eiffel in the late 1980s. Object-oriented modeling languages appeared in the 1980s as methodologists, faced with a new genre of object-oriented programming languages and increasingly complex applications, began to experiment with alternative approaches to analysis and design. The number of object-oriented methods increased from fewer than 10 to more than 50 during the period between 1989 and 1994. Many users of these methods had trouble finding a modeling language that met their needs completely, thus fueling the so-called method wars. A few methods gained prominence, including Booch's method, Jacobson's OOSE (Object-Oriented Software Engineering), and Rumbaugh's OMT (Object Modeling Technique). Other important methods included Fusion, Shlaer-Mellor, and Coad-Yourdon. Each of these was a complete method, although each was recognized as having strengths and weaknesses. In simple terms, the Booch method was particularly expressive during the design and construction phases of projects; OOSE provided excellent support for use cases as a way to drive requirements capture, analysis, and high-level design; and OMT was most useful for analysis and data-intensive information systems.

A critical mass of ideas started to form by the mid 1990s when Grady Booch (Rational Software Corporation), James Rumbaugh (General Electric), Ivar Jacobson (Objectory), and others began to adopt ideas from each other's methods, which collectively were becoming recognized as the leading object-oriented methods worldwide. As the primary authors of the Booch, OMT, and OOSE methods, we were motivated to create a unified modeling language for three reasons. First, our methods were already evolving toward each other independently. It made sense to continue that evolution together rather than apart, eliminating the potential for any unnecessary and gratuitous differences that would further confuse users. Second, by unifying our methods, we could bring some stability to the object-oriented marketplace, allowing projects to settle on one mature modeling language and letting tool builders focus on delivering more useful features. Third, we expected that our collaboration would yield improvements for all three earlier methods, helping us to capture lessons learned and to address problems that none of our methods previously handled well.

As we began our unification, we established three goals for our work:

1. To model systems, from concept to executable artifact, using object-oriented techniques
2. To address the issues of scale inherent in complex, mission-critical systems
3. To create a modeling language usable by both humans and machines

Devising a language for use in object-oriented analysis and design is not unlike designing a programming language. First, we had to constrain the problem: Should the language encompass requirements specification? Should the language be sufficient to permit visual programming? Second, we had to strike a balance between expressiveness and simplicity. Too simple a language would limit the breadth of problems that could be solved; too complex a language would overwhelm the mortal developer. In the case of unifying existing methods, we also had to be sensitive to the installed base. Make too many changes and we would confuse existing users; resist advancing the language and we would miss the opportunity to engage a much broader set of users and to make the language simpler. The UML definition strives to make the best trade-offs in each of these areas.

The UML effort started officially in October 1994 when Rumbaugh joined Booch at Rational. Our project's initial focus was the unification of the Booch and OMT methods. The version 0.8 draft of the Unified Method (as it was then called) was released in October 1995. Around the same time, Jacobson joined Rational and the scope of the UML project was expanded to incorporate OOSE. Our efforts resulted in the release of the UML version 0.9 documents in June 1996. Throughout 1996, we invited and received feedback from the general software engineering community. During this time, it also became clear that many software organizations saw the UML as strategic to their business. We established a UML consortium, with several organizations willing to dedicate resources to work toward a strong and complete UML definition. Those partners contributing to the UML 1.0 definition included Digital Equipment Corporation, Hewlett-Packard, I-Logix, Intellicorp, IBM, ICON Computing, MCI Systemhouse, Microsoft, Oracle, Rational, Texas Instruments, and Unisys. This collaboration resulted in the UML 1.0, a modeling language that was well-defined, expressive, powerful, and applicable to a wide spectrum of problem domains. Mary Loomis was instrumental in convincing the Object Management Group (OMG) to issue a request for proposals (RFP) for a standard modeling language. UML 1.0 was offered for standardization to the OMG in January 1997 in response to their RFP.

Between January 1997 and July 1997, the original group of partners was expanded to include virtually all of the other submitters and contributors of the original OMG response, including Andersen Consulting, Ericsson, ObjecTime Limited, Platinum Technology, PTech, Reich Technologies, Softeam, Sterling Software, and Taskon. A semantics task force was formed, led by Cris Kobryn of MCI Systemhouse and administered by Ed Eykholt of Rational, to formalize the UML specification and to integrate the UML with other standardization efforts. A revised version of the UML (version 1.1) was offered to the OMG for standardization in July 1997. In September 1997, this version was accepted by the OMG Analysis and Design Task Force (ADTF) and the OMG Architecture Board and then put up for vote by the entire OMG membership. UML 1.1 was adopted by the OMG on November 14, 1997.

For several years, UML was maintained by an OMG Revision Task Force, which produced versions 1.3, 1.4, and 1.5. From 2000 to 2003, a new and expanded set of partners produced an updated specification of UML, version 2.0. This version was reviewed for a year by a Finalization Task Force (FTF) headed by Bran Selic of IBM, and the official version of UML 2.0 was adopted by the OMG in early 2005. UML 2.0 is a major revision of UML 1 and includes a large number of additional features. In addition, many changes were made to previous constructs based on experience with the previous version. The actual UML specification documents are found on the OMG Website at www.omg.org.

UML is the work of a large number of individuals, and the ideas in it come from a wide range of previous works. It would be a major historical research project to reconstruct a complete list of sources, and even more difficult to identify the many predecessors who have influenced UML in manners large and small. As with all scientific research and engineering practice, UML is a small hill atop a large mountain of previous experience.

Part 1
GETTING STARTED

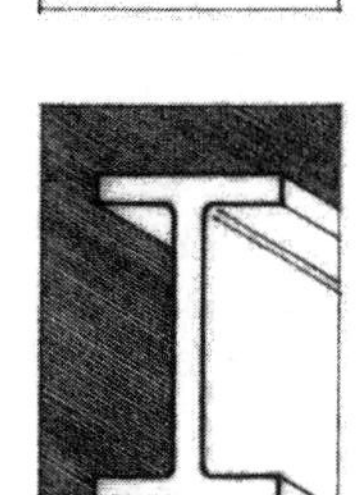

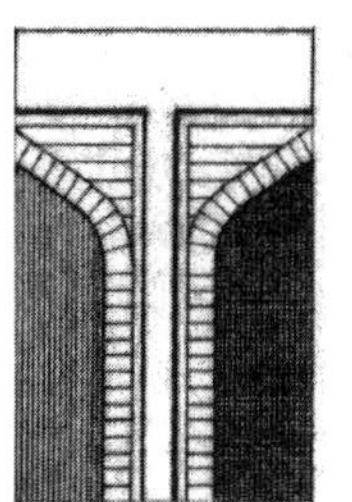
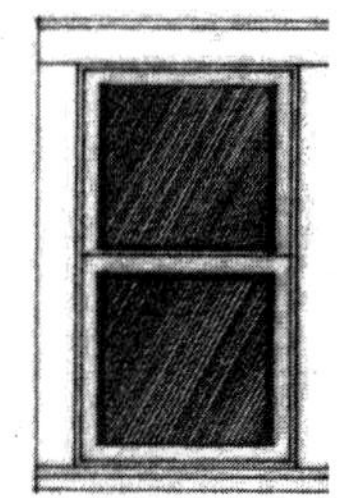

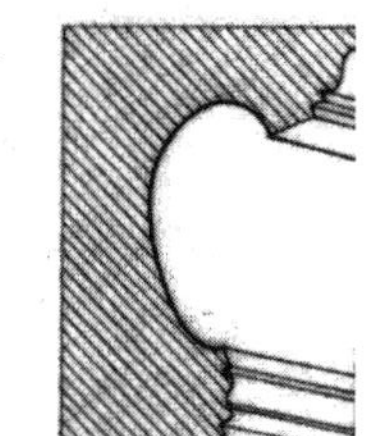

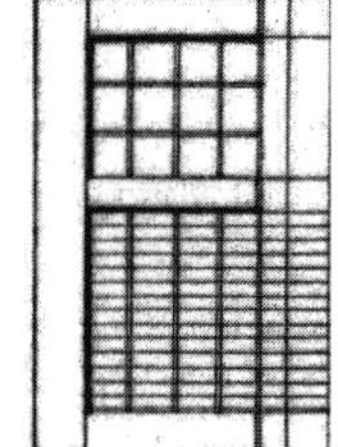
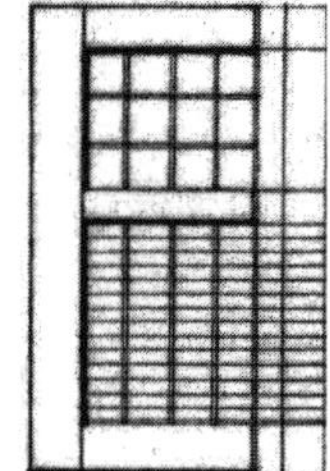

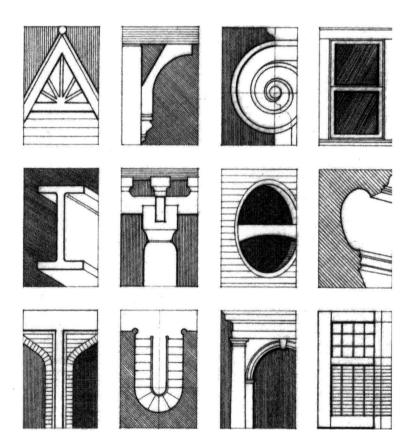

Chapter 1
Why We Model

In this chapter

- The importance of modeling
- Four principles of modeling
- The essential blueprints of a software system
- Object-oriented modeling

A successful software organization is one that consistently deploys quality software that meets the needs of its users. An organization that can develop such software in a timely and predictable fashion, with an efficient and effective use of resources, both human and material, is one that has a sustainable business.

There's an important implication in this message: The primary product of a development team is not beautiful documents, world-class meetings, great slogans, or Pulitzer prize–winning lines of source code. Rather, it is good software that satisfies the evolving needs of its users and the business. Everything else is secondary.

Unfortunately, many software organizations confuse "secondary" with "irrelevant." To deploy software that satisfies its intended purpose, you have to meet and engage users in a disciplined fashion, to expose the real requirements of your system. To develop software of lasting quality, you have to craft a solid architectural foundation that's resilient to change. To develop software rapidly, efficiently, and effectively, with a minimum of software scrap and rework, you need to have the right people, the right tools, and the right focus. To do all this consistently and predictably, with an appreciation for the lifetime costs of the system, you must have a sound development process that can adapt to the changing needs of your business and technology.

Modeling is a central part of all the activities that lead up to the deployment of good software. We build models to communicate the desired structure and behavior of our system. We build models to visualize and control the system's architecture. We build models to better understand the system we are building, often exposing opportunities for simplification and reuse. And we build models to manage risk.

The Importance of Modeling

If you want to build a dog house, you can pretty much start with a pile of lumber, some nails, and a few basic tools such as a hammer, saw, and tape measure. In a few hours, with little prior planning, you'll likely end up with a dog house that's reasonably functional, and you can probably do it with no one else's help. As long as it's big enough and doesn't leak too much, your dog will be happy. If it doesn't work out, you can always start over, or get a less demanding dog.

If you want to build a house for your family, you can start with a pile of lumber, some nails, and a few basic tools, but it's going to take you a lot longer, and your family will certainly be more demanding than the dog. In this case, unless you've already done it a few dozen times before, you'll be better served by doing some detailed planning before you pound the first nail or lay the foundation. At the very least, you'll want to make some sketches of how you want the house to look. If you want to build a quality house that meets the needs of your family and of local building codes, you'll need to draw some blueprints as well, so that you can think through the intended use of the rooms and the practical details of lighting, heating, and plumbing. Given these plans, you can start to make reasonable estimates of the amount of time and materials this job will require. Although it is humanly possible to build a house yourself, you'll find it is much more efficient to work with others, possibly subcontracting out many key work products or buying pre-built materials. As long as you stay true to your plans and stay within the limitations of time and money, your family will most likely be satisfied. If it doesn't work out, you can't exactly get a new family, so it is best to set expectations early and manage change carefully.

If you want to build a high-rise office building, it would be infinitely stupid for you to start with a pile of lumber, some nails, and a few basic tools. Because you are probably using other people's money, they will insist upon having input into the size, shape, and style of the building. Often, they will change their minds, even after you've started building. You will want to do extensive planning, because the cost of failure is high. You will be just a part of a much larger group responsible for developing and deploying the building, so the team will need all sorts of blueprints and models to communicate with one another. As long as you get the right people and the right tools and actively manage the process of transforming an architectural concept into reality, you will likely end up with a building that will satisfy its tenants. If you want to keep constructing buildings, then you will want to be certain to balance the desires of your tenants with the realities of building technology, and you will want to treat the rest of your team professionally, never placing them at any risk or driving them so hard that they burn out.

Curiously, a lot of software development organizations start out wanting to build high rises but approach the problem as if they were knocking out a dog house.

Sometimes, you get lucky. If you have the right people at the right moment and if all the planets align properly, then you might, just might, get your team to push out a software product that dazzles its users. Typically, however, you can't get all the right people (the right ones are often already overcommitted), it's never the right moment (yesterday would have been better), and the planets never seem to align (instead, they keep moving out of your control). Given the increasing demand to develop software quickly, development teams often fall back on the only thing they really know how to do well—pound out lines of code. Heroic programming efforts are legend in this industry, and it often seems that working harder is the proper reaction to any crisis in development. However, these are not necessarily the right lines of code, and some projects are of such a magnitude that even adding more hours to the workday is not enough to get the job done.

If you really want to build the software equivalent of a house or a high rise, the problem is more than just a matter of writing lots of software—in fact, the trick is in creating the right software and in figuring out how to write less software. This makes quality software development an issue of architecture and process and tools. Even so, many projects start out looking like dog houses but grow to the magnitude of a high rise simply because they are a victim of their own success. There comes a time when, if there was no consideration given to architecture, process, or tools, the dog house, now grown into a high rise, collapses of its own weight. The collapse of a dog house may annoy your dog; the failure of a high rise will materially affect its tenants.

Unsuccessful software projects fail in their own unique ways, but all successful projects are alike in many ways. There are many elements that contribute to a successful software organization; one common thread is the use of modeling.

Modeling is a proven and well-accepted engineering technique. We build architectural models of houses and high rises to help their users visualize the final product. We may even build mathematical models to analyze the effects of winds or earthquakes on our buildings.

Modeling is not just a part of the building industry. It would be inconceivable to deploy a new aircraft or an automobile without first building models—from computer models to physical wind tunnel models to full-scale prototypes. New electrical devices, from microprocessors to telephone switching systems, require some degree of modeling in order to better understand the system and to communicate those ideas to others. In the motion picture industry, storyboarding, which is a form of modeling, is central to any production. In the fields of sociology, economics, and business management, we build models so that we can validate our theories or try out new ones with minimal risk and cost.

What, then, is a model? Simply put,

> *A model is a simplification of reality.*

A model provides the blueprints of a system. Models may encompass detailed plans, as well as more general plans that give a 30,000-foot view of the system under consideration. A good model includes those elements that have broad effect and omits those minor elements that are not relevant to the given level of abstraction. Every system may be described from different aspects using different models, and each model is therefore a semantically closed abstraction of the system. A model may be structural, emphasizing the organization of the system, or it may be behavioral, emphasizing the dynamics of the system.

Why do we model? There is one fundamental reason.

> *We build models so that we can better understand the system we are developing.*

Through modeling, we achieve four aims.

How UML addresses these four things is discussed in Chapter 2.

1. Models help us to visualize a system as it is or as we want it to be.
2. Models permit us to specify the structure or behavior of a system.
3. Models give us a template that guides us in constructing a system.
4. Models document the decisions we have made.

Modeling is not just for big systems. Even the software equivalent of a dog house can benefit from some modeling. However, it's definitely true that the larger and more complex the system, the more important modeling becomes, for one very simple reason:

We build models of complex systems because we cannot comprehend such a system in its entirety.

There are limits to the human ability to understand complexity. Through modeling, we narrow the problem we are studying by focusing on only one aspect at a time. This is essentially the approach of "divide-and-conquer" that Edsger Dijkstra spoke of years ago: Attack a hard problem by dividing it into a series of smaller problems that you can solve. Furthermore, through modeling, we amplify the human intellect. A model properly chosen can enable the modeler to work at higher levels of abstraction.

Saying that one ought to model does not necessarily make it so. In fact, a number of studies suggest that most software organizations do little if any formal modeling. Plot the use of modeling against the complexity of a project and you'll find that the simpler the project, the less likely it is that formal modeling will be used.

The operative word here is "formal." In reality, in even the simplest project, developers do some amount of modeling, albeit very informally. A developer might sketch out an idea on a blackboard or a scrap of paper to visualize a part of a system, or the team might use CRC cards to work through a scenario or the design of a mechanism. There's nothing wrong with any of these models. If it works, by all means use it. However, these informal models are often *ad hoc* and do not provide a common language that can easily be shared with others. Just as there exists a common language of blueprints for the construction industry, a common language for electrical engineering, and a common language for mathematical modeling, so too can a development organization benefit by using a common language for software modeling.

Every project can benefit from some modeling. Even in the realm of disposable software, where it's sometimes more effective to throw away inadequate software because of the productivity offered by visual programming languages, modeling can help the development team better visualize the plan of their system and allow them to develop more rapidly by helping them build the right thing. The more complex your project, the more likely it is that you will fail or that you will build the wrong thing if you do no modeling at all. All interesting and useful systems have a natural tendency to become more complex over time. So, although you might think you don't need to model today, as your system evolves you will regret that decision, after it is too late.

Principles of Modeling

The use of modeling has a rich history in all the engineering disciplines. That experience suggests four basic principles of modeling. First,

> *The choice of what models to create has a profound influence on how a problem is attacked and how a solution is shaped.*

In other words, choose your models well. The right models will brilliantly illuminate the most wicked development problems, offering insight that you simply could not gain otherwise; the wrong models will mislead you, causing you to focus on irrelevant issues.

Setting aside software for a moment, suppose you are trying to tackle a problem in quantum physics. Certain problems, such as the interaction of photons in space-time, are full of wonderfully hairy mathematics. Choose a different model and suddenly this inherent complexity becomes doable, if not exactly easy. In this field, this is precisely the value of Feynmann diagrams, which provide a graphical rendering of a very complex problem. Similarly, in a totally different domain, suppose you are constructing a new building and you are concerned about how it might behave in high winds. If you build a physical model and then subject it to wind tunnel tests, you might learn some interesting things, although materials in the small don't flex exactly as they do in the large. Hence, if you build a mathematical model and then subject it to simulations, you will learn some different things, and you will also probably be able to play with more new scenarios than if you were using a physical model. By rigorously and continuously testing your models, you'll end up with a far higher level of confidence that the system you have modeled will behave as you expect it to in the real world.

In software, the models you choose can greatly affect your world view. If you build a system through the eyes of a database developer, you will likely focus on entity-relationship models that push behavior into triggers and stored procedures. If you build a system through the eyes of a structured analyst, you will likely end up with models that are algorithmic-centric, with data flowing from process to process. If you build a system through the eyes of an object-oriented developer, you'll end up with a system whose architecture is centered around a sea of classes and the patterns of interaction that direct how those classes work together. Executable models can greatly help testing. Any of these approaches might be right for a given application and development culture, although experience suggests that the object-oriented view is superior in crafting resilient architectures, even for systems that might have a large database or computational element. That fact notwithstanding, the point is that each world view leads to a different kind of system, with different costs and benefits.

Second,

Every model may be expressed at different levels of precision.

If you are building a high rise, sometimes you need a 30,000-foot view—for instance, to help your investors visualize its look and feel. Other times, you need to get down to the level of the studs—for instance, when there's a tricky pipe run or an unusual structural element.

The same is true with software models. Sometimes a quick and simple executable model of the user interface is exactly what you need; at other times you have to get down and dirty with the bits, such as when you are specifying cross-system interfaces or wrestling with networking bottlenecks. In any case, the best kinds of models are those that let you choose your degree of detail, depending on who is doing the viewing and why they need to view it. An analyst or an end user will want to focus on issues of what; a developer will want to focus on issues of how. Both of these stakeholders will want to visualize a system at different levels of detail at different times.

Third,

The best models are connected to reality.

A physical model of a building that doesn't respond in the same way as do real materials has only limited value; a mathematical model of an aircraft that assumes only ideal conditions and perfect manufacturing can mask some potentially fatal characteristics of the real aircraft. It's best to have models that have a clear connection to reality, and where that connection is weak, to know exactly how those models are divorced from the real world. All models simplify reality; the trick is to be sure that your simplifications don't mask any important details.

In software, the Achilles' heel of structured analysis techniques is the fact that there is a basic disconnect between its analysis model and the system's design model. Failing to bridge this chasm causes the system as conceived and the system as built to diverge over time. In object-oriented systems, it is possible to connect all the nearly independent views of a system into one semantic whole.

Fourth,

No single model or view is sufficient. Every nontrivial system is best approached through a small set of nearly independent models with multiple viewpoints.

If you are constructing a building, there is no single set of blueprints that reveal all its details. At the very least, you'll need floor plans, elevations, electrical plans, heating plans, and plumbing plans. And within any kind of model, you need multiple views to capture the breadth of the system, such as blueprints of different floors.

The operative phrase here is "nearly independent." In this context, it means having models that can be built and studied separately but that are still interrelated. As in the case of a building, you can study electrical plans in isolation, but you can also see how they map to the floor plan and perhaps even their interaction with the routing of pipes in the plumbing plan.

The five views of an architecture are discussed in Chapter 2.

The same is true of object-oriented software systems. To understand the architecture of such a system, you need several complementary and interlocking views: a use case view (exposing the requirements of the system), a design view (capturing the vocabulary of the problem space and the solution space), an interaction view (showing the interactions among the parts of the system and between the system and the environment), an implementation view (addressing the physical realization of the system), and a deployment view (focusing on system engineering issues). Each of these views may have structural, as well as behavioral, aspects. Together, these views represent the blueprints of software.

Depending on the nature of the system, some views may be more important than others. For example, in data-intensive systems, views addressing static design will dominate. In GUI-intensive systems, static and dynamic use case views are quite important. In hard real time systems, dynamic process views tend to be more important. Finally, in distributed systems, such as one finds in Web-intensive applications, implementation and deployment models are the most important.

Object-Oriented Modeling

Civil engineers build many kinds of models. Most commonly, there are structural models that help people visualize and specify parts of systems and the way those parts relate to one another. Depending on the most important business or engineering concerns, engineers might also build dynamic models—for instance, to help them to study the behavior of a structure in the presence of an earthquake. Each kind of model is organized differently, and each has its own focus. In software, there are several ways to approach a model. The two most common ways are from an algorithmic perspective and from an object-oriented perspective.

The traditional view of software development takes an algorithmic perspective. In this approach, the main building block of all software is the procedure or function. This view leads developers to focus on issues of control and the decomposition of larger algorithms into smaller ones. There's nothing inherently evil about such a point of view except that it tends to yield brittle systems. As requirements change (and they will) and the system grows (and it will), systems built with an algorithmic focus turn out to be very hard to maintain.

The contemporary view of software development takes an object-oriented perspective. In this approach, the main building block of all software systems is the object or class. Simply put, an object is a thing, generally drawn from the vocabulary of the problem space or the solution space. A class is a description of a set of objects that are similar enough (from the modeler's viewpoint) to share a specification. Every object has identity (you can name it or otherwise distinguish it from other objects), state (there's generally some data associated with it), and behavior (you can do things to the object, and it can do things to other objects as well).

For example, consider a simple three-tier architecture for a billing system, involving a user interface, business services, and a database. In the user interface, you will find concrete objects, such as buttons, menus, and dialog boxes. In the database, you will find concrete objects, such as tables representing entities from the problem domain, including customers, products, and orders. In the middle layer, you will find objects such as transactions and business rules, as well as higher-level views of problem entities, such as customers, products, and orders.

The object-oriented approach to software development is decidedly a part of the mainstream simply because it has proven to be of value in building systems in all sorts of problem domains and encompassing all degrees of size and complexity. Furthermore, most contemporary languages, operating systems, and tools are object-oriented in some fashion, giving greater cause to view the world in terms of objects. Object-oriented development provides the conceptual foundation for assembling systems out of components using technology such as J2EE or .NET.

These questions are discussed in Chapter 2.

A number of consequences flow from the choice of viewing the world in an object-oriented fashion: What is the structure of a good object-oriented architecture? What artifacts should the project create? Who should create them? How should they be measured?

Visualizing, specifying, constructing, and documenting object-oriented systems is exactly the purpose of the Unified Modeling Language.

Chapter 2

INTRODUCING THE UML

In this chapter

- Overview of the UML
- Three steps to understanding the UML
- Software architecture
- The software development process

The Unified Modeling Language (UML) is a standard language for writing software blueprints. The UML may be used to visualize, specify, construct, and document the artifacts of a software-intensive system.

The UML is appropriate for modeling systems ranging from enterprise information systems to distributed Web-based applications and even to hard real time embedded systems. It is a very expressive language, addressing all the views needed to develop and then deploy such systems. Even though it is expressive, the UML is not difficult to understand and to use. Learning to apply the UML effectively starts with forming a conceptual model of the language, which requires learning three major elements: the UML's basic building blocks, the rules that dictate how these building blocks may be put together, and some common mechanisms that apply throughout the language.

The UML is only a language, so it is just one part of a software development method. The UML is process independent, although optimally it should be used in a process that is use case driven, architecture-centric, iterative, and incremental.

An Overview of the UML

The UML is a language for

- Visualizing
- Specifying
- Constructing
- Documenting

the artifacts of a software-intensive system.

The UML Is a Language

A language provides a vocabulary and the rules for combining words in that vocabulary for the purpose of communication. A *modeling* language is a language whose vocabulary and rules focus on the conceptual and physical representation of a system. A modeling language such as the UML is thus a standard language for software blueprints.

The basic principles of modeling are discussed in Chapter 1.

Modeling yields an understanding of a system. No one model is ever sufficient. Rather, you often need multiple models that are connected to one another to understand anything but the most trivial system. For software-intensive systems, this requires a language that addresses the different views of a system's architecture as it evolves throughout the software development life cycle.

The vocabulary and rules of a language such as the UML tell you how to create and read well-formed models, but they don't tell you what models you should create and when you should create them. That's the role of the software development process. A well-defined process will guide you in deciding what artifacts to produce, what activities and what workers to use to create them and manage them, and how to use those artifacts to measure and control the project as a whole.

The UML Is a Language for Visualizing

For many programmers, the distance between thinking of an implementation and then pounding it out in code is close to zero. You think it, you code it. In fact, some things are best cast directly in code. Text is a wonderfully minimal and direct way to write expressions and algorithms.

In such cases, the programmer is still doing some modeling, albeit entirely mentally. He or she may even sketch out a few ideas on a white board or on a napkin. However, there are several problems with this. First, communicating those conceptual models to others is error-prone unless everyone involved speaks the same language. Typically, projects and organizations develop their own language, and it is difficult to understand what's going on if you are an outsider or new to the group. Second, there are some things about a software system you can't understand unless you build models that transcend the textual programming language. For example, the meaning of a class hierarchy can be inferred, but not directly grasped, by staring at the code for all the classes in the hierarchy. Similarly, the physical distribution and possible migration of the objects in a Web-based system can be inferred, but not directly grasped, by studying the system's code. Third, if the developer who cut the code never wrote down the models that are in his or her head, that information would be lost forever or, at best, only partially recreatable from the implementation once that developer moved on.

Writing models in the UML addresses the third issue: An explicit model facilitates communication.

Some things are best modeled textually; others are best modeled graphically. Indeed, in all interesting systems, there are structures that transcend what can be represented in a programming language. The UML is such a graphical language. This addresses the second problem described earlier.

The complete semantics of the UML are discussed in The Unified Modeling Language Reference Manual.

The UML is more than just a bunch of graphical symbols. Rather, behind each symbol in the UML notation is a well-defined semantics. In this manner, one developer can write a model in the UML, and another developer, or even another tool, can interpret that model unambiguously. This addresses the first issue described earlier.

The UML Is a Language for Specifying

In this context, *specifying* means building models that are precise, unambiguous, and complete. In particular, the UML addresses the specification of all the important analysis, design, and implementation decisions that must be made in developing and deploying a software-intensive system.

The UML Is a Language for Constructing

The UML is not a visual programming language, but its models can be directly connected to a variety of programming languages. This means that it is possible to map from a model in the UML to a programming language such as Java, C++, or Visual Basic, or even to tables in a relational database or the persistent store of an object-oriented database. Things that are best expressed graphically are done so graphically in the UML, whereas things that are best expressed textually are done so in the programming language.

Modeling the structure of a system is discussed in Parts 2 and 3.

This mapping permits forward engineering—the generation of code from a UML model into a programming language. The reverse is also possible: You can reconstruct a model from an implementation back into the UML. Reverse engineering is not magic. Unless you encode that information in the implementation, information is lost when moving forward from models to code. Reverse engineering thus requires tool support with human intervention. Combining these two paths of forward code generation and reverse engineering yields round-trip engineering, meaning the ability to work in either a graphical or a textual view, while tools keep the two views consistent.

Modeling the behavior of a system is discussed in Parts 4 and 5.

In addition to this direct mapping, the UML is sufficiently expressive and unambiguous to permit the direct execution of models, the simulation of systems, and the instrumentation of running systems.

The UML Is a Language for Documenting

A healthy software organization produces all sorts of artifacts in addition to raw executable code. These artifacts include (but are not limited to)

- Requirements
- Architecture
- Design
- Source code
- Project plans
- Tests
- Prototypes
- Releases

Depending on the development culture, some of these artifacts are treated more or less formally than others. Such artifacts are not only the deliverables of a project, they are also critical in controlling, measuring, and communicating about a system during its development and after its deployment.

The UML addresses the documentation of a system's architecture and all of its details. The UML also provides a language for expressing requirements and for tests. Finally, the UML provides a language for modeling the activities of project planning and release management.

Where Can the UML Be Used?

The UML is intended primarily for software-intensive systems. It has been used effectively for such domains as

- Enterprise information systems
- Banking and financial services
- Telecommunications
- Transportation
- Defense/aerospace
- Retail
- Medical electronics
- Scientific
- Distributed Web-based services

The UML is not limited to modeling software. In fact, it is expressive enough to model nonsoftware systems, such as workflow in the legal system, the structure and behavior of a patient healthcare system, software engineering in aircraft combat systems, and the design of hardware.

A Conceptual Model of the UML

To understand the UML, you need to form a conceptual model of the language, and this requires learning three major elements: the UML's basic building blocks, the rules that dictate how those building blocks may be put together, and some common mechanisms that apply throughout the UML. Once you have grasped these ideas, you will be able to read UML models and create some basic ones. As you gain more experience in applying the UML, you can build on this conceptual model, using more advanced features of the language.

Building Blocks of the UML

The vocabulary of the UML encompasses three kinds of building blocks:

1. Things
2. Relationships
3. Diagrams

Things are the abstractions that are first-class citizens in a model; relationships tie these things together; diagrams group interesting collections of things.

Things in the UML There are four kinds of things in the UML:

1. Structural things
2. Behavioral things
3. Grouping things
4. Annotational things

These things are the basic object-oriented building blocks of the UML. You use them to write well-formed models.

Structural Things *Structural things* are the nouns of UML models. These are the mostly static parts of a model, representing elements that are either conceptual or physical. Collectively, the structural things are called *classifiers*.

Classes are discussed in Chapters 4 and 9.

A *class* is a description of a set of objects that share the same attributes, operations, relationships, and semantics. A class implements one or more interfaces. Graphically, a class is rendered as a rectangle, usually including its name, attributes, and operations, as in Figure 2-1.

Window
origin size
open() close() move() display()

Figure 2-1: Classes

Interfaces are discussed in Chapter 11.

An *interface* is a collection of operations that specify a service of a class or component. An interface therefore describes the externally visible behavior of that element. An interface might represent the complete behavior of a class or component or only a part of that behavior. An interface defines a set of operation specifications (that is, their signatures) but never a set of operation implementations. The declaration of an interface looks like a class with the keyword «interface» above the name; attributes are not relevant, except sometimes to show constants. An interface rarely stands alone, however. An interface provided by a class to the outside world is shown as a small circle attached to the class box by a line. An interface required by a class from some other class is shown as a small semicircle attached to the class box by a line, as in Figure 2-2.

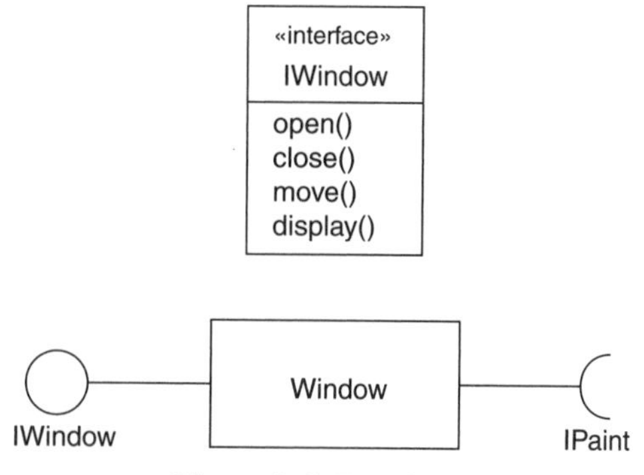

Figure 2-2: Interfaces

Collaborations are discussed in Chapter 28.

A *collaboration* defines an interaction and is a society of roles and other elements that work together to provide some cooperative behavior that's bigger than the sum of all the elements. Collaborations have structural, as well as behavioral, dimensions. A given class or object might participate in several collaborations. These collaborations therefore represent the implementation of patterns that make up a system. Graphically, a collaboration is rendered as an ellipse with dashed lines, sometimes including only its name, as in Figure 2-3.

Figure 2-3: Collaborations

Use cases are discussed in Chapter 17.

A *use case* is a description of sequences of actions that a system performs that yield observable results of value to a particular actor. A use case is used to structure the behavioral things in a model. A use case is realized by a collaboration. Graphically, a use case is rendered as an ellipse with solid lines, usually including only its name, as in Figure 2-4.

Figure 2-4: Use Cases

The remaining three things—active classes, components, and nodes—are all class-like, meaning they also describe sets of entities that share the same attributes, operations, relationships, and semantics. However, these three are different enough and are necessary for modeling certain aspects of an object-oriented system, so they warrant special treatment.

Active classes are discussed in Chapter 23.

An *active class* is a class whose objects own one or more processes or threads and therefore can initiate control activity. An active class is just like a class except that its objects represent elements whose behavior is concurrent with other elements. Graphically, an active class is rendered as a class with double lines on the left and right; it usually includes its name, attributes, and operations, as in Figure 2-5.

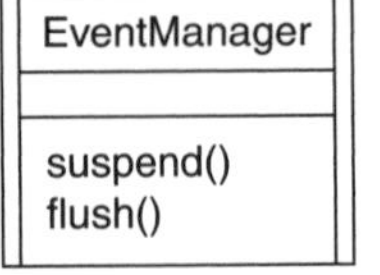

Figure 2-5: Active Classes

Components and internal structure are discussed in Chapter 15.

A component is a modular part of the system design that hides its implementation behind a set of external interfaces. Within a system, components sharing the same interfaces can be substituted while preserving the same logical behavior. The implementation of a component can be expressed by wiring together parts and connectors; the parts can include smaller components. Graphically, a component is rendered like a class with a special icon in the upper right corner, as in Figure 2-6.

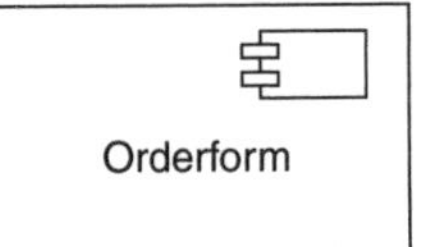

Figure 2-6: Components

The remaining two elements—artifacts and nodes—are also different. They represent physical things, whereas the previous five things represent conceptual or logical things.

Artifacts are discussed in Chapter 26.

An *artifact* is a physical and replaceable part of a system that contains physical information ("bits"). In a system, you'll encounter different kinds of deployment artifacts, such as source code files, executables, and scripts. An artifact typically represents the physical packaging of source or run-time information. Graphically, an artifact is rendered as a rectangle with the keyword «artifact» above the name, as in Figure 2-7.

«artifact»
window.dll

Figure 2-7: Artifacts

Nodes are discussed in Chapter 27.

A *node* is a physical element that exists at run time and represents a computational resource, generally having at least some memory and, often, processing capability. A set of components may reside on a node and may also migrate from node to node. Graphically, a node is rendered as a cube, usually including only its name, as in Figure 2-8.

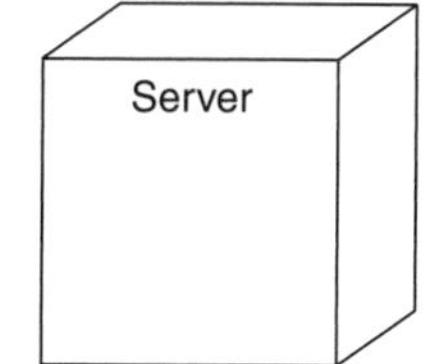

Figure 2-8: Nodes

These elements—classes, interfaces, collaborations, use cases, active classes, components, artifacts, and nodes—are the basic structural things that you may include in a UML model. There are also variations on these, such as actors, signals, and utilities (kinds of classes); processes and threads (kinds of active classes); and applications, documents, files, libraries, pages, and tables (kinds of artifacts).

Use cases, which are used to structure the behavioral things in a model, are discussed in Chapter 17; interactions are discussed in Chapter 16.

Behavioral Things *Behavioral things* are the dynamic parts of UML models. These are the verbs of a model, representing behavior over time and space. In all, there are three primary kinds of behavioral things.

First, an *interaction* is a behavior that comprises a set of messages exchanged among a set of objects or roles within a particular context to accomplish a specific purpose. The behavior of a society of objects or of an individual operation may be specified with an interaction. An interaction involves a number of other elements, including messages, actions, and connectors (the connection between objects). Graphically, a message is rendered as a directed line, almost always including the name of its operation, as in Figure 2-9.

Figure 2-9: Messages

State machines are discussed in Chapter 22.

Second, a *state machine* is a behavior that specifies the sequences of states an object or an interaction goes through during its lifetime in response to events, together with its responses to those events. The behavior of an individual class or a collaboration of classes may be specified with a state machine. A state machine involves a number of other elements, including states, transitions (the flow from state to state), events (things that trigger a transition), and activities (the response to a transition). Graphically, a state is rendered as a rounded rectangle, usually including its name and its substates, if any, as in Figure 2-10.

Figure 2-10: States

Third, an activity is a behavior that specifies the sequence of steps a computational process performs. In an interaction, the focus is on the set of objects that interact. In a state machine, the focus is on the life cycle of one object at a time. In an activity, the focus is on the flows among steps without regard to which object performs each step. A step of an activity is called an *action.* Graphically, an action is rendered as a rounded rectangle with a name indicating its purpose. States and actions are distinguished by their different contexts.

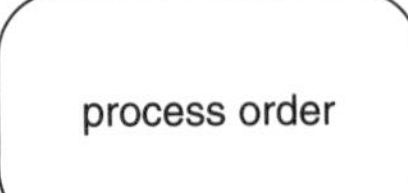

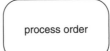

Figure 2-11: Actions

These three elements—interactions, state machines, and activities—are the basic behavioral things that you may include in a UML model. Semantically, these elements are usually connected to various structural elements, primarily classes, collaborations, and objects.

Grouping Things *Grouping things* are the organizational parts of UML models. These are the boxes into which a model can be decomposed. There is one primary kind of grouping thing, namely, packages.

Packages are discussed in Chapter 12.

A *package* is a general-purpose mechanism for organizing the design itself, as opposed to classes, which organize implementation constructs. Structural things, behavioral things, and even other grouping things may be placed in a package. Unlike components (which exist at run time), a package is purely conceptual (meaning that it exists only at development time). Graphically, a package is rendered as a tabbed folder, usually including only its name and, sometimes, its contents, as in Figure 2-12.

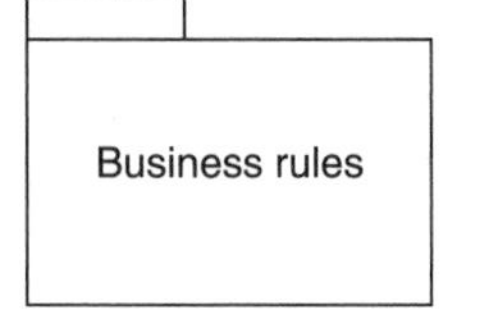

Figure 2-12: Packages

Packages are the basic grouping things with which you may organize a UML model. There are also variations, such as frameworks, models, and subsystems (kinds of packages).

Notes are discussed in Chapter 6.

Annotational Things *Annotational things* are the explanatory parts of UML models. These are the comments you may apply to describe, illuminate, and remark about any element in a model. There is one primary kind of annotational thing, called a note. A *note* is simply a symbol for rendering constraints and comments attached to an element or a collection of elements. Graphically, a note is rendered as a rectangle with a dog-eared corner, together with a textual or graphical comment, as in Figure 2-13.

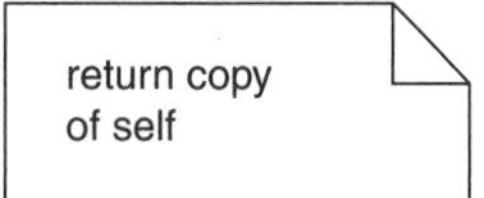

Figure 2-13: Notes

This element is the one basic annotational thing you may include in a UML model. You'll typically use notes to adorn your diagrams with constraints or comments that are best expressed in informal or formal text. There are also variations on this element, such as requirements (which specify some desired behavior from the perspective of outside the model).

Relationships in the UML There are four kinds of relationships in the UML:

1. Dependency
2. Association
3. Generalization
4. Realization

These relationships are the basic relational building blocks of the UML. You use them to write well-formed models.

Dependencies are discussed in Chapters 5 and 10.

First, a *dependency* is a semantic relationship between two model elements in which a change to one element (the independent one) may affect the semantics of the other element (the dependent one). Graphically, a dependency is rendered as a dashed line, possibly directed, and occasionally including a label, as in Figure 2-14.

Figure 2-14: Dependencies

Associations are discussed in Chapters 5 and 10.

Second, an *association* is a structural relationship among classes that describes a set of links, a link being a connection among objects that are instances of the classes. Aggregation is a special kind of association, representing a structural relationship between a whole and its parts. Graphically, an association is rendered as a solid line, possibly directed, occasionally including a label, and often containing other adornments, such as multiplicity and end names, as in Figure 2-15.

Figure 2-15: Associations

Generalizations are discussed in Chapters 5 and 10.

Third, a *generalization* is a specialization/generalization relationship in which the specialized element (the child) builds on the specification of the generalized element (the parent). The child shares the structure and the behavior of the parent. Graphically, a generalization relationship is rendered as a solid line with a hollow arrowhead pointing to the parent, as in Figure 2-16.

Figure 2-16: Generalizations

Realizations are discussed in Chapter 10.

Fourth, a *realization* is a semantic relationship between classifiers, wherein one classifier specifies a contract that another classifier guarantees to carry out. You'll encounter realization relationships in two places: between interfaces and the classes or components that realize them, and between use cases and the collaborations that realize them. Graphically, a realization relationship is rendered as a cross between a generalization and a dependency relationship, as in Figure 2-17.

Figure 2-17: Realizations

These four elements are the basic relational things you may include in a UML model. There are also variations on these four, such as refinement, trace, include, and extend.

The five views of an architecture are discussed later in this chapter.

Diagrams in the UML A *diagram* is the graphical presentation of a set of elements, most often rendered as a connected graph of vertices (things) and paths (relationships). You draw diagrams to visualize a system from different perspectives, so a diagram is a projection into a system. For all but the most trivial systems, a diagram represents an elided view of the elements that make up a system. The same element may appear in all diagrams, only a few diagrams (the most common case), or in no diagrams at all (a very rare case). In theory, a diagram may contain any combination of things and relationships. In practice, however, a small number of common combinations arise, which are consistent with the five most useful views that comprise the architecture of a software-intensive system. For this reason, the UML includes thirteen kinds of diagrams:

1. Class diagram
2. Object diagram
3. Component diagram
4. Composite structure diagram
5. Use case diagram
6. Sequence diagram
7. Communication diagram
8. State diagram
9. Activity diagram
10. Deployment diagram
11. Package diagram
12. Timing diagram
13. Interaction overview diagram

Class diagrams are discussed in Chapter 8.

A *class diagram* shows a set of classes, interfaces, and collaborations and their relationships. These diagrams are the most common diagram found in modeling object-oriented systems. Class diagrams address the static design view of a system. Class diagrams that include active classes address the static process view of a system. Component diagrams are variants of class diagrams.

Object diagrams are discussed in Chapter 14.

An *object diagram* shows a set of objects and their relationships. Object diagrams represent static snapshots of instances of the things found in class diagrams. These diagrams address the static design view or static process view of a system as do class diagrams, but from the perspective of real or prototypical cases.

Component diagrams and internal structure are discussed in Chapter 15.

A *component diagram* is shows an encapsulated class and its interfaces, ports, and internal structure consisting of nested components and connectors. Component diagrams address the static design implementation view of a system. They are important for building large systems from smaller parts. (UML distinguishes a *composite structure diagram*, applicable to any class, from a component diagram, but we combine the discussion because the distinction between a component and a structured class is unnecessarily subtle.)

Use case diagrams are discussed in Chapter 18.

A *use case diagram* shows a set of use cases and actors (a special kind of class) and their relationships. Use case diagrams address the static use case view of a system. These diagrams are especially important in organizing and modeling the behaviors of a system.

Interaction diagrams are discussed in Chapter 19.

Both sequence diagrams and communication diagrams are kinds of interaction diagrams. An *interaction diagram* shows an interaction, consisting of a set of objects or roles, including the messages that may be dispatched among them. Interaction diagrams address the dynamic view of a system. A *sequence diagram* is an interaction diagram that emphasizes the time-ordering of messages; a *communication diagram* is an interaction diagram that emphasizes the structural organization of the objects or roles that send and receive messages. Sequence diagrams and communication diagrams represent similar basic concepts, but each diagram emphasizes a different view of the concepts. Sequence diagrams emphasize temporal ordering, and communication diagrams emphasize the data structure through which messages flow. A *timing diagram* (not covered in this book) shows the actual times at which messages are exchanged.

State diagrams are discussed in Chapter 25.

A *state diagram* shows a state machine, consisting of states, transitions, events, and activities. A state diagrams shows the dynamic view of an object. They are especially important in modeling the behavior of an interface, class, or collaboration and emphasize the event-ordered behavior of an object, which is especially useful in modeling reactive systems.

Activity diagrams are discussed in Chapter 20.

An *activity diagram* shows the structure of a process or other computation as the flow of control and data from step to step within the computation. Activity diagrams address the dynamic view of a system. They are especially important in modeling the function of a system and emphasize the flow of control among objects.

Deployment diagrams are discussed in Chapter 31.

A *deployment diagram* shows the configuration of run-time processing nodes and the components that live on them. Deployment diagrams address the static deployment view of an architecture. A node typically hosts one or more artifacts.

Artifact diagrams are discussed in Chapter 30.

An *artifact diagram* shows the physical constituents of a system on the computer. Artifacts include files, databases, and similar physical collections of bits. Artifacts are often used in conjunction with deployment diagrams. Artifacts also show the classes and components that they implement. (UML treats artifact diagrams as a variety of deployment diagram, but we discuss them separately.)

Package diagrams are discussed in Chapter 12.

A *package diagram* shows the decomposition of the model itself into organization units and their dependencies.

A *timing diagram* is an interaction diagram that shows actual times across different objects or roles, as opposed to just relative sequences of messages. An *interaction overview diagram* is a hybrid of an activity diagram and a sequence diagram. These diagrams have specialized uses and so are not discussed in this book. See the *UML Reference Manual* for more details.

This is not a closed list of diagrams. Tools may use the UML to provide other kinds of diagrams, although these are the most common ones that you will encounter in practice.

Rules of the UML

The UML's building blocks can't simply be thrown together in a random fashion. Like any language, the UML has a number of rules that specify what a well-formed model should look like. A *well-formed model* is one that is semantically self-consistent and in harmony with all its related models.

The UML has syntactic and semantic rules for

- Names What you can call things, relationships, and diagrams
- Scope The context that gives specific meaning to a name
- Visibility How those names can be seen and used by others
- Integrity How things properly and consistently relate to one another
- Execution What it means to run or simulate a dynamic model

Models built during the development of a software-intensive system tend to evolve and may be viewed by many stakeholders in different ways and at different times. For this reason, it is common for the development team to not only build models that are well-formed, but also to build models that are

- Elided Certain elements are hidden to simplify the view
- Incomplete Certain elements may be missing
- Inconsistent The integrity of the model is not guaranteed

These less-than-well-formed models are unavoidable as the details of a system unfold and churn during the software development life cycle. The rules of the UML encourage you—but do not force you—to address the most important analysis, design, and implementation questions that push such models to become well-formed over time.

Common Mechanisms in the UML

A building is made simpler and more harmonious by the conformance to a pattern of common features. A house may be built in the Victorian or French country style largely by using certain architectural patterns that define those styles. The same is true of the UML. It is made simpler by the presence of four common mechanisms that apply consistently throughout the language.

1. Specifications
2. Adornments
3. Common divisions
4. Extensibility mechanisms

Specifications The UML is more than just a graphical language. Rather, behind every part of its graphical notation there is a specification that provides a textual statement of the syntax and semantics of that building block. For example, behind a class icon is a specification that provides the full set of attributes, operations (including their full signatures), and behaviors that the class embodies; visually, that class icon might only show a small part of this specification. Furthermore, there might be another view of that class that presents a completely different set of parts yet is still consistent with the class's underlying specification. You use the UML's graphical notation to visualize a system; you use the UML's specification to state the system's details. Given this split, it's possible to build up a model incrementally by drawing diagrams and then adding semantics to the model's specifications, or directly by creating a specification, perhaps by reverse engineering an existing system, and then creating diagrams that are projections into those specifications.

The UML's specifications provide a semantic backplane that contains all the parts of all the models of a system, each part related to one another in a consistent fashion. The UML's diagrams are thus simply visual projections into that backplane, each diagram revealing a specific interesting aspect of the system.

Notes and other adornments are discussed in Chapter 6.

Adornments Most elements in the UML have a unique and direct graphical notation that provides a visual representation of the most important aspects of the element. For example, the notation for a class is intentionally designed to be easy to draw, because classes are the most common element found in modeling object-oriented systems. The class notation also exposes the most important aspects of a class, namely its name, attributes, and operations.

A class's specification may include other details, such as whether it is abstract or the visibility of its attributes and operations. Many of these details can be rendered as graphical or textual adornments to the class's basic rectangular notation. For example, Figure 2-18 shows a class, adorned to indicate that it is an abstract class with two public, one protected, and one private operation.

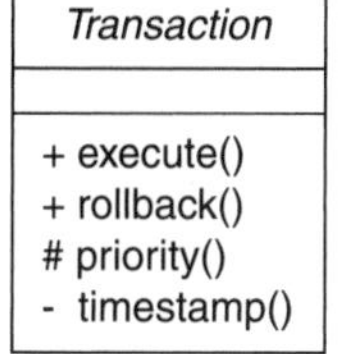

Figure 2-18: Adornments

Every element in the UML's notation starts with a basic symbol, to which can be added a variety of adornments specific to that symbol.

Common Divisions In modeling object-oriented systems, the world often gets divided in several ways.

Objects are discussed in Chapter 13.

First, there is the division of class and object. A class is an abstraction; an object is one concrete manifestation of that abstraction. In the UML, you can model classes as well as objects, as shown in Figure 2-19. Graphically, the UML distinguishes an object by using the same symbol as its class and then simply underlying the object's name.

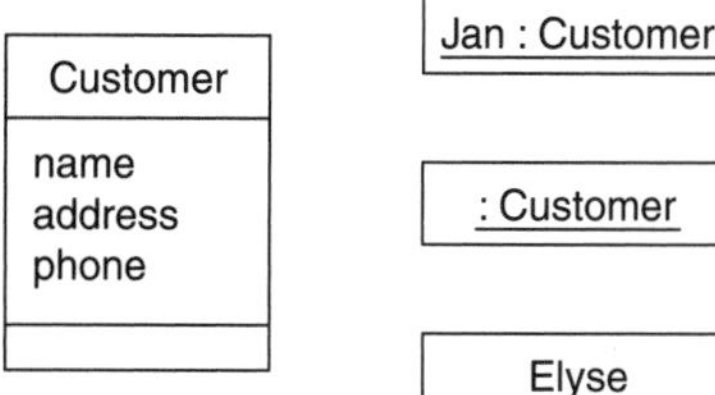

Figure 2-19: Classes and Objects

In this figure, there is one class, named `Customer`, together with three objects: `Jan` (which is marked explicitly as being a `Customer` object), `:Customer` (an anonymous `Customer` object), and `Elyse` (which in its specification is marked as being a kind of `Customer` object, although it's not shown explicitly here).

Almost every building block in the UML has this same kind of class/object dichotomy. For example, you can have use cases and use case executions, components and component instances, nodes and node instances, and so on.

Interfaces are discussed in Chapter 11.

Second, there is the separation of interface and implementation. An interface declares a contract, and an implementation represents one concrete realization of that contract, responsible for faithfully carrying out the interface's complete semantics. In the UML, you can model both interfaces and their implementations, as shown in Figure 2-20.

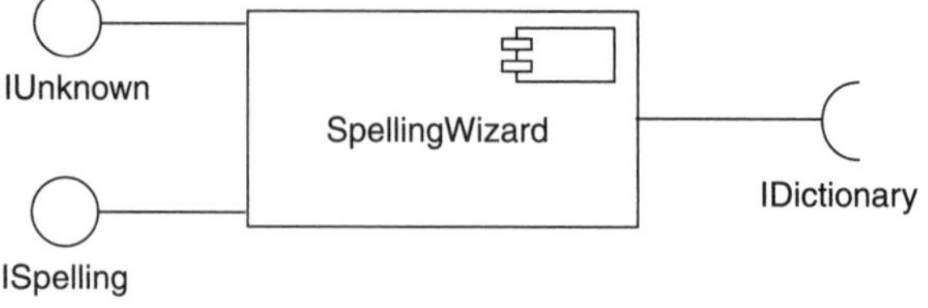

Figure 2-20: Interfaces and Implementations

In this figure, there is one component named `SpellingWizard.dll` that provides (implements) two interfaces, `IUnknown` and `ISpelling`. It also requires an interface, `IDictionary`, that must be provided by another component.

Almost every building block in the UML has this same kind of interface/implementation dichotomy. For example, you can have use cases and the collaborations that realize them, as well as operations and the methods that implement them.

Third, there is the separation of type and role. The type declares the class of an entity, such as an object, an attribute, or a parameter. A role describes the meaning of an entity within its context, such as a class, component, or collaboration. Any entity that forms part of the structure of another entity, such as an attribute, has both characteristics: It derives some of its meaning from its inherent type and some of its meaning from its role within its context (Figure 2-21).

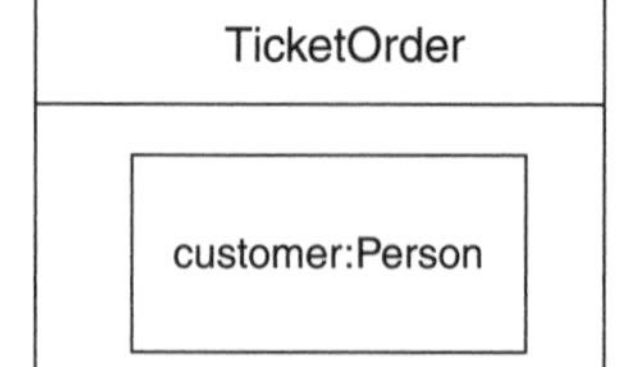

Figure 2-21: Part with role and type

The UML's extensibility mechanisms are discussed in Chapter 6.

Extensibility Mechanisms The UML provides a standard language for writing software blueprints, but it is not possible for one closed language to ever be sufficient to express all possible nuances of all models across all domains across all time. For this reason, the UML is opened-ended, making it possible for you to extend the language in controlled ways. The UML's extensibility mechanisms include

- Stereotypes
- Tagged values
- Constraints

A *stereotype* extends the vocabulary of the UML, allowing you to create new kinds of building blocks that are derived from existing ones but that are specific to your problem. For example, if you are working in a programming language, such as Java or C++, you will often want to model exceptions. In these languages, exceptions are just classes, although they are treated in very special ways. Typically, you only want to allow them to be thrown and caught, nothing else. You can make exceptions first-class citizens in your models—meaning that they are treated like basic building blocks—by marking them with an appropriate stereotype, as for the class `Overflow` in Figure 2-19.

A *tagged value* extends the properties of a UML stereotype, allowing you to create new information in the stereotype's specification. For example, if you are working on a shrink-wrapped product that undergoes many releases over time, you often want to track the version and author of certain critical abstractions. Version and author are not primitive UML concepts. They can be added to any building block, such as a class, by introducing new tagged values to that building block. In Figure 2-19, for example, the class `EventQueue` is extended by marking its version and author explicitly.

A *constraint* extends the semantics of a UML building block, allowing you to add new rules or modify existing ones. For example, you might want to constrain the `EventQueue` class so that all additions are done in order. As Figure 2-22 shows, you can add a constraint that explicitly marks these for the operation `add`.

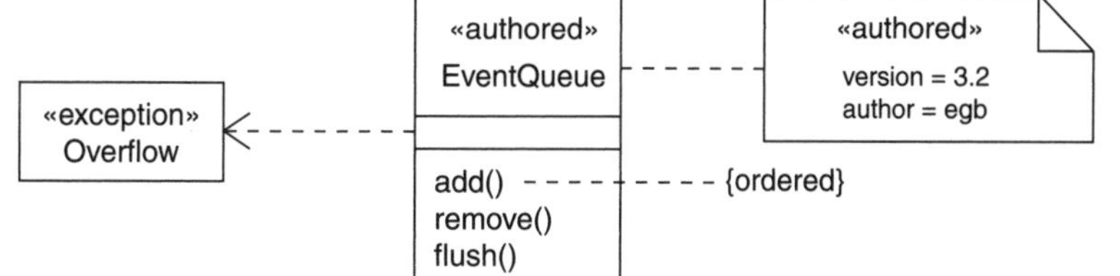

Figure 2-22: Extensibility Mechanisms

Collectively, these three extensibility mechanisms allow you to shape and grow the UML to your project's needs. These mechanisms also let the UML adapt to new software technology, such as the likely emergence of more powerful distributed programming languages. You can add new building blocks, modify the specification of existing ones, and even change their semantics. Naturally, it's important that you do so in controlled ways so that through these extensions, you remain true to the UML's purpose—the communication of information.

Architecture

The need for viewing complex systems from different perspectives is discussed in Chapter 1.

Visualizing, specifying, constructing, and documenting a software-intensive system demands that the system be viewed from a number of perspectives. Different stakeholders—end users, analysts, developers, system integrators, testers, technical writers, and project managers—each bring different agendas to a project, and each looks at that system in different ways at different times over the project's life. A system's architecture is perhaps the most important artifact that can be used to manage these different viewpoints and thus control the iterative and incremental development of a system throughout its life cycle.

Architecture is the set of significant decisions about

- The organization of a software system
- The selection of the structural elements and their interfaces by which the system is composed
- Their behavior, as specified in the collaborations among those elements
- The composition of these structural and behavioral elements into progressively larger subsystems
- The architectural style that guides this organization: the static and dynamic elements and their interfaces, their collaborations, and their composition

Software architecture is not only concerned with structure and behavior but also with usage, functionality, performance, resilience, reuse, comprehensibility, economic and technology constraints and trade-offs, and aesthetic concerns.

Modeling the architecture of a system is discussed in Chapter 32.

As Figure 2-23 illustrates, the architecture of a software-intensive system can best be described by five interlocking views. Each view is a projection into the organization and structure of the system, focused on a particular aspect of that system.

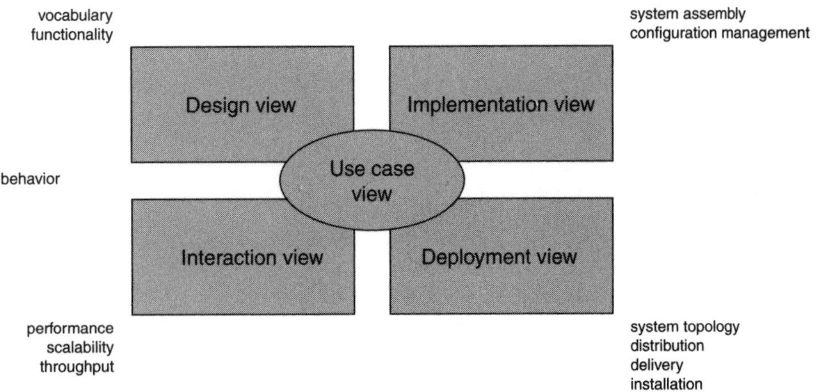

Figure 2-23: Modeling a System's Architecture

The *use case view* of a system encompasses the use cases that describe the behavior of the system as seen by its end users, analysts, and testers. This view doesn't really specify the organization of a software system. Rather, it exists to specify the forces that shape the system's architecture. With the UML, the static aspects of this view are captured in use case diagrams; the dynamic aspects of this view are captured in interaction diagrams, state diagrams, and activity diagrams.

The *design view* of a system encompasses the classes, interfaces, and collaborations that form the vocabulary of the problem and its solution. This view primarily supports the functional requirements of the system, meaning the services that the system should provide to its end users. With the UML, the static aspects of this view are captured in class diagrams and object diagrams; the dynamic aspects of this view are captured in interaction diagrams, state diagrams, and activity diagrams. The internal structure diagram of a class is particularly useful.

The *interaction view* of a system shows the flow of control among its various parts, including possible concurrency and synchronization mechanisms. This view primarily addresses the performance, scalability, and throughput of the system. With the UML, the static and dynamic aspects of this view are captured in the same kinds of diagrams as for the design view, but with a focus on the active classes that control the system and the messages that flow between them.

The *implementation view* of a system encompasses the artifacts that are used to assemble and release the physical system. This view primarily addresses the configuration management of the system's releases, made up of somewhat independent files that can be assembled in various ways to produce a running system. It is also concerned with the mapping from logical classes and components to physical artifacts. With the UML, the static aspects of this view are captured in artifact diagrams; the dynamic aspects of this view are captured in interaction diagrams, state diagrams, and activity diagrams.

The *deployment view* of a system encompasses the nodes that form the system's hardware topology on which the system executes. This view primarily addresses the distribution, delivery, and installation of the parts that make up the physical system. With the UML, the static aspects of this view are captured in deployment diagrams; the dynamic aspects of this view are captured in interaction diagrams, state diagrams, and activity diagrams.

Each of these five views can stand alone so that different stakeholders can focus on the issues of the system's architecture that most concern them. These five views also interact with one another: Nodes in the deployment view hold components in the implementation view that, in turn, represent the physical realization of classes, interfaces, collaborations, and active classes from the design and process views. The UML permits you to express each of these five views.

Software Development Life Cycle

The Rational Unified Process is summarized in Appendix B; a more complete treatment of this process is discussed in The Unified Software Development Process *and* The Rational Unified Process.

The UML is largely process-independent, meaning that it is not tied to any particular software development life cycle. However, to get the most benefit from the UML, you should consider a process that is

- Use case driven
- Architecture-centric
- Iterative and incremental

Use case driven means that use cases are used as a primary artifact for establishing the desired behavior of the system, for verifying and validating the system's architecture, for testing, and for communicating among the stakeholders of the project.

Architecture-centric means that a system's architecture is used as a primary artifact for conceptualizing, constructing, managing, and evolving the system under development.

An *iterative process* is one that involves managing a stream of executable releases. An *incremental process* is one that involves the continuous integration of the system's architecture to produce these releases, with each new release embodying incremental improvements over the other. Together, an iterative and incremental process is *risk-driven*, meaning that each new release is focused on attacking and reducing the most significant risks to the success of the project.

This use case driven, architecture-centric, and iterative/incremental process can be broken into phases. A *phase* is the span of time between two major milestones of the process, when a well-defined set of objectives are met, artifacts are completed, and decisions are made whether to move into the next phase. As Figure 2-24 shows, there are four phases in the software development life cycle: inception, elaboration, construction, and transition. In the diagram, workflows are plotted against these phases, showing their varying degrees of focus over time.

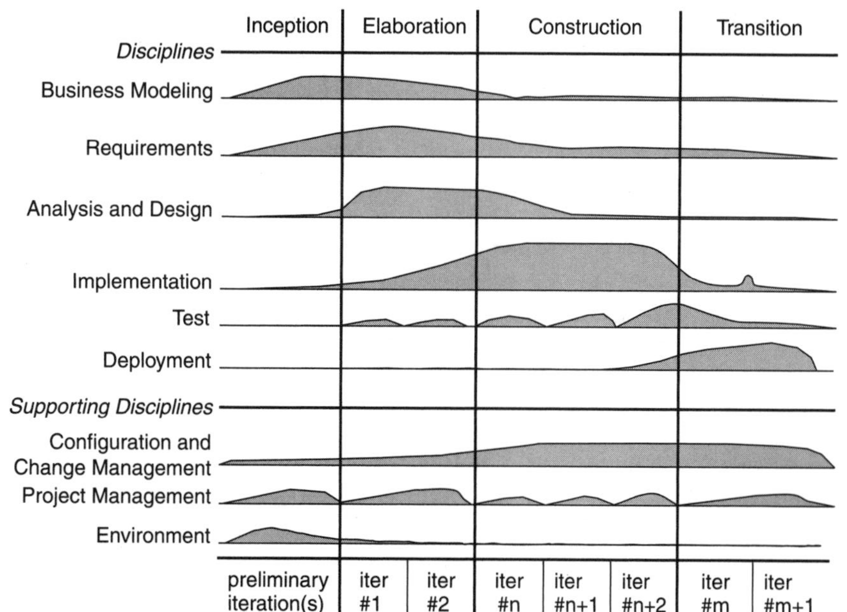

Figure 2-24: Software Development Life Cycle

Inception is the first phase of the process, when the seed idea for the development is brought up to the point of being—at least internally—sufficiently well-founded to warrant entering into the elaboration phase.

Elaboration is the second phase of the process, when the product requirements and architecture are defined. In this phase, the requirements are articulated, prioritized, and baselined. A system's requirements may range from general vision statements to precise evaluation criteria, each specifying particular functional or nonfunctional behavior and each providing a basis for testing.

Construction is the third phase of the process, when the software is brought from an executable architectural baseline to being ready to be transitioned to the user community. Here also, the system's requirements and especially its evaluation criteria are constantly reexamined against the business needs of the project, and resources are allocated as appropriate to actively attack risks to the project.

Transition is the fourth phase of the process, when the software is delivered to the user community. Rarely does the software development process end here, for even during this phase, the system is continuously improved, bugs are eradicated, and features that didn't make an earlier release are added.

One element that distinguishes this process and that cuts across all four phases is an iteration. An *iteration* is a distinct set of work tasks, with a baselined plan and evaluation criteria that results in an executable system that can be run, tested, and evaluated. The executable system need not be released externally. Because the iteration yields an executable product, progress can be judged and risks can be reevaluated after each iteration. This means that the software development life cycle can be characterized as involving a continuous stream of executable releases of the system's architecture with a midcourse correction after each iteration to mitigate potential risk. It is this emphasis on architecture as an important artifact that drives the UML to focus on modeling the different views of a system's architecture.

Chapter 3
HELLO, WORLD!

In this chapter

- Classes and artifacts
- Static models and dynamic models
- Connections among models
- Extending the UML

Brian Kernighan and Dennis Ritchie, the authors of the C programming language, point out that "the only way to learn a new programming language is by writing programs in it." The same is true of the UML. The only way to learn the UML is by writing models in it.

The first program many developers write when approaching a new programming language is a simple one, involving little more than printing the string "Hello, World!" This is a reasonable starting point, because mastering this trivial application provides some instant gratification. It also covers all the infrastructure needed to get something running.

This is where we begin with the UML. Modeling "Hello, World!" is about the simplest use of the UML you'll ever find. However, this application is deceptively easy because underneath it all there are some interesting mechanisms that make it work. These mechanisms can easily be modeled with the UML, providing a richer view of this simple application.

Key Abstractions

In Java, the applet for printing "Hello, World!" in a Web browser is quite simple:

```
import java.awt.Graphics;
class HelloWorld extends java.applet.Applet {
  public void paint (Graphics g) {
    g.drawString("Hello, World!", 10, 10);
  }
}
```

The first line of code:

```
import java.awt.Graphics;
```

makes the class `Graphics` directly available to the code that follows. The `java.awt` prefix specifies the Java package in which the class `Graphics` lives.

The second line of code:

```
class HelloWorld extends java.applet.Applet {
```

introduces a new class named `HelloWorld` and specifies that it is a kind of class just like `Applet`, which lives in the package `java.applet`.

The next three lines of code:

```
public void paint (Graphics g) {
  g.drawString("Hello, World!", 10, 10);
}
```

declare an operation named `paint`, whose implementation invokes another operation, named `drawString`, responsible for printing the string `"Hello, World!"` at the given coordinates. In the usual object-oriented fashion, `drawString` is an operation on a parameter named `g`, whose type is the class `Graphics`.

Classes are discussed in Chapters 4 and 9.

Modeling this application in the UML is straightforward. As Figure 3-1 shows, you can represent the class `HelloWorld` graphically as a rectangular icon. Its `paint` operation is shown here as well, with all its formal parameters elided and its implementation specified in the attached note.

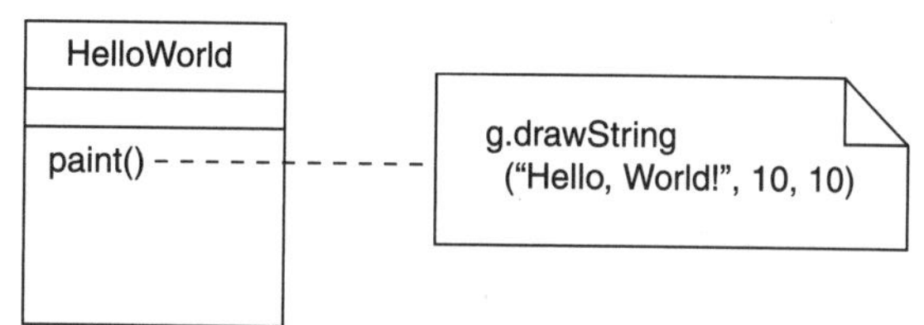

Figure 3-1: Key Abstractions for `HelloWorld`

Note: The UML is not a visual programming language, although, as the figure shows, the UML does allow—but does not require—a tight coupling to a variety of programming languages, such as Java. The UML is designed to allow models to be transformed into code and to allow code to be reengineered back into models. Some things are best written in the syntax of a textual programming language (for example, mathematical expressions), whereas other things are best visualized graphically in the UML (for example, hierarchies of classes).

This class diagram captures the basics of the "Hello, World!" application, but it leaves out a number of things. As the preceding code specifies, two other classes—`Applet` and `Graphics`—are involved in this application and each is used in a different way. The class `Applet` is used as the parent of `HelloWorld`, and the class `Graphics` is used in the signature and implementation of one of its operations, `paint`. You can represent these classes and their different relationships to the class `HelloWorld` in a class diagram, as shown in Figure 3-2.

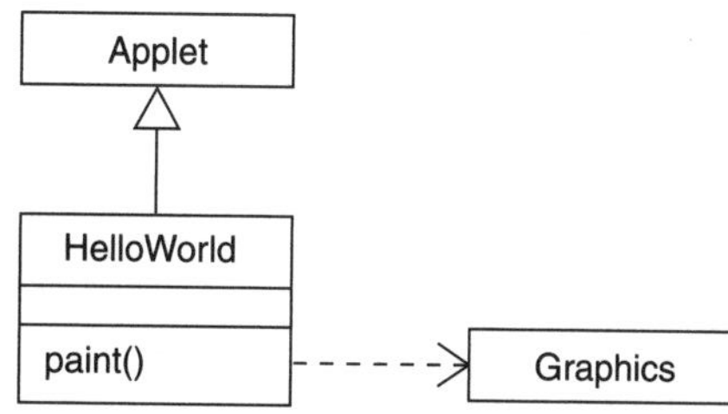

Figure 3-2: Immediate Neighbors Surrounding `HelloWorld`

Relationships are discussed in Chapters 5 and 10.

The `Applet` and `Graphics` classes are represented graphically as rectangular icons. No operations are shown for either of them, so their icons are elided. The directed line with the hollow arrowhead from `HelloWorld` to `Applet` represents generalization, which in this case means that `HelloWorld` is a child of `Applet`. The dashed directed line from `HelloWorld` to `Graphics` represents a dependency relationship, which means that `HelloWorld` uses `Graphics`.

This is not the end of the framework upon which `HelloWorld` is built. If you study the Java libraries for `Applet` and `Graphics`, you will discover that both of these classes are part of a larger hierarchy. Tracing just the classes that `Applet` extends and implements, you can generate another class diagram, shown in Figure 3-3.

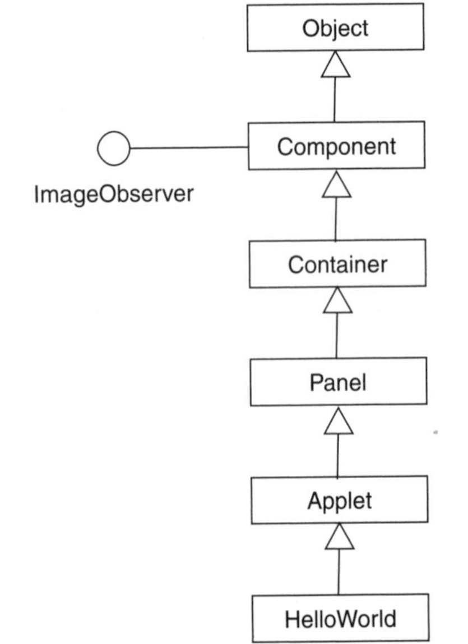

Figure 3-3: `HelloWorld` Inheritance Hierarchy

Note: This figure is a good example of a diagram generated by reverse engineering an existing system. Reverse engineering is the creation of a model from code.

This figure makes it clear that `HelloWorld` is just a leaf in a larger hierarchy of classes. `HelloWorld` is a child of `Applet`; `Applet` is a child of `Panel`; `Panel` is a child of `Container`; `Container` is a child of `Component`; and `Component` is a child of `Object`, which is the parent class of every class in Java. This model thus matches the Java library—each child extends some parent.

Interfaces are discussed in Chapter 11.

The relationship between `ImageObserver` and `Component` is a bit different, and the class diagram reflects this difference. In the Java library, `ImageObserver` is an interface, which, among other things, means that it has no implementation and instead requires that other classes implement it. You can show that class `Component` implements interface `ImageObserver` by the solid line from the rectangle (Component) to a provided interface circle (ImageObserver).

As these figures show, HelloWorld collaborates directly with only two classes (Applet and Graphics), and these two classes are but a small part of the larger library of predefined Java classes. To manage this large collection, Java organizes its interfaces and classes in a number of different packages. The root package in the Java environment is named, not surprisingly, java. Nested inside this package are several other packages, which contain other packages, interfaces, and classes. Object lives in the package lang, so its full path name is java.lang.Object. Similarly, Panel, Container, and Component live in awt; the class Applet lives in the package applet. The interface ImageObserver lives in the package image, which in turn lives in the package awt, so its full path name is the rather lengthy string java.awt.image.ImageObserver.

Packages are discussed in Chapter 12.

You can visualize this packaging in a class diagram, shown in Figure 3-4. As this figure shows, packages are represented in the UML as a tabbed folders. Packages may be nested, and the dashed directed lines represent dependencies among these packages. For example, HelloWorld depends on the package java.applet, and java.applet depends on the package java.awt.

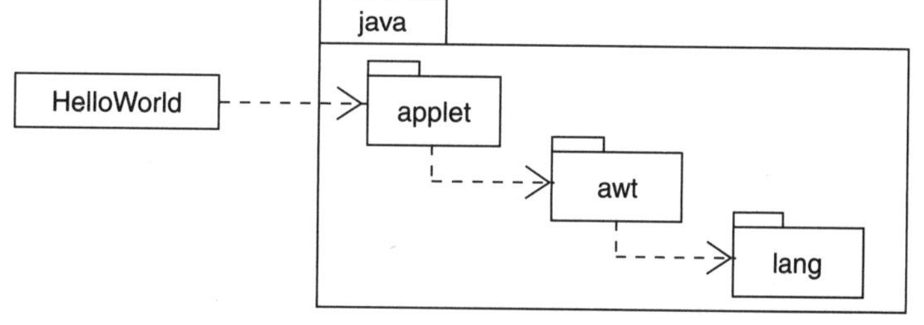

Figure 3-4: HelloWorld Packaging

Mechanisms

Patterns and frameworks are discussed in Chapter 29.

The hardest part of mastering a library as rich as Java's is learning how its parts work together. For example, how does HelloWorld's paint operation get invoked? What operations must you use if you want to change the behavior of this applet, such as making it print the string in a different color? To answer these and other questions, you must have a conceptual model of the way these classes work together dynamically.

Processes and threads are discussed in Chapter 23.

Studying the Java library reveals that `HelloWorld`'s `paint` operation is inherited from `Component`. This still begs the question of how this operation is invoked. The answer is that `paint` is called as part of running the thread that encloses the applet, as Figure 3-5 illustrates.

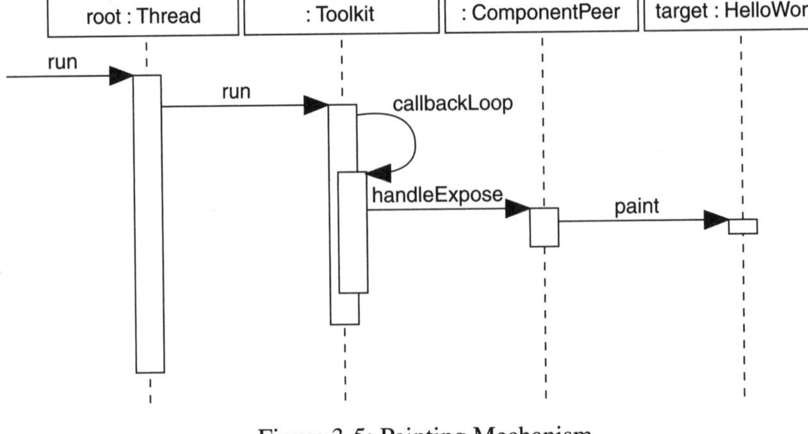

Figure 3-5: Painting Mechanism

Instances are discussed in Chapter 13.

This figure shows the collaboration of several objects, including one instance of the class `HelloWorld`. The other objects are a part of the Java environment, so, for the most part, they live in the background of the applets you create. This shows a collaboration among objects that can be applied many times. Each column shows a role in the collaboration, that is, a part that can be played by a different object in each execution. In the UML, roles are represented just like classes, except they have both role names and types. The middle two roles in this diagram are anonymous, because their types are enough to identify them within the collaboration (but the colon and the absence of an underline mark them as roles). The initial `Thread` is called `root`, and the `HelloWorld` role has the name `target` known by the `ComponentPeer` role.

Sequence diagrams are discussed in Chapter 19.

You can model the ordering of events using a sequence diagram, as in Figure 3-5. Here, the sequence begins by running the `Thread` object, which in turn calls the `Toolkit`'s `run` operation. The `Toolkit` object then calls one of its own operations (`callbackLoop`), which then calls the `ComponentPeer`'s `handleExpose` operation. The `ComponentPeer` object then calls its target's `paint` operation. The `ComponentPeer` object assumes that its target is a `Component`, but in this case the target is actually a child of `Component` (namely, `HelloWorld`), so `HelloWorld`'s `paint` operation is dispatched polymorphically.

Artifacts

"Hello, World!" is implemented as an applet, so it never stands alone but instead is typically a part of some Web page. The applet starts when its enclosing page is opened, triggered by some browser mechanism that runs the applet's `Thread` object. However, it's not the `HelloWorld` class that's directly a part of the Web page. Rather, it's a binary form of the class, created by a Java compiler that transforms the source code representing that class into an artifact that can be executed. This suggests a very different perspective of the system. Whereas all the earlier diagrams represented a logical view of the applet, what's going on here is a view of the applet's physical artifacts.

Artifacts are discussed in Chapter 26.

You can model this physical view using an artifact diagram, as in Figure 3-6.

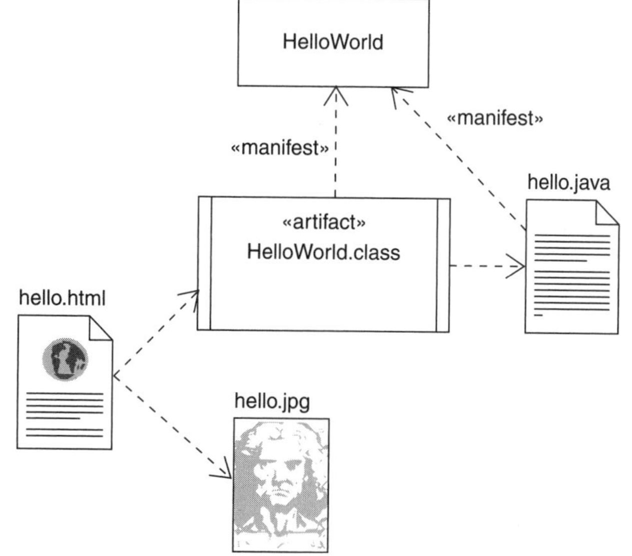

Figure 3-6: `HelloWorld` Artifacts

The logical class `HelloWorld` is shown at the top as a class rectangle. Each of the other icons in this figure represents a UML artifact in the implementation view of the system. An artifact is a physical representation, such as a file. The artifact called `hello.java` represents the source code for the logical class `HelloWorld`, so it is a file that may be manipulated by development environments and configuration management tools. This source code can be transformed into the binary applet `hello.class` by a Java compiler, making it suitable for execution by a computer's Java virtual machine. Both the source code and the binary applet manifest—physically implement—the logical class. This is shown by the dashed arrows with the keyword «`manifest`».

The UML's extensibility mechanisms are discussed in Chapter 6.

The icon for an artifact is a rectangle with the keyword «`artifact`» above the name. The binary applet `HelloWorld.class` is a variation of this basic symbol, with its lines made thicker, indicating that it is an executable artifact (just like an active class). The icon for the `hello.java` artifact has been replaced with a user-defined icon, representing a text file. The icon for the Web page `hello.html` has been similarly tailored by extending the UML's notation. As the figure indicates, this Web page has another artifact, `hello.jpg`, which is represented by a user-defined artifact icon, in this case providing a thumbnail sketch of the graphics image. Because these latter three artifacts use user-defined graphical symbols, their names are placed outside the icon. The dependencies among the artifacts are shown by dashed arrows.

Note: The relationships among the class (`HelloWorld`), its source code (`hello.java`), and its object code (`HelloWorld.class`) are rarely modeled explicitly, although it is sometimes useful to do so to visualize the physical configuration of a system. On the other hand, it is common to visualize the organization of a Web-based system such as this by using artifact diagrams to model its pages and other executable artifacts.

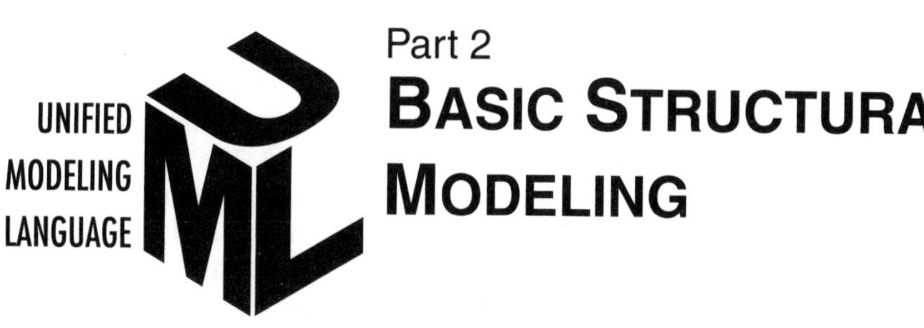

Part 2

Basic Structural Modeling

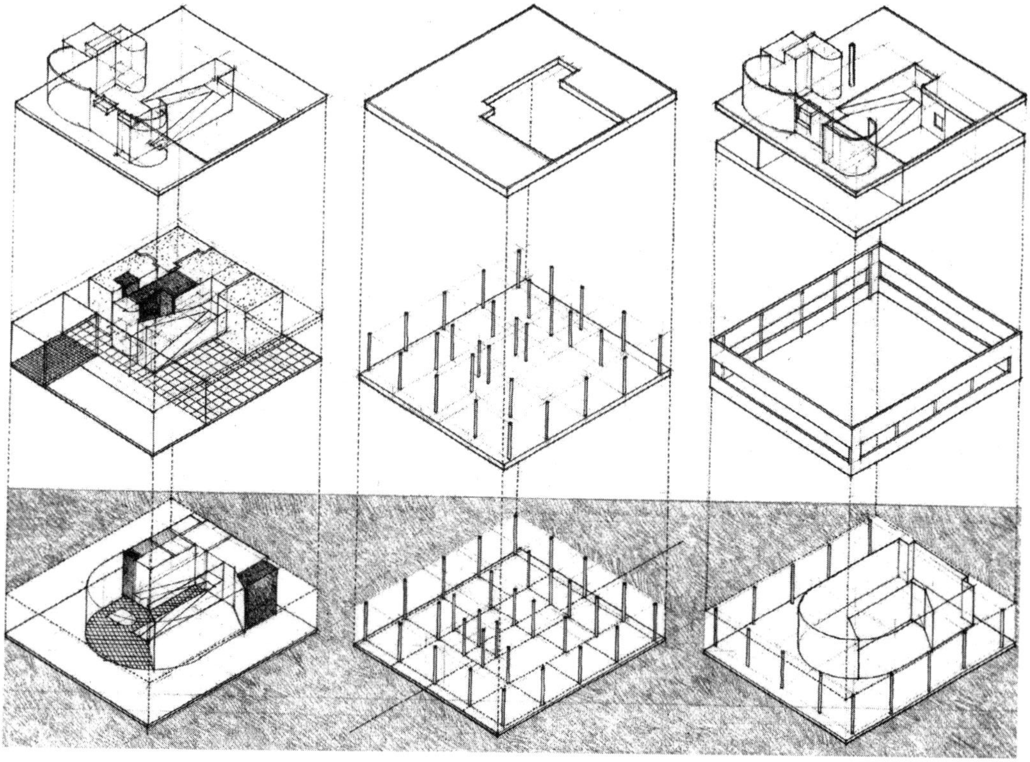

Chapter 4

CLASSES

In this chapter

- Classes, attributes, operations, and responsibilities
- Modeling the vocabulary of a system
- Modeling the distribution of responsibilities in a system
- Modeling nonsoftware things
- Modeling primitive types
- Making quality abstractions

Classes are the most important building block of any object-oriented system. A class is a description of a set of objects that share the same attributes, operations, relationships, and semantics. A class implements one or more interfaces.

Advanced features of classes are discussed in Chapter 9.

You use classes to capture the vocabulary of the system you are developing. These classes may include abstractions that are part of the problem domain, as well as classes that make up an implementation. You can use classes to represent software things, hardware things, and even things that are purely conceptual.

Well-structured classes have crisp boundaries and form a part of a balanced distribution of responsibilities across the system.

Getting Started

Modeling a system involves identifying the things that are important to your particular view. These things form the vocabulary of the system you are modeling. For example, if you are building a house, things like walls, doors, windows, cabinets, and lights are some of the things that will be important to you as a home owner. Each of these things can be distinguished from the other.

Each of them also has a set of properties. Walls have a height and a width and are solid. Doors also have a height and a width and are solid as well, but have the additional behavior that allows them to open in one direction. Windows are similar to doors in that both are openings that pass through walls, but windows and doors have slightly different properties. Windows are usually (but not always) designed so that you can look out of them instead of pass through them.

Individual walls, doors, and windows rarely exist in isolation, so you must also consider how specific instances of these things fit together. The things you identify and the relationships you choose to establish among them will be affected by how you expect to use the various rooms of your home, how you expect traffic to flow from room to room, and the general style and feel you want this arrangement to create.

Users will be concerned about different things. For example, the plumbers who help build your house will be interested in things like drains, traps, and vents. You, as a home owner, won't necessarily care about these things except insofar as they interact with the things in your view, such as where a drain might be placed in a floor or where a vent might intersect with the roof line.

Objects are discussed in Chapter 13.

In the UML, all of these things are modeled as classes. A class is an abstraction of the things that are a part of your vocabulary. A class is not an individual object, but rather represents a whole set of objects. Thus, you may conceptually think of "wall" as a class of objects with certain common properties, such as height, length, thickness, load-bearing or not, and so on. You may also think of individual instances of wall, such as "the wall in the southwest corner of my study."

In software, many programming languages directly support the concept of a class. That's excellent, because it means that the abstractions you create can often be mapped directly to a programming language, even if these are abstractions of nonsoftware things, such as "customer," "trade," or "conversation."

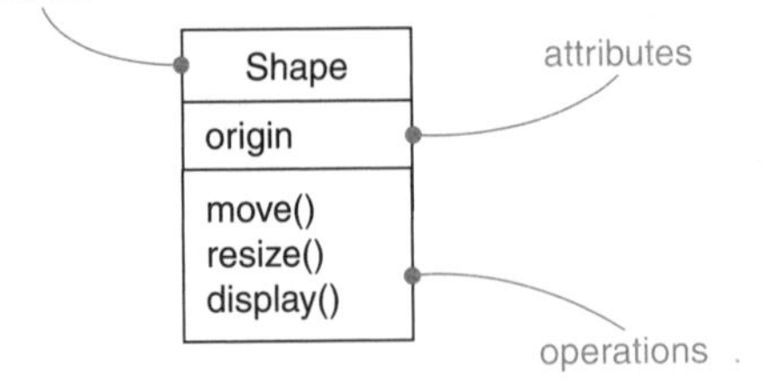

Figure 4-1: Classes

The UML provides a graphical representation of class, as well, as Figure 4-1 shows. This notation permits you to visualize an abstraction apart from any specific programming language and in a way that lets you emphasize the most important parts of an abstraction: its name, attributes, and operations.

Terms and Concepts

A *class* is a description of a set of objects that share the same attributes, operations, relationships, and semantics. Graphically, a class is rendered as a rectangle.

Names

A class name must be unique within its enclosing package, as discussed in Chapter 12.

Every class must have a name that distinguishes it from other classes. A *name* is a textual string. That name alone is known as a *simple name*; a *qualified name* is the class name prefixed by the name of the package in which that class lives. A class may be drawn showing only its name, as Figure 4-2 shows.

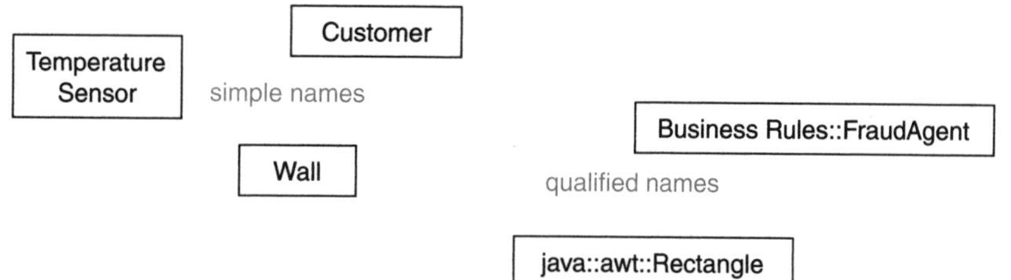

Figure 4-2: Simple and Qualified Names

Note: A class name may be text consisting of any number of letters, numbers, and certain punctuation marks (except for marks such as the double colon, which is used to separate a class name and the name of its enclosing package) and may continue over several lines. In practice, class names are short nouns or noun phrases drawn from the vocabulary of the system you are modeling. Typically, you capitalize the first letter of every word in a class name, as in `Customer` or `TemperatureSensor`.

Attributes

Attributes are related to the semantics of aggregation, as discussed in Chapter 10.

An *attribute* is a named property of a class that describes a range of values that instances of the property may hold. A class may have any number of attributes or no attributes at all. An attribute represents some property of the thing you are modeling that is shared by all objects of that class. For example, every wall has a height, width, and thickness; you might model your customers in such a way that each has a name, address, phone number, and date of birth. An attribute is therefore an abstraction of the kind of data or state an object of the class might encompass. At a given moment, an object of a class will have specific values for every one of its class's attributes. Graphically, attributes are listed in a compartment just below the class name. Attributes may be drawn showing only their names, as shown in Figure 4-3.

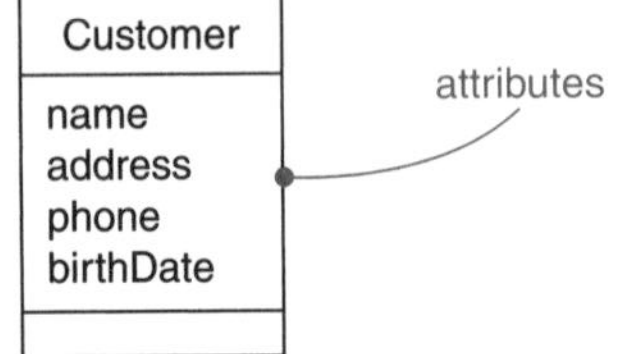

Figure 4-3: Attributes

Note: An attribute name may be text, just like a class name. In practice, an attribute name is a short noun or noun phrase that represents some property of its enclosing class. Typically, you capitalize the first letter of every word in an attribute name except the first letter, as in `name` or `loadBearing`.

You can specify other features of an attribute, such as marking it read-only or shared by all objects of the class, as discussed in Chapter 9.

You can further specify an attribute by stating its class and possibly a default initial value, as shown Figure 4-4.

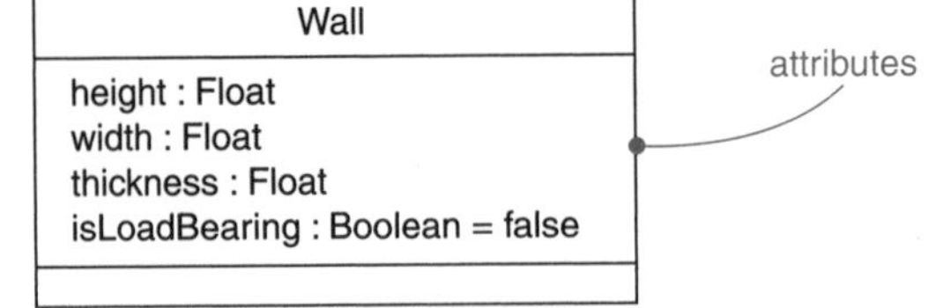

Figure 4-4: Attributes and Their Class

Operations

You can further specify the implementation of an operation by using a note, as described in Chapter 6, or by using an activity diagram, as discussed in Chapter 20.

An *operation* is the implementation of a service that can be requested from any object of the class to affect behavior. In other words, an operation is an abstraction of something you can do to an object that is shared by all objects of that class. A class may have any number of operations or no operations at all. For example, in a windowing library such as the one found in Java's `awt` package, all objects of the class `Rectangle` can be moved, resized, or queried for their properties. Often (but not always), invoking an operation on an object changes the object's data or state. Graphically, operations are listed in a compartment just below the class attributes. Operations may be drawn showing only their names, as in Figure 4-5.

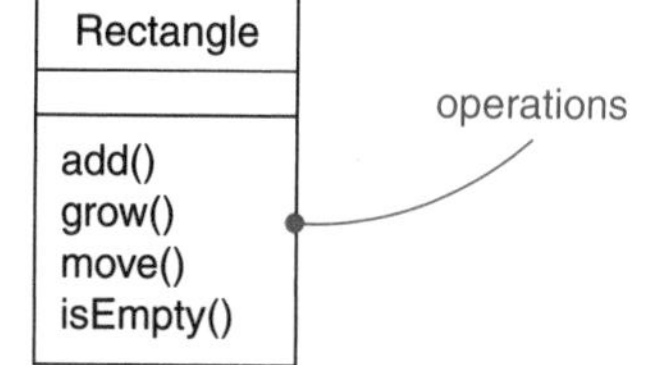

Figure 4-5: Operations

Note: An operation name may be text, just like a class name. In practice, an operation name is a short verb or verb phrase that represents some behavior of its enclosing class. Typically, you capitalize the first letter of every word in an operation name except the first letter, as in `move` or `isEmpty`.

You can specify other features of an operation, such as marking it polymorphic or constant, or specifying its visibility, as discussed in Chapter 9.

You can specify an operation by stating its signature, which includes the name, type, and default value of all parameters and (in the case of functions) a return type, as shown in Figure 4-6.

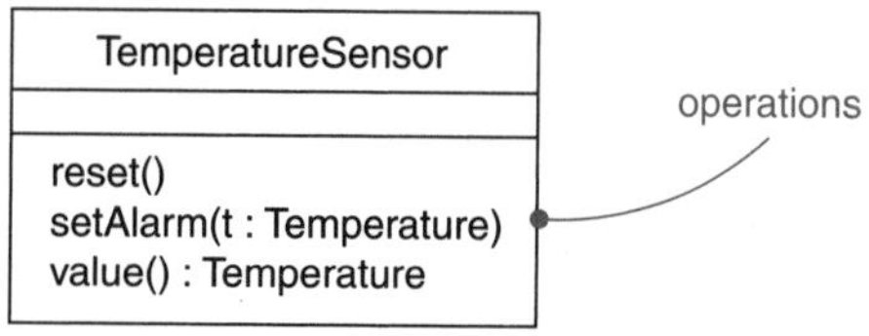

TemperatureSensor
reset()
setAlarm(t : Temperature)
value() : Temperature
operations

Figure 4-6: Operations and Their Signatures

Organizing Attributes and Operations

When drawing a class, you don't have to show every attribute and every operation at once. In fact, in most cases, you can't (there are too many of them to put in one figure) and you probably shouldn't (only a subset of these attributes and operations are likely to be relevant to a specific view). For these reasons, you can elide a class, meaning that you can choose to show only some or none of a class's attributes and operations. You can indicate that there are more attributes or properties than shown by ending each list with an ellipsis ("..."). You can also suppress the compartment entirely, in which case you can't tell if there are any attributes or operations or how many there are.

Stereotypes are discussed in Chapter 6.

To better organize long lists of attributes and operations, you can also prefix each group with a descriptive category by using stereotypes, as shown in Figure 4-7.

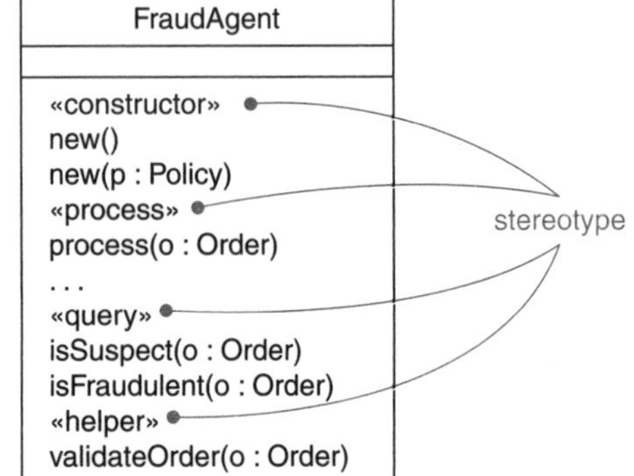

Figure 4-7: Stereotypes for Class Features

Responsibilities

Responsibilities are an example of a defined stereotype, as discussed in Chapter 6.

A *responsibility* is a contract or an obligation of a class. When you create a class, you are making a statement that all objects of that class have the same kind of state and the same kind of behavior. At a more abstract level, these corresponding attributes and operations are just the features by which the class's responsibilities are carried out. A `Wall` class is responsible for knowing about height, width, and thickness; a `FraudAgent` class, as you might find in a credit card application, is responsible for processing orders and determining if they are legitimate, suspect, or fraudulent; a `TemperatureSensor` class is responsible for measuring temperature and raising an alarm if the temperature reaches a certain point.

Modeling the semantics of a class is discussed in Chapter 9.

When you model classes, a good starting point is to specify the responsibilities of the things in your vocabulary. Techniques like CRC cards and use case-based analysis are especially helpful here. A class may have any number of responsibilities, although, in practice, every well-structured class has at least one responsibility and at most just a handful. As you refine your models, you will translate these responsibilities into a set of attributes and operations that best fulfill the class's responsibilities.

You can also draw the responsibilities of a class in a note, as discussed in Chapter 6.

Graphically, responsibilities can be drawn in a separate compartment at the bottom of the class icon, as shown in Figure 4-8.

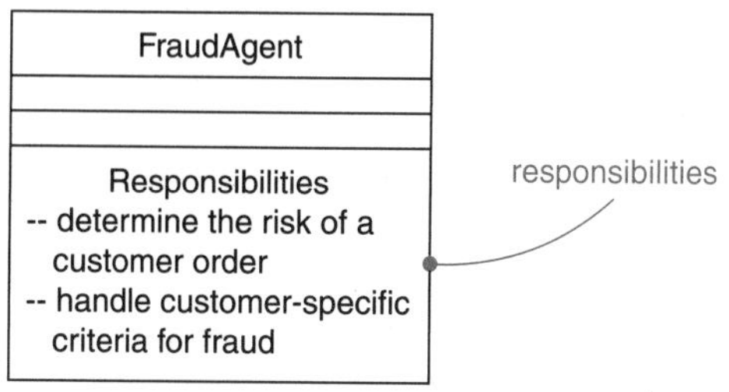

Figure 4-8: Responsibilities

Note: Responsibilities are just free-form text. In practice, a single responsibility is written as a phrase, a sentence, or (at most) a short paragraph.

Other Characteristics

Advanced class concepts are discussed in Chapter 9.

Attributes, operations, and responsibilities are the most common features you'll need when you create abstractions. In fact, for most models you build, the basic form of these three features will be all you need to convey the most important semantics of your classes. Sometimes, however, you'll need to visualize or specify other characteristics, such as the visibility of individual attributes and operations; language-specific features of an operation, such as whether it is polymorphic or constant; or even the exceptions that objects of the class might produce or handle. These and many other features can be expressed in the UML, but they are treated as advanced concepts.

Interfaces are discussed in Chapter 11.

When you build models, you will soon discover that almost every abstraction you create is some kind of class. Sometimes you will want to separate the implementation of a class from its specification, and this can be expressed in the UML by using interfaces.

Internal structure is discussed in Chapter 15.

When you start designing the implementation of a class, you need to model its internal structure as a set of connected parts. You can expand a top-level class through several layers of internal structure to get the eventual design.

Active classes, components, and nodes are discussed in Chapters 23, 25, and 27, and artifacts are discussed in Chapter 26.

When you start building more complex models, you will also find yourself encountering the same kinds of entities over and over again, such as classes that represent concurrent processes and threads, or classifiers that represent physical things, such as applets, Java Beans, files, Web pages, and hardware. Because these kinds of entities are so common and because they represent important architectural abstractions, the UML provides active classes (representing processes and threads) and classifiers, such as artifacts (representing physical software components) and nodes (representing hardware devices).

Class diagrams are discussed in Chapter 8.

Finally, classes rarely stand alone. Rather, when you build models, you will typically focus on groups of classes that interact with one another. In the UML, these societies of classes form collaborations and are usually visualized in class diagrams.

Common Modeling Techniques

Modeling the Vocabulary of a System

You'll use classes most commonly to model abstractions that are drawn from the problem you are trying to solve or from the technology you are using to implement a solution to that problem. Each of these abstractions is a part of the vocabulary of your system, meaning that, together, they represent the things that are important to users and to implementers.

Use cases are discussed in Chapter 17.

For users, most abstractions are not that hard to identify because, typically, they are drawn from the things that users already use to describe their system. Techniques such as CRC cards and use case-based analysis are excellent ways to help users find these abstractions. For implementers, these abstractions are typically just the things in the technology that are parts of the solution.

To model the vocabulary of a system,

- Identify those things that users or implementers use to describe the problem or solution. Use CRC cards and use case-based analysis to help find these abstractions.

- For each abstraction, identify a set of responsibilities. Make sure that each class is crisply defined and that there is a good balance of responsibilities among all your classes.
- Provide the attributes and operations that are needed to carry out these responsibilities for each class.

Figure 4-9 shows a set of classes drawn from a retail system, including `Customer`, `Order`, and `Product`. This figure includes a few other related abstractions drawn from the vocabulary of the problem, such as `Shipment` (used to track orders), `Invoice` (used to bill orders), and `Warehouse` (where products are located prior to shipment). There is also one solution-related abstraction, `Transaction`, which applies to orders and shipments.

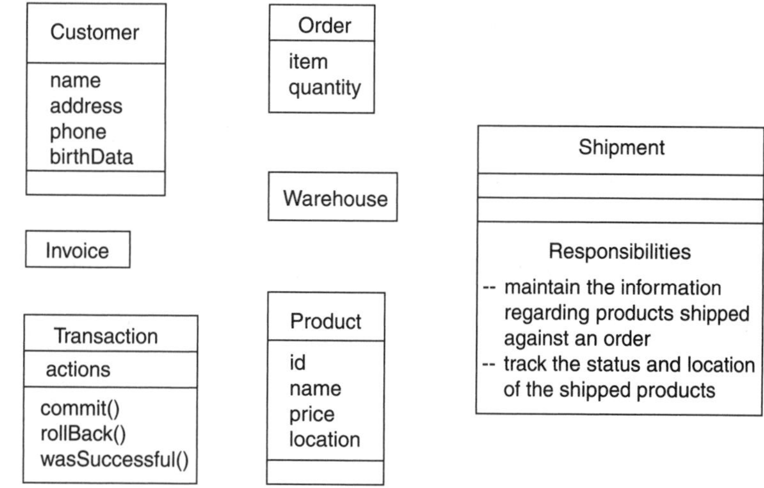

Figure 4-9: Modeling the Vocabulary of a System

Packages are discussed in Chapter 12.

As your models get larger, many of the classes you find will tend to cluster together in groups that are conceptually and semantically related. In the UML, you can use packages to model these clusters of classes.

Modeling behavior is discussed in Parts 4 and 5.

Your models will rarely be completely static. Instead, most abstractions in your system's vocabulary will interact with one another in dynamic ways. In the UML, there are a number of ways to model this dynamic behavior.

Modeling the Distribution of Responsibilities in a System

Once you start modeling more than just a handful of classes, you will want to be sure that your abstractions provide a balanced set of responsibilities. What this means is that you don't want any one class to be too big or too small. Each class should do one thing well. If you abstract classes that are too big, you'll find that your models are hard to change and are not very reusable. If you abstract classes that are too small, you'll end up with many more abstractions than you can reasonably manage or understand. You can use the UML to help you visualize and specify this balance of responsibilities.

To model the distribution of responsibilities in a system,

- Identify a set of classes that work together closely to carry out some behavior.
- Identify a set of responsibilities for each of these classes.
- Look at this set of classes as a whole, split classes that have too many responsibilities into smaller abstractions, collapse tiny classes that have trivial responsibilities into larger ones, and reallocate responsibilities so that each abstraction reasonably stands on its own.
- Consider the ways in which those classes collaborate with one another, and redistribute their responsibilities accordingly so that no class within a collaboration does too much or too little.

Collaborations are discussed in Chapter 28.

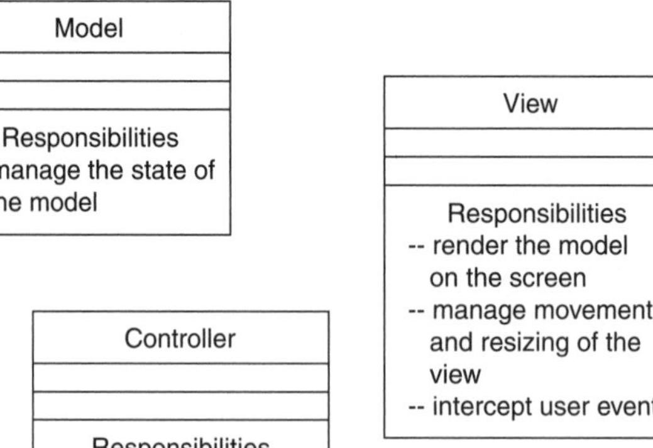

Figure 4-10: Modeling the Distribution of Responsibilities in a System

This set of classes forms a pattern, as discussed in Chapter 29.

For example, Figure 4-10 shows a set of classes drawn from Smalltalk, showing the distribution of responsibilities among `Model`, `View`, and `Controller` classes. Notice how all these classes work together such that no one class does too much or too little.

Modeling Nonsoftware Things

Sometimes, the things you model may never have an analog in software. For example, the people who send invoices and the robots that automatically package orders for shipping from a warehouse might be a part of the workflow you model in a retail system. Your application might not have any software that represents them (unlike customers in the example above, since your system will probably want to maintain information about them).

To model nonsoftware things,

Stereotypes are discussed in Chapter 6.

Nodes are discussed in Chapter 27.

- Model the thing you are abstracting as a class.
- If you want to distinguish these things from the UML's defined building blocks, create a new building block by using stereotypes to specify these new semantics and to give a distinctive visual cue.
- If the thing you are modeling is some kind of hardware that itself contains software, consider modeling it as a kind of node as well, so that you can further expand on its structure.

Note: The UML is mainly intended for modeling software-intensive systems, although, in conjunction with textual hardware modeling languages, such as VHDL, the UML can be quite expressive for modeling hardware systems. The OMG has also produced a UML extension called SysML intended for systems modeling.

External things are often modeled as actors, as discussed in Chapter 17.

As Figure 4-11 shows, it's perfectly normal to abstract humans (like `AccountsReceivableAgent`) and hardware (like `Robot`) as classes, because each represents a set of objects with a common structure and a common behavior.

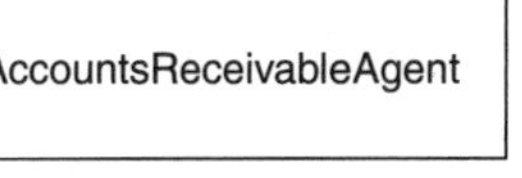

Figure 4-11: Modeling Nonsoftware Things

Modeling Primitive Types

Types are discussed in Chapter 11.

At the other extreme, the things you model may be drawn directly from the programming language you are using to implement a solution. Typically, these abstractions involve primitive types, such as integers, characters, strings, and even enumeration types, that you might create yourself.

To model primitive types,

- Model the thing you are abstracting as a class or an enumeration, which is rendered using class notation with the appropriate stereotype.
- If you need to specify the range of values associated with this type, use constraints.

Constraints are described in Chapter 6.

Types are discussed in Chapter 11.

As Figure 4-12 shows, these things can be modeled in the UML as types or enumerations, which are rendered just like classes but are explicitly marked via stereotypes. Primitive types such as integers (represented by the class `Int`) are modeled as types, and you can explicitly indicate the range of values these things can take on by using a constraint; the semantics of primitive types must be defined externally to UML. Enumeration types, such as `Boolean` and `Status`, can be modeled as enumerations, with their individual literals listed within the attribute compartment (note that they are not attributes). Enumeration types may also define operations.

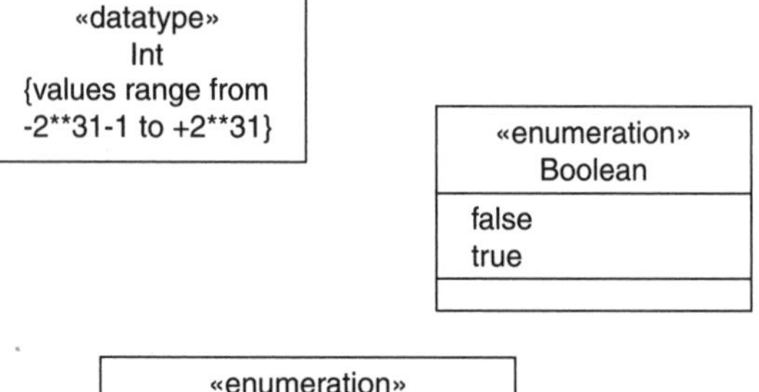

Figure 4-12: Modeling Primitive Types

Note: Some languages, such as C and C++, let you set an integer value for an enumeration literal. You can model this in the UML by attaching a note to an enumeration literal as implementation guidance. Integer values are not needed for logical modeling.

Hints and Tips

When you model classes in the UML, remember that every class should map to some tangible or conceptual abstraction in the domain of the end user or the implementer. A well-structured class

- Provides a crisp abstraction of something drawn from the vocabulary of the problem domain or the solution domain.
- Embodies a small, well-defined set of responsibilities and carries them all out very well.
- Provides a clear separation of the abstraction's specification and its implementation.
- Is understandable and simple, yet extensible and adaptable.

When you draw a class in the UML,

- Show only those properties of the class that are important to understanding the abstraction in its context.
- Organize long lists of attributes and operations by grouping them according to their category.
- Show related classes in the same class diagrams.

Chapter 5
RELATIONSHIPS

In this chapter

- Dependency, generalization, and association relationships
- Modeling simple dependencies
- Modeling single inheritance
- Modeling structural relationships
- Creating webs of relationships

When you build abstractions, you'll discover that very few of your classes stand alone. Instead, most of them collaborate with others in a number of ways. Therefore, when you model a system, not only must you identify the things that form the vocabulary of your system, you must also model how these things stand in relation to one another.

Advanced features of relationships are discussed in Chapter 10.

In object-oriented modeling, there are three kinds of relationships that are especially important: *dependencies*, which represent using relationships among classes (including refinement, trace, and bind relationships); *generalizations*, which link generalized classes to their specializations; and *associations*, which represent structural relationships among objects. Each of these relationships provides a different way of combining your abstractions.

Building webs of relationships is not unlike creating a balanced distribution of responsibilities among your classes. Over-engineer, and you'll end up with a tangled mess of relationships that make your model incomprehensible; under-engineer, and you'll have missed a lot of the richness of your system embodied in the way things collaborate.

Getting Started

If you are building a house, things like walls, doors, windows, cabinets, and lights will form part of your vocabulary. None of these things stands alone, however. Walls connect to other walls. Doors and windows are placed in walls to form openings for people and for light. Cabinets and lights are physically attached to walls and ceilings. You group walls, doors, windows, cabinets, and lights together to form higher-level things, such as rooms.

Not only will you find structural relationships among these things, you'll find other kinds of relationships as well. For example, your house certainly has windows, but there are probably many kinds of windows. You might have large bay windows that don't open, as well as small kitchen windows that do. Some of your windows might open up and down; others, like patio windows, will slide left and right. Some windows have a single pane of glass; others have double. No matter their differences, there is some essential "window-ness" about each of them: Each is an opening in a wall, and each is designed to let in light, air, and sometimes, people.

In the UML, the ways that things can connect to one another, either logically or physically, are modeled as relationships. In object-oriented modeling, there are three kinds of relationships that are most important: dependencies, generalizations, and associations.

1. *Dependencies* are using relationships. For example, pipes depend on the water heater to heat the water they carry.

2. *Associations* are structural relationships among instances. For example, rooms consist of walls and other things; walls themselves may have embedded doors and windows; pipes may pass through walls.

3. *Generalizations* connect generalized classes to more-specialized ones in what is known as subclass/superclass or child/parent relationships. For example, a picture window is a kind of window with very large, fixed panes; a patio window is a kind of window with panes that open side to side.

Other kinds of relationships, such as realization and refinement, are discussed in Chapter 10.

These three kinds of relationships cover most of the important ways in which things collaborate with one another. Not surprisingly, they also map well to the ways that are provided by most object-oriented programming languages to connect objects.

The UML provides a graphical representation for each of these kinds of relationships, as Figure 5-1 shows. This notation permits you to visualize relationships apart from any specific programming language, and in a way that lets you emphasize the most important parts of a relationship: its name, the things it connects, and its properties.

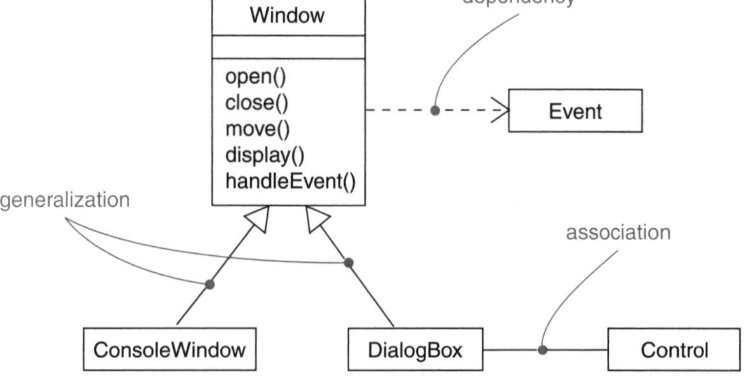

Figure 5-1: Relationships

Terms and Concepts

A *relationship* is a connection among things. In object-oriented modeling, the three most important relationships are dependencies, generalizations, and associations. Graphically, a relationship is rendered as a path, with different kinds of lines used to distinguish the kinds of relationships.

Dependencies

A *dependency* is a relationship that states that one thing (for example, class `Window`) uses the information and services of another thing (for example, class `Event`), but not necessarily the reverse. Graphically, a dependency is rendered as a dashed directed line, directed to the thing being depended on. Choose dependencies when you want to show one thing using another.

Notes are discussed in Chapter 6; packages are discussed in Chapter 12.

Most often, you will use dependencies between classes to show that one class uses operations from another class or it uses variables or arguments typed by the other class; see Figure 5-2. This is very much a using relationship—if the used class changes, the operation of the other class may be affected as well, because the used class may now present a different interface or behavior. In the UML you can also create dependencies among many other things, especially notes and packages.

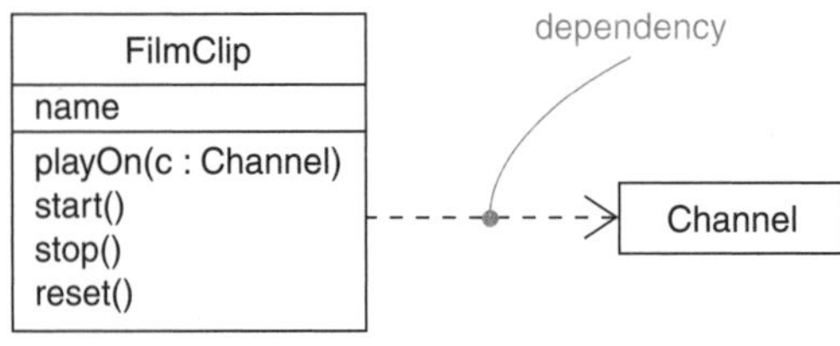

Figure 5-2: Dependencies

Different kinds of dependencies are discussed in Chapter 10; stereotypes are discussed in Chapter 6.

Note: A dependency can have a name, although names are rarely needed unless you have a model with many dependencies and you need to refer to or distinguish among dependencies. More commonly, you'll use stereotypes to distinguish different flavors of dependencies.

Generalizations

A *generalization* is a relationship between a general kind of thing (called the superclass or parent) and a more specific kind of thing (called the subclass or child). Generalization is sometimes called an "is-a-kind-of" relationship: one thing (like the class `BayWindow`) is-a-kind-of a more general thing (for example, the class `Window`). An objects of the child class may be used for a variable or parameter typed by the parent, but not the reverse. In other words, generalization means that the child is substitutable for a declaration of the parent. A child inherits the properties of its parents, especially their attributes and operations. Often—but not always—the child has attributes and operations in addition to those found in its parents. An implementation of an operation in a child overrides an implementation of the same operation of the parent; this is known as polymorphism. To be the same, two operations must have the same signature (same name and parameters). Graphically, generalization is rendered as a solid directed line with a large unfilled triangular arrowhead, pointing to the parent, as shown in Figure 5-3. Use generalizations when you want to show parent/child relationships.

A class may have zero, one, or more parents. A class that has no parents and one or more children is called a root class or a base class. A class that has no children is called a leaf class. A class that has exactly one parent is said to use single inheritance; a class with more than one parent is said to use multiple inheritance.

Packages are discussed in Chapter 12.

Most often, you will use generalizations among classes and interfaces to show inheritance relationships. In the UML, you can also create generalizations among other kinds of classifiers, such as nodes.

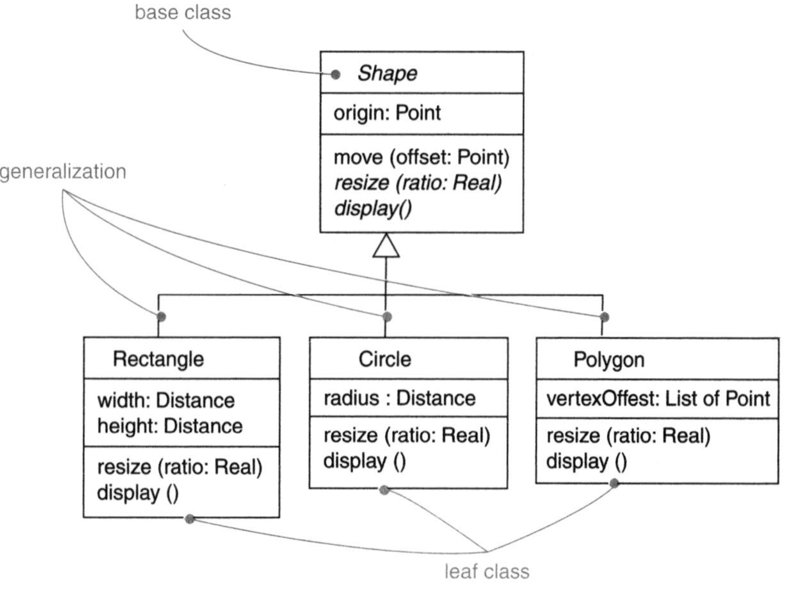

Figure 5-3: Generalization

Note: A generalization with a name indicates a decomposition of the subclasses of a superclass on a particular aspect, called a generalization set. Multiple generalization sets are orthogonal; the superclass is intended to be specialized using multiple inheritance to select one subclass from each generalization set. This is an advanced topic that we do not cover in this book.

Associations

Associations and dependencies (but not generalization relationships) may be reflective, as discussed in Chapter 10.

An *association* is a structural relationship that specifies that objects of one thing are connected to objects of another. Given an association connecting two classes, you can relate objects of one class to objects of the other class. It's quite legal to have both ends of an association circle back to the same class. This means that, given an object of the class, you can link to other objects of the same class. An association that connects exactly two classes is called a binary association. Although it's not as common, you can have associations that connect more than two classes; these are called *n-ary associations*. Graphically, an association is rendered as a solid line connecting the same or different classes. Use associations when you want to show structural relationships.

Beyond this basic form, there are four adornments that apply to associations.

Don't confuse name direction with association navigation, as discussed in Chapter 10.

Name An association can have a name, and you use that name to describe the nature of the relationship. So that there is no ambiguity about its meaning, you can give a direction to the name by providing a direction triangle that points in the direction you intend to read the name, as shown in Figure 5-4.

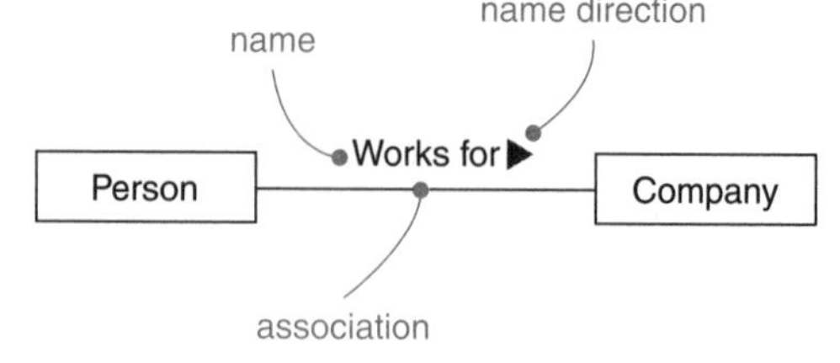

Figure 5-4: Association Names

Note: Although an association may have a name, you typically don't need to include one if you explicitly provide end names for the association. If you have more than one association connecting the same classes, it is necessary to use either association names or association end names to distinguish them. If an association has more than one end on the same class, it is necessary to use association end names to distinguish the ends. If there is only one association between a pair of classes, some modelers omit the names, but it is better to provide them to make the purpose of the association clear.

Roles are related to the semantics of interfaces, as discussed in Chapter 11.

Role When a class participates in an association, it has a specific role that it plays in that relationship; a role is just the face the class at the far end of the association presents to the class at the near end of the association. You can explicitly name the role a class plays in an association. The role played by an end of an association is called an *end name* (in UML1, it was called a *role name*). In Figure 5-5, the class `Person` playing the role of `employee` is associated with the class `Company` playing the role of `employer`.

Note: The same class can play the same or different roles in other associations.

Note: An attribute may be regarded as a one-way association owned by a class. The attribute name corresponds to the end name on the association end away from the class.

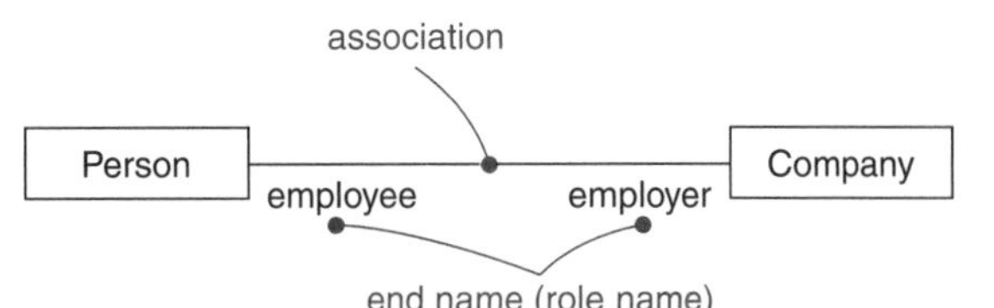

Figure 5-5: Association End Names (Role Names)

An instance of an association is called a link, as discussed in Chapter 16.

Multiplicity An association represents a structural relationship among objects. In many modeling situations, it's important for you to state how many objects may be connected across an instance of an association. This "how many" is called the multiplicity of an association's role. It represents a range of integers specifying the possible size of the set of related objects. It is written as an expression with a minimum and maximum value, which may be the same; two dots are used to separate the minimum and maximum values. When you state a multiplicity at the far end of an association, you are specifying that, for each object of the class at the near end, how many objects at the near end may exist. The number of objects must be in the given range. You can show a multiplicity of exactly one (`1`), zero or one (`0..1`), many (`0..*`), or one or more (`1..*`). You can give an integer range (such as `2..5`). You can even state an exact number (for example, `3`, which is equivalent to `3..3`).

For example, in Figure 5-6, each company object has as employee one or more person objects (multiplicity `1..*`); each person object has as employer zero or more company objects (multiplicity `*`, which is equivalent to `0..*`).

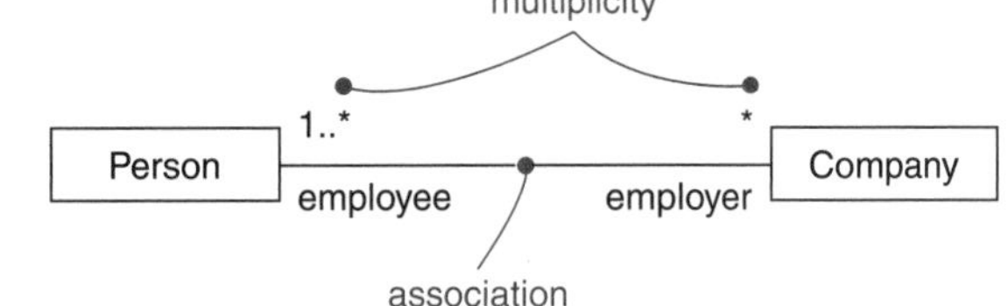

Figure 5-6: Multiplicity

Aggregation has a number of important variations, as discussed in Chapter 10.

Aggregation A plain association between two classes represents a structural relationship between peers, meaning that both classes are conceptually at the same level, no one more important than the other. Sometimes you will want to model a "whole/part" relationship, in which one class represents a larger thing (the "whole"), which consists of smaller things (the "parts"). This kind of relationship is called aggregation, which represents a "has-a" relationship, meaning that an object of the whole has objects of the part. Aggregation is really just a special kind of association and is specified by adorning a plain association with an unfilled diamond at the whole end, as shown in Figure 5-7.

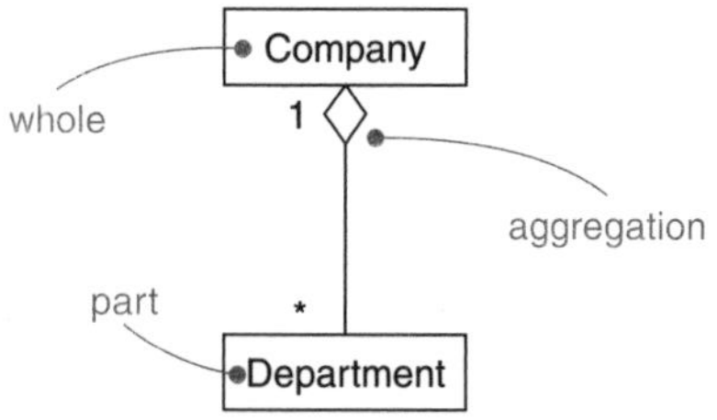

Figure 5-7: Aggregation

Note: The meaning of this simple form of aggregation is entirely conceptual. The open diamond distinguishes the "whole" from the "part," no more, no less. This means that simple aggregation does not change the meaning of navigation across the association between the whole and its parts, nor does it link the lifetimes of the whole and its parts. See the section on composition in Chapter 10 for a tighter form of aggregation.

Other Features

Advanced relationship concepts are discussed in Chapter 10.

Plain, unadorned dependencies, generalizations, and associations with names, multiplicities, and roles are the most common features you'll need when creating abstractions. In fact, for most of the models you build, the basic form of these three relationships will be all you need to convey the most important semantics of your relationships. Sometimes, however, you'll need to visualize or specify other features, such as composite aggregation, navigation, discriminants, association classes, and special kinds of dependencies and generalizations. These and many other features can be expressed in the UML, but they are treated as advanced concepts.

Class diagrams are discussed in Chapter 8.

Dependencies, generalizations, and associations are all static things defined at the level of classes. In the UML, these relationships are usually visualized in class diagrams.

Links are discussed in Chapter 16.

When you start modeling at the object level, and especially when you start working with dynamic collaborations of these objects, you'll encounter links, which are instances of associations representing connections among objects across which messages may be sent.

Drawing Styles

Relationships are shown in diagrams by lines from one icon to another. The lines have various adornments, such as arrowheads or diamonds, to distinguish different kinds of relationships. Typically, modelers choose one of two styles for drawing lines:

- Oblique lines at any angle. Use one line segment unless multiple segments are needed to avoid other icons.
- Rectilinear lines drawn parallel to the sides of the page. Unless a lines connects two icons that align, the line must be drawn as a series of line segments connected by right angles.This is the style mostly used in this book.

With care, most line crossings can be avoided. If a line crossing is necessary and there is ambiguity about how the paths are connected, a small arc can be used to indicate a line crossing.

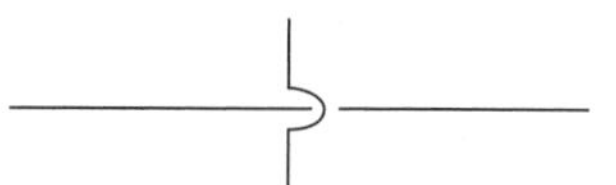

Figure 5-8: Line Crossing Symbol

Common Modeling Techniques

Modeling Simple Dependencies

A common kind of dependency relationship is the connection between a class that uses another class as a parameter to an operation.

To model this using relationship,

- Create a dependency pointing from the class with the operation to the class used as a parameter in the operation.

For example, Figure 5-9 shows a set of classes drawn from a system that manages the assignment of students and instructors to courses in a university. This figure shows a dependency from `CourseSchedule` to `Course`, because `Course` is used in both the `add` and `remove` operations of `CourseSchedule`.

If you provide the full signature of the operation as in this figure, you don't normally need to show the dependency as well, because the use of the class is already explicit in the signature. However, you'll want to show this dependency sometimes, especially if you've elided operation signatures or if your model shows other relationships to the used class.

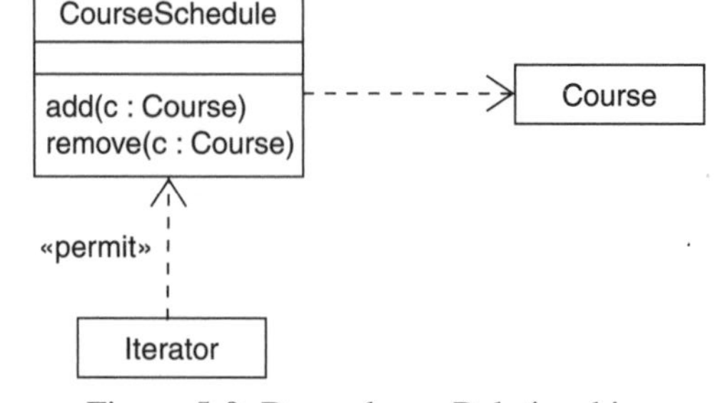

Figure 5-9: Dependency Relationships

Other relationship stereotypes are discussed in Chapter 10.

This figure shows one other dependency, this one not involving classes in operations but rather modeling a common C++ idiom. The dependency from `Iterator` shows that the `Iterator` uses the `CourseSchedule`; the `CourseSchedule` knows nothing about the `Iterator`. The dependency is marked with the stereotype «`permit`», which is similar to the `friend` statement in C++.

Modeling Single Inheritance

In modeling the vocabulary of your system, you will often run across classes that are structurally or behaviorally similar to others. You could model each of these as distinct and unrelated abstractions. A better way would be to extract any common structural and behavioral features and place them in more-general classes from which the specialized ones inherit.

To model inheritance relationships,

- Given a set of classes, look for responsibilities, attributes, and operations that are common to two or more classes.
- Elevate these common responsibilities, attributes, and operations to a more general class. If necessary, create a new class to which you can assign these elements (but be careful about introducing too many levels).
- Specify that the more-specific classes inherit from the more-general class by placing a generalization relationship that is drawn from each specialized class to its more-general parent.

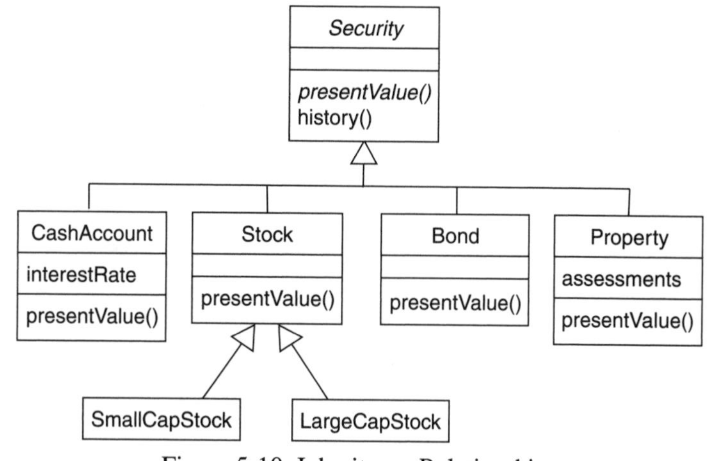

Figure 5-10: Inheritance Relationships

For example, Figure 5-10 shows a set of classes drawn from a trading application. You will find a generalization relationship from four classes—CashAccount, Stock, Bond, and Property—to the more-general class named Security. Security is the parent, and CashAccount, Stock, Bond, and Property are all children. Each of these specialized classes is a kind of Security. You'll notice that Security includes two operations: presentValue and history. Because Security is their parent, CashAccount, Stock, Bond, and Property all inherit these two operations, and for that matter, any other attributes and operations of Security that may be elided in this figure.

Abstract classes and operations are discussed in Chapter 9.

You may notice that the names Security and presentValue are written a bit differently than others. There's a reason for this. When you build hierarchies as in Figure 5-10, you often encounter nonleaf classes that are incomplete or are simply ones for which you don't want there to be any objects. Such classes are called *abstract.* You can specify a class as abstract in the UML by writing its name in italics, such as for the class Security. This convention applies to operations such presentValue and means that the given operation provides a signature but is otherwise incomplete, so it must be implemented by some method at a lower level of abstraction. In fact, as the figure shows, all four of the immediate children of Security are concrete (meaning that they are nonabstract) and must each provide a concrete implementation of the operation presentValue.

Your generalization/specialization hierarchies don't have to be limited to only two levels. In fact, as Figure 5-10 shows, it is common to have more than two layers of inheritance. SmallCapStock and LargeCapStock are both children of Stock, which, in turn, is a child of Security. Security is therefore a root class because it has no parents. `SmallCapStock` and `LargeCapStock` are both leaf classes because they have no children. `Stock` has a parent as well as children, so it is neither a root nor a leaf class.

Multiple inheritance is discussed in Chapter 10.

Although it is not shown here, you can also create classes that have more than one parent. This is called multiple inheritance and means that the given class has all the attributes, operations, and associations of all its parents.

Of course, there can be no cycles in an inheritance lattice; a given class cannot be its own ancestor.

Modeling Structural Relationships

When you model with dependencies or generalization relationships, you may be modeling classes that represent different levels of importance or different levels of abstraction. Given a dependency between two classes, one class depends on another but the other class has no knowledge of the one. Given a generalization relationship between two classes, the child inherits from its parent but the parent has no specific knowledge of its children. In short, dependency and generalization relationships are asymmetric.

Associations are, by default, bidirectional; you can limit their direction, as discussed in Chapter 10.

When you model with association relationships, you are modeling classes that are peers of one another. Given an association between two classes, both rely on the other in some way, and you can often navigate in either direction. Whereas dependency is a using relationship and generalization is an is-a-kind-of relationship, an association specifies a structural path across which objects of the classes interact.

To model structural relationships,

- For each pair of classes, if you need to navigate from objects of one to objects of another, specify an association between the two. This is a data-driven view of associations.
- For each pair of classes, if objects of one class need to interact with objects of the other class other than as local variables in a procedure or parameters to an operation, specify an association between the two. This is more of a behavior-driven view of associations.
- For each of these associations, specify a multiplicity (especially when the multiplicity is not *, which is the default), as well as role names (especially if they help to explain the model).
- If one of the classes in an association is structurally or organizationally a whole compared with the classes at the other end that look like parts, mark this as an aggregation by adorning the association at the end near the whole with a diamond.

Use cases are discussed in Chapter 17.

How do you know when objects of a given class must interact with objects of another class? The answer is that CRC cards and use case analysis help tremendously by forcing you to consider structural and behavioral scenarios. Where you find that two or more classes interact using data relationships, specify an association.

Figure 5-11 shows a set of classes drawn from an information system for a school. Starting at the bottom left of this diagram, you will find the classes named `Student`, `Course`, and `Instructor`. There's an association between `Student` and `Course`, specifying that students attend courses. Furthermore, every student may attend any number of courses and every course may have any number of students. Similarly, you'll find an association between `Course` and `Instructor`, specifying that instructors teach courses. For every course there is at least one instructor and every instructor may teach zero or more courses. Each course belongs to exactly one department.

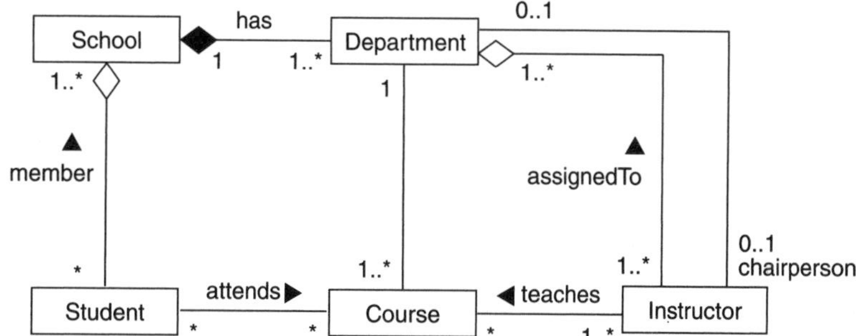

Figure 5-11: Structural Relationships

The aggregation relationship between `School` and `Department` is composite aggregation, as discussed in Chapter 10. Composition is a tight form of aggregation implying ownership.

The relationships between `School` and the classes `Student` and `Department` are a bit different. Here you'll see aggregation relationships. A school has zero or more students, each student may be a registered member of one or more schools, a school has one or more departments, and each department belongs to exactly one school. You could leave off the aggregation adornments and use plain associations, but by specifying that `School` is a whole and that `Student` and `Department` are some of its parts, you make clear which one is organizationally superior to the other. Thus, schools are somewhat defined by the students and departments they have. Similarly, students and departments don't really stand alone outside the school to which they belong. Rather, they get some of their identity from their school.

You'll also see that there are two associations between `Department` and `Instructor`. One of these associations specifies that every instructor is assigned to one or more departments and that each department has one or more instructors. This is modeled as an aggregation because organizationally, departments are at a higher level in the school's structure than are instructors. The other association specifies that for every department, there is exactly one instructor who is the department chair. The way this model is specified, an instructor can be the chair of no more than one department, and some instructors are not chairs of any department.

Note: Your school might not have departments. You might have chairs who are not instructors, or you might even have students who are also instructors. That doesn't mean that the model here is wrong, it's just different. You cannot model in isolation, and every model like this depends on how you intend to use these models.

Hints and Tips

When you model relationships in the UML,

- Use dependencies only when the relationship you are modeling is not structural.
- Use generalization only when you have an "is-a-kind-of" relationship; multiple inheritance can often be replaced with aggregation.
- Beware of introducing cyclical generalization relationships.
- Keep your generalization relationships generally balanced; inheritance lattices should not be too deep (more than five levels or so should be questioned) nor too wide (instead, look for the possibility of intermediate abstract classes).
- Use associations primarily where there are structural relationships among objects. Do not use them to show transient relationships such as parameters or local variables of procedures.

When you draw a relationship in the UML,

- Use either rectilinear or oblique lines consistently. Rectilinear lines give a visual cue that emphasizes the connections among related things all pointing to one common thing. Oblique lines are often more space-efficient in complex diagrams. Using both kinds of lines in one diagram is useful for drawing attention to different groups of relationships.
- Avoid lines that cross unless absolutely necessary.
- Show only those relationships that are necessary to understand a particular grouping of things. Superfluous relationships (especially redundant associations) should be avoided.

Chapter 6
COMMON MECHANISMS

In this chapter

- Notes
- Stereotypes, tagged values, and constraints
- Modeling comments
- Modeling new building blocks
- Modeling new properties
- Modeling new semantics
- Extending the UML

These common mechanisms are discussed in Chapter 2.

The UML is made simpler by the presence of four common mechanisms that apply throughout the language: specifications, adornments, common divisions, and extensibility mechanisms. This chapter explains the use of two of these common mechanisms: adornments and extensibility mechanisms.

Notes are the most important kind of adornment that stands alone. A note is a graphical symbol for rendering constraints or comments attached to an element or a collection of elements. You use notes to attach information to a model, such as requirements, observations, reviews, and explanations.

The UML's extensibility mechanisms permit you to extend the language in controlled ways. These mechanisms include stereotypes, tagged values, and constraints. A stereotype extends the vocabulary of the UML, allowing you to create new kinds of building blocks that are derived from existing ones but that are specific to your problem. A tagged value extends the properties of a UML stereotype, allowing you to create new information in that element's specification. A constraint extends the semantics of a UML building block, allowing you to add new rules or modify existing ones. You use these mechanisms to tailor the UML to the specific needs of your domain and your development culture.

Getting Started

Sometimes you just have to color outside the lines. For example, at a job site, an architect might scribble a few notes on the building's blueprints to communicate a subtle detail to the construction workers. In a recording studio, a composer might invent a new musical notation to represent some unusual effect she wants from a guitarist. In both cases, there already exist well-defined languages—the language of structural blueprints and the language of musical notation—but sometimes you have to bend or extend those languages in controlled ways to communicate your intent.

Modeling is all about communication. The UML already gives you all the tools you need to visualize, specify, construct, and document the artifacts of a wide range of software-intensive systems. However, you might find circumstances in which you'll want to bend or extend the UML. This happens to human languages all the time (that's why new dictionaries get published every year), because no static language can ever be sufficient to cover everything you'll want to communicate for all time. When using a modeling language such as the UML, remember that you are doing so to communicate, and that means you'll want to stick to the core language unless there's compelling reason to deviate. When you find yourself needing to color outside the lines, you should do so only in controlled ways. Otherwise, you will make it impossible for anyone to understand what you've done.

Notes are the mechanism provided by the UML to let you capture arbitrary comments and constraints to help illuminate the models you've created. Notes may represent artifacts that play an important role in the software development life cycle, such as requirements, or they may simply represent free-form observations, reviews, or explanations.

The UML provides a graphical representation for comments and constraints, called a note, as Figure 6-1 shows. This notation permits you to visualize a comment directly. In conjunction with the proper tools, notes also give you a placeholder to link to or embed other documents.

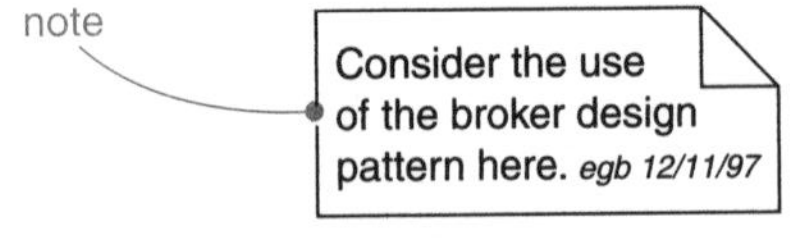

Figure 6-1: Notes

Stereotypes, tagged values, and constraints are the mechanisms provided by the UML to let you add new building blocks, create new properties, and specify new semantics. For example, if you are modeling a network, you might want to have symbols for routers and hubs; you can use stereotyped nodes to make these things appear as primitive building blocks. Similarly, if you are part of your project's release team, responsible for assembling, testing, and then deploying releases, you might want to keep track of the version number and test results for each major subsystem. You can use tagged values to add this information to your models. Finally, if you are modeling hard real time systems, you might want to adorn your models with information about time budgets and deadlines; you can use constraints to capture timing requirements.

The UML provides a textual representation for stereotypes, tagged values, and constraints, as Figure 6-2 shows. Stereotypes also let you introduce new graphical symbols so that you can provide visual cues to your models that speak the language of your domain and your development culture.

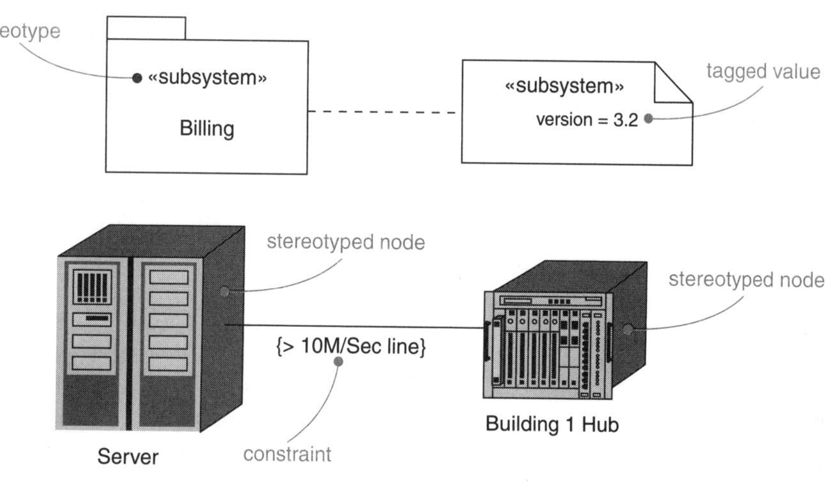

Figure 6-2: Stereotypes, Tagged Values, and Constraints

Terms and Concepts

A *note* is a graphical symbol for rendering constraints or comments attached to an element or a collection of elements. Graphically, a note is rendered as a rectangle with a dog-eared corner, together with a textual or graphical comment.

A *stereotype* is an extension of the vocabulary of the UML, allowing you to create new kinds of building blocks similar to existing ones but specific to your problem. Graphically, a stereotype is rendered as a name enclosed by guillemets (French quotation marks of the form « »), placed above the name of another element.

Optionally the stereotyped element may be rendered by using a new icon associated with that stereotype.

A *tagged value* is a property of a stereotype, allowing you to create new information in an element bearing that stereotype. Graphically, a tagged value is rendered as a string of the form `name = value` within a note attached to the object.

A *constraint* is a textual specification of the semantics of a UML element, allowing you to add new rules or to modify existing ones. Graphically, a constraint is rendered as a string enclosed by brackets and placed near the associated element or connected to that element or elements by dependency relationships. As an alternative, you can render a constraint in a note.

Notes

A note that renders a comment has no semantic impact, meaning that its contents do not alter the meaning of the model to which it is attached. This is why notes are used to specify things like requirements, observations, reviews, and explanations, in addition to rendering constraints.

Notes may be attached to more than one element by using dependencies, as discussed in Chapter 5.

A note may contain any combination of text or graphics. If your implementation allows it, you can put a live URL inside a note, or even link to or embed another document. In this way, you can use the UML to organize all the artifacts you might generate or use during development, as Figure 6-3 illustrates.

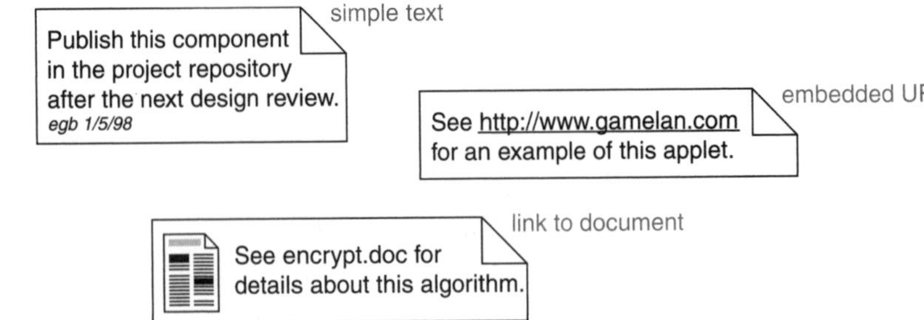

Figure 6-3: Notes

Other Adornments

The basic notation for an association, along with some of its adornments, are discussed in Chapters 5 and 10.

Adornments are textual or graphical items that are added to an element's basic notation and are used to visualize details from the element's specification. For example, the basic notation for an association is a line, but this may be adorned with such details as the role and multiplicity of each end. In using the UML, the general rule to follow is this: Start with the basic notation for each element and then add other adornments only as they are necessary to convey specific information that is important to your model.

Most adornments are rendered by placing text near the element of interest or by adding a graphic symbol to the basic notation. However, sometimes you'll want to adorn an element with more detail than can be accommodated by simple text or graphics. In the case of such things as classes, components, and nodes, you can add an extra compartment below the usual compartments to provide this information, as Figure 6-4 shows.

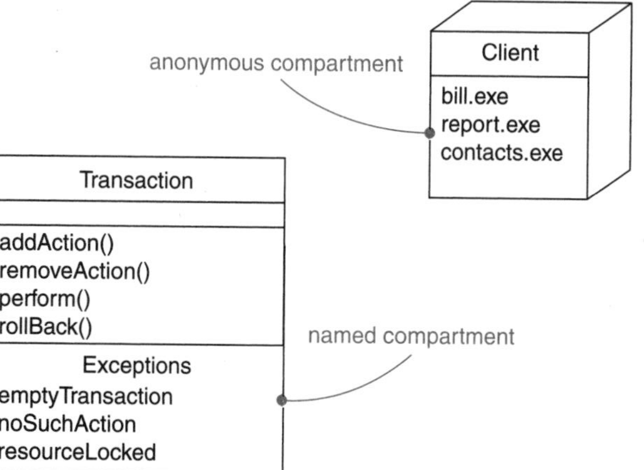

Figure 6-4: Extra Compartments

Note: Unless it's obvious by its content, it's good practice to name any extra compartment explicitly so that there is no confusion about its meaning. It's also good practice to use extra compartments sparingly, because if overused, they make diagrams cluttered.

Stereotypes

These four basic elements of the UML are discussed in Chapter 2.

The UML provides a language for structural things, behavioral things, grouping things, and notational things. These four basic kinds of things address the overwhelming majority of the systems you'll need to model. However, sometimes you'll want to introduce new things that speak the vocabulary of your domain and look like primitive building blocks.

The Rational Unified Process is summarized in Appendix B.

A stereotype is not the same as a parent class in a parent/child generalization relationship. Rather, you can think of a stereotype as a metatype (a type that defines other types), because each one creates the equivalent of a new class in the UML's metamodel. For example, if you are modeling a business process, you'll want to introduce things like workers, documents, and policies. Similarly, if you are following a development process, such as the Rational Unified Process, you'll want to model using boundary, control, and entity classes. This is where the real value of stereotypes comes in. When you stereotype an element such as a node or a class, you are in effect extending the UML by creating a new building block just like an existing one but with its own special modeling properties (each stereotype may provide its own set of tagged values), semantics (each stereotype may provide its own constraints), and notation (each stereotype may provide its own icon).

In its simplest form, a stereotype is rendered as a name enclosed by guillemets (for example, `«name»`) and placed above the name of another element. As a visual cue, you may define an icon for the stereotype and render that icon to the right of the name (if you are using the basic notation for the element) or use that icon as the basic symbol for the stereotyped item. All three of these approaches are illustrated in Figure 6-5.

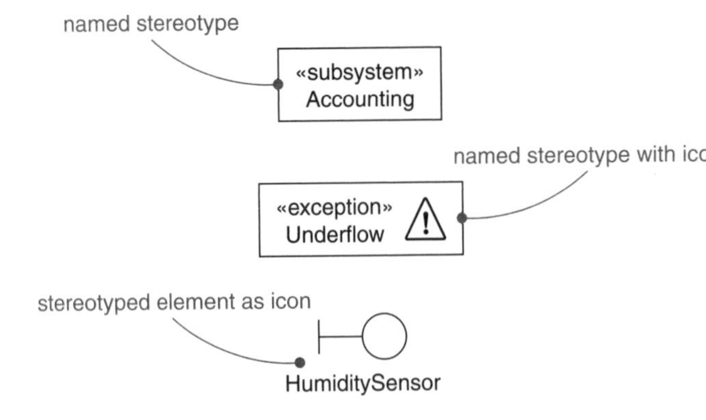

Figure 6-5: Stereotypes

Note: When you define an icon for a stereotype, consider using color as an accent to provide a subtle visual cue (but use color sparingly). The UML lets you use any shape for such icons, and if your implementation permits it, these icons might appear as primitive tools so that users who create UML diagrams will have a palette of things that look basic to them and speak the vocabulary of their domain.

Tagged Values

Every thing in the UML has its own set of properties: classes have names, attributes, and operations; associations have names and two or more ends, each with its own properties; and so on. With stereotypes, you can add new things to the UML; with tagged values, you can add new properties to a stereotype.

Attributes are discussed in Chapters 4 and 9.

You define tags that apply to individual stereotypes so that everything with that stereotype has that tagged value. A tagged value is not the same as a class attribute. Rather, you can think of a tagged value as metadata because its value applies to the element specification, not to its instances. For example, as Figure 6-6 shows, you can specify the required capacity of a server class or require that only one kind of server be used in a given system.

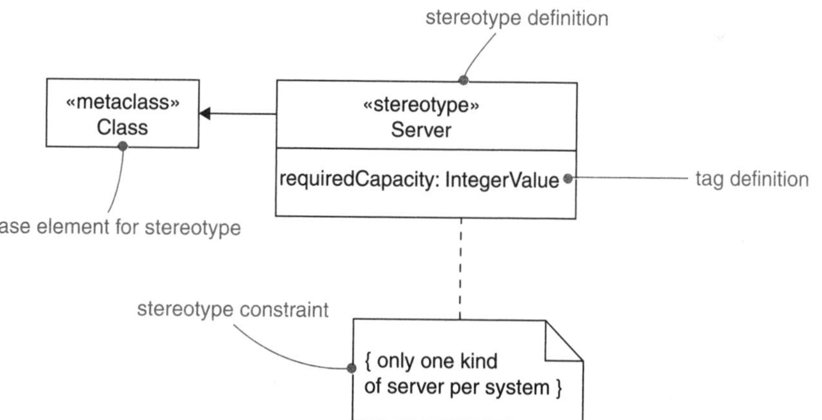

Figure 6-6: Stereotype and Tag Definitions

Tagged values are placed in a note attached to the affected element, as shown in Figure 6-7. Each tagged value comprises a string that includes a name (the tag), a separator (the symbol =), and a value (of the tag).

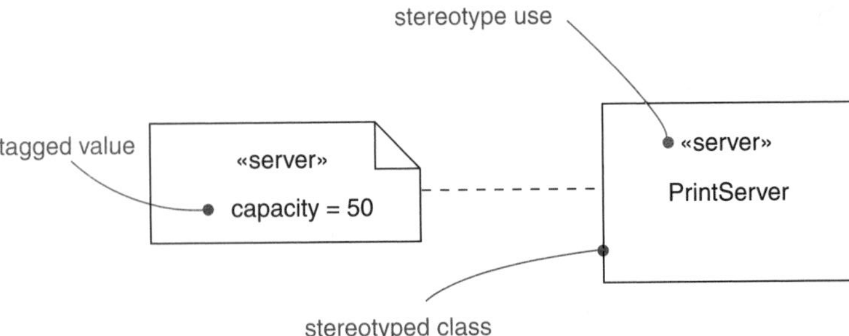

Figure 6-7: Tagged Values

Note: One of the most common uses of tagged values is to specify properties that are relevant to code generation or configuration management. For example, you can use tagged values to specify the programming language to which you map a particular class. Similarly, you can use tagged values to specify the author and version of a component.

Constraints

Time and space constraints, commonly used when modeling real time systems, are discussed in Chapter 24.

Everything in the UML has its own semantics. Generalization (usually, if you know what's good for you) implies the Liskov substitution principle, and multiple associations connected to one class denote distinct relationships. With constraints, you can add new semantics or extend existing rules. A constraint specifies conditions that a run-time configuration must satisfy to conform to the model. For example, as Figure 6-8 shows, you might want to specify that, across a given association, communication is secure; a configuration that violates this constraint is inconsistent with the model. Similarly, you might want to specify that among a set of associations connected to a given class, a particular instance may have links of only one association in the set.

Constraints may be attached to more than one element by using dependencies, as discussed in Chapter 5.

Note: Constraints may be written as free-form text. If you want to specify your semantics more precisely, you can use the UML's Object Constraint Language (OCL), described further in *The Unified Modeling Language Reference Manual.*

A constraint is rendered as a string enclosed by brackets and placed near the associated element. This notation is also used as an adornment to the basic notation of an element to visualize parts of an element's specification that have no graphical cue. For example, some properties of associations (order and changeability) are rendered using constraint notation.

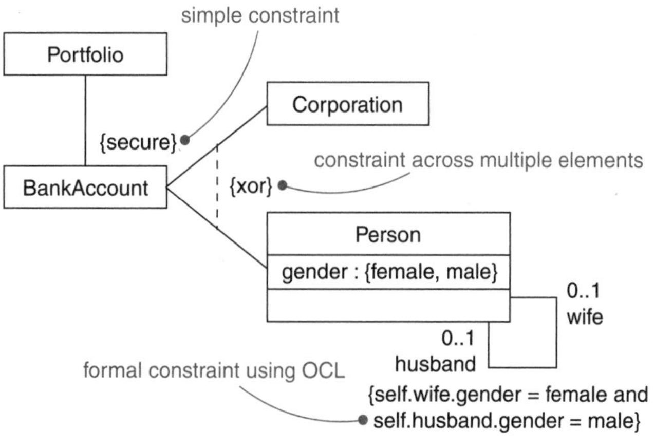

Figure 6-8: Constraint

Standard Elements

Classifiers are discussed in Chapter 9.

The UML defines a number of standard stereotypes for classifiers, components, relationships, and other modeling elements. There is one standard stereotype, mainly of interest to tool builders, that lets you model stereotypes themselves.

- `stereotype` Specifies that the classifier is a stereotype that may be applied to other elements

You'll use this stereotype when you want to explicitly model the stereotypes you've defined for your project.

Profiles

Often it is useful to define a version of UML tailored to a particular purpose or domain area. For example, if you want to use a UML model for code generation in a particular language, it is helpful to define stereotypes that can be applied to elements to give hints to the code generator (like an Ada pragma). The stereotypes you define would be different for Java and C++, however. As another example, you might want to use UML for modeling databases. Some of the UML capabilities, such as dynamic modeling, are less important, but you want to add concepts such as candidate keys and indexes. You can tailor UML using profiles.

A *profile* is a UML model with a set of predefined stereotypes, tagged values, constraints, and base classes. It also selects a subset of the UML element kinds for use so that a modeler is not confused by element kinds that are not needed for the particular application area. A profile defines, in effect, a specialized version of UML for a particular area. Because it is built on ordinary UML elements, it does not represent a new language, and it can be supported by ordinary UML tools.

Most modelers will not construct their own profiles. Most profiles will be constructed by tool builders, framework builders, and similar designers of generic capabilities. Many modelers will use profiles, however. It is the same as traditional subroutine libraries—a few experts built them but many programmers used them. We expect profiles to be constructed for programming languages and databases, for different implementation platforms, for different modeling tools, and for various business domain application areas.

Common Modeling Techniques

Modeling Comments

The most common purpose for which you'll use notes is to write down free-form observations, reviews, or explanations. By putting these comments directly in your models, your models can become a common repository for all the disparate artifacts you'll create during development. You can even use notes to visualize requirements and show how they tie explicitly to the parts of your model.

To model a comment,

- Put your comment as text in a note and place it adjacent to the element to which it refers. You can show a more explicit relationship by connecting a note to its elements using a dependency relationship.
- Remember that you can hide or make visible the elements of your model as you see fit. This means that you don't have to make your comments visible everywhere the elements to which it is attached are visible. Rather, expose your comments in your diagrams only insofar as you need to communicate that information in that context.
- If your comment is lengthy or involves something richer than plain text, consider putting your comment in an external document and linking or embedding that document in a note attached to your model.

- As your model evolves, keep those comments that record significant decisions that cannot be inferred from the model itself, and—unless they are of historic interest—discard the others.

Simple generalization is discussed in Chapter 5; advanced forms of generalization are discussed in Chapter 10.

For example, Figure 6-9 shows a model that's a work in progress of a class hierarchy, showing some requirements that shape the model, as well as some notes from a design review.

In this example, most of the comments are simple text (such as the note to Mary), but one of them (the note at the bottom of the diagram) provides a hyperlink to another document.

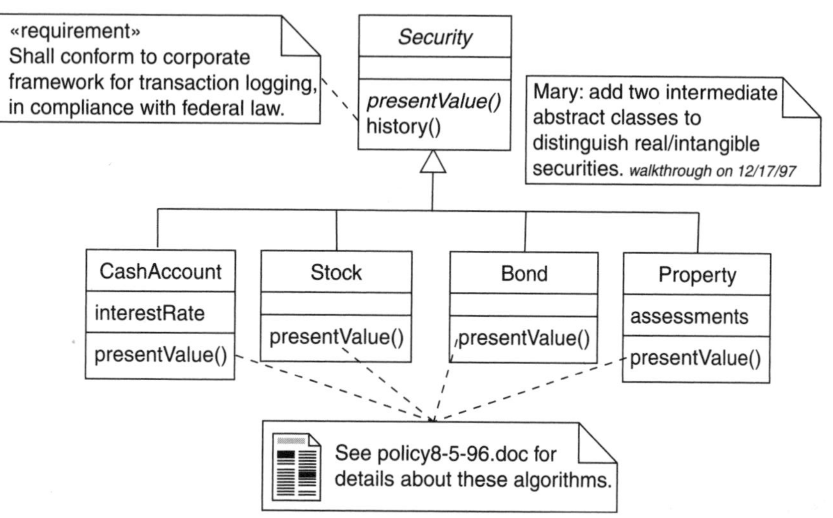

Figure 6-9: Modeling Comments

Modeling New Properties

The basic properties of the UML's building blocks—attributes and operations for classes, the contents of packages, and so on—are generic enough to address most of the things you'll want to model. However, if you want to extend the properties of these basic building blocks, you need to define stereotypes and tagged values.

To model new properties,

- First, make sure there's not already a way to express what you want by using basic UML.

- If you're convinced there's no other way to express these semantics, define a stereotype and add the new properties to the stereotype. The rules of generalization apply—tagged values defined for one kind of stereotype apply to its children.

Subsystems are discussed in Chapter 32.

For example, suppose you want to tie the models you create to your project's configuration management system. Among other things, this means keeping track of the version number, current check in/check out status, and perhaps even the creation and modification dates of each subsystem. Because this is process-specific information, it is not a basic part of the UML, although you can add this information as tagged values. Furthermore, this information is not just a class attribute either. A subsystem's version number is part of its metadata, not part of the model.

Figure 6-10 shows three subsystems, each of which has been extended with the «`versioned`» stereotype to include its version number and status.

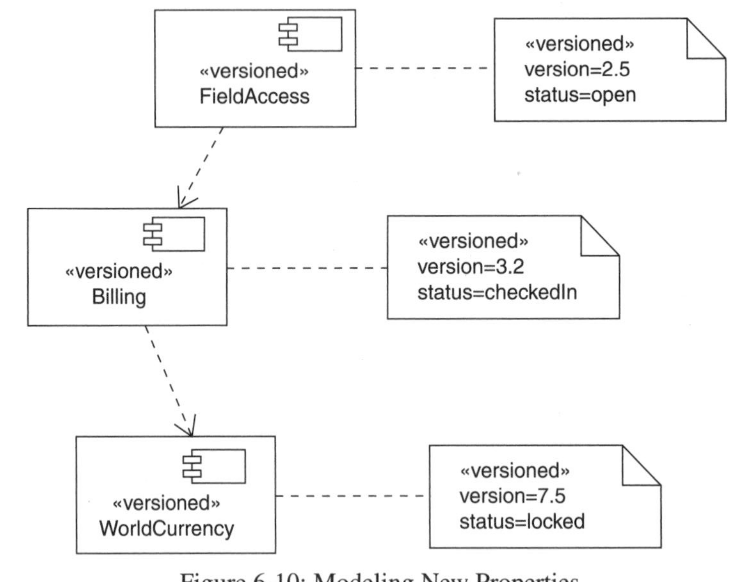

Figure 6-10: Modeling New Properties

Note: The values of tags such as `version` and `status` are things that can be set by tools. Rather than setting these values in your model by hand, you can use a development environment that integrates your configuration management tools with your modeling tools to maintain these values for you.

Modeling New Semantics

When you create a model using the UML, you work within the rules the UML lays down. That's a good thing, because it means that you can communicate your intent without ambiguity to anyone else who knows how to read the UML. However, if you find yourself needing to express new semantics about which the UML is silent or that you need to modify the UML's rules, then you need to write a constraint.

To model new semantics,

- First, make sure there's not already a way to express what you want by using basic UML.
- If you're convinced there's no other way to express these semantics, write your new semantics in a constraint placed near the element to which it refers. You can show a more explicit relationship by connecting a constraint to its elements using a dependency relationship.
- If you need to specify your semantics more precisely and formally, write your new semantics using OCL.

For example, Figure 6-11 models a small part of a corporate human resources system.

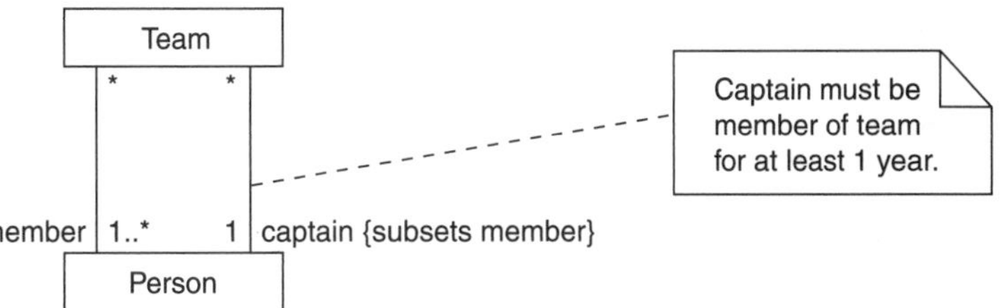

Figure 6-11: Modeling New Semantics

This diagram shows that each `Person` may be a member of zero or more `Teams` and that each `Team` must have at least one `Person` as a member. This diagram goes on to indicate that each `Team` must have exactly one `Person` as a captain and every `Person` may be the captain of zero or more `Teams`. All of these semantics can be expressed using simple UML. However, to assert that a captain must also be a member of the same team is something that cuts across multiple associations and cannot be expressed using simple UML. To state this invariant, you have to write a constraint that shows the manager as a subset of the members of the `Team`, connecting the two associations with a constraint. There is also a constraint that the captain must be a member for at least 1 year.

Hints and Tips

When you adorn a model with notes,

- Use notes only for those requirements, observations, reviews, and explanations that you can't express simply or meaningfully using existing features of the UML.
- Use notes as a kind of electronic sticky note, to keep track of your work in progress.

When you draw notes,

- Don't clutter your models with large blocks of comments. Rather, if you really need a long comment, use notes as a placeholder to link to or embed a document that contains the full comment.

When you extend a model with stereotypes, tagged values, or constraints,

- Standardize on a small set of stereotypes, tagged values, and constraints to use on your project, and avoid letting individual developers create lots of new extensions.
- Chose short, meaningful names for your stereotypes and tagged values.
- Where precision can be relaxed, use free-form text for specifying constraints. If you need more rigor, use the OCL to write constraint expressions.

When you draw a stereotype, tagged value, or constraint,

- Use graphical stereotypes sparingly. You can totally change the basic notation of the UML with stereotypes, but in so doing you'll make it impossible for anyone else to understand your models.
- Consider using simple color or shading for graphical stereotypes, as well as more complicated icons. Simple notations are generally the best, and even the most subtle visual cues can go a long way in communicating meaning.

Chapter 7 DIAGRAMS

In this chapter

- Diagrams, views, and models
- Modeling different views of a system
- Modeling different levels of abstraction
- Modeling complex views
- Organizing diagrams and other artifacts

Modeling is discussed in Chapter 1.

When you model something, you create a simplification of reality so that you can better understand the system you are developing. Using the UML, you build your models from basic building blocks, such as classes, interfaces, collaborations, components, nodes, dependencies, generalizations, and associations.

Diagrams are the means by which you view these building blocks. A diagram is a graphical presentation of a set of elements, most often rendered as a connected graph of vertices (things) and arcs (relationships). You use diagrams to visualize your system from different perspectives. Because no complex system can be understood in its entirety from only one perspective, the UML defines a number of diagrams so that you can focus on different aspects of your system independently.

Good diagrams make the system you are developing understandable and approachable. Choosing the right set of diagrams to model your system forces you to ask the right questions about your system and helps to illuminate the implications of your decisions.

Getting Started

When you work with an architect to design a house, you start with three things: a list of wants (such as "I want a house with three bedrooms" and "I want to pay no more than *x*"), a few simple sketches or pictures from other houses representing some of its key features (such as a picture of an entry with a circular staircase), and some general idea of style (such as "We'd like a French country look with hints of California coastal"). The job of the architect is to take these incomplete, ever-changing, and possibly contradictory requirements and turn them into a design.

To do that, the architect will probably start with a blueprint of a basic floor plan. This artifact provides a vehicle for you and your architect to visualize the final house, to specify details, and to document decisions. At each review, you'll want to make some changes, such as moving walls about, rearranging rooms, and placing windows and doors. Early on, these blueprints change often. As the design matures and you become satisfied that you have a design that best fits all the constraints of form, function, time, and money, these blueprints will stabilize to the point at which they can be used for constructing your house. Even while your house is being built, you'll probably change some of these diagrams and create some new ones as well.

Along the way, you'll want to see views of the house other than just the floor plan. For example, you'll want to see elevations showing the house from different sides. As you start specifying details so that the job can be meaningfully costed, your architect will need to create electrical plans, plans for heating and ventilation, and plans for water and sewer connections. If your design requires some unusual feature (such as a long, unsupported span over the basement) or you have a feature that's important to you (such as the placement of a fireplace so that you can install a home theater), you and your architect will want to create some sketches that highlight those details.

The practice of creating diagrams to visualize systems from different perspectives is not limited to the construction industry. You'll find this in every engineering discipline involving the creation of complex systems, from civil engineering to aeronautical engineering, ship building, manufacturing, and software.

The five views of an architecture are discussed in Chapter 2.

In the context of software, there are five complementary views that are most important in visualizing, specifying, constructing, and documenting a software architecture: the use case view, the design view, the interaction view, the implementation view, and the deployment view. Each of these views involves structural modeling (modeling static things) as well as behavioral modeling (modeling dynamic things). Together, these different views capture the most important decisions about the system. Individually, each of these views lets you focus attention on one perspective of the system so that you can reason about your decisions with clarity.

Modeling the architecture of a system is discussed in Chapter 32.

When you view a software system from any perspective using the UML, you use diagrams to organize the elements of interest. The UML defines different kinds of diagrams, which you can mix and match to assemble each view. For example, the static aspects of a system's implementation view might be visualized using class diagrams; the dynamic aspects of the same implementation view might be visualized using interaction diagrams.

Of course, you are not limited to the predefined diagram types. In the UML, diagram types are defined because they represent the most common packaging of viewed elements. To fit the needs of your project or organization, you can create your own kinds of diagrams to view UML elements in different ways.

This incremental and iterative process is summarized in Appendix B.

You'll use the UML's diagrams in two basic ways: to specify models from which you'll construct an executable system (forward engineering) and to reconstruct models from parts of an executable system (reverse engineering). Either way, just like a building architect, you'll tend to create your diagrams incrementally (crafting them one piece at a time) and iteratively (repeating the process of "design a little, build a little").

Terms and Concepts

Systems, models, and views are discussed in Chapter 32.

A *system* is a collection of subsystems organized to accomplish a purpose and described by a set of models, possibly from different viewpoints. A *subsystem* is a grouping of elements, some of which constitute a specification of the behavior offered by the other contained elements. A *model* is a semantically closed abstraction of a system, meaning that it represents a complete and self-consistent simplification of reality, created in order to better understand the system. In the context of architecture, a *view* is a projection into the organization and structure of a system's model, focused on one aspect of that system. A *diagram* is the graphical presentation of a set of elements, most often rendered as a connected graph of vertices (things) and arcs (relationships).

To put it another way, a system represents the thing you are developing, viewed from different perspectives by different models, with those views presented in the form of diagrams.

A diagram is just a graphical projection into the elements that make up a system. For example, you might have several hundred classes in the design of a corporate human resources system. You could never visualize the structure or behavior of that system by staring at one large diagram containing all these classes and all their relationships. Instead, you'd want to create several diagrams, each focused on one view. For example, you might find one class diagram that includes classes, such as `Person`, `Department`, and `Office`, assembled to construct a database schema. You might find some of these same classes, along with other classes, in another diagram that presents an API that's used by client applications. You'd likely see some of these same classes mentioned in an interaction diagram, specifying the semantics of a transaction that reassigns a `Person` to a new `Department`.

As this example shows, the same thing in a system (such as the class `Person`) may appear multiple times in the same diagram or even in different diagrams. In each case, it's the same thing. Each diagram provides a view into the elements that make up the system.

In modeling real systems, no matter what the problem domain, you'll find yourself creating the same kinds of diagrams, because they represent common views into common models. Typically, you'll view the static parts of a system using one of the following diagrams.

1. Class diagram
2. Component diagram
3. Composite structure diagram
4. Object diagram
5. Deployment diagram
6. Artifact diagram

You'll often use five additional diagrams to view the dynamic parts of a system.

1. Use case diagram
2. Sequence diagram
3. Communication diagram
4. State diagram
5. Activity diagram

Packages are discussed in Chapter 12.

Every diagram you create will most likely be one of these nine or occasionally of another kind, defined for your project or organization. Every diagram must have a name that's unique in its context so that you can refer to a specific diagram and distinguish one from another. For anything but the most trivial system, you'll want to organize your diagrams into packages.

You can project any combination of elements in the UML in the same diagram. For example, you might show both classes and objects in the same diagram (a common thing to do), or you might even show both classes and components in the same diagram (legal, but less common). Although there's nothing that prevents you from placing wildly disparate kinds of modeling elements in the same diagram, it's more common for you to have roughly the same kinds of things in one diagram. In fact, the UML's defined diagrams are named after the element you'll most often place in each. For example, if you want to visualize a set of classes and their relationships, you'll use a class diagram. Similarly, if you want to visualize a set of components, you'll use a component diagram.

Structural Diagrams

The UML's structural diagrams exist to visualize, specify, construct, and document the static aspects of a system. You can think of the static aspects of a system as representing its relatively stable skeleton and scaffolding. Just as the static aspects of a house encompass the existence and placement of such things as walls, doors, windows, pipes, wires, and vents, so too do the static aspects of a software system encompass the existence and placement of such things as classes, interfaces, collaborations, components, and nodes.

The UML's structural diagrams are roughly organized around the major groups of things you'll find when modeling a system.

1. Class diagram	Classes, interfaces, and collaborations
2. Component diagram	Components
3. Composite structure diagram	Internal structure
4. Object diagram	Objects
5. Artifact diagram	Artifacts
6. Deployment diagram	Nodes

Class diagrams are discussed in Chapter 8.

Class Diagram A *class diagram* shows a set of classes, interfaces, and collaborations and their relationships. Class diagrams are the most common diagram found in modeling object-oriented systems. You use class diagrams to illustrate the static design view of a system. Class diagrams that include active classes are used to address the static process view of a system.

Composite structure diagrams and component diagrams are discussed in Chapter 15.

Component Diagram An *component diagram* shows the internal parts, connectors, and ports that implement a component. When the component is instantiated, copies of its internal parts are also instantiated.

Composite Structure Diagram An *composite structure diagram* shows the internal structure of a class or a collaboration. The difference between components and composite structure is small and this book treats them both as component diagrams.

Object diagrams are discussed in Chapter 14.

Object Diagram An *object diagram* shows a set of objects and their relationships. You use object diagrams to illustrate data structures, the static snapshots of instances of the things found in class diagrams. Object diagrams address the static design view or static process view of a system just as class diagrams do, but from the perspective of real or prototypical cases.

Artifact diagrams are discussed in Chapter 30.

Artifact Diagram An *artifact diagram* shows a set of artifacts and their relationships to other artifacts and to the classes that they implement. You use artifact diagrams to show the physical implementation units of the system. (UML considers artifacts to be part of deployment diagrams, but we separate them for convenience of discussion.)

Deployment diagrams are discussed in Chapter 31.

Deployment Diagram A *deployment diagram* shows a set of nodes and their relationships. You use deployment diagrams to illustrate the static deployment view of an architecture. Deployment diagrams are related to component diagrams in that a node typically encloses one or more components.

Note: There are some common variants of these four diagrams, named after their primary purpose. For example, you might create a subsystem diagram to illustrate the structural decomposition of a system into subsystems. A subsystem diagram is just a class diagram that contains, primarily, subsystems.

Behavioral Diagrams

The UML's behavioral diagrams are used to visualize, specify, construct, and document the dynamic aspects of a system. You can think of the dynamic aspects of a system as representing its changing parts. Just as the dynamic aspects of a house encompass airflow and traffic through the rooms of a house, so too do the dynamic aspects of a software system encompass such things as the flow of messages over time and the physical movement of components across a network.

The UML's behavioral diagrams are roughly organized around the major ways you can model the dynamics of a system.

1. Use case diagram	Organizes the behaviors of the system
2. Sequence diagram	Focuses on the time ordering of messages
3. Communication diagram	Focuses on the structural organization of objects that send and receive messages
4. State diagram	Focuses on the changing state of a system driven by events

5. Activity diagram — Focuses on the flow of control from activity to activity

Use case diagrams are discussed in Chapter 18.

Use Case Diagram A *use case diagram* shows a set of use cases and actors (a special kind of class) and their relationships. You apply use case diagrams to illustrate the static use case view of a system. Use case diagrams are especially important in organizing and modeling the behaviors of a system.

Interaction diagram is the collective name given to sequence diagrams and communication diagrams. All sequence diagrams and communication diagrams are interaction diagrams, and an interaction diagram is either a sequence diagram or a communication diagram. These diagrams share the same underlying model, although in practice they emphasize different things. (Timing diagrams are another kind of interaction diagram that are not covered in this book.)

Sequence diagrams are discussed in Chapter 19.

Sequence Diagram A *sequence diagram* is an interaction diagram that emphasizes the time ordering of messages. A sequence diagram shows a set of roles and the messages sent and received by the instances playing the roles. You use sequence diagrams to illustrate the dynamic view of a system.

Communication diagrams are discussed in Chapter 19.

Communication Diagram A *communication diagram* is an interaction diagram that emphasizes the structural organization of the objects that send and receive messages. A communication diagram shows a set of roles, connectors among those roles, and messages sent and received by the instances playing the roles. You use communication diagrams to illustrate the dynamic view of a system.

State diagrams are discussed in Chapter 25.

State Diagram A *state diagram* shows a state machine, consisting of states, transitions, events, and activities. You use state diagrams to illustrate the dynamic view of a system. They are especially important in modeling the behavior of an interface, class, or collaboration. State diagrams emphasize the event-ordered behavior of an object, which is especially useful in modeling reactive systems.

Activity diagrams, a special case of state diagrams, are discussed in Chapter 20.

Activity Diagram An *activity diagram* shows the flow from step to step within a computation. An activity shows a set of actions, the sequential or branching flow from action to action, and values that are produced or consumed by actions. You use activity diagrams to illustrate the dynamic view of a system. Activity diagrams are especially important in modeling the function of a system. Activity diagrams emphasize the flow of control within the execution of a behavior.

Note: There are obvious practical limitations to illustrating something that's inherently dynamic (the behavior of a system) using diagrams (inherently static artifacts, especially when you draw them on a sheet of paper, a whiteboard, or the back of an envelope). Rendered on a computer display, there are opportunities for animating behavioral diagrams so that they either simulate an executable system or mirror the actual behavior of a system that's executing. The UML allows you to create dynamic diagrams and to use color or other visual cues to "run" the diagram. Some tools have already demonstrated this advanced use of the UML.

Common Modeling Techniques

Modeling Different Views of a System

When you model a system from different views, you are in effect constructing your system simultaneously from multiple dimensions. By choosing the right set of views, you set up a process that forces you to ask good questions about your system and to expose risks that need to be attacked. If you do a poor job of choosing these views or if you focus on one view at the expense of all others, you run the risk of hiding issues and deferring problems that will eventually destroy any chance of success.

To model a system from different views,

- Decide which views you need to best express the architecture of your system and to expose the technical risks to your project. The five views of an architecture described earlier are a good starting point.
- For each of these views, decide which artifacts you need to create to capture the essential details of that view. For the most part, these artifacts will consist of various UML diagrams.
- As part of your process planning, decide which of these diagrams you'll want to put under some sort of formal or semi-formal control. These are the diagrams for which you'll want to schedule reviews and to preserve as documentation for the project.
- Allow room for diagrams that are thrown away. Such transitory diagrams are still useful for exploring the implications of your decisions and for experimenting with changes.

For example, if you are modeling a simple monolithic application that runs on a single machine, you might need only the following handful of diagrams.

- Use case view — Use case diagrams
- Design view — Class diagrams (for structural modeling)
- Interaction view — Interaction diagrams (for behavioral modeling)
- Implementation view — Composite structure diagrams
- Deployment view — None required

If yours is a reactive system or if it focuses on process flow, you'll probably want to include state diagrams and activity diagrams, respectively, to model your system's behavior.

Similarly, if yours is a client/server system, you'll probably want to include component diagrams and deployment diagrams to model the physical details of your system.

Finally, if you are modeling a complex, distributed system, you'll need to employ the full range of the UML's diagrams in order to express the architecture of your system and the technical risks to your project, as in the following.

- Use case view — Use case diagrams
Sequence diagrams
- Design view — Class diagrams (for structural modeling)
Interaction diagrams (for behavioral modeling)
State diagrams (for behavioral modeling)
Activity diagrams
- Interaction view — Interaction diagrams (for behavioral modeling)
- Implementation view — Class diagrams
Composite structure diagrams
- Deployment view — Deployment diagrams

Modeling Different Levels of Abstraction

Not only do you need to view a system from several angles, you'll also find people involved in development who need the same view of the system but at different levels of abstraction. For example, given a set of classes that capture the vocabulary of your problem space, a programmer might want a detailed view down to the level of each class's attributes, operations, and relationships. On the other hand, an analyst who's walking through some use case scenarios with an end user will likely want only a much elided view of these same classes. In this context, the programmer is working at a lower level of abstraction, and the analyst and end user are working at a higher level of abstraction, but all are working from the same model. In fact, because diagrams are just a graphical presentation of the elements that make up a model, you can create several diagrams against the same model or different models, each hiding or exposing different sets of these elements and each showing different levels of detail.

Basically, there are two ways to model a system at different levels of abstraction: by presenting diagrams with different levels of detail against the same model or by creating models at different levels of abstraction with diagrams that trace from one model to another.

To model a system at different levels of abstraction by presenting diagrams with different levels of detail,

- Consider the needs of your readers, and start with a given model.
- If your reader is using the model to construct an implementation, she'll need diagrams that are at a lower level of abstraction, which means that they'll need to reveal a lot of detail. If she is using the model to present a conceptual model to an end user, she'll need diagrams that are at a higher level of abstraction, which means that they'll hide a lot of detail.
- Depending on where you land in this spectrum of low-to-high levels of abstraction, create a diagram at the right level of abstraction by hiding or revealing the following four categories of things from your model:

Messages are discussed in Chapter 16; transitions are discussed in Chapter 22; stereotypes are discussed in Chapter 6.

1. *Building blocks and relationships*: Hide those that are not relevant to the intent of your diagram or the needs of your reader.
2. *Adornments*: Reveal only the adornments of these building blocks and relationships that are essential to understanding your intent.
3. *Flow*: In the context of behavioral diagrams, expand only those messages or transitions that are essential to understanding your intent.
4. *Stereotypes*: In the context of stereotypes used to classify lists of things, such as attributes and operations, reveal only those stereotyped items that are essential to understanding your intent.

The main advantage of this approach is that you are always modeling from a common semantic repository. The main disadvantage of this approach is that changes from diagrams at one level of abstraction may make obsolete diagrams at a different level of abstraction.

To model a system at different levels of abstraction by creating models at different levels of abstraction,

- Consider the needs of your readers and decide on the level of abstraction that each should view, forming a separate model for each level.

Trace dependencies are discussed in Chapter 32.

- In general, populate your models that are at a high level of abstraction with simple abstractions and your models that are at a low level of abstraction with detailed abstractions. Establish trace dependencies among the related elements of different models.
- In practice, if you follow the five views of an architecture, there are four common situations you'll encounter when modeling a system at different levels of abstraction:

Use cases are discussed in Chapter 17; collaborations are discussed in Chapter 28; components are discussed in Chapter 15; nodes are discussed in Chapter 27.

1. *Use cases and their realization*: Use cases in a use case model will trace to collaborations in a design model.
2. *Collaborations and their realization*: Collaborations will trace to a society of classes that work together to carry out the collaboration.
3. *Components and their design*: Components in an implementation model will trace to the elements in a design model.
4. *Nodes and their components*: Nodes in a deployment model will trace to components in an implementation model.

The main advantage of the approach is that diagrams at different levels of abstraction remain more loosely coupled. This means that changes in one model will have less direct effect on other models. The main disadvantage of this approach is that you must spend resources to keep these models and their diagrams synchronized. This is especially true when your models parallel different phases of the software development life cycle, such as when you decide to maintain an analysis model separate from a design model.

Interaction diagrams are discussed in Chapter 19.

For example, suppose you are modeling a system for Web commerce—one of the main use cases of such a system would be for placing an order. If you're an analyst or an end user, you'd probably create some interaction diagrams at a high level of abstraction that show the action of placing an order, as in Figure 7-1.

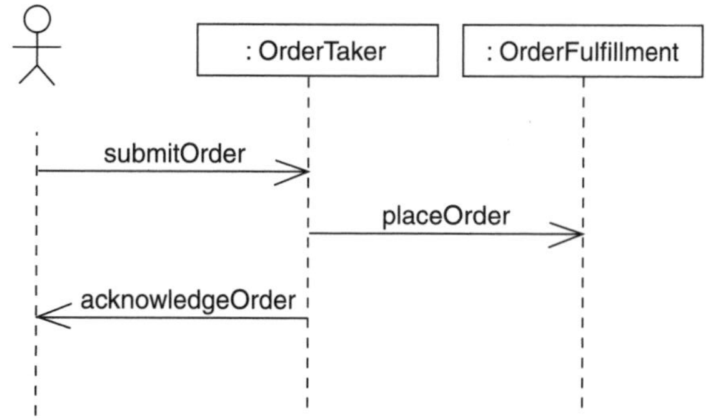

Figure 7-1: Interaction Diagram at a High Level of Abstraction

On the other hand, a programmer responsible for implementing this scenario would have to build on this diagram, expanding certain messages and adding other players in this interaction, as in Figure 7-2.

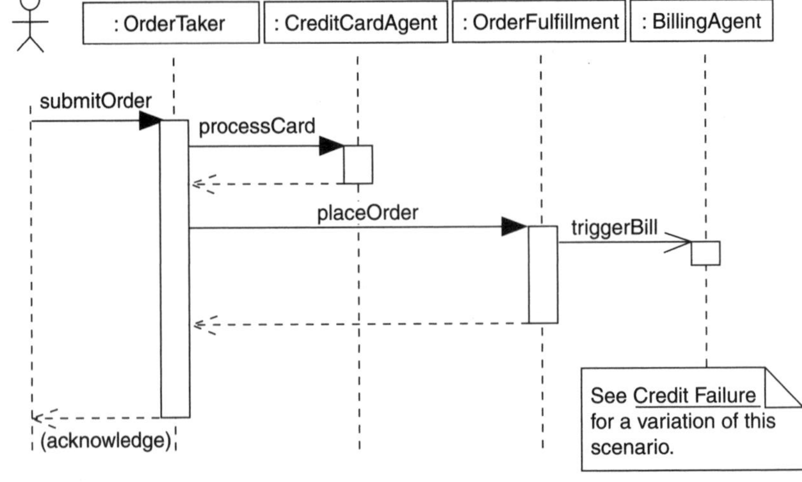

Figure 7-2: Interaction at a Low Level of Abstraction

Both of these diagrams work against the same model, but at different levels of detail. The second diagram has additional messages and roles. It's reasonable to have many diagrams such as these, especially if your tools make it easy to navigate from one diagram to another.

Modeling Complex Views

No matter how you break up your models, there are times when you'll find it necessary to create large and complex diagrams. For example, if you want to analyze the entire schema of a database encompassing 100 or more abstractions, it really is valuable to study a diagram showing all these classes and their associations. In so doing, you'll be able to see common patterns of collaboration. If you were to show this model at a higher level of abstraction by eliding some detail, you'd lose the information necessary to make these insights.

To model complex views,

Packages are discussed in Chapter 12; collaborations are discussed in Chapter 28.

- First, convince yourself that there is no meaningful way to present this information at a higher level of abstraction, perhaps eliding some parts of the diagram and retaining the detail in other parts.
- If you've hidden as much detail as you can and your diagram is still complex, consider grouping some of the elements in packages or in

higher-level collaborations, then render only those packages or collaborations in your diagram.

- If your diagram is still complex, use notes and color as visual cues to draw the reader's attention to the points you want to make.
- If your diagram is still complex, print it in its entirety and hang it on a convenient large wall. You lose the interactivity that an online version of the diagram brings, but you can step back from the diagram and study it for common patterns.

Hints and Tips

When you create a diagram,

- Remember that the purpose of a diagram in the UML is not to draw pretty pictures but to visualize, specify, construct, and document. Diagrams are a means to the end of deploying an executable system.
- Not all diagrams are meant to be preserved. Consider building up diagrams on the fly by querying the elements in your models, and use these diagrams to reason about your system as it is being built. Many of these kinds of diagrams can be thrown away after they have served their purpose (but the semantics upon which they were created will remain as a part of the model).
- Avoid extraneous or redundant diagrams. They clutter your models.
- Reveal only enough detail in each diagram to address the issues for which it was intended. Extraneous information can distract the reader from the key point you're trying to make.
- On the other hand, don't make your diagrams minimalist unless you really need to present something at a very high level of abstraction. Oversimplification can hide details that are important to reasoning about your models.
- Keep a balance between the structural and behavioral diagrams in your system. Very few systems are totally static or totally dynamic.
- Don't make your diagrams too big (ones that run more than one printed page are hard to understand) or too small (consider joining several trivial diagrams into one).
- Give each diagram a meaningful name that clearly expresses its intent.
- Keep your diagrams organized. Group them into packages according to view.
- Don't obsess over the format of a diagram. Let tools help you.

A well-structured diagram

- Is focused on communicating one aspect of a system's view.
- Contains only those elements that are essential to understanding that aspect.
- Provides detail consistent with its level of abstraction (expose only those adornments that are essential to understanding).
- Is not so minimalist that it misinforms the reader about semantics that are important.

When you draw a diagram,

- Give it a name that communicates its purpose.
- Lay out its elements to minimize lines that cross.
- Organize its elements spatially so that things that are semantically close are laid out physically close.
- Use notes and color as visual cues to draw attention to important features of your diagram. Use color with care, however, because many people are color blind; color should only be used as a highlight, not to convey essential information.

Chapter 8

CLASS DIAGRAMS

In this chapter

- Modeling simple collaborations
- Modeling a logical database schema
- Forward and reverse engineering

Class diagrams are the most common diagram found in modeling object-oriented systems. A class diagram shows a set of classes, interfaces, and collaborations and their relationships.

You use class diagrams to model the static design view of a system. For the most part, this involves modeling the vocabulary of the system, modeling collaborations, or modeling schemas. Class diagrams are also the foundation for a couple of related diagrams: component diagrams and deployment diagrams.

Class diagrams are important not only for visualizing, specifying, and documenting structural models, but also for constructing executable systems through forward and reverse engineering.

Getting Started

When you build a house, you start with a vocabulary that includes basic building blocks, such as walls, floors, windows, doors, ceilings, and joists. These things are largely structural (walls have height, width, and thickness), but they're also somewhat behavioral (different kinds of walls can support different loads, doors open and close, there are constraints on the span of a unsupported floor). In fact, you can't consider these structural and behavioral features independently. Rather, when you build your house, you must consider how they interact. The process of architecting your house thus involves assembling these things in a unique and pleasing manner intended to satisfy all your functional and nonfunctional requirements. The blueprints you create to visualize your house and to specify its details to your contractors for construction are, in effect, graphical presentations of these things and their relationships.

Building software has much the same characteristics except that, given the fluidity of software, you have the ability to define your own basic building blocks from scratch. With the UML, you use class diagrams to visualize the static aspects of these building blocks and their relationships and to specify their details for construction, as you can see in Figure 8-1.

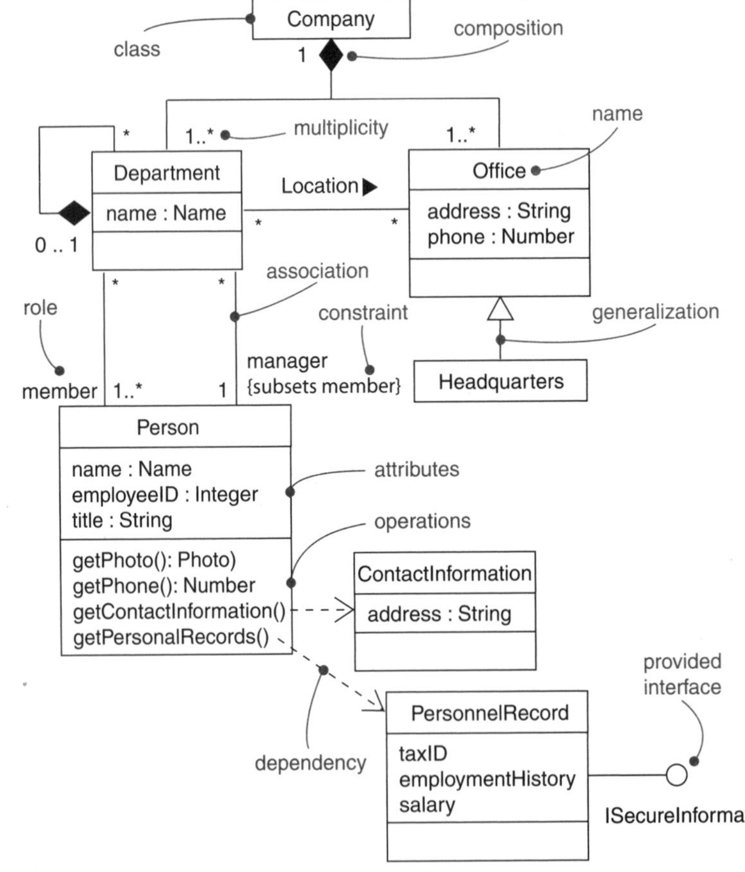

Figure 8-1: A Class Diagram

Terms and Concepts

A *class diagram* is a diagram that shows a set of classes, interfaces, and collaborations and their relationships. Graphically, a class diagram is a collection of vertices and arcs.

Common Properties

The general properties of diagrams are discussed in Chapter 7.

A class diagram is just a special kind of diagram and shares the same common properties as do all other diagrams—a name and graphical content that are a projection into a model. What distinguishes a class diagram from other kinds of diagrams is its particular content.

Contents

Classes are discussed in Chapters 4 and 9; interfaces are discussed in Chapter 11; relationships are discussed in Chapters 5 and 10; packages are discussed in Chapter 12; subsystems are discussed in Chapter 32; instances are discussed in Chapter 13.

Class diagrams commonly contain the following things:

- Classes
- Interfaces
- Dependency, generalization, and association relationships

Like all other diagrams, class diagrams may contain notes and constraints.

Class diagrams may also contain packages or subsystems, both of which are used to group elements of your model into larger chunks. Sometimes you'll want to place instances in your class diagrams as well, especially when you want to visualize the (possibly dynamic) type of an instance.

Note: Component diagrams and deployment diagrams are similar to class diagrams, except that instead of containing classes they contain components and nodes, respectively.

Common Uses

Design views are discussed in Chapter 2.

You use class diagrams to model the static design view of a system. This view primarily supports the functional requirements of a system—the services the system should provide to its end users.

When you model the static design view of a system, you'll typically use class diagrams in one of three ways.

Modeling the vocabulary of a system is discussed in Chapter 4.

1. To model the vocabulary of a system

Modeling the vocabulary of a system involves making a decision about which abstractions are a part of the system under consideration and which fall outside its boundaries. You use class diagrams to specify these abstractions and their responsibilities.

Collaborations are discussed in Chapter 28.

2. To model simple collaborations

A collaboration is a society of classes, interfaces, and other elements that work together to provide some cooperative behavior that's bigger than the sum of all the elements. For example, when you're modeling the semantics of a transaction in a distributed system, you can't just stare at a single class to understand what's going on. Rather, these semantics are carried out by a set of classes that work together. You use class diagrams to visualize and specify this set of classes and their relationships.

Persistence is discussed in Chapter 24; modeling physical databases is discussed in Chapter 30.

3. To model a logical database schema

Think of a schema as the blueprint for the conceptual design of a database. In many domains, you'll want to store persistent information in a relational database or in an object-oriented database. You can model schemas for these databases using class diagrams.

Common Modeling Techniques

Modeling Simple Collaborations

No class stands alone. Rather, each works in collaboration with others to carry out some semantics greater than each individual. Therefore, in addition to capturing the vocabulary of your system, you'll also need to turn your attention to visualizing, specifying, constructing, and documenting the various ways these things in your vocabulary work together. You use class diagrams to represent such collaborations.

To model a collaboration,

Mechanisms such as this are often coupled to use cases, as discussed in Chapter 17; scenarios are threads through a use case, as discussed in Chapter 16.

- Identify the mechanism you'd like to model. A mechanism represents some function or behavior of the part of the system you are modeling that results from the interaction of a society of classes, interfaces, and other things.
- For each mechanism, identify the classes, interfaces, and other collaborations that participate in this collaboration. Identify the relationships among these things as well.
- Use scenarios to walk through these things. Along the way, you'll discover parts of your model that were missing and parts that were just plain semantically wrong.
- Be sure to populate these elements with their contents. For classes, start with getting a good balance of responsibilities. Then, over time, turn these into concrete attributes and operations.

For example, Figure 8-2 shows a set of classes drawn from the implementation of an autonomous robot. The figure focuses on the classes involved in the mechanism for moving the robot along a path. You'll find one abstract class (`Motor`) with two concrete children, `SteeringMotor` and `MainMotor`. Both of these classes inherit the five operations of their parent, `Motor`. The two classes are, in turn, shown as parts of another class, `Driver`. The class `PathAgent` has a one-to-one association to `Driver` and a one-to-many association to `CollisionSensor`. No attributes or operations are shown for `PathAgent`, although its responsibilities are given.

There are many more classes involved in this system, but this diagram focuses only on those abstractions that are directly involved in moving the robot. You'll see some of these same classes in other diagrams. For example, although not shown here, the class `PathAgent` collaborates with at least two other classes (`Environment` and `GoalAgent`) in a higher-level mechanism for managing the conflicting goals the robot might have at a given moment. Similarly, also not shown here, the classes `CollisionSensor` and `Driver` (and its parts) collaborate with another class (`FaultAgent`) in a mechanism responsible for continuously checking the robot's hardware for errors. By focusing on each of these collaborations in different diagrams, you provide an understandable view of the system from several angles.

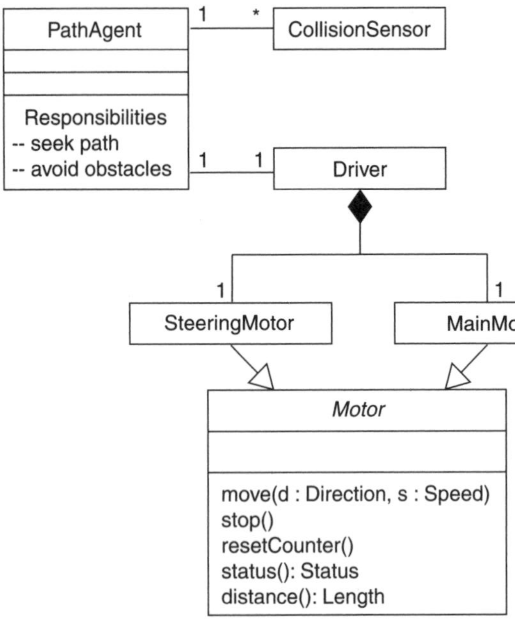

Figure 8-2: Modeling Simple Collaborations

Modeling a Logical Database Schema

Modeling the distribution and of objects is discussed in Chapter 24; modeling physical databases is discussed in Chapter 30.

Many of the systems you'll model will have persistent objects, which means that they can be stored in a database for later retrieval. Most often, you'll use a relational database, an object-oriented database, or a hybrid object/relational database for persistent storage. The UML is well-suited to modeling logical database schemas, as well as physical databases themselves.

The UML's class diagrams are a superset of entity-relationship (E-R) diagrams, a common modeling tool for logical database design. Whereas classical E-R diagrams focus only on data, class diagrams go a step further by permitting the modeling of behavior as well. In the physical database, these logical operations are generally turned into triggers or stored procedures.

To model a schema,

- Identify those classes in your model whose state must transcend the lifetime of their applications.

Stereotypes are discussed in Chapter 6.

- Create a class diagram that contains these classes. You can define your own set of stereotypes and tagged values to address database-specific details.
- Expand the structural details of these classes. In general, this means specifying the details of their attributes and focusing on the associations and their multiplicities that relate these classes.
- Watch for common patterns that complicate physical database design, such as cyclic associations and one-to-one associations. Where necessary, create intermediate abstractions to simplify your logical structure.
- Consider also the behavior of these classes by expanding operations that are important for data access and data integrity. In general, to provide a better separation of concerns, business rules concerned with the manipulation of sets of these objects should be encapsulated in a layer above these persistent classes.
- Where possible, use tools to help you transform your logical design into a physical design.

Note: Logical database design is beyond the scope of this book. The focus here is simply to show how you can model schemas using the UML. In practice, you'll end up using stereotypes tuned to the kind of database (relational or object-oriented) you are using.

Figure 8-3 shows a set of classes drawn from an information system for a school. This figure expands upon an earlier class diagram, and you'll see the details of these classes revealed to a level sufficient to construct a physical database. Starting at the bottom-left of this diagram, you will find the classes named `Student`, `Course`, and `Instructor`. There's an association between `Student` and `Course`, specifying that students attend courses. Furthermore, every student may attend any number of courses, and every course may have any number of students.

Modeling primitive types is discussed in Chapter 4; aggregation is discussed in Chapters 5 and 10.

This diagram exposes the attributes of all six of these classes. Notice that the types of all the attributes are primitive types. When you are modeling a schema, you'll generally want to model the relationship to any nonprimitive types using an explicit association rather than an attribute.

Two of these classes (`School` and `Department`) expose several operations for manipulating their parts. These operations are included because they are important to maintain data integrity (adding or removing a `Department`, for example, will have some rippling effects). There are many other operations that you might consider for these and the other classes, such as querying the prerequisites of a course before assigning a student. These function more as business rules than as operations for database integrity, so they are best placed at a higher level of abstraction than this schema.

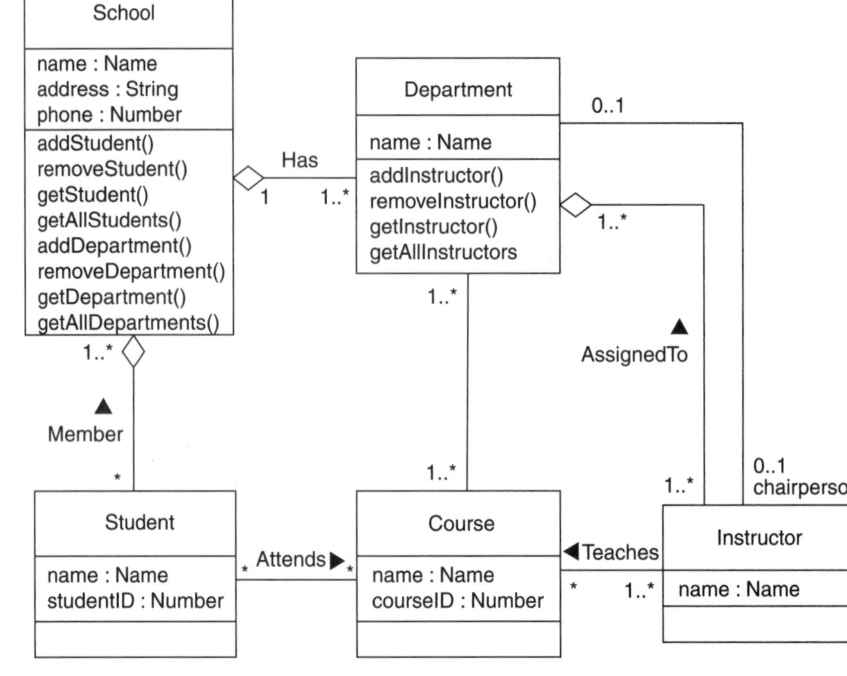

Figure 8-3: Modeling a Schema

Forward and Reverse Engineering

The importance of modeling is discussed in Chapter 1.

Modeling is important, but you have to remember that the primary product of a development team is software, not diagrams. Of course, the reason for creating models is to be able to deliver software that satisfies the evolving goals of its users and the business at the right time. For this reason, it's important that the models you create and the implementations you deploy map to one another and do so in a way that minimizes or even eliminates the cost of keeping your models and your implementation in sync with one another.

Activity diagrams are discussed in Chapter 20.

For some uses of the UML, the models you create will never map to code. For example, if you are modeling a business process using activity diagrams, many of the activities you model will involve people, not computers. In other cases, you'll want to model systems whose parts are, from your level of abstraction, just a piece of hardware (although at another level of abstraction, it's a good bet that this hardware contains an embedded computer and software).

In most cases though, the models you create will map to code. The UML does not specify a particular mapping to any object-oriented programming language, but the UML was designed with such mappings in mind. This is especially true for class diagrams, whose contents have a clear mapping to all the industrial-strength object-oriented languages, such as Java, C++, Smalltalk, Eiffel, Ada, ObjectPascal, and Forte. The UML was also designed to map to a variety of commercial object-based languages, such as Visual Basic.

Stereotypes and tagged values are discussed in Chapter 6.

Note: The mapping of the UML to specific implementation languages for forward and reverse engineering is beyond the scope of this book. In practice, you'll end up using stereotypes and tagged values tuned to the programming language you are using.

Forward engineering is the process of transforming a model into code through a mapping to an implementation language. Forward engineering results in a loss of information, because models written in the UML are semantically richer than any current object-oriented programming language. In fact, this is a major reason why you need models in addition to code. Structural features, such as collaborations, and behavioral features, such as interactions, can be visualized clearly in the UML, but not so clearly from raw code.

To forward engineer a class diagram,

- Identify the rules for mapping to your implementation language or languages of choice. This is something you'll want to do for your project or your organization as a whole.
- Depending on the semantics of the languages you choose, you may want to constrain your use of certain UML features. For example, the UML permits you to model multiple inheritance, but Smalltalk permits only single inheritance. You can choose to prohibit developers from modeling with multiple inheritance (which makes your models language-dependent), or you can develop idioms that transform these richer features into the implementation language (which makes the mapping more complex).
- Use tagged values to guide implementation choices in your target language. You can do this at the level of individual classes if you need precise control. You can also do so at a higher level, such as with collaborations or packages.
- Use tools to generate code.

Patterns are discussed in Chapter 29.

Figure 8-4 illustrates a simple class diagram specifying an instantiation of the chain of responsibility pattern. This particular instantiation involves three classes: `Client`, `EventHandler`, and `GUIEventHandler`. The classes `Client` and `EventHandler` are abstract, whereas `GUIEventHandler` is concrete. `EventHandler` has the usual operation expected of this pattern (`handleRequest`), although two private attributes have been added for this instantiation.

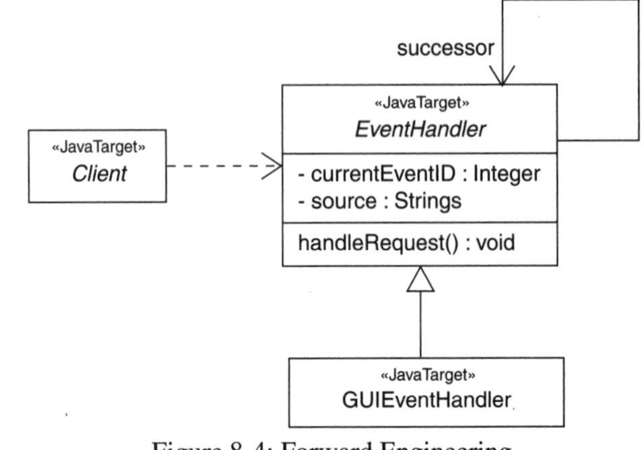

Figure 8-4: Forward Engineering

All of these classes specify a mapping to Java, as noted in their stereotype. Forward engineering the classes in this diagram to Java is straightforward, using a tool. Forward engineering the class `EventHandler` yields the following code.

```
public abstract class EventHandler {

  EventHandler successor;
  private Integer currentEventID;
  private String source;

  EventHandler() {}
  public void handleRequest() {}

}
```

Reverse engineering is the process of transforming code into a model through a mapping from a specific implementation language. Reverse engineering results in a flood of information, some of which is at a lower level of detail than you'll need to build useful models. At the same time, reverse engineering is incomplete. There is a loss of information when forward engineering models into code, and so you can't completely recreate a model from code unless your tools encode information in the source comments that goes beyond the semantics of the implementation language.

To reverse engineer a class diagram,

- Identify the rules for mapping from your implementation language or languages of choice. This is something you'll want to do for your project or your organization as a whole.
- Using a tool, point to the code you'd like to reverse engineer. Use your tool to generate a new model or modify an existing one that was previously forward engineered. It is unreasonable to expect to reverse engineer a single concise model from a large body of code. You need to select portion of the code and build the model from the bottom.
- Using your tool, create a class diagram by querying the model. For example, you might start with one or more classes, then expand the diagram by following specific relationships or other neighboring classes. Expose or hide details of the contents of this class diagram as necessary to communicate your intent.
- Manually add design information to the model to express the intent of the design that is missing or hidden in the code.

Hints and Tips

When you create class diagrams in the UML, remember that every class diagram is just a graphical presentation of the static design view of a system. No single class diagram need capture everything about a system's design view. Collectively, all the class diagrams of a system represent the system's complete static design view; individually, each represents just one aspect.

A well-structured class diagram

- Is focused on communicating one aspect of a system's static design view.
- Contains only elements that are essential to understanding that aspect.
- Provides detail consistent with its level of abstraction, with only those adornments that are essential to understanding.
- Is not so minimalist that it misinforms the reader about important semantics.

When you draw a class diagram,

- Give it a name that communicates its purpose.
- Lay out its elements to minimize lines that cross.
- Organize its elements spatially so that things that are semantically close are laid out physically close.
- Use notes and color as visual cues to draw attention to important features of your diagram.
- Try not to show too many kinds of relationships. In general, one kind of relationship will tend to dominate each class diagram.

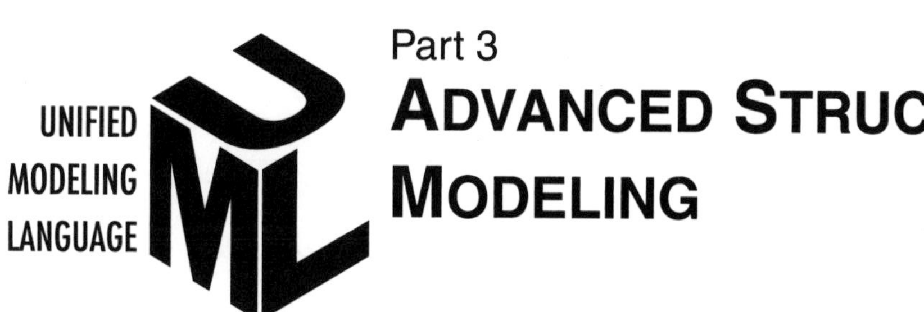

Part 3

Advanced Structural Modeling

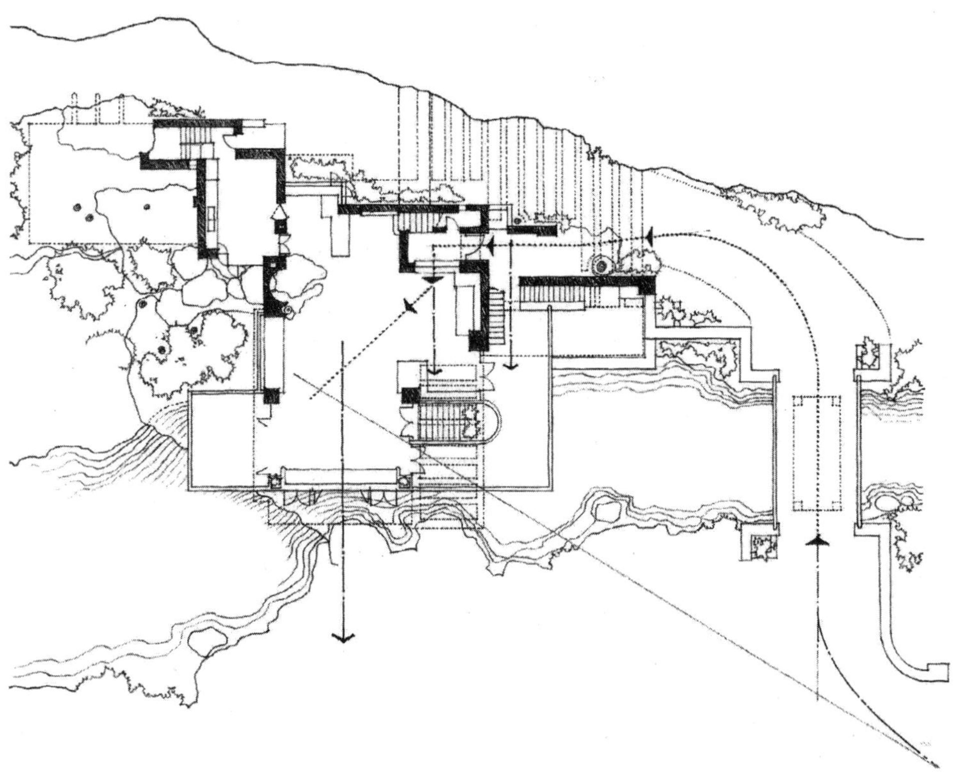

Chapter 9
ADVANCED CLASSES

In this chapter

- Classifiers, special properties of attributes and operations, and different kinds of classes
- Modeling the semantics of a class
- Choosing the right kind of classifier

Classes are indeed the most important building block of any object-oriented system. However, classes are just one kind of an even more general building block in the UML—classifiers. A classifier is a mechanism that describes structural and behavioral features. Classifiers include classes, interfaces, datatypes, signals, components, nodes, use cases, and subsystems.

The basic properties of classes are discussed in Chapter 4.

Classifiers (and especially classes) have a number of advanced features beyond the simpler properties of attributes and operations described in the previous part: You can model multiplicity, visibility, signatures, polymorphism, and other characteristics. In the UML, you can model the semantics of a class so that you can state its meaning to whatever degree of formality you like.

In the UML, there are several kinds of classifiers and classes; it's important that you choose the one that best models your abstraction of the real world.

Getting Started

Architecture is discussed in Chapter 2.

When you build a house, at some point in the project you'll make an architectural decision about your building materials. Early on, it's sufficient to simply state wood, stone, or steel. That's a level of detail sufficient for you to move forward. The material you choose will be affected by the requirements of your project—steel and concrete would be a good choice if you are building in an area susceptible to hurricanes, for example. As you move forward, the material you choose will affect your design decisions that follow—choosing wood versus steel will affect the mass that can be supported, for example.

As your project continues, you'll have to refine these basic design decisions and add more detail sufficient for a structural engineer to validate the safety of the design and for a builder to proceed with construction. For example, you might have to specify not just wood, but wood of a certain grade that's been treated for resistance to insects.

Responsibilities are discussed in Chapter 6.

It's the same when you build software. Early in a project, it's sufficient to say that you'll include a `Customer` class that carries out certain responsibilities. As you refine your architecture and move to construction, you'll have to decide on a structure for the class (its attributes) and a behavior (its operations) that are sufficient and necessary to carry out those responsibilities. Finally, as you evolve to the executable system, you'll need to model details, such as the visibility of individual attributes and operations, the concurrency semantics of the class as a whole and its individual operations, and the interfaces the class realizes.

Forward and reverse engineering is discussed in Chapters 8, 14, 18, 19, 20, 25, 30, and 31.

The UML provides a representation for a number of advanced properties, as Figure 9-1 shows. This notation permits you to visualize, specify, construct, and document a class to any level of detail you wish, even sufficient to support forward and reverse engineering of models and code.

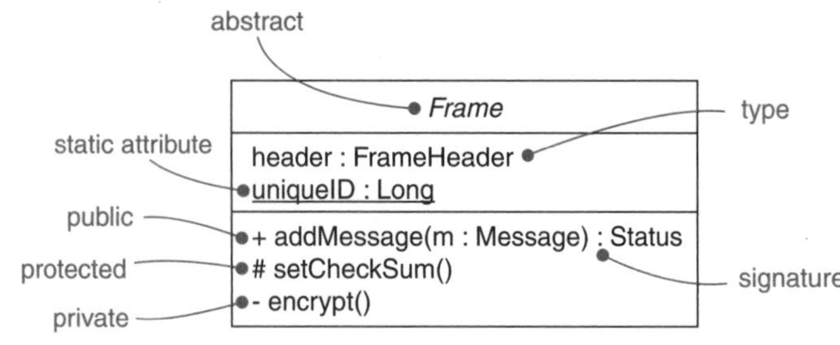

Figure 9-1: Advanced Classes

Terms and Concepts

A *classifier* is a mechanism that describes structural and behavioral features. Classifiers include classes, associations, interfaces, datatypes, signals, components, nodes, use cases, and subsystems.

Classifiers

Modeling the vocabulary of a system is discussed in Chapter 4; the class/object dichotomy is discussed in Chapter 2.

When you model, you'll discover abstractions that represent things in the real world and things in your solution. For example, if you are building a Web-based ordering system, the vocabulary of your project will likely include a `Customer` class (representing people who order products) and a `Transaction` class (an implementation artifact, representing an atomic action). In the deployed system, you might have a `Pricing` component, with instances living on every client node. Each of these abstractions will have instances; separating the essence and the instance of the things in your world is an important part of modeling.

Instances are discussed in Chapter 13; packages are discussed in Chapter 12; generalization is discussed in Chapters 5 and 10; associations are discussed in Chapters 5 and 10; messages are discussed in Chapter 16; interfaces are discussed in Chapter 11; datatypes are discussed in Chapters 4 and 11; signals are discussed in Chapter 21; components are discussed in Chapter 15; nodes are discussed in Chapter 27; use cases are discussed in Chapter 17; subsystems are discussed in Chapter 32.

Some things in the UML don't have instances—for example, packages and generalization relationships. In general, those modeling elements that can have instances are called classifiers. Even more important, a classifier has structural features (in the form of attributes) as well as behavioral features (in the form of operations). Every instance of a given classifier shares the same feature definitions, but each instance has its own value for each attribute.

The most important kind of classifier in the UML is the class. A class is a description of a set of objects that share the same attributes, operations, relationships, and semantics. Classes are not the only kind of classifier, however. The UML provides a number of other kinds of classifiers to help you model.

- Interface — A collection of operations that are used to specify a service of a class or a component
- Datatype — A type whose values are immutable, including primitive built-in types (such as numbers and strings) as well as enumeration types (such as Boolean)
- Association — A description of a set of links, each of which relates two or more objects.
- Signal — The specification of an asynchronous message communicated between instances
- Component — A modular part of a system that hides its implementation behind a set of external interfaces
- Node — A physical element that exists at run time and that represents a computational resource, generally having at least some memory and often processing capability
- Use case — A description of a set of a sequence of actions, including variants, that a system performs that yields an observable result of value to a particular actor
- Subsystem — A component that represents a major part of a system

For the most part, every kind of classifier may have both structural and behavioral features. Furthermore, when you model with any of these classifiers, you may use all the advanced features described in this chapter to provide the level of detail you need to capture the meaning of the abstraction.

Graphically, the UML distinguishes among these different classifiers, as Figure 9-2 shows.

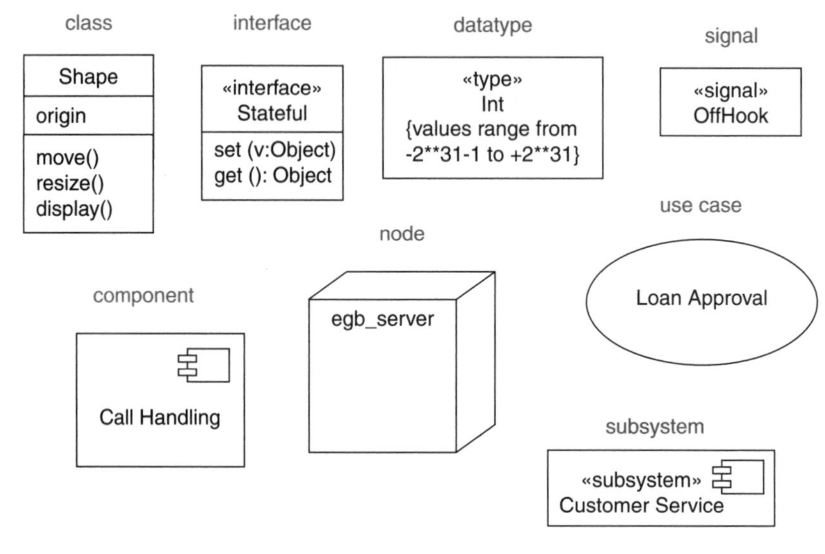

Figure 9-2: Classifiers

Note: A minimalist approach would have used one icon for all classifiers; however, a distinctive visual cue was deemed important. Similarly, a maximal approach would have used different icons for each kind of classifier. That doesn't make sense either because, for example, classes and datatypes aren't that different. The design of the UML strikes a balance—some classifiers have their own icon, and others use special keywords (such as `type`, `signal`, and `subsystem`).

Visibility

One of the design details you can specify for an attribute or operation is visibility. The visibility of a feature specifies whether it can be used by other classifiers. In the UML, you can specify any of four levels of visibility.

A classifier can see another classifier if it is in scope and if there is an explicit or implicit relationship to the target; relationships are discussed in Chapters 5 and 10; descendants come from generalization relationships, as discussed in Chapter 5; permission allows a classifier to share its private features, as discussed in Chapter 10.

1. `public` Any outside classifier with visibility to the given classifier can use the feature; specified by prepending the symbol + .
2. `protected` Any descendant of the classifier can use the feature; specified by prepending the symbol # .
3. `private` Only the classifier itself can use the feature; specified by prepending the symbol – .
3. `package` Only classifiers declared in the same package can use the feature; specified by prepending the symbol ~.

Figure 9-3 shows a mix of public, protected, and private figures for the class `Toolbar`.

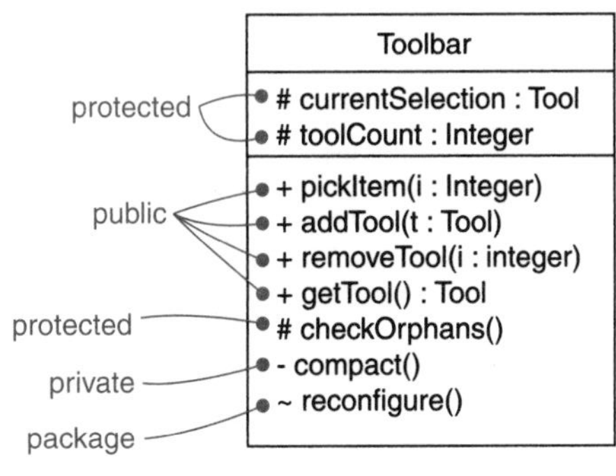

Figure 9-3: Visibility

When you specify the visibility of a classifier's features, you generally want to hide all its implementation details and expose only those features that are necessary to carry out the responsibilities of the abstraction. That's the very basis of information hiding, which is essential to building solid, resilient systems. If you don't explicitly adorn a feature with a visibility symbol, you can usually assume that it is public.

Note: The UML's visibility property matches the semantics common among most programming languages, including C++, Java, Ada, and Eiffel. Note that languages differ slightly in their semantics of visibility, however.

Instance and Static Scope

Instances are discussed in Chapter 13.

Another important detail you can specify for a classifier's attributes and operations is scope. The scope of a feature specifies whether each instance of the classifier has its own distinct value of the feature or whether there is just a single value of the feature shared by all instances of the classifier. In the UML, you can specify two kinds of owner scope.

1. `instance` Each instance of the classifier holds its own value for the feature. This is the default and requires no additional notation.
2. `static` There is just one value of the feature for all instances of the classifier. This has also been called *class scope*. This is notated by underlining the feature string.

As Figure 9-4 (a simplification of the first figure) shows, a feature that is static scoped is rendered by underlining the feature's name. No adornment means that the feature is instance scoped.

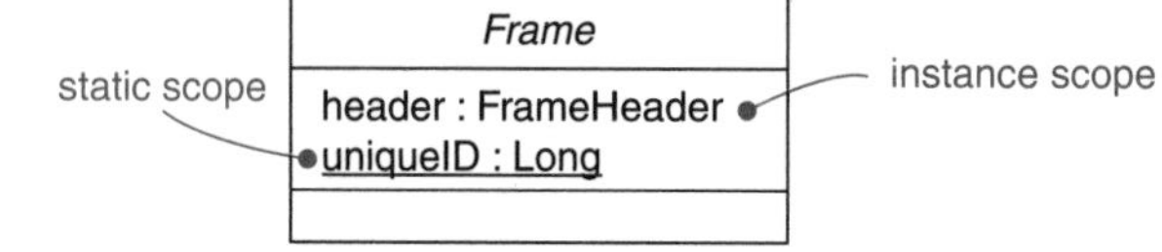

Figure 9-4: Owner Scope

In general, most features of the classifiers you model will be instance scoped. The most common use of static scoped features is for private attributes that must be shared among all instances of a class, such as for generating unique IDs for new instances of a class.

Note: Static scope maps to what C++ and Java call static attributes and operations.

Static scope works somewhat differently for operations. An instance operation has an implicit parameter corresponding to the object being manipulated. A static operation has no such parameter; it behaves like a traditional global procedure that has no target object. Static operations are used for operations that create instances or operations that manipulate static attributes.

Abstract, Leaf, and Polymorphic Elements

Generalization is discussed in Chapters 5 and 10; instances are discussed in Chapter 13.

You use generalization relationships to model a lattice of classes, with more-generalized abstractions at the top of the hierarchy and more-specific ones at the bottom. Within these hierarchies, it's common to specify that certain classes are abstract—meaning that they may not have any direct instances. In the UML, you specify that a class is abstract by writing its name in italics. For example, as Figure 9-5 shows, `Icon`, `RectangularIcon`, and `ArbitraryIcon` are all abstract classes. By contrast, a concrete class (such as `Button` and `OKButton`) may have direct instances.

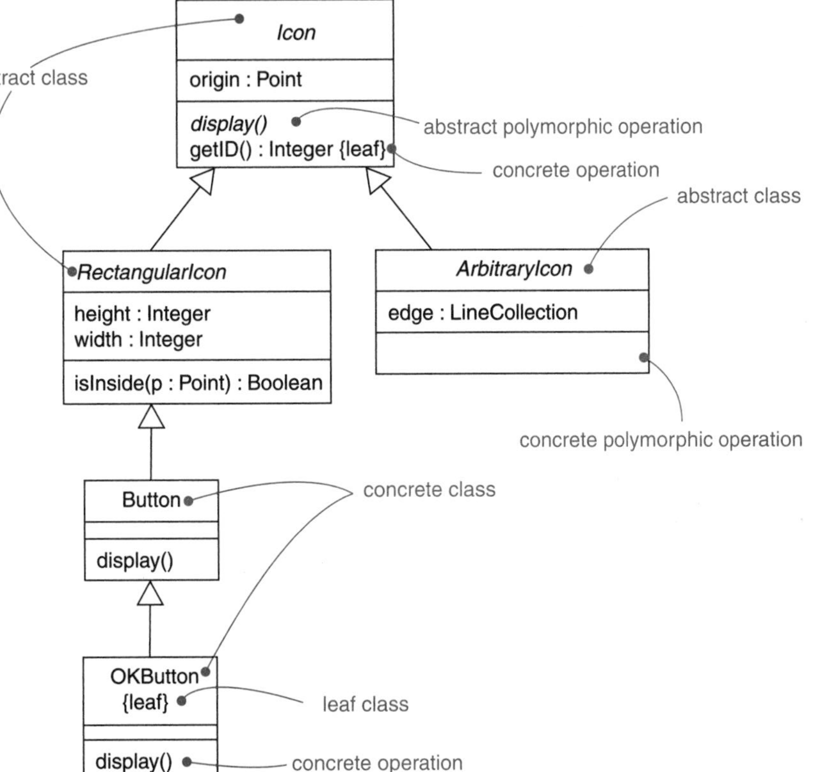

Figure 9-5: Abstract and Concrete Classes and Operations

Whenever you use a class, you'll probably want to inherit features from other, more-general classes, and have other, more-specific classes inherit features from it. These are the normal semantics you get from classes in the UML. However, you can also specify that a class may have no children. Such an element is called a leaf class and is specified in the UML by writing the property `leaf` below the class's name. For example, in the figure, `OKButton` is a leaf class, so it may have no children.

Messages are discussed in Chapter 16.

Operations have similar properties. Typically, an operation is polymorphic, which means that, in a hierarchy of classes, you can specify operations with the same signature at different points in the hierarchy. An operation in a child class overrides the behavior of a similar operation in the parent class. When a message is dispatched at run time, the operation in the hierarchy that is invoked is chosen polymorphically—that is, a match is determined at run time according to the type of the object. For example, `display` and `isInside` are both polymorphic operations. Furthermore, the operation *`Icon::display()`* is abstract, meaning that it is incomplete and requires a child to supply an implementation of the operation. In the UML, you specify an abstract operation by writing its name in italics, just as you do for a class. By contrast, `Icon::getID()` is a leaf operation, so designated by the property `leaf`. This means that the operation is not polymorphic and may not be overridden. (This is similar to a Java `final` operation.)

Note: Abstract operations map to what C++ calls pure virtual operations; leaf operations in the UML map to C++ nonvirtual operations.

Multiplicity

Instances are discussed in Chapter 13.

Whenever you use a class, it's reasonable to assume that there may be any number of instances of that class (unless, of course, it is an abstract class and may not have any direct instances, although there may be any number of instances of its concrete children). Sometimes, though, you'll want to restrict the number of instances a class may have. Most often, you'll want to specify zero instances (in which case, the class is a utility class that exposes only static-scoped attributes and operations), one instance (a singleton class), a specific number of instances, or many instances (the default case).

Multiplicity applies to associations as well, as discussed in Chapters 5 and 10.

Attributes are related to the semantics of association, as discussed in Chapter 10.

The number of instances a class may have is called its multiplicity. Multiplicity is a specification of the range of allowable cardinalities an entity may assume. In the UML, you can specify the multiplicity of a class by writing a multiplicity expression in the upper-right corner of the class icon. For example, in Figure 9-6, `NetworkController` is a singleton class. Similarly, there are exactly three instances of the class `ControlRod` in the system. Multiplicity applies to attributes, as well. You can specify the multiplicity of an attribute by writing a suitable expression in brackets just after the attribute name. For example, in the figure, there are two or more `consolePort` instances in the instance of `NetworkController`.

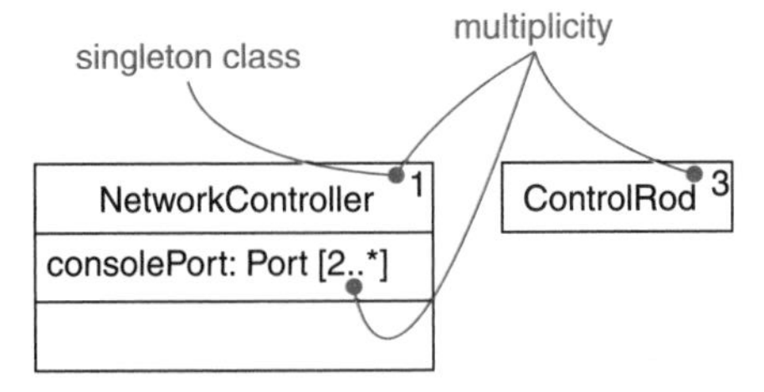

Figure 9-6: Multiplicity

Structured classifiers are discussed in Chapter 15.

Note: The multiplicity of a class applies within a given context. There is an implied context for the entire system at the top level. The entire system can be regarded as a structured classifier.

Attributes

At the most abstract level, when you model a class's structural features (that is, its attributes), you simply write each attribute's name. That's usually enough information for the average reader to understand the intent of your model. As the previous parts have described, however, you can also specify the visibility, scope, and multiplicity of each attribute. There's still more. You can also specify the type, initial value, and changeability of each attribute.

You can also use stereotypes to designate sets of related attributes, such as housekeeping attributes, as discussed in Chapter 6.

In its full form, the syntax of an attribute in the UML is

```
[visibility] name
['':' type] ['[' multiplicity] ']']
['=' initial-value]
[property-string {',' property-string}]
```

For example, the following are all legal attribute declarations:

- `origin` Name only
- `+ origin` Visibility and name
- `origin : Point` Name and type
- `name : String[0..1]` Name, type, and multiplicity
- `origin : Point = (0,0)` Name, type, and initial value
- `id: Integer {readonly}` Name and property

Unless otherwise specified, attributes are always changeable. You can use the `readonly` property to indicate that the attribute's value may not be changed after the object is initialized.

You'll mainly want to use `readonly` when modeling constants or attributes that are initialized at the creation of an instance and not changed thereafter.

Note: The `readonly` property maps to `const` in C++.

Operations

Signals are discussed in Chapter 21.

At the most abstract level, when you model a class's behavioral features (that is, its operations and its signals), you will simply write each operation's name. That's usually enough information for the average reader to understand the intent of your model. As the previous parts have described, however, you can also specify the visibility and scope of each operation. There's still more: You can also specify the parameters, return type, concurrency semantics, and other properties of each operation. Collectively, the name of an operation plus its parameters (including its return type, if any) is called the operation's signature.

Note: The UML distinguishes between operation and method. An operation specifies a service that can be requested from any object of the class to affect behavior; a method is an implementation of an operation. Every nonabstract operation of a class must have a method, which supplies an executable algorithm as a body (generally designated in some programming language or structured text). In an inheritance lattice, there may be many methods for the same operation, and polymorphism selects which method in the hierarchy is dispatched during run time.

You can also use stereotypes to designate sets of related operations, such as helper functions, as discussed in Chapter 6.

In its full form, the syntax of an operation in the UML is

```
[visibility] name ['(' parameter-list ')']
['.' return-type]
[property-string {',' property-string}]
```

For example, the following are all legal operation declarations:

■ `display`	Name only
■ `+ display`	Visibility and name
■ `set(n : Name, s : String)`	Name and parameters
■ `getID() : Integer`	Name and return type
■ `restart() {guarded}`	Name and property

In an operation's signature, you may provide zero or more parameters, each of which follows the syntax

```
[direction] name : type [= default-value]
```

Direction may be any of the following values:

- `in` An input parameter; may not be modified
- `out` An output parameter; may be modified to communicate information to the caller
- `inout` An input parameter; may be modified to communicate information to the caller

---

Note: An out or inout parameter is equivalent to a return parameter and an `in` parameter. `Out` and `inout` are provided for compatibility with older programming languages. Use explicit return parameters instead.

In addition to the `leaf` and `abstract` properties described earlier, there are defined properties that you can use with operations.

1. `query` Execution of the operation leaves the state of the system unchanged. In other words, the operation is a pure function that has no side effects.
2. `sequential` Callers must coordinate outside the object so that only one flow is in the object at a time. In the presence of multiple flows of control, the semantics and integrity of the object cannot be guaranteed.
3. `guarded` The semantics and integrity of the object is guaranteed in the presence of multiple flows of control by sequentializing all calls to all of the object's guarded operations. In effect, exactly one operation at a time can be invoked on the object, reducing this to sequential semantics.
4. `concurrent` The semantics and integrity of the object is guaranteed in the presence of multiple flows of control by treating the operation as atomic. Multiple calls from concurrent flows of control may occur simultaneously to one object on any concurrent operation, and all may proceed concurrently with correct semantics; concurrent operations must be designed so that they perform correctly in case of a concurrent sequential or guarded operation on the same object.
5. `static` The operation does not have an implicit parameter for the target object; it behaves like a traditional global procedure.

Active objects, processes, and threads are discussed in Chapter 23.

The concurrency properties (`sequential`, `guarded`, `concurrent`) address the concurrency semantics of an operation, properties that are relevant only in the presence of active objects, processes, or threads.

Template Classes

The basic properties of classes are discussed in Chapter 4.

A template is a parameterized element. In such languages as C++ and Ada, you can write template classes, each of which defines a family of classes. (You can also write template functions, each of which defines a family of functions.) A template may include slots for classes, objects, and values, and these slots serve as the template's parameters. You can't use a template directly; you have to instantiate it first. Instantiation involves binding these formal template parameters to actual ones. For a template class, the result is a concrete class that can be used just like any ordinary class.

The most common use of template classes is to specify containers that can be instantiated for specific elements, making them type-safe. For example, the following C++ code fragment declares a parameterized `Map` class.

```
template<class Item, class VType, int Buckets>
class Map {
public:
  virtual map(const Item&, const VType&);
  virtual Boolean isMappen(const Item&) const;
  ...
};
```

You might then instantiate this template to map `Customer` objects to `Order` objects.

```
m : Map<Customer, Order, 3>;
```

You can model template classes in the UML as well. As Figure 9-7 shows, you render a template class just as you do an ordinary class, but with an additional dashed box in the upper-right corner of the class icon, which lists the template parameters.

Dependencies are discussed in Chapters 5 and 10; stereotypes are discussed in Chapter 6.

As the figure goes on to show, you can model the instantiation of a template class in two ways. First, you can do so implicitly, by declaring a class whose name provides the binding. Second, you can do so explicitly, by using a dependency stereotyped as `bind`, which specifies that the source instantiates the target template using the actual parameters.

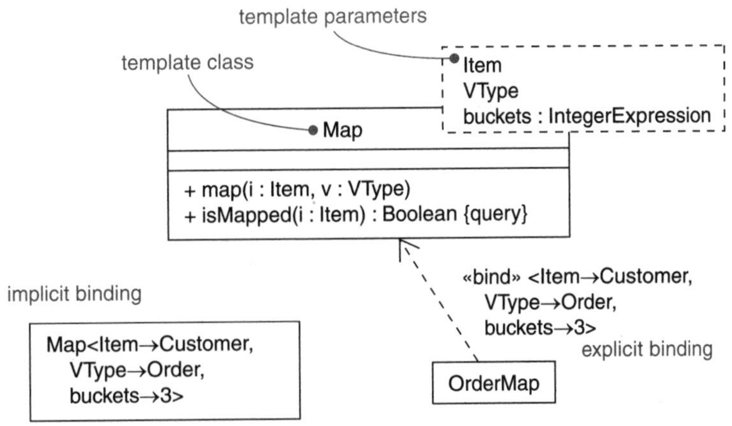

template parameters
template class
Item
VType
buckets : IntegerExpression
Map
+ map(i : Item, v : VType)
+ isMapped(i : Item) : Boolean {query}
implicit binding
Map<Item→Customer,
VType→Order,
buckets→3>
«bind» <Item→Customer,
VType→Order,
buckets→3>
explicit binding
OrderMap

Figure 9-7: Template Classes

Standard Elements

The UML's extensibility mechanisms are discussed in Chapter 6.

All of the UML's extensibility mechanisms apply to classes. Most often, you'll use tagged values to extend class properties (such as specifying the version of a class) and stereotypes to specify new kinds of components (such as model-specific components).

The UML defines four standard stereotypes that apply to classes.

1. `metaclass` Specifies a classifier whose objects are all classes
2. `powertype` Specifies a classifier whose objects are classes that are the children of a given parent class
3. `stereotype` Specifies that the classifier is a stereotype that may be applied to other elements
4. `utility` Specifies a class whose attributes and operations are all static scoped

---

Note: A number of other standard stereotypes or keywords that apply to classes are discussed elsewhere.

Common Modeling Techniques

Modeling the Semantics of a Class

The common uses of classes are discussed in Chapter 4.

The most common purpose for which you'll use classes is to model abstractions that are drawn from the problem you are trying to solve or from the technology you are using to implement a solution to that problem. Once you've identified those abstractions, the next thing you'll need to do is specify their semantics.

Modeling is discussed in Chapter 1; you can also model the semantics of an operation using an activity diagram, as discussed in Chapter 20.

In the UML, you have a wide spectrum of modeling possibilities at your disposal, ranging from the very informal (responsibilities) to the very formal (OCL—Object Constraint Language). Given these choices, you must decide the level of detail that is appropriate to communicate the intent of your model. If the purpose of your model is to communicate with end users and domain experts, you'll tend to lean toward the less formal. If the purpose of your model is to support round-trip engineering, which flows between models and code, you'll tend to lean toward the more formal. If the purpose of your model is to rigorously and mathematically reason about your models and prove their correctness, you'll lean toward the very formal.

Note: Less formal does not mean less accurate. It means less complete and less detailed. Pragmatically, you'll want to strike a balance between informal and very formal. This means providing enough detail to support the creation of executable artifacts, but still hiding those details so that you do not overwhelm the reader of your models.

To model the semantics of a class, choose among the following possibilities, arranged from informal to formal.

Responsibilities are discussed in Chapter 4.

Specifying the body of a method is discussed in Chapter 3.

- Specify the responsibilities of the class. A responsibility is a contract or obligation of a type or class and is rendered in a note attached to the class, or in an extra compartment in the class icon.
- Specify the semantics of the class as a whole using structured text, rendered in a note (stereotyped as `semantics`) attached to the class.
- Specify the body of each method using structured text or a programming language, rendered in a note attached to the operation by a dependency relationship.

Specifying the semantics of an operation is discussed in Chapter 20. State machines are discussed in Chapter 22; collaborations are discussed in Chapter 28; internal structures are discussed in Chapter 15. OCL is discussed in The Unified Modeling Language Reference Manual.

- Specify the pre- and postconditions of each operation, plus the invariants of the class as a whole, using structured text. These elements are rendered in notes (stereotyped as `precondition`, `postcondition`, and `invariant`) attached to the operation or class by a dependency relationship.
- Specify a state machine for the class. A state machine is a behavior that specifies the sequences of states an object goes through during its lifetime in response to events, together with its responses to those events.
- Specify internal structure of the class.
- Specify a collaboration that represents the class. A collaboration is a society of roles and other elements that work together to provide some cooperative behavior that's bigger than the sum of all the elements. A collaboration has a structural part as well as a dynamic part, so you can use collaborations to specify all dimensions of a class's semantics.
- Specify the pre- and postconditions of each operation, plus the invariants of the class as a whole, using a formal language such as OCL.

Pragmatically, you'll end up doing some combination of these approaches for the different abstractions in your system.

Note: When you specify the semantics of a class, keep in mind whether your intent is to specify what the class does or how it does it. Specifying the semantics of what a class does represents its public, outside view; specifying the semantics of how a class does it represents its private, inside view. You'll want to use a mixture of these two views, emphasizing the outside view for clients of the class and emphasizing the inside view for those who implement the class.

Hints and Tips

When you model classifiers in the UML, remember that there is a wide range of building blocks at your disposal, from interfaces to classes to components, and so on. You must choose the one that best fits your abstraction. A well-structured classifier

- Has both structural and behavioral aspects.
- Is tightly cohesive and loosely coupled.
- Exposes only those features necessary for clients to use the class and hides all others.
- Is unambiguous in its intent and semantics.

- Is not so overly specified that it eliminates all degrees of freedom for its implementers.
- Is not so underspecified that it renders the meaning of the classifier as ambiguous.

When you draw a classifier in the UML,

- Show only those properties of the classifier that are important to understand the abstraction in its context.
- Chose a stereotyped version that provides the best visual cue to the intent of the classifier.

Chapter 10
Advanced Relationships

In this chapter

- Advanced dependency, generalization, association, realization, and refinement relationships
- Modeling webs of relationships
- Creating webs of relationships

The basic properties of relationships are discussed in Chapter 5; interfaces are discussed in Chapter 11; components are discussed in Chapter 15; use cases are discussed in Chapter 17; collaborations are discussed in Chapter 28.

When you model the things that form the vocabulary of your system, you must also model how those things stand in relationship to one another. Relationships can be complex, however. Visualizing, specifying, constructing, and documenting webs of relationships require a number of advanced features.

Dependencies, generalizations, and associations are the three most important relational building blocks of the UML. These relationships have a number of properties beyond those described in the previous part. You can also model multiple inheritance, navigation, composition, refinement, and other characteristics. Using a fourth kind of relationship—realization—you can model the connection between an interface and a class or component, or between a use case and a collaboration. In the UML, you can model the semantics of relationships to any degree of formality.

Managing complex webs of relationships requires that you use the right relationships at the level of detail so that you neither under- nor over-engineer your system.

Getting Started

Use cases and scenarios are discussed in Chapter 17.

If you are building a house, deciding where to place each room in relation to others is a critical task. At one level of abstraction, you might decide to put the master bedroom on the main level, away from the front of the house. You might next think through common scenarios to help you reason about the use of this room arrangement. For example, consider bringing in groceries from the garage. It wouldn't make sense to walk from the garage through your bedroom to get to the kitchen, so that's an arrangement you'd reject.

You can form a fairly complete picture of your house's floor plan just by thinking through these basic relationships and use cases. However, that's not enough. You can end up with some real flaws in your design if you don't consider more-complex relationships.

For example, you might like the arrangement of rooms on each floor, but rooms on different floors might interact in unforeseen ways. Suppose you place your teenager daughter's room right above your bedroom. Now, suppose your teenager decides to learn how to play the drums. You'd clearly want to reject that floor plan, too.

Similarly, you have to consider how underlying mechanisms in the house might interact with your floor plan. For example, you'll increase the cost of construction if you don't arrange your rooms so that you have common walls in which to run pipes and drains.

Forward and reverse engineering are discussed in Chapters 8, 14, 18, 19, 20, 25, 30, and 31.

It's the same when you build software. Dependencies, generalizations, and associations are the most common relationships you'll encounter when modeling software-intensive systems. However, you need a number of advanced features of these relationships in order to capture the details of many systems—details that are important for you to consider so that you avoid real flaws in your design.

The UML provides a representation for a number of advanced properties, as Figure 10-1 shows. This notation permits you to visualize, specify, construct, and document webs of relationships to any level of detail you wish, even sufficient to support forward and reverse engineering of models and code.

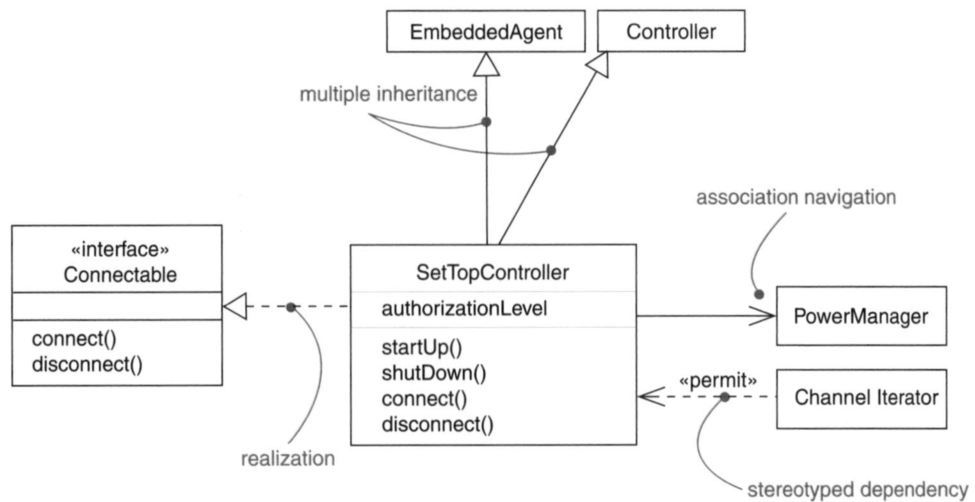

Figure 10-1: Advanced Relationships

Terms and Concepts

A *relationship* is a connection among things. In object-oriented modeling, the four most important relationships are dependencies, generalizations, associations, and realizations. Graphically, a relationship is rendered as a path, with different kinds of lines used to distinguish the different relationships.

Dependencies

The basic properties of dependencies are discussed in Chapter 5.

A *dependency* is a using relationship, specifying that a change in the specification of one thing (for example, class `SetTopController`) may affect another thing that uses it (for example, class `ChannelIterator`), but not the reverse. Graphically, a dependency is rendered as a dashed line, directed to the thing that is depended on. Apply dependencies when you want to show one thing using another.

The UML's extensibility mechanisms are discussed in Chapter 6.

A plain, unadorned dependency relationship is sufficient for most of the using relationships you'll encounter. However, if you want to specify a shade of meaning, the UML defines a number of stereotypes that may be applied to dependency relationships. There are a number of stereotypes, which can be organized into several groups.

Class diagrams are discussed in Chapter 8.

First, there are stereotypes that apply to dependency relationships among classes and objects in class diagrams.

1. `bind` — Specifies that the source instantiates the target template using the given actual parameters

Templates and `bind` dependencies are discussed in Chapter 9.

You'll use `bind` when you want to model the details of template classes. For example, the relationship between a template container class and an instantiation of that class would be modeled as a `bind` dependency. `Bind` includes a list of actual arguments that map to the formal arguments of the template.

2. `derive` — Specifies that the source may be computed from the target

Attributes are discussed in Chapters 4 and 9; associations are discussed in Chapter 5 and later in this chapter.

You'll use `derive` when you want to model the relationship between two attributes or two associations, one of which is concrete and the other is conceptual. For example, a `Person` class might have the attribute `BirthDate` (which is concrete) as well as the attribute `Age` (which can be derived from `BirthDate`, so is not separately manifest in the class). You'd show the relationship between `Age` and `BirthDate` by using a `derive` dependency, showing `Age` derived from `BirthDate`.

3. `permit` — Specifies that the source is given special visibility into the target

`Permit` dependencies are discussed in Chapter 5.

You'll use `permit` when you want to allow a class to access private features of another class, such as found with C++ `friend` classes.

4. `instanceOf` — Specifies that the source object is an instance of the target classifier. Ordinarily shown using text notation in the form `source : Target`
5. `instantiate` — Specifies that the source creates instances of the target

The class/object dichotomy is discussed in Chapter 2.

These last two stereotypes let you model class/object relationships explicitly. You can use `instanceOf` when you want to model the relationship between a class and an object in the same diagram, or between a class and its metaclass; usually, however, this is shown using text syntax. You'll use `instantiate` when you want to specify that a class creates objects of another class.

6. `powertype` — Specifies that the target is a powertype of the source; a powertype is a classifier whose objects are the children of a given parent

Modeling logical databases is discussed in Chapter 8; modeling physical databases is discussed in Chapter 30.

You'll use `powertype` when you want to model classes that classify other classes, such as you'll find when modeling databases.

7. `refine` — Specifies that the source is at a finer degree of abstraction than the target

You'll use `refine` when you want to model classes that represent the same concept at different levels of abstraction. For example, during analysis you might encounter a `Customer` class which, during design, you refine into a more detailed `Customer` class, complete with its implementation.

8. `use` — Specifies that the semantics of the source element depends on the semantics of the public part of the target

You'll apply `use` when you want to explicitly mark a dependency as a using relationship, in contrast to the shades of dependencies other stereotypes provide.

Packages are discussed in Chapter 12.

Continuing, there are two stereotypes that apply to dependency relationships among packages.

1. `import` — Specifies that the public contents of the target package enter the public namespace of the source, as if they had been declared in the source.
2. `access` — Specifies that the public contents of the target package enter the private namespace of the source. The unqualified names may be used within the source, but they may not be re-exported.

You'll use `import` and `access` when you want to use elements declared in other packages. Importing elements avoids the need to use a fully qualified name to reference an element from another package within a text expression.

Use cases are discussed in Chapter 17.

Two stereotypes apply to dependency relationships among use cases:

1. `extend` — Specifies that the target use case extends the behavior of the source
2. `include` — Specifies that the source use case explicitly incorporates the behavior of another use case at a location specified by the source

You'll use `extend` and `include` (and simple generalization) when you want to decompose use cases into reusable parts.

Interactions are discussed in Chapter 16.

One stereotype you'll encounter in the context of interactions among objects is

- `send` Specifies that the source class sends the target event

State machines are discussed in Chapter 22.

You'll use `send` when you want to model an operation (such as found in the action associated with a state transition) dispatching a given event to a target object (which in turn might have an associated state machine). The `send` dependency in effect lets you tie independent state machines together.

Systems and models are discussed in Chapter 32.

Finally, one stereotype that you'll encounter in the context of organizing the elements of your system into subsystems and models is

- `trace` Specifies that the target is a historical predecessor of the source from an earlier stage of development

The five views of an architecture are discussed in Chapter 2.

You'll use `trace` when you want to model the relationships among elements in different models. For example, in the context of a system's architecture, a use case in a use case model (representing a functional requirement) might trace to a package in the corresponding design model (representing the artifacts that realize that use case).

Note: All relationships, including generalization, association, and realization, are conceptually kinds of dependencies. Generalization, association, and realization have enough important semantics about them that they are treated as distinct kinds of relationships in the UML. The stereotypes listed above represent shades of dependencies, each of which has its own semantics, but each of which is not so semantically distant from plain dependencies to warrant treatment as distinct kinds of relationships. This is a judgment call on the part of the UML, but experience shows that this approach strikes a balance between highlighting the important kinds of relationships you'll encounter and not overwhelming the modeler with too many choices. You won't go wrong if you model generalization, association, and realization first, then view all other relationships as kinds of dependencies.

Generalizations

The basic properties of generalizations are discussed in Chapter 5.

A *generalization* is a relationship between a general classifier (called the superclass or parent) and a more specific classifier (called the subclass or child). For example, you might encounter the general class `Window` with its more specific subclass, `MultiPaneWindow`. With a generalization relationship from the child to the parent, the child (`MultiPaneWindow`) will inherit all the structure and behavior of the parent (`Window`). The child may even add new structure and behavior, or it may override the behavior of the parent. In a generalization relationship, instances of the child may be used anywhere instances of the parent apply—meaning that the child is substitutable for the parent.

Most of the time, you'll find single inheritance sufficient. A class that has exactly one parent is said to use single inheritance. There are times, however, when a class incorporates aspects of multiple classes. Then multiple inheritance models those relationships better. For example, Figure 10-2 shows a set of classes drawn from a financial services application. The class `Asset` has three children: `BankAccount`, `RealEstate`, and `Security`. Two of these children (`BankAccount` and `Security`) have their own children. For example, `Stock` and `Bond` are both children of `Security`.

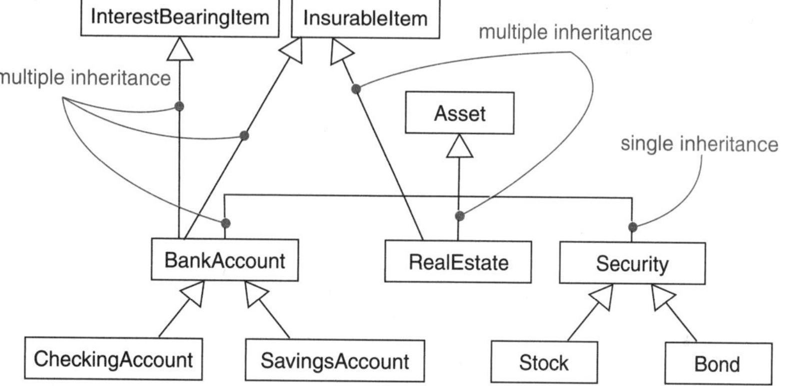

Figure 10-2: Multiple Inheritance

Two of these children (`BankAccount` and `RealEstate`) inherit from multiple parents. `RealEstate`, for example, is a kind of `Asset` as well as a kind of `InsurableItem`, and `BankAccount` is a kind of `Asset` as well as a kind of `InterestBearingItem` and an `InsurableItem`.

Some superclasses are only used to add behavior (usually) and structure (occasionally) to classes that inherit their main structure from ordinary superclasses. These additive classes are called mixins; they do not stand alone but are always used as supplementary superclasses in a multiple inheritance relationship. For example, `InterestBearingItem` and `InsurableItem` are mixins in Figure 10-2.

Note: Use multiple inheritance carefully. You'll run into problems if a child has multiple parents whose structure or behavior overlap. In many cases, multiple inheritance can be replaced by delegation, in which a child inherits from only one parent and then uses aggregation to obtain the structure and behavior of more subordinate parents. For example, instead of specializing `Vehicle` into `LandVehicle`, `WaterVehicle`, and `AirVehicle` on one dimension and into `GasPowered`, `WindPowered`, and `MusclePowered` on another dimension, let `Vehicle` contain a `meansOfPropulsion` as a part. The main downside with this approach is that you lose the semantics of substitutability with these subordinate parents.

The UML's extensibility mechanisms are discussed in Chapter 6.

A plain, unadorned generalization relationship is sufficient for most of the inheritance relationships you'll encounter. However, if you want to specify a shade of meaning, the UML defines four constraints that may be applied to generalization relationships:

1. `complete` — Specifies that all children in the generalization have been specified in the model (although some may be elided in the diagram) and that no additional children are permitted
2. `incomplete` — Specifies that not all children in the generalization have been specified (even if some are elided) and that additional children are permitted

The general properties of diagrams are discussed in Chapter 7.

Unless otherwise stated, you can assume that any diagram shows only a partial view of an inheritance lattice, so it is elided. However, elision is different from the completeness of a model. Specifically, you'll use the `complete` constraint when you want to show explicitly that you've fully specified a hierarchy in the model (although no one diagram may show that hierarchy); you'll use `incomplete` to show explicitly that you have not stated the full specification of the hierarchy in the model (although one diagram may show everything in the model).

3. `disjoint` — Specifies that objects of the parent may have no more than one of the children as a type. For example, class `Person` can be specialized into disjoint classes `Man` and `Woman`.
4. `overlapping` — Specifies that objects of the parent may have more than one of the children as a type. For example, class `Vehicle` can be specialized into overlapping subclasses `LandVehicle` and `WaterVehicle` (an amphibious vehicle is both).

Types and interfaces are discussed in Chapter 11; interactions are discussed in Chapter 16.

These two constraints apply only in the context of multiple inheritance. You'll use `disjoint` to show that the classes in a set are mutually incompatible; a subclass may not inherit from more than one. You'll use `overlapping` to indicate that a class can multiply inherit from more than one class in the set.

Note: In most cases, an object has one type at run time; that's a case of static classification. If an object can change its type during run time, that's a case of dynamic classification. Modeling dynamic classification is complex. But in the UML, you can use a combination of multiple inheritance (to show the potential types of an object) and types and interactions (to show the changing type of an object during run time).

Associations

The basic properties of associations are discussed in Chapter 5.

An *association* is a structural relationship, specifying that objects of one thing are connected to objects of another. For example, a `Library` class might have a one-to-many association to a `Book` class, indicating that each `Book` instance is owned by one `Library` instance. Furthermore, given a `Book`, you can find its owning `Library`, and given a `Library`, you can navigate to all its `Books`. Graphically, an association is rendered as a solid line connecting the same or different classes. You use associations when you want to show structural relationships.

There are four basic adornments that apply to an association: a name, the role at each end of the association, the multiplicity at each end of the association, and aggregation. For advanced uses, there are a number of other properties you can use to model subtle details, such as navigation, qualification, and various flavors of aggregation.

Navigation Given a plain, unadorned association between two classes, such as `Book` and `Library`, it's possible to navigate from objects of one kind to objects of the other kind. Unless otherwise specified, navigation across an association is bidirectional. However, there are some circumstances in which you'll want to limit navigation to just one direction. For example, as Figure 10-3 shows, when modeling the services of an operating system, you'll find an association between `User` and `Password` objects. Given a `User`, you'll want to be able to find the corresponding `Password` objects; but given a `Password`, you don't want to be able to identify the corresponding `User`. You can explicitly represent the direction of navigation by adorning an association with an arrowhead pointing to the direction of traversal.

Note: Specifying a direction of traversal does not necessarily mean that you can't ever get from objects at one end of an association to objects at the other end. Rather, navigation is a statement of knowledge of one class by another. For example, in the previous figure, it might still be possible to find the `User` objects associated with a `Password` through other associations that involve yet other classes not shown. Specifying that an association is navigable is a statement that, given an object at one end, you can easily and directly get to objects at the other end, usually because the source object stores some references to objects of the target.

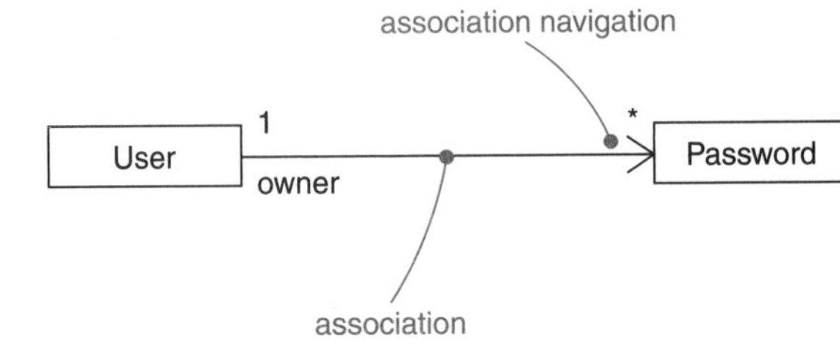

Figure 10-3: Navigation

Public, protected, private, and package visibility are discussed in Chapter 9.

Visibility Given an association between two classes, objects of one class can see and navigate to objects of the other unless otherwise restricted by an explicit statement of navigation. However, there are circumstances in which you'll want to limit the visibility across that association relative to objects outside the association. For example, as Figure 10-4 shows, there is an association between `UserGroup` and `User` and another between `User` and `Password`. Given a `User` object, it's possible to identify its corresponding `Password` objects. However, a `Password` is private to a `User`, so it shouldn't be accessible from the outside (unless, of course, the `User` explicitly exposes access to the `Password`, perhaps through some public operation). Therefore, as the figure shows, given a `UserGroup` object, you can navigate to its `User` objects (and vice versa), but you cannot in turn see the `User` object's `Password` objects; they are private to the `User`. In the UML, you can specify three levels of visibility for an association end, just as you can for a class's features by appending a visibility symbol to a role name. Unless otherwise noted, the visibility of a role is public. Private visibility indicates that objects at that end are not accessible to any objects outside the association; protected visibility indicates that objects at that end are not accessible to any objects outside the association, except for children of the other end. Package visibility indicates that classes declared in the same package can see the given element; this does not apply to association ends.

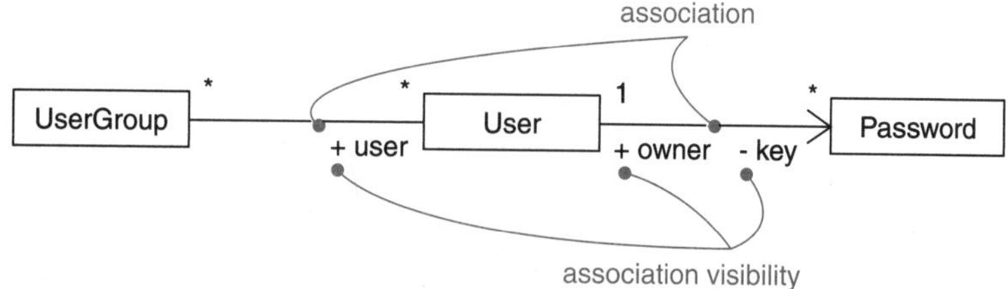

Figure 10-4: Visibility

Attributes are discussed in Chapters 4 and 9.

Qualification In the context of an association, one of the most common modeling idioms you'll encounter is the problem of lookup. Given an object at one end of an association, how do you identify an object or set of objects at the other end? For example, consider the problem of modeling a work desk at a manufacturing site at which returned items are processed to be fixed. As Figure 10-5 shows, you'd model an association between two classes, `WorkDesk` and `ReturnedItem`. In the context of the `WorkDesk`, you'd have a `jobId` that would identify a particular `ReturnedItem`. In that sense, `jobId` is an attribute of the association. It's not a feature of `ReturnedItem` because items really have no knowledge of things like repairs or jobs. Then, given an object of `WorkDesk` and given a particular value for `jobId`, you can navigate to zero or one objects of `ReturnedItem`. In the UML, you'd model this idiom using a qualifier, which is an association attribute whose values identify a subset of objects (usually a single object) related to an object across an association. You render a qualifier as a small rectangle attached to the end of an association, placing the attributes in the rectangle, as the figure shows. The source object, together with the values of the qualifier's attributes, yield a target object (if the target multiplicity is at most one) or a set of objects (if the target multiplicity is many).

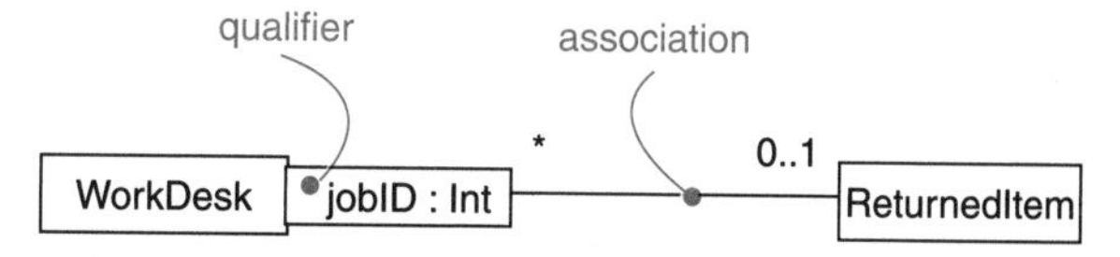

Figure 10-5: Qualification

Simple aggregation is discussed in Chapter 5.

Composition Aggregation turns out to be a simple concept with some fairly deep semantics. Simple aggregation is entirely conceptual and does nothing more than distinguish a "whole" from a "part." Simple aggregation does not change the meaning of navigation across the association between the whole and its parts, nor does it link the lifetimes of the whole and its parts.

An attribute is essentially a shorthand for composition; attributes are discussed in Chapters 4 and 9.

However, there is a variation of simple aggregation—composition—that does add some important semantics. Composition is a form of aggregation, with strong ownership and coincident lifetime as part of the whole. Parts with non-fixed multiplicity may be created after the composite itself, but once created they live and die with it. Such parts can also be explicitly removed before the death of the composite.

This means that, in a composite aggregation, an object may be a part of only one composite at a time. For example, in a windowing system, a `Frame` belongs to exactly one `Window`. This is in contrast to simple aggregation, in which a part may be shared by several wholes. For example, in the model of a house, a `Wall` may be a part of one or more `Room` objects.

In addition, in a composite aggregation the whole is responsible for the disposition of its parts, which means that the composite must manage the creation and destruction of its parts. For example, when you create a `Frame` in a windowing system, you must attach it to an enclosing `Window`. Similarly, when you destroy the `Window`, the `Window` object must in turn destroy its `Frame` parts.

As Figure 10-6 shows, composition is really just a special kind of association and is specified by adorning a plain association with a filled diamond at the whole end.

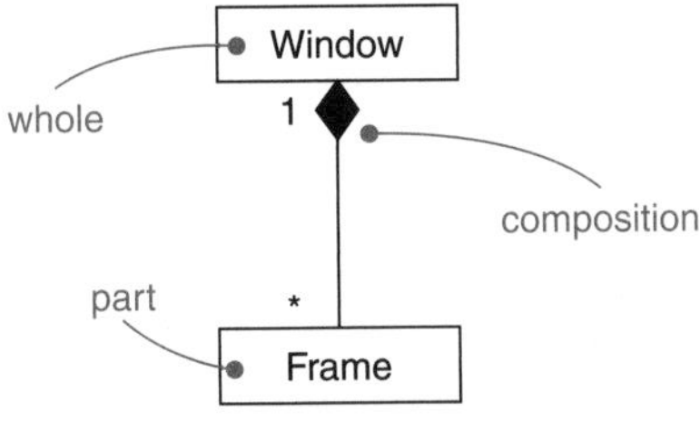

Figure 10-6: Composition

Internal structure is discussed in Chapter 15.

Note: Alternately, you can show composition by using a structured class and nesting the symbols of the parts within the symbol of the composite. This form is most useful when you want to emphasize the relationships among the parts that apply only in the context of the whole.

Attributes are discussed in Chapters 4 and 9.

Association Classes In an association between two classes, the association itself might have properties. For example, in an employer/employee relationship between a `Company` and a `Person`, there is a `Job` that represents the properties of that relationship that apply to exactly one pairing of the `Person` and `Company`. It wouldn't be appropriate to model this situation with a `Company` to `Job` association together with a `Job` to `Person` association.

That wouldn't tie a specific instance of the `Job` to the specific pairing of `Company` and `Person`.

In the UML, you'd model this as an association class, which is a modeling element that has both association and class properties. An association class can be seen as an association that also has class properties or as a class that also has association properties. You render an association class as a class symbol attached by a dashed line to an association line as in Figure 10-7.

Note: Sometimes you'll want to have the same properties for several different association classes. However, you can't attach an association class to more than one association, since an association class is the association itself. To achieve that effect, define a class (`C`) and then have each association class that needs those features inherit from `C` or use `C` as the type of an attribute.

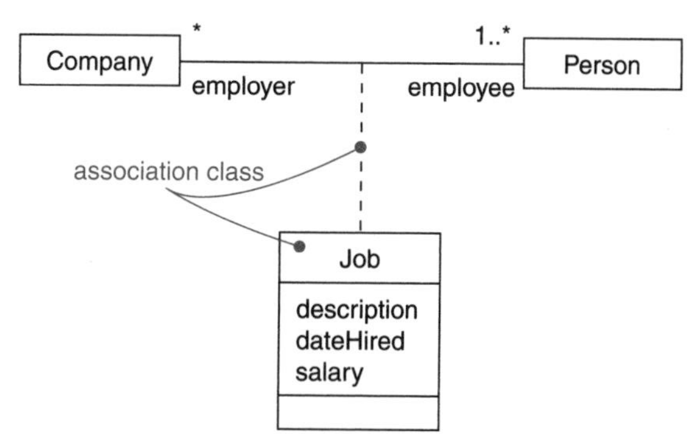

Figure 10-7: Association Classes

The UML's extensibility mechanisms are discussed in Chapter 6.

Constraints These simple and advanced properties of associations are sufficient for most of the structural relationships you'll encounter. However, if you want to specify a shade of meaning, the UML defines five constraints that may be applied to association relationships.

First, you can specify whether the objects at one end of an association (with a multiplicity greater than one) are ordered or unordered.

1. `ordered` Specifies that the set of objects at one end of an association are in an explicit order.

For example, in a `User/Password` association, the `Passwords` associated with the `User` might be kept in a least-recently used order and would be marked as `ordered`. If this keyword is absent, the objects are unordered.

These changeability properties apply to attributes as well, as discussed in Chapter 9; links are discussed in Chapter 16.

Second, you can specify that the objects at one end of an association are unique—that is, they form a set—or whether they are nonunique—that is, they form a bag.

2. `set` The objects are unique with no duplicates.
3. `bag` The objects are nonunique, may be duplicates.
4. `ordered set` The objects are unique but ordered.
5. `list` or `sequence` The objects are ordered, may be duplicates.

Finally, there is a constraint that restricts the changeability of the instances of an association.

6. `readonly` A link, once added from an object on the opposite end of the association, may not be modified or deleted. The default in the absence of this constraint is unlimited changeability.

Note: To be precise, `ordered` and `readOnly` are properties of an association end. However, they are rendered using constraint notation.

Realizations

A *realization* is a semantic relationship between classifiers in which one classifier specifies a contract that another classifier guarantees to carry out. Graphically, a realization is rendered as a dashed directed line with a large open arrowhead pointing to the classifier that specifies the contract.

Interfaces are discussed in Chapter 11; classes are discussed in Chapters 4 and 9; components are discussed in Chapter 15; the five views of an architecture are discussed in Chapter 2.

Realization is different enough from dependency, generalization, and association relationships that it is treated as a separate kind of relationship. Semantically, realization is somewhat of a cross between dependency and generalization, and its notation is a combination of the notation for dependency and generalization. You'll use realization in two circumstances: in the context of interfaces and in the context of collaborations.

Most of the time you'll use realization to specify the relationship between an interface and the class or component that provides an operation or service for it. An interface is a collection of operations that are used to specify a service of a class or a component. Therefore, an interface specifies a contract that a class or component must carry out. An interface may be realized by many such classes or components, and a class or component may realize many interfaces. Perhaps the most interesting thing about interfaces is that they let you separate the specification of a contract (the interface itself) from its implementation (by a class or a component). Furthermore, interfaces span the logical and physical parts of a system's architecture. For example, as Figure 10-8 shows, a class (such as `AccountBusinessRules` in an order entry system) in a system's design view might realize a given interface (such as `IRuleAgent`). That same interface (`IRuleAgent`) might also be realized by a component (such as `acctrule.dll`) in the system's implementation view. Note that you can represent realization in two ways: in the canonical form (using the `interface` stereotype and the dashed directed line with a large open arrowhead) and in an elided form (using the interface lollipop notation for a provided interface).

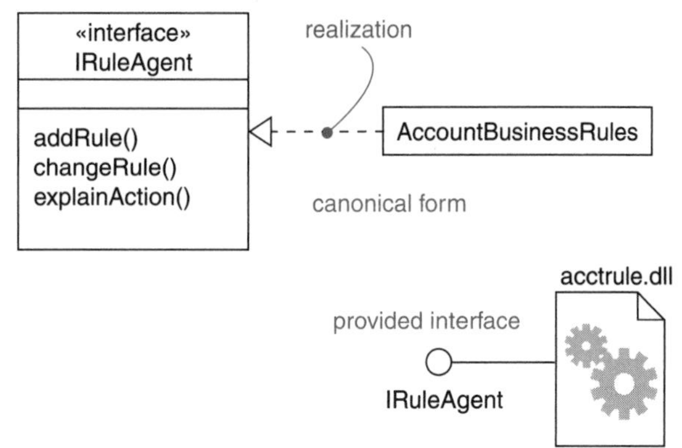

Figure 10-8: Realization of an Interface

Use cases are discussed in Chapter 17; collaborations are discussed in Chapter 28.

You'll also use realization to specify the relationship between a use case and the collaboration that realizes that use case, as Figure 10-9 shows. In this circumstance, you'll almost always use the dashed arrow form of realization.

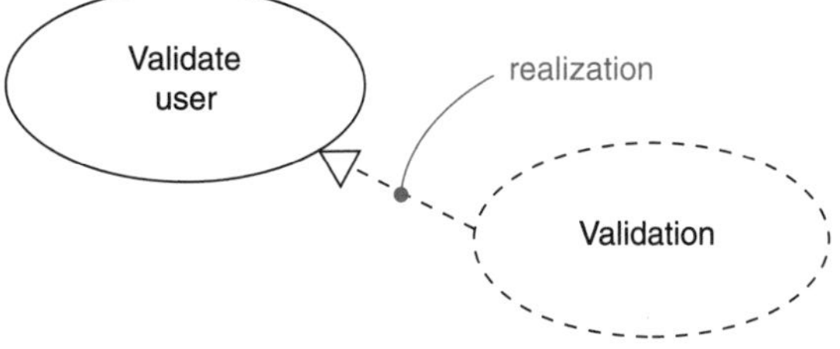

Figure 10-9: Realization of a Use Case

Note: When a class or a component realizes an interface, it means that clients can rely on the class or component to faithfully carry out the behavior specified by the interface. That means the class or component implements all the operations of the interface, responds to all its signals, and in all ways follows the protocol established by the interface for clients who use those operations or send those signals.

Common Modeling Techniques

Modeling Webs of Relationships

Modeling the vocabulary of a system and modeling the distribution of responsibilities in a system are discussed in Chapter 4.

When you model the vocabulary of a complex system, you may encounter dozens, if not hundreds or thousands, of classes, interfaces, components, nodes, and use cases. Establishing a crisp boundary around each of these abstractions is hard. Establishing the myriad of relationships among these abstractions is even harder: This requires you to form a balanced distribution of responsibilities in the system as a whole, with individual abstractions that are tightly cohesive and with relationships that are expressive, yet loosely coupled.

When you model these webs of relationships,

Use cases are discussed in Chapter 17.

- Don't begin in isolation. Apply use cases and scenarios to drive your discovery of the relationships among a set of abstractions.
- In general, start by modeling the structural relationships that are present. These reflect the static view of the system and are therefore fairly tangible.
- Next, identify opportunities for generalization/specialization relationships; use multiple inheritance sparingly.
- Only after completing the preceding steps should you look for dependencies; they generally represent more-subtle forms of semantic connection.
- For each kind of relationship, start with its basic form and apply advanced features only as absolutely necessary to express your intent.

The five views of an architecture are discussed in Chapter 2; the Rational Unified Process is summarized in Appendix B.

- Remember that it is both undesirable and unnecessary to model all relationships among a set of abstractions in a single diagram or view. Rather, build up your system's relationships by considering different views on the system. Highlight interesting sets of relationships in individual diagrams.

The key to successfully modeling complex webs of relationships is to do so in an incremental fashion. Build up relationships as you add to the structure of a system's architecture. Simplify those relationships as you discover opportunities for common mechanisms. At every release in your development process, assess the relationships among the key abstractions in your system.

Note: In practice—and especially if you are following an incremental and iterative development process—the relationships in your models will derive from explicit decisions by the modeler as well as from the reverse engineering of your implementation.

Hints and Tips

When you model advanced relationships in the UML, remember that there is a wide range of building blocks at your disposal, from simple associations to more-detailed properties of navigation, qualification, aggregation, and so on. You must choose the relationship and the details of that relationship to best fit your abstraction. A well-structured relationship

- Exposes only those features necessary for clients to use the relationship and hides all others.
- Is unambiguous in its intent and semantics.
- Is not so overly specified that it eliminates all degrees of freedom by its implementers.
- Is not so underspecified that it renders the meaning of the relationship ambiguous.

When you draw a relationship in the UML,

- Show only those properties of the relationship that are important to understanding the abstraction in its context.
- Choose a stereotyped version that provides the best visual cue to the intent of the relationship.

Chapter 11

INTERFACES, TYPES, AND ROLES

In this chapter

- Interfaces, types, roles, and realization
- Modeling the seams in a system
- Modeling static and dynamic types
- Making interfaces understandable and approachable

Interfaces define a line between the specification of what an abstraction does and the implementation of how that abstraction does it. An interface is a collection of operations that are used to specify a service of a class or a component.

You use interfaces to visualize, specify, construct, and document the seams within your system. Types and roles provide a mechanism for you to model the static and dynamic conformance of an abstraction to an interface in a specific context.

A well-structured interface provides a clear separation between the outside view and the inside view of an abstraction, making it possible to understand and approach an abstraction without having to dive into the details of its implementation.

Getting Started

Designing houses is discussed in Chapter 1.

It wouldn't make a lot of sense to design a house that required you to rip up the foundation every time you needed to repaint the walls. Similarly, you wouldn't want to live in a place that required you to rewire the building whenever you needed to change a light bulb. The owner of a high rise wouldn't be thrilled to have to move doors or replace all electrical and phone jacks whenever a new tenant moved in.

Centuries of building experience have provided lots of pragmatic construction-related information to help builders avoid these obvious—and some not so obvious—problems that arise when a building grows and changes over time. In software terms, we call this designing with a clear separation of concerns. For example, in a well-structured building, the skin or facade of the structure can be modified or replaced without disturbing the rest of the building. Similarly, the furnishings inside a building can easily be moved about without changing the infrastructure. Services that run through the walls for electrical, heating, plumbing, and waste disposal facilities can be changed with some degree of scrap and rework, but you still don't have to rend the fabric of the building to do so.

Not only do standard building practices help you build buildings that can evolve over time, but there are many standard interfaces to which you can build, permitting you to use common, off-the-shelf components whose use ultimately helps reduce the cost of construction and maintenance. For example, there are standard sizes for lumber, making it easy to build walls that are multiples of a common size. There are standard sizes of doors and windows, which means that you don't have to hand-craft every opening in your building. There are even standards for electrical outlets and telephone plugs (although these vary from country to country) that make it easier for you to mix and match electronic equipment.

Frameworks are discussed in Chapter 29.

In software, it's important to build systems with a clear separation of concerns so that as the system evolves, changes in one part of the system don't ripple through, damaging other parts of the system. One important way of achieving this degree of separation is by specifying clear seams in your system, which draw a line between those parts that may change independently. Furthermore, by choosing the right interfaces, you can pick standard components, libraries, and frameworks to implement those interfaces without having to build them yourself. As you discover better implementations, you can replace the old ones without disturbing their users.

Classes are discussed in Chapters 4 and 9; components are discussed in Chapter 15.

In the UML, you use interfaces to model the seams in a system. An interface is a collection of operations used to specify a service of a class or a component. By declaring an interface, you can state the desired behavior of an abstraction independent of an implementation of that abstraction. Clients can build against that interface, and you can build or buy any implementation of that interface as long as the implementation satisfies the responsibilities and the contract denoted by the interface.

Packages are discussed in Chapter 12; subsystems are discussed in Chapter 32.

Many programming languages support the concept of interfaces, including Java and CORBA IDL. Interfaces are not only important for dividing the specification and the implementation of a class or component, but as you scale up to larger systems, you can use interfaces to specify the outside view of a package or subsystem.

Components are discussed in Chapter 15.

The UML provides a graphical representation for interfaces, as Figure 11-1 shows. This notation permits you to visualize the specification of an abstraction apart from any implementation.

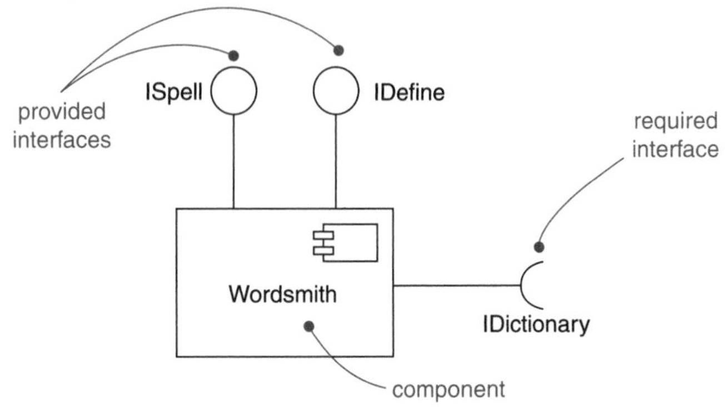

Figure 11-1: Interfaces

Terms and Concepts

An *interface* is a collection of operations that are used to specify a service of a class or a component. A *type* is a stereotype of a class used to specify a domain of objects, together with the operations (but not the methods) applicable to the object. A *role* is the behavior of an entity participating in a particular context.

Graphically, an interface may be rendered as a stereotyped class in order to expose its operations and other properties. To show the relationship between a class and its interfaces, a special notation is provided. A provided interface (one that represents services provided by the class) is shown as a small circle attached to the class box. A required interface (one that represents services required by a class of another class) is shown as a small semicircle attached to the class box.

Note: Interfaces may also be used to specify a contract for a use case or subsystem.

Names

An interface name must be unique within its enclosing package, as discussed in Chapter 12.

Every interface must have a name that distinguishes it from other interfaces. A *name* is a textual string. That name alone is known as a *simple name*; a *path name* is the interface name prefixed by the name of the package in which that interface lives. An interface may be drawn showing only its name, as in Figure 11-2.

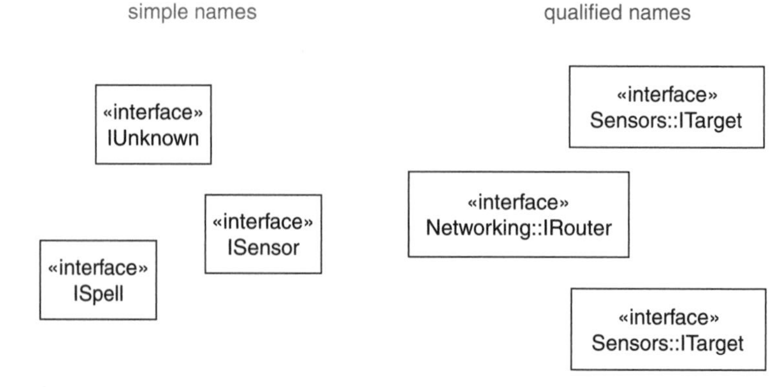

Figure 11-2: Simple and Path Names

Note: An interface name may be text consisting of any number of letters, numbers, and certain punctuation marks (except for marks such as the colon, which is used to separate an interface name and the name of its enclosing package) and may continue over several lines. In practice, interface names are short nouns or noun phrases drawn from the vocabulary of the system you are modeling.

Operations

Operations are discussed in Chapters 4 and 9; the UML's extensibility mechanisms are discussed in Chapter 6.

An interface is a named collection of operations used to specify a service of a class or of a component. Unlike classes or types, interfaces do not specify any implementation (so they may not include any methods, which provide the implementation of an operation). Like a class, an interface may have any number of operations. These operations may be adorned with visibility properties, concurrency properties, stereotypes, tagged values, and constraints.

When you declare an interface, you render an interface as a stereotyped class, listing its operations in the appropriate compartment. Operations may be drawn showing only their name, or they may be augmented to show their full signature and other properties, as in Figure 11-3.

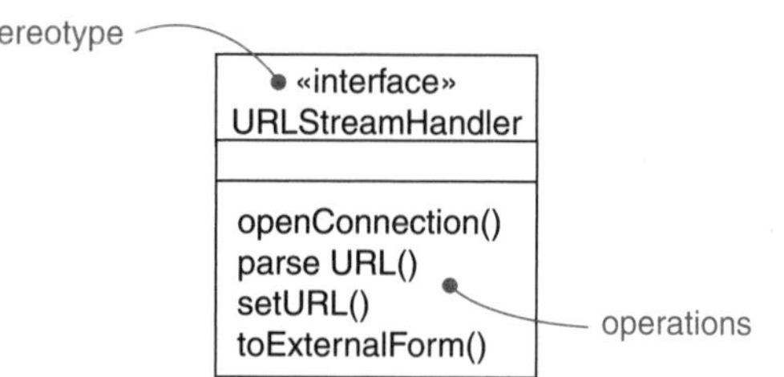

Figure 11-3: Operations

Events are discussed in Chapter 21.

Note: You can also associate signals with an interface.

Relationships

Relationships are discussed in Chapters 5 and 10.

Like a class, an interface may participate in generalization, association, and dependency relationships. In addition, an interface may participate in realization relationships. Realization is a semantic relationship between two classifiers in which one classifier specifies a contract that another classifier guarantees to carry out.

An interface specifies a contract for a class or a component without dictating its implementation. A class or component may realize many interfaces. In so doing, it commits to carry out all these contracts faithfully, which means that it provides a set of methods that properly implement the operations defined in the interface. The set of services that it agrees to provide are its *provided interface*. Similarly, a class or a component may depend on many interfaces. In so doing, it expects that these contracts will be honored by some set of components that realize them. The set of services that a class requires from other classes are its *required interface*. This is why we say that an interface represents a seam in a system. An interface specifies a contract, and the client and the supplier on each side of the contract may change independently, as long as each fulfills its obligations to the contract.

As Figure 11-4 illustrates, you can show that an element realizes an interface in two ways. First, you can use the simple form in which the interface and its realization relationship are rendered as a line between the class box and a small circle (for a provided interface) or a small semicircle (for a required interface). This form is useful when you simply want to expose the seams in your system; it is usually the preferred form. However, the limitation of this style is that you can't directly visualize the operations or signals provided by the interface. Second, you can use the expanded form in which you render an interface as a stereotyped class, which allows you to visualize its operations and other properties, and then draw a realization relationship (for a provided interface) or a dependency (for a required interface) from the classifier or component to the interface box. In the UML, a realization relationship is rendered as a dashed directed line with a large triangular arrowhead pointing to the interface. This notation is a cross between generalization and dependency.

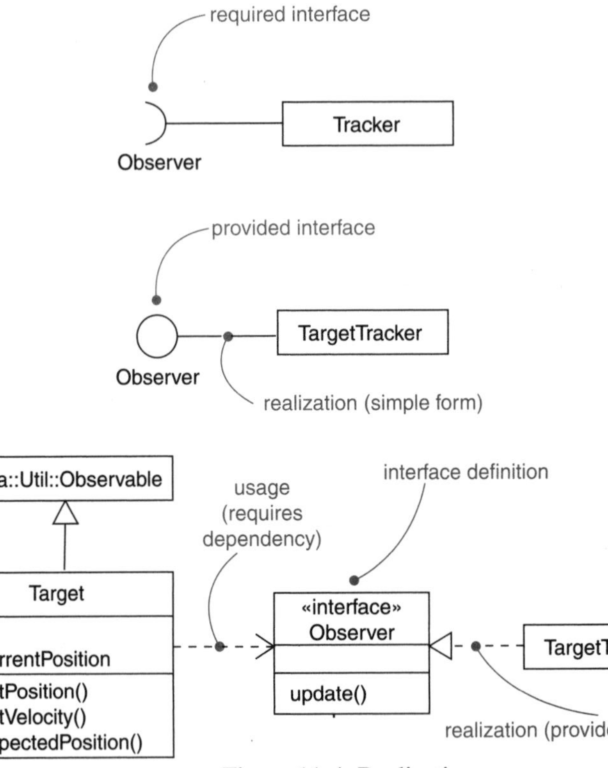

Figure 11-4: Realizations

Abstract classes are discussed in Chapter 4; components are discussed in Chapter 15.

Note: Interfaces are similar to abstract classes. For example, neither may have direct instances. An abstract class can implement its concrete operations, however. An interface is more like an abstract class in which all of the operations are also abstract.

Understanding an Interface

Operations and their properties are discussed in Chapter 9; concurrency semantics are discussed in Chapter 24.

When you are handed an interface, the first thing you'll see is a set of operations that specify a service of a class or a component. Look a little deeper and you'll see the full signature of those operations, along with any of their special properties, such as visibility, scope, and concurrency semantics.

These properties are important, but for complex interfaces they aren't enough to help you understand the semantics of the service they represent, much less know how to use those operations properly. In the absence of any other information, you'd have to dive into some abstraction that realizes the interface to figure out what each operation does and how those operations are meant to work together. However, that defeats the purpose of an interface, which is to provide a clear separation of concerns in a system.

Preconditions, postconditions, and invariants are discussed in Chapter 9; state machines are discussed in Chapter 22; collaborations are discussed in Chapter 28; OCL is discussed in Chapter 6.

In the UML, you can supply much more information to an interface to make it understandable and approachable. First, you may attach pre- and postconditions to each operation and invariants to the class or component as a whole. By doing this, a client who needs to use an interface will be able to understand what the interface does and how to use it, without having to dive into an implementation. If you need to be rigorous, you can use the UML's OCL to formally specify the semantics. Second, you can attach a state machine to the interface. You can use this state machine to specify the legal partial ordering of an interface's operations. Third, you can attach collaborations to the interface. You can use collaborations to specify the expected behavior of the interface through a series of interaction diagrams.

Common Modeling Techniques

Modeling the Seams in a System

Components are discussed in Chapter 15; systems are discussed in Chapter 32.

The most common purpose for which you'll use interfaces is to model the seams in a system composed of software components, such as Eclipse, .NET, or Java Beans. You'll reuse some components from other systems or buy them off the shelf; you will create others from scratch. In any case, you'll need to write glue code that weaves these components together. This requires you to understand the interfaces provided and required by each component.

Identifying the seams in a system involves identifying clear lines of demarcation in your architecture. On either side of those lines, you'll find components that may change independently, without affecting the components on the other side, as long as the components on both sides conform to the contract specified by that interface.

Patterns and frameworks are discussed in Chapter 29.

When you reuse a component from another system or when you buy it off the shelf, you'll probably be handed a set of operations with some minimal documentation about the meaning of each one. That's useful, but it's not sufficient. It's more important for you to understand the order in which to call each operation and what underlying mechanisms the interface embodies. Unfortunately, given a poorly documented component, the best you can do is to build up, by trial and error, a conceptual model for how that interface works. You can then document your understanding by modeling that seam in the system using interfaces in the UML so that, later, you and others can approach that component more easily. Similarly, when you create your own component, you'll need to understand its context, which means specifying the interfaces it relies on to do its job as well as the interfaces it presents to the world that others might build on.

Note: Most component systems, such as Eclipse, .NET, and Enterprise Java Beans, provide for component introspection, meaning that you can programmatically query an interface to determine its operations. Doing so is the first step in understanding the nature of any under-documented component.

To model the seams in a system,

- Within the collection of classes and components in your system, draw a line around those that tend to be tightly coupled relative to other sets of classes and components.

Collaborations are discussed in Chapter 28.

- Refine your grouping by considering the impact of change. Classes or components that tend to change together should be grouped together as collaborations.
- Consider the operations and the signals that cross these boundaries, from instances of one set of classes or components to instances of other sets of classes and components.
- Package logically related sets of these operations and signals as interfaces.
- For each such collaboration in your system, identify the interfaces it requires from (imports) and those it provides to others (exports). You

model the importing of interfaces by dependency relationships, and you model the exporting of interfaces by realization relationships.

Behavioral modeling is discussed in Parts 4 and 5.

- For each such interface in your system, document its dynamics by using pre- and postconditions for each operation, and use cases and state machines for the interface as a whole.

For example, Figure 11-5 shows the seams that surround the component `Ledger` drawn from a financial system. This component provides (realizes) three interfaces: `IUnknown`, `ILedger`, and `IReports`. In this diagram, `IUnknown` is shown in its expanded form; the other two are shown in their simple form, as lollipops. These three interfaces are realized by `Ledger` and are exported to other components for them to build on.

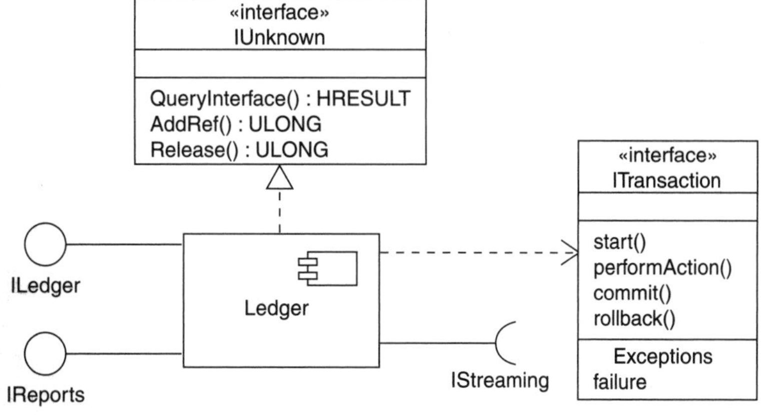

Figure 11-5: Modeling the Seams in a System

As this diagram also shows, `Ledger` requires (uses) two interfaces, `IStreaming` and `ITransaction`, the latter of which is shown in its expanded form. These two interfaces are required by the `Ledger` component for its proper operation. Therefore, in a running system, you must supply components that realize these two interfaces. By identifying interfaces such as `ITransaction`, you've effectively decoupled the components on either side of the interface, permitting you to employ any component that conforms to that interface.

Use cases are discussed in Chapter 17.

Interfaces such as `ITransaction` are more than just a pile of operations. This particular interface makes some assumptions about the order in which its operations should be called. Although not shown here, you could attach use cases to this interface and enumerate the common ways you'd use it.

Modeling Static and Dynamic Types

Instances are discussed in Chapter 13.

Most object-oriented programming languages are statically typed, which means that the type of an object is bound at the time the object is created. Even so, that object will likely play different roles over time. This means that clients using that object interact with the object through different sets of interfaces, representing interesting, possibly overlapping, sets of operations.

Class diagrams are discussed in Chapter 8.

Modeling the static nature of an object can be visualized in a class diagram. However, when you are modeling things like business objects, which naturally change their types throughout a workflow, it's sometimes useful to explicitly model the dynamic nature of that object's type. In these circumstances, an object can gain and lose types during its life. You can also model the object's life cycle using a state machine.

To model a dynamic type,

Associations and generalizations are discussed in Chapters 5 and 10; interaction diagrams are discussed in Chapter 19; dependencies are discussed in Chapters 5 and 10.

- Specify the different possible types of that object by rendering each type as a class (if the abstraction requires structure and behavior) or as an interface (if the abstraction requires only behavior).
- Model all the roles the class of the object may take on at any point in time. You can mark them with the «`dynamic`» stereotype. (This is not a predefined UML stereotype, but one that you can add.)
- In an interaction diagram, properly render each instance of the dynamically typed class. Display the type of the instance in brackets below the object's name, just like a state. (We are using UML syntax in a novel way, but one that we feel is consistent with the intent of states.)

For example, Figure 11-6 shows the roles that instances of the class `Person` might play in the context of a human resources system.

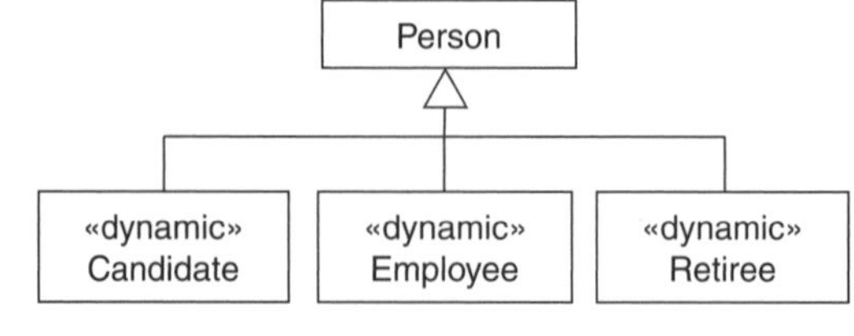

Figure 11-6: Modeling Static Types

This diagram specifies that instances of the `Person` class may be any of the three types—namely, `Candidate`, `Employee`, or `Retiree`.

Hints and Tips

When you model an interface in the UML, remember that every interface should represent a seam in the system, separating specification from implementation. A well-structured interface:

- Is simple yet complete, providing all the operations necessary yet sufficient to specify a single service.
- Is understandable, providing sufficient information to both use and realize the interface without having to examine an existing use or implementation.
- Is approachable, providing information to guide the user to its key properties without being overwhelmed by the details of a pile of operations.

When you draw an interface in the UML,

- Use the lollipop or socket notation whenever you simply need to specify the presence of a seam in the system. Most of the time, you'll need this for components, not classes.
- Use the expanded form when you need to visualize the details of the service itself. Most of the time you'll need this for specifying the seams in a system attached to a package or a subsystem.

Chapter 12
PACKAGES

In this chapter

- Packages, visibility, importing, and exporting
- Modeling groups of elements
- Modeling architectural views
- Scaling up to large systems

Visualizing, specifying, constructing, and documenting large systems involves manipulating potentially large numbers of classes, interfaces, components, nodes, diagrams, and other elements. As you scale up to systems such as these, you will find it necessary to organize these things into larger chunks. In the UML, the package is a general-purpose mechanism for organizing modeling elements into groups.

You use packages to arrange your modeling elements into larger chunks that you can manipulate as a group. You can control the visibility of these elements so that some things are visible outside the package while others are hidden. You can also use packages to present different views of your system's architecture.

Well-designed packages group elements that are semantically close and that tend to change together. Well-structured packages are therefore loosely coupled and very cohesive, with tightly controlled access to the package's contents.

Getting Started

The differences between building a dog house and building a high rise are discussed in Chapter 1.

Dog houses aren't complex: you have four walls, one of them with a dog-size hole, and a roof. When you build a dog house, you really need only a small pile of lumber. There's not a lot more structure than that.

Houses are more complex. Walls, ceilings, and floors come together in larger abstractions that we call rooms. Even these rooms are organized into larger chunks: the public area, the sleeping area, the working area, and so on. These larger groups may not manifest themselves as anything to do with the physical house itself but may just be names we give to logically related rooms in the house, which we apply when we talk about how we'll use the house.

High rise buildings are very complex. Not only are there elementary structures, such as walls, ceilings, and floors, but there are larger chunks, such as public areas, the retail wing, and office spaces. These chunks are probably grouped into even larger chunks, such as rental space and building service area. These larger chunks may have nothing to do with the final high rise itself but are simply artifacts we use to organize our plans for the high rise.

Every large system is layered in this way. In fact, about the only way you can understand a complex system is by chunking your abstractions into ever-larger groups. Most of these modest-size chunks (such as rooms) are, in their own right, class-like abstractions for which there are many instances. Most of these larger chunks are purely conceptual (such as a retail wing), for which there are no real instances. They are not distinct objects in the physical system but, rather, they represent views on the system itself. These latter kinds of chunks have no separate identity in the deployed system; they represent groupings of parts selected across the system.

Software architecture is discussed in Chapter 2; modeling the architecture of a system is discussed in Chapter 32.

In the UML, the chunks that organize a model are called packages. A package is a general-purpose mechanism for organizing elements into groups. Packages help you organize the elements in your models so that you can more easily understand them. Packages also let you control access to their contents so that you can control the seams in your system's architecture.

The UML provides a graphical representation of package, as Figure 12-1 shows. This notation permits you to visualize groups of elements that can be manipulated as a whole and in a way that lets you control the visibility of and access to individual elements.

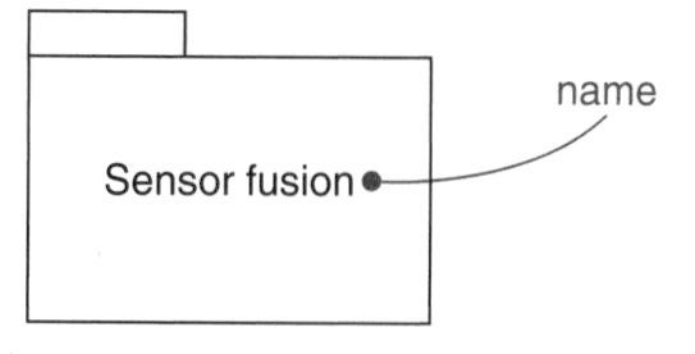

Figure 12-1: Packages

Terms and Concepts

A *package* is a general-purpose mechanism for organizing the model itself into a hierarchy; it has no meaning to the execution. Graphically, a package is rendered as a tabbed folder. The name of the package goes in the folder (if its contents are not shown) or in the tab (if the contents of the folder are shown).

Names

A package name must be unique within its enclosing package.

Every package must have a name that distinguishes it from other packages. A *name* is a textual string. That name alone is known as a *simple name*; a *qualified name* is the package name prefixed by the name of the package in which that package lives, if any. A double colon (::) separates package names. A package is typically drawn showing only its name, as in Figure 12-2. Just as with classes, you may draw packages adorned with tagged values or with additional compartments to expose their details.

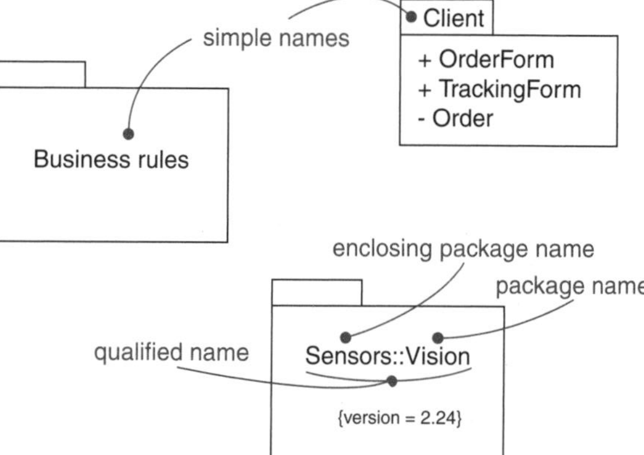

Figure 12-2: Simple and Qualified Package Names

Note: A package name may be text consisting of any number of letters, numbers, and certain punctuation marks (except for marks such as the colon, which is used to separate a package name and the name of its enclosing package) and may continue over several lines. In practice, package names are short grouping nouns or noun phrases drawn from the vocabulary of the model.

Owned Elements

Composition is discussed in Chapter 10.

A package may own other elements, including classes, interfaces, components, nodes, collaborations, use cases, diagrams, and even other packages. Ownership is a composite relationship, which means that the element is declared in the package. If the package is destroyed, the element is destroyed. Every element is uniquely owned by exactly one package.

Note: The package owns the model elements declared within it. These may include elements such as classes, associations, generalizations, dependencies, and notes. It does not own elements that are merely referenced within a package.

A package forms a namespace, which means that elements of the same kind must be named uniquely within the context of its enclosing package. For example, you can't have two classes named `Queue` owned by the same package, but you can have a class named `Queue` in package `P1` and another (and different) class named `Queue` in package `P2`. The classes `P1::Queue` and `P2::Queue` are, in fact, different classes and can be distinguished by their path names. Different kinds of elements may have the same name.

Note: It is best to avoid duplicate names in different packages, if possible, to avoid the danger of confusion.

Elements of different kinds may have the same name within a package. Thus, you can have a class named `Timer`, as well as a component named `Timer`, within the same package. In practice, however, to avoid confusion, it's best to name elements uniquely for all kinds within a package.

Importing is discussed later in this chapter.

Packages may own other packages. This means that it's possible to decompose your models hierarchically. For example, you might have a class named `Camera` that lives in the package `Vision` that in turn lives in the package `Sensors`. The full name of this class is `Sensors::Vision::Camera`. In practice, it's best to avoid deeply nested packages. Two to three levels of nesting is about the limit that's manageable. More than nesting, you'll use importing to organize your packages.

These semantics of ownership make packages an important mechanism for dealing with scale. Without packages, you'd end up with large, flat models in which all elements would have to be named uniquely—an unmanageable situation, especially when you've brought in classes and other elements developed by multiple teams. Packages help you control the elements that compose your system as they evolve at different rates over time.

As Figure 12-3 shows, you can explicitly show the contents of a package either textually or graphically. Note that when you show these owned elements, you place the name of the package in the tab. In practice, you usually won't want to show the contents of packages this way. Instead, you'll use graphical tools to zoom into the contents of a package.

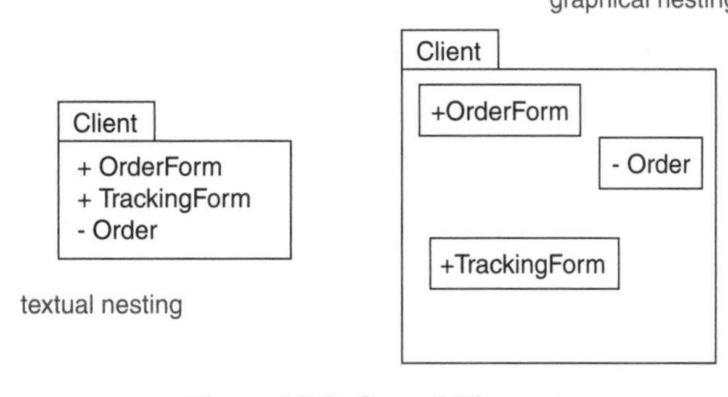

Figure 12-3: Owned Elements

Note: The UML assumes that there is an anonymous, root package in a model, the consequence of which is that elements of each kind at the top of a model must be uniquely named.

Visibility

Visibility is discussed in Chapter 9.

You can control the visibility of the elements owned by a package just as you can control the visibility of the attributes and operations owned by a class. Typically, an element owned by a package is public, which means that it is visible to the contents of any package that imports the element's enclosing package. Conversely, protected elements can only be seen by children, and private elements cannot be seen outside the package in which they are declared. In Figure 12-3, `OrderForm` is a public part of the package `Client`, and `Order` is a private part. A package that imports `Client` can see `OrderForm`, but it cannot see `Order`. As viewed from the outside, the fully qualified name of `OrderForm` would be `Client::OrderForm`.

You specify the visibility of an element owned by a package by prefixing the element's name with an appropriate visibility symbol. Public elements are rendered by prefixing their name with a + symbol, as for `OrderForm` in Figure 12-3. Collectively, the public parts of a package constitute the package's interface.

Just as with classes, you can designate an element as protected or private, rendered by prefixing the element's name with a # symbol and a - symbol, respectively. Protected elements are visible only to packages that inherit from another package; private elements are not visible outside the package at all.

Package visibility indicates that a class is visible to other classes declared in the same package but is invisible to classes declared in other packages. Show package visibility by prefixing a ~ symbol to the name of the class.

Importing and Exporting

Suppose you have two classes named `A` and `B` sitting side by side. Because they are peers, `A` can see `B` and `B` can see `A`, so both can depend on the other. Just two classes makes for a trivial system, so you really don't need any kind of packaging.

Now, imagine having a few hundred such classes sitting side by side. There's no limit to the tangled web of relationships that you can weave. Furthermore, there's no way that you can understand such a large, unorganized group of classes. That's a very real problem for large systems—simple, unrestrained access does not scale up. For these situations, you need some kind of controlled packaging to organize your abstractions.

Dependency relationships are discussed in Chapter 5; the UML's extensibility mechanisms are discussed in Chapter 6.

So suppose that instead you put `A` in one package and `B` in another package, both packages sitting side by side. Suppose also that `A` and `B` are both declared as public parts of their respective packages. This is a very different situation. Although `A` and `B` are both public, accessing one of the classes from within the other package requires a qualified name. However, if `A`'s package imports `B`'s package, `A` can now see `B` directly, although still `B` cannot see `A` without a qualified name. Importing adds the public elements from the target package to the public namespace of the importing package. In the UML, you model an import relationship as a dependency adorned with the stereotype `import`. By packaging your abstractions into meaningful chunks and then controlling their access by importing, you can control the complexity of large numbers of abstractions.

Note: Actually, two stereotypes apply here—`import` and `access`—and both specify that the source package has direct access to the public contents of the target package. `Import` adds the contents of the target to the source's public namespace, so you don't have to qualify their names. This admits the possibility of name clashes, which you must avoid to keep the model well-formed. `Access` adds the contents of the target package to the sources's private namespace. The only difference is that you cannot re-export the imported elements if a third package imports the original source package. Most of the time you'll use `import`.

Interfaces are discussed in Chapter 11.

The public parts of a package are called its exports. For example, in Figure 12-4, the package `GUI` exports two classes, `Window` and `Form`. `EventHandler` is not exported by `GUI`; `EventHandler` is a protected part of the package.

The parts that one package exports are visible to the contents of those packages that have visibility to the package. In this example, `Policies` explicitly imports the package `GUI`. The classes `GUI::Window` and `GUI::Form` are therefore made visible to the contents of the package `Policies` using their simple names `Window` and `Form`. However, `GUI::EventHandler` is not visible because it is protected. Because the package `Server` doesn't import `GUI`, the contents of `Server` may access the public contents of `GUI`, but must use qualified names to do so, for example, `GUI::WINDOW`. Similarly, the contents of `GUI` don't have permission to access any of the contents of `Server` because they are private; they are inaccessible even using qualified names.

Import and access dependencies are transitive. In this example, `Client` imports `Policies` and `Policies` imports `GUI`, so `Client` transitively imports `GUI`. Therefore, the contents of `Client` have access to the exports of `Policies` as well as access to the exports of `GUI`. If `Policies` accesses `GUI`, instead of importing it, `Client` does not add the elements of `GUI` to its namespace, but it can still reference them using qualified names (such as `GUI::Window`).

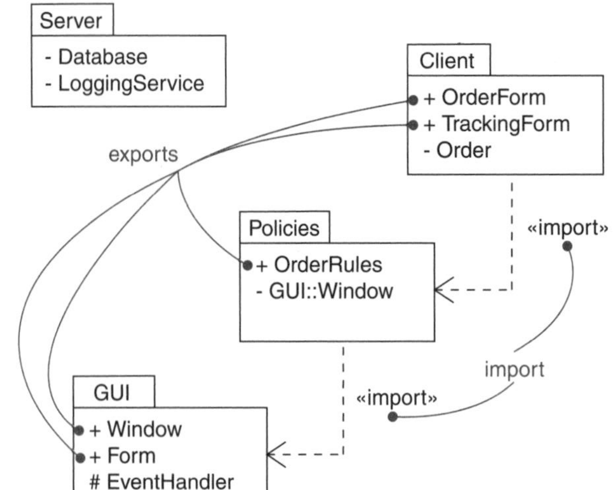

Figure 12-4: Importing and Exporting

Note: If an element is visible within a package, it is visible within all packages nested inside the package. Nested packages can see everything that their containing packages can see. A name in a nested package can hide a name in a containing package, in which case a qualified name is required to reference it.

Common Modeling Techniques

Modeling Groups of Elements

The most common purpose for which you'll use packages is to organize modeling elements into groups that you can name and manipulate as a set. If you are developing a trivial application, you won't need packages at all. All your abstractions will fit nicely into one package. For every other system, however, you'll find that many of your system's classes, interfaces, components, and nodes tend to naturally fall into groups. You model these groups as packages.

There is one important distinction between classes and packages: Classes are abstractions of things found in your problem or solution; packages are mechanisms you use to organize the things in your model. Packages do not appear in a running system; they are strictly mechanisms to organize the design.

The five views of an architecture are discussed in Chapter 2.

Most of the time you'll use packages to group the same basic kind of elements. For example, you might separate all the classes and their corresponding relationships from your system's design view into a series of packages using the UML's import dependencies to control access among these packages. You might organize all the components in your system's implementation view in a similar fashion.

You can also use packages to group different kinds of elements. For example, for a system being developed by a geographically distributed team, you might use packages as your unit of configuration management, putting in them all the classes and diagrams that each team can check in and check out separately. In fact, it's common to use packages to group modeling elements and their associated diagrams.

To model groups of elements,

- Scan the modeling elements in a particular architectural view and look for clumps defined by elements that are conceptually or semantically close to one another.
- Surround each of these clumps in a package.
- For each package, distinguish which elements should be accessible outside the package. Mark them public, and all others protected or private. When in doubt, hide the element.
- Explicitly connect packages that build on others via import dependencies.
- In the case of families of packages, connect specialized packages to their more general part via generalizations.

For example, Figure 12-5 shows a set of packages that organize the classes in an information system's design view into a classic three-tier architecture. The elements in the package `User Services` provide the visual interface for presenting information and gathering data. The elements in the package `Data Services` maintain, access, and update data. The elements in the package `Business Services` bridge the elements in the other two packages and encompass all the classes and other elements that manage requests from the user to execute a business task, including business rules that dictate the policies for manipulating data.

The documentation tagged value is discussed in Chapter 6.

In a trivial system, you could lump all your abstractions into one package. However, by organizing your classes and other elements of the system's design view into three packages, you not only make your model more understandable, but you can control access to the elements of your model by hiding some and exporting others.

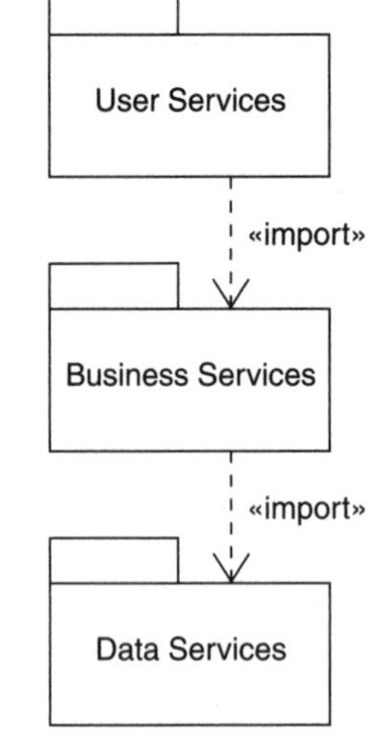

Figure 12-5: Modeling Groups of Elements

Note: When you render models such as these, you'll typically want to expose elements that are central to each package. To make clear the purpose of each package, you can also expose a documentation tagged value for each package.

Modeling Architectural Views

The five views of an architecture are discussed in Chapter 2.

Using packages to group related elements is important; you can't develop complex models without doing so. This approach works well for organizing related elements, such as classes, interfaces, components, nodes, and diagrams. As you consider the different views of a software system's architecture, you need even larger chunks. You can use packages to model the views of an architecture.

Views are related to models, as discussed in Chapter 32.

Remember that a view is a projection into the organization and structure of a system, focused on a particular aspect of that system. This definition has two implications. First, you can decompose a system into almost orthogonal packages, each of which addresses a set of architecturally significant decisions. For example, you might have a design view, an interaction view, an implementation view, a deployment view, and a use case view. Second, these packages own all the abstractions germane to that view. For example, all the components in your model would belong to the package that represents the implementation view. Packages can reference elements owned by other packages, however.

To model architectural views,

- Identify the set of architectural views that are significant in the context of your problem. In practice, this typically includes a design view, an interaction view, an implementation view, a deployment view, and a use case view.
- Place the elements (and diagrams) that are necessary and sufficient to visualize, specify, construct, and document the semantics of each view into the appropriate package.
- As necessary, further group these elements into their own packages.

There will typically be dependencies across the elements in different views. So, in general, let each view at the top of a system be open to all others at that level.

Modeling systems is discussed in Chapter 32.

For example, Figure 12-6 illustrates a canonical top-level decomposition that's appropriate for even the most complex system you might encounter.

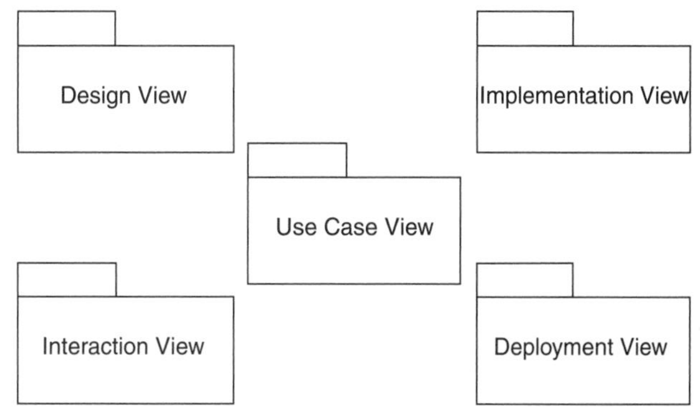

Figure 12-6: Modeling Architectural Views

Hints and Tips

When you model packages in the UML, remember that they exist only to help you organize the elements of your model. If you have abstractions that manifest themselves as objects in the real system, don't use packages. Instead, use modeling elements such as classes or components. A well-structured package

- Is cohesive, providing a crisp boundary around a set of related elements.
- Is loosely coupled, exporting only those elements other packages really need to see, and importing only those elements necessary and sufficient for the elements in the package to do their job.
- Is not deeply nested, because there are limits to the human understanding of deeply nested structures.
- Owns a balanced set of contents; relative to one another in a system, packages should not be too large (split them up if necessary) or too small (combine elements that you manipulate as a group).

When you draw a package in the UML,

- Use the simple form of a package icon unless it's necessary for you to explicitly reveal the contents of that package.
- When you do reveal a package's contents, show only elements that are necessary to understand the meaning of that package in context.
- Especially if you are using packages to model things under configuration management, reveal the values of tags associated with versioning.

Chapter 13

INSTANCES

In this chapter

- Instances and objects
- Modeling concrete instances
- Modeling prototypical instances
- The real and conceptual world of instances

See Chapter 15 for a discussion of internal structure, which is preferable when dealing with prototypical objects and roles.

The terms "instance" and "object" are largely synonymous, so, for the most part, they may be used interchangeably. An instance is a concrete manifestation of an abstraction to which a set of operations may be applied and which may have a state that stores the effects of the operation.

You use instances to model concrete things that live in the real world. Almost every building block in the UML participates in this class/object dichotomy. For example, you can have use cases and use case instances, nodes and node instances, associations and association instances, and so on.

Getting Started

Suppose you've set out to build a house for your family. By saying "house" rather than "car," you've already begun to narrow the vocabulary of your solution space. House is an abstraction of "a permanent or semipermanent dwelling, the purpose of which is to provide shelter." Car is "a mobile, powered vehicle, the purpose of which is to transport people from place to place." As you work to reconcile the many competing requirements that shape your problem, you'll want to refine your abstraction of this house. For example, you might choose "a three-bedroom house with a walkout basement," a kind of house, albeit a more specialized one.

When your builder finally hands you the keys to your house and you and your family walk through the front door, you are now dealing with something concrete and specific. It's no longer just a three-bedroom house with a walk-out, but it's "my three-bedroom house with a walkout basement, located at 835 S. Moore Street." If you are terminally sentimental, you might even name your house something like Sanctuary or Our Money Pit.

There's a fundamental difference between a three-bedroom house with a walk-out basement and my three-bedroom house named Sanctuary. The former is an abstraction representing a certain kind of house with various properties; the latter is a concrete instance of that abstraction, representing some thing that manifests itself in the real world, with real values for each of those properties.

An abstraction denotes the ideal essence of a thing; an instance denotes a concrete manifestation. You'll find this separation of abstraction and instance in everything you model. For a given abstraction, you can have innumerable instances. For a given instance, there is some abstraction that specifies the characteristics common to all such instances.

Classes are discussed in Chapters 4 and 9; components are discussed in Chapter 15; nodes are discussed in Chapter 27; use cases are discussed in Chapter 17. UML actually uses the term instance specification, *but that is a metamodel subtlety.*

In the UML, you can represent abstractions and their instances. Almost every building block in the UML—most notably classes, components, nodes, and use cases—may be modeled in terms of their essence or in terms of their instances. Most of the time, you'll work with them as abstractions. When you want to model concrete manifestations, you'll need to work with their instances.

The UML provides a graphical representation for instances, as Figure 13-1 shows. This notation permits you to visualize named instances, as well as anonymous ones.

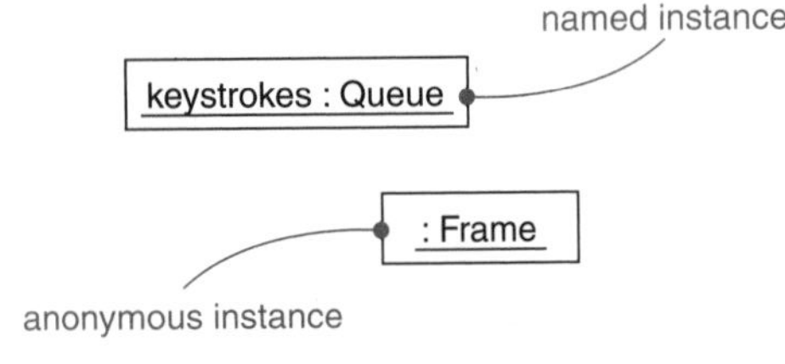

Figure 13-1: Instances

Terms and Concepts

The UML's class/object dichotomy is discussed in Chapter 2.

An *instance* is a concrete manifestation of an abstraction to which a set of operations can be applied and which has a state that stores the effects of the operations. *Instance* and *object* are largely synonymous. Graphically, an instance specification is rendered by underlining its name.

Associations are discussed in Chapters 5 and 10; links are discussed in Chapters 14 and 16.

Note: From common usage, the concrete manifestation of a class is called an object. Objects are instances of classes, so it's excruciatingly proper to say that all objects are instances, although some instances are not objects (for example, an instance of an association is really not an object, it's just an instance, also known as a link). Only power modelers will really care about this subtle distinction.

Abstractions and Instances

Classifiers are discussed in Chapter 9.

Instances don't stand alone; they are almost always tied to an abstraction. Most instances you'll model with the UML will be instances of classes (and these things are called objects), although you can have instances of other things, such as components, nodes, use cases, and associations. In the UML, an instance is easily distinguishable from an abstraction. To indicate an instance, you underline its name.

In a general sense, an object is something that takes up space in the real or conceptual world, and you can do things to it. For example, an instance of a node is typically a computer that physically sits in a room; an instance of a component takes up some space on the file system; an instance of a customer record consumes some amount of physical memory. Similarly, an instance of a flight envelope for an aircraft is something you can manipulate mathematically.

Abstract classes are discussed in Chapter 9; interfaces are discussed in Chapter 11.

You can use the UML to model these physical instances, but you can also model things that are not so concrete. For example, an abstract class, by definition, may not have any direct instances. However, you can model indirect instances of abstract classes to show the use of a prototypical instance of that abstract class. Literally, no such object might exist. But pragmatically, this instance lets you name one of any potential instances of concrete children of that abstract class. This same touch applies to interfaces. By their very definition, interfaces may not have any direct instances, but you can model a prototypical instance of an interface, representing one of any potential instances of concrete classes that realize that interface.

Object diagrams are discussed in Chapter 14.

When you model instances, you'll place them in object diagrams (if you want to visualize their structural details) or in interaction and activity diagrams (if you want to visualize their participation in dynamic situations). Although typically not necessary, you can place objects in class diagrams if you want to explicitly show the relationship of an object to its abstraction.

Types

Interaction diagrams are discussed in Chapter 19; activity diagrams are discussed in Chapter 20; dynamic typing is discussed in Chapter 11; classifiers are discussed in Chapter 9.

An instance has a type. The type of an actual instance must be a concrete classifier, but an instance specification (that does not represent a single instance) could have an abstract type. In notation, the name of the instance is followed by a colon followed by the type, for example, `t : Transaction`.

The classifier of an instance is usually static. For example, once you create an instance of a class, its class won't change during the lifetime of that object. In some modeling situations and in some programming languages, however, it is possible to change the abstraction of an instance. For example, a `Caterpillar` object might become a `Butterfly` object. It's the same object, but of a different abstraction.

Note: During development, it's also possible for you to have instances with no associated classifier, which you can render as an object but with its abstraction name missing, as in Figure 13-2. You can introduce orphan objects such as these when you need to model very abstract behavior, although you must eventually tie such instances to an abstraction if you want to enforce any degree of semantics about the object.

Names

Operations are discussed in Chapters 4 and 9; components are discussed in Chapter 15; nodes are discussed in Chapter 27.

An instance may have a name that distinguishes it from other instances within its context. Typically, an object lives within the context of an operation, a component, or a node. A *name* is a textual string, such as `t` and `myCustomer` in Figure 13-2. That name alone is known as a *simple name.* The abstraction of the instance may be a simple name (such as `Transaction`) or it may be a *path name* (such as `Multimedia::AudioStream`) which is the abstraction's name prefixed by the name of the package in which that abstraction lives.

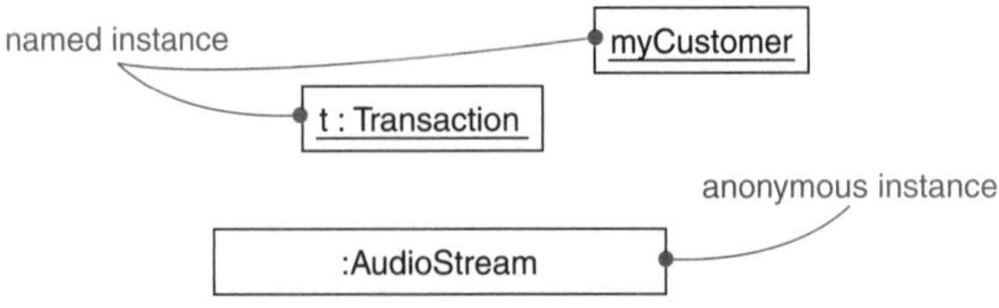

Figure 13-2: Named and Anonymous Instances

When you explicitly name an object, you are really giving it a name (such as `myCustomer`) that's usable by a human. You can also simply name an object (such as `myCustomer`) and elide its abstraction if it's obvious in the given context. In many cases, however, the real name of an object is known only to the computer on which that object lives. In such cases, you can render an anonymous object (such as `:AudioStream`). Each occurrence of an anonymous object is considered distinct from all other occurrences. If you don't even know the object's associated abstraction, you must at least give it an explicit name (such as `agent:`).

Roles and structured classes are discussed in Chapter 15.

The name and the type of an object form one string in the notation, for example, `t : Transaction`. For an object (as opposed to a role within a structured class), the entire string is underlined.

Note: An instance name may be text consisting of any number of letters, numbers, and certain punctuation marks (except for marks such as the colon, which is used to separate the name of the instance from the name of its abstraction) and may continue over several lines. In practice, instance names are short nouns or noun phrases drawn from the vocabulary of the system you are modeling. Typically, you capitalize the first letter of all but the first word in an instance name, as in `t` or `myCustomer`.

Operations

Operations are discussed in Chapters 4 and 9; polymorphism is discussed in Chapter 9.

Not only is an object something that usually takes up space in the real world, it is also something you can do things to. The operations you can perform on an object are declared in the object's abstraction. For example, if the class `Transaction` defines the operation `commit`, then given the instance `t : Transaction`, you can write expressions such as `t.commit()`. The execution of this expression means that `t` (the object) is operated on by `commit` (the operation). Depending on the inheritance lattice associated with `Transaction`, this operation may or may not be invoked polymorphically.

State

An object also has state, which in this sense encompasses all the properties of the object plus the current values of each of these properties (also including links and related objects, depending on your viewpoint). These properties include the attributes and associations of the object, as well as all its aggregate parts. An object's state is therefore dynamic. So when you visualize its state, you are really specifying the value of its state at a given moment in time and space. It's possible to show the changing state of an object by showing it multiple times in the same interaction diagram, but with each occurrence representing a different state.

Attributes are discussed in Chapter 4; interaction diagrams are discussed in Chapter 19. Another way to show the changing state of an individual object over time is via state machines, which are discussed in Chapter 22.

When you operate on an object, you typically change its state; when you query an object, you don't change its state. For example, when you make an airline reservation (represented by the object `r : Reservation`), you might set the value of one of its attributes (for example, `price = 395.75`). If you change your reservation, perhaps by adding a new leg to your itinerary, then its state might change (for example, `price = 1024.86`).

As Figure 13-3 shows, you can use the UML to render the value of an object's attributes. For example, `myCustomer` is shown with the attribute `id` having the value "`432-89-1783`." In this case, `id`'s type (`SSN`) is shown explicitly, although it can be elided (as for `active = True`), because its type can be found in the declaration of `id` in `myCustomer`'s associated class.

You can associate a state machine with a class, which is especially useful when modeling event-driven systems or when modeling the lifetime of a class. In these cases, you can also show the state of this machine for a given object at a given time. The state is shown in square brackets following the type. For example, as Figure 13-3 shows, the object `c` (an instance of the class `Phone`) is indicated in the state `WaitingForAnswer`, a named state defined in the state machine for `Phone`.

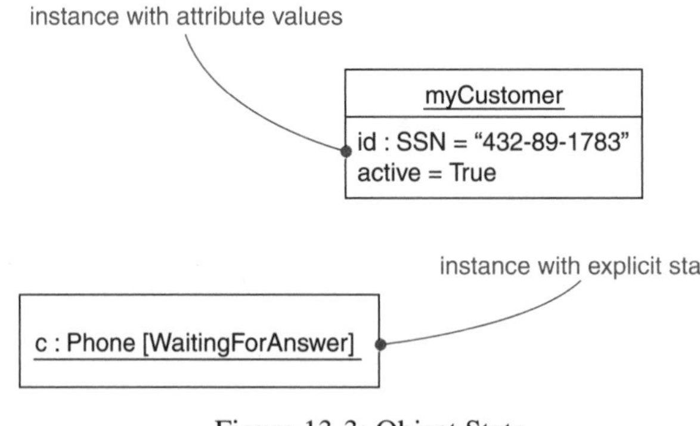

Figure 13-3: Object State

Note: Because an object may be in several states simultaneously, you can also show a list of its current states.

Other Features

Processes and threads are discussed in Chapter 23.

Processes and threads are an important element of a system's process view, so the UML provides a visual cue to distinguish elements that are active (those that are part of a process or thread and represent a root of a flow of control) from those that are passive. You can declare active classes that reify a process or thread, and in turn you can distinguish an instance of an active class, as in Figure 13-4.

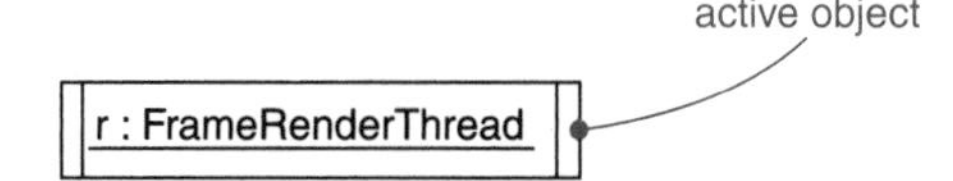

Figure 13-4: Active Objects

Interaction diagrams are discussed in Chapter 19.

Note: Most often you'll use active objects in the context of interaction diagrams that model multiple flows of control. Each active object represents the root of a flow of control and may be used to name distinct flows.

Links are discussed in Chapters 14 and 16; static-scoped attributes and operations are discussed in Chapter 9.

There are two other elements in the UML that may have instances. The first is an association. An instance of an association is a link. A link is a semantic connection among a list of objects. A link is rendered as a line, just like an association, but it can be distinguished from an association because links connect objects.

The second kind of instance is a static (class-scoped) attribute. A static attribute is, in effect, an object owned by the class that is accessible by all instances of the class. It is therefore shown in a class declaration as an underlined attribute.

Standard Elements

The UML's extensibility mechanisms are discussed in Chapter 6.

All of the UML's extensibility mechanisms apply to objects. Usually, however, you don't stereotype an instance directly, nor do you give it its own tagged values. Instead, an object's stereotype and tagged values derive from the stereotype and tagged values of its associated abstraction. For example, as shown in Figure 13-5, you can explicitly indicate an object's stereotype as well as its abstraction.

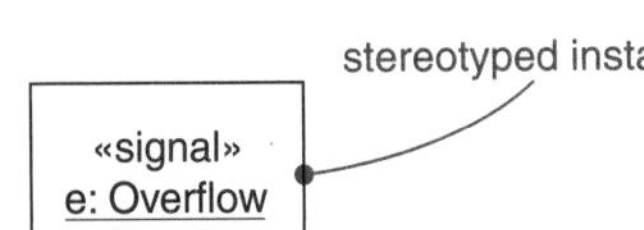

Figure 13-5: Stereotyped Objects

The UML defines two standard stereotypes that apply to the dependency relationships among objects and among classes:

1. `instanceOf` Specifies that the client object is an instance of the supplier classifier. This is rarely shown graphically; it is usually shown using text notation following a colon.
2. `instantiate` Specifies that the client class creates instances of the supplier class

Common Modeling Techniques

Modeling Concrete Instances

When you model concrete instances, you are in effect visualizing things that live in the real world. You can't exactly see an instance of a `Customer` class, for example, unless that customer is standing beside you; in a debugger, you might be able to see a representation of that object, however.

Component diagrams are discussed in Chapter 15; deployment diagrams are discussed in Chapter 31; object diagrams are discussed in Chapter 14.

One of the things for which you'll use objects is to model concrete instances that exist in the real world. For example, if you want to model the topology of your organization's network, you'll use deployment diagrams containing instances of nodes. Similarly, if you want to model the components that live on the physical nodes in this network, you'll use component diagrams containing instances of the components. Finally, suppose you have a debugger connected to your running system; it can present the structural relationships among instances by rendering an object diagram.

To model concrete instances,

- Identify those instances necessary and sufficient to visualize, specify, construct, or document the problem you are modeling.

- Render these objects in the UML as instances. Where possible, give each object a name. If there is no meaningful name for the object, render it as an anonymous object.
- Expose the stereotype, tagged values, and attributes (with their values) of each instance necessary and sufficient to model your problem.
- Render these instances and their relationships in an object diagram or other diagram appropriate to the kind of the instance.

For example, Figure 13-6 shows an object diagram drawn from the execution of a credit card validation system, perhaps as seen by a debugger that's probing the running system.

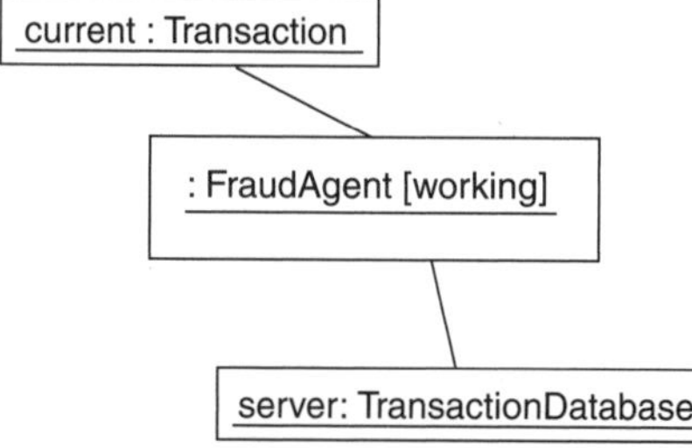

Figure 13-6: Modeling Concrete Instances

Hints and Tips

When you model instances in the UML, remember that every instance should denote a concrete manifestation of some abstraction, typically a class, component, node, use case, or association. A well-structured instance

- Is explicitly associated with a specific abstraction.
- Has a unique name drawn from the vocabulary of the problem domain or the solution domain.

When you draw an instance in the UML,

- Render the name of the abstraction of which it is an instance unless it's obvious by context.
- Show the instance's stereotype and state only as necessary to understand the object in its context.
- If visible, organize long lists of attributes and their values by grouping them according to their category.

Chapter 14
Object Diagrams

In this chapter

- Modeling object structures
- Forward and reverse engineering

Object diagrams model the instances of things contained in class diagrams. An object diagram shows a set of objects and their relationships at a point in time.

You use object diagrams to model the static design view or static process view of a system. This involves modeling a snapshot of the system at a moment in time and rendering a set of objects, their state, and their relationships.

Object diagrams are not only important for visualizing, specifying, and documenting structural models, but also for constructing the static aspects of systems through forward and reverse engineering.

Getting Started

If you are not used to the game, soccer looks like a terribly simple sport—an unruly mob of people madly running about a field chasing a white ball. Looking at the blurred image of bodies in motion, there hardly seems to be any subtlety or style to it.

Freeze the motion for a moment, then classify the individual players, and a very different picture of the game emerges. No longer just a mass of humanity, you'll be able to distinguish the forwards, halfbacks, and fullbacks. Dig a bit deeper and you'll understand how these players collaborate: following strategies for goal-tending, moving the ball, stealing the ball, and attacking. In a winning team, you won't find players placed randomly around the field.

Instead, at every moment of the game, you'll find their placement on the field and their relationship to other players well calculated.

Trying to visualize, specify, construct, or document a software-intensive system is similar. If you were to trace the control flow of a running system, you'd quickly lose sight of the bigger picture for how the system's parts are organized, especially if you have multiple threads of control. Similarly, if you have a complex data structure, just looking at the state of one object at a time doesn't help much. Rather, you need to study a snapshot of the object, its neighbors, and its relationships to these neighbors. In all but the simplest object-oriented systems, you'd find a multitude of objects present, each standing in precise relationship with others. In fact, when an object-oriented system breaks, it's typically not because of a failure in logic, but because of broken connections among objects or a mangled state in individual objects.

Class diagrams are discussed in Chapter 8; interactions are discussed in Chapter 16; interaction diagrams are discussed in Chapter 19.

With the UML, you use class diagrams to visualize the static aspects of your system's building blocks. You use interaction diagrams to visualize the dynamic aspects of your system, consisting of instances of these building blocks and messages dispatched among them. An object diagram covers a set of instances of the things found in a class diagram. An object diagram, therefore, expresses the static part of an interaction, consisting of the objects that collaborate but without any of the messages passed among them. In both cases, an object diagram freezes a moment in time, as in Figure 14-1.

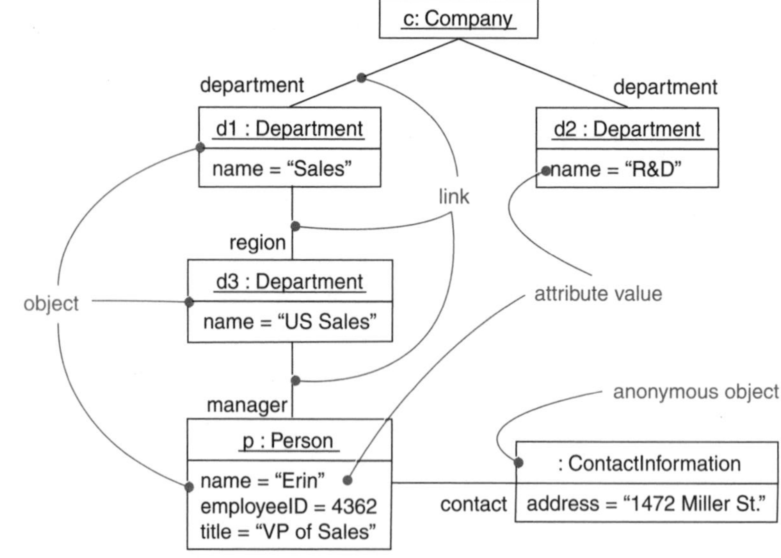

Figure 14-1: An Object Diagram

Terms and Concepts

An *object diagram* is a diagram that shows a set of objects and their relationships at a point in time. Graphically, an object diagram is a collection of vertices and arcs.

Common Properties

The general properties of diagrams are discussed in Chapter 7.

An object diagram is a special kind of diagram and shares the same common properties as all other diagrams—that is, a name and graphical contents that are a projection into a model. What distinguishes an object diagram from all other kinds of diagrams is its particular content.

Contents

Objects are discussed in Chapter 13; links are discussed in Chapter 16.

Object diagrams commonly contain

- Objects
- Links

Like all other diagrams, object diagrams may contain notes and constraints.

Sometimes you'll want to place classes in your object diagrams as well, especially when you want to visualize the classes behind each instance.

Class diagrams are discussed in Chapter 8; interaction diagrams are discussed in Chapter 19.

Note: An object diagram correlates with a class diagram: The class diagram describes the general situation, and the instance diagram describes specific instances derived from the class diagram.An object diagram contains primarily objects and links. Deployment diagrams may also occur in generic and instance forms: General deployment diagrams describe node types, and instance deployment diagrams describe a concrete configuration of node instances described by those types.

Common Uses

Design views are discussed in Chapter 2.

You use object diagrams to model the static design view or static process view of a system just as you do with class diagrams, but from the perspective of real or prototypical instances. This view primarily supports the functional requirements of a system—that is, the services the system should provide to its end users. Object diagrams let you model static data structures.

When you model the static design view or static interaction view of a system, you typically use object diagrams to model object structures.

Interaction diagrams are discussed in Chapter 19.

Modeling object structures involves taking a snapshot of the objects in a system at a given moment in time. An object diagram represents one static frame in the dynamic storyboard represented by an interaction diagram. You use object diagrams to visualize, specify, construct, and document the existence of certain instances in your system, together with their relationships to one another. You can show dynamic behavior and execution as a sequence of frames.

Common Modeling Techniques

Modeling Object Structures

When you construct a class diagram, a component diagram, or a deployment diagram, what you are really doing is capturing a set of abstractions that are interesting to you as a group and, in that context, exposing their semantics and their relationships to other abstractions in the group. These diagrams show only potentiality. If class `A` has a one-to-many association to class `B`, then for one instance of `A` there might be five instances of `B`; for another instance of `A` there might be only one instance of `B`. Furthermore, at a given moment in time, that instance of `A`, along with the related instances of `B`, will each have certain values for their attributes and state machines.

If you freeze a running system or just imagine a moment of time in a modeled system, you'll find a set of objects, each in a specific state and each in a particular relationship to other objects. You can use object diagrams to visualize, specify, construct, and document the structure of these snapshots. Object diagrams are especially useful for modeling complex data structures.

When you model your system's design view, a set of class diagrams can be used to completely specify the semantics of your abstractions and their relationships. With object diagrams, however, you cannot completely specify the object structure of your system. For an individual class, there may be a multitude of possible instances, and for a set of classes in relationship to one another, there may be many times more possible configurations of these objects. Therefore, when you use object diagrams, you can only meaningfully expose interesting sets of concrete or prototypical objects. This is what it means to model an object structure—an object diagram shows one set of objects in relation to one another at one moment in time.

To model an object structure,

Mechanisms such as these are often coupled to use cases, as discussed in Chapters 17 and 29.

- Identify the mechanism you'd like to model. A mechanism represents some function or behavior of the part of the system you are modeling that results from the interaction of a society of classes, interfaces, and other things.
- Create a collaboration to describe a mechanism.
- For each mechanism, identify the classes, interfaces, and other elements that participate in this collaboration; identify the relationships among these things as well.
- Consider one scenario that walks through this mechanism. Freeze that scenario at a moment in time, and render each object that participates in the mechanism.
- Expose the state and attribute values of each such object, as necessary, to understand the scenario.
- Similarly, expose the links among these objects, representing instances of associations among them.

For example, Figure 14-2 shows a set of objects drawn from the implementation of an autonomous robot. This figure focuses on some of the objects involved in the mechanism used by the robot to calculate a model of the world in which it moves. There are many more objects involved in a running system, but this diagram focuses on only those abstractions that are directly involved in creating this world view.

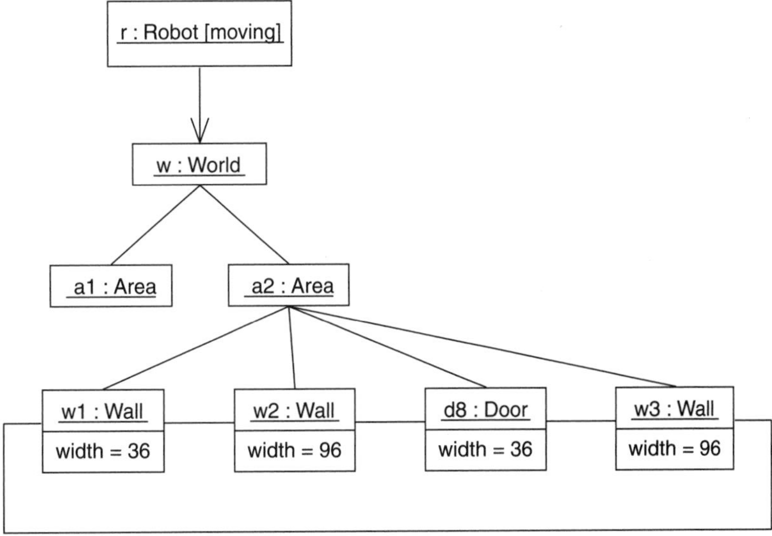

Figure 14-2: Modeling Object Structures

As this figure indicates, one object represents the robot itself (`r`, an instance of `Robot`), and `r` is currently in the state marked `moving`. This object has a link to `w`, an instance of `World`, which represents an abstraction of the robot's world model.

At this moment in time, `w` is linked to two instances of `Area`. One of them (`a2`) is shown with its own links to three `Wall` objects and one `Door` object. Each of these walls is marked with its current width, and each is shown linked to its neighboring walls. As this object diagram suggests, the robot has recognized this enclosed area, which has walls on three sides and a door on the fourth.

Reverse Engineering

Reverse engineering (the creation of a model from code) an object diagram can be useful. In fact, while you are debugging your system, this is something that you or your tools will do all the time. For example, if you are chasing down a dangling link, you'll want to literally or mentally draw an object diagram of the affected objects to see where, at a given moment in time, an object's state or its relationship to other objects is broken.

To reverse engineer an object diagram,

- Chose the target you want to reverse engineer. Typically, you'll set your context inside an operation or relative to an instance of one particular class.
- Using a tool or simply walking through a scenario, stop execution at a certain moment in time.
- Identify the set of interesting objects that collaborate in that context and render them in an object diagram.
- As necessary to understand their semantics, expose these object's states.
- As necessary to understand their semantics, identify the links that exist among these objects.
- If your diagram ends up overly complicated, prune it by eliminating objects that are not germane to the questions about the scenario you need answered. If your diagram is too simplistic, expand the neighbors of certain interesting objects and expose each object's state more deeply.
- You will usually have to manually add or label structure that is not explicit in the target code. The missing information supplies the design intent that is only implicit in the final code.

Hints and Tips

When you create object diagrams in the UML, remember that every object diagram is just a graphical representation of the static design view or static interaction view of a system. This means that no single object diagram need capture everything about a system's design or process view. In fact, for all but trivial systems, you'll encounter hundreds if not thousands of objects, most of them anonymous. So it's impossible to completely specify all the objects of a system or all the ways in which these objects may be associated. Consequently, object diagrams reflect some of the concrete or prototypical objects that live in the running system.

A well-structured object diagram

- Is focused on communicating one aspect of a system's static design view or static process view.
- Represents one frame in the dynamic storyboard represented by an interaction diagram.
- Contains only those elements that are essential to understanding that aspect.
- Provides detail consistent with its level of abstraction; you should expose only those attribute values and other adornments that are essential to understanding.
- Is not so minimalist as to misinform the reader about semantics that are important.

When you draw an object diagram,

- Give it a name that communicates its purpose.
- Lay out its elements to minimize lines that cross.
- Organize its elements spatially so that things that are semantically close are laid out to be physically close.
- Use notes and color as visual cues to draw attention to important features of your diagram.
- Include the values and state of each object as necessary to communicate your intent.

Chapter 15
Components

In this chapter

- Components, interfaces, and realization
- Internal structure, ports, parts, and connectors
- Wiring subcomponents together
- Modeling an API

A component is a logical, replaceable part of a system that conforms to and provides the realization of a set of interfaces.

Good components define crisp abstractions with well-defined interfaces, making it possible to easily replace older components with newer, compatible ones.

Interfaces bridge your logical and design models. For example, you may specify an interface for a class in a logical model, and that same interface will carry over to some design component that realizes it.

Interfaces allow you to build the implementation of a component using smaller components by wiring ports on the components together.

Getting Started

When you are building a house, you may choose to install a home entertainment system. It is possible to buy a single unit that includes everything: television screen, tuner, VCR, DVD player, and speakers. Such a system is easy to install and works great if it meets your needs. A one-piece unit is not very flexible, however. You have to take the combination of features that the manufacturer provides. You probably won't be able to get high-quality speakers. If you want to install a new high-definition television screen, you have to throw away the entire unit and replace it, including the VCR and DVD player that may still be working fine. If you have a collection of records (some of you readers may remember what those are), you are out of luck.

You can plug the amplifier input into the video output, because they happen to use the same kinds of plugs. Software has the advantage of an unlimited number of "plug" types.

A more flexible approach is to build your entertainment system out of individual components, each focused on a single functionality. A monitor displays the picture; individual speakers play the sound, and they can be placed wherever your room and ears allow; the tuner, VCR, and DVD player are each separate units, their capabilities adjusted to your videophile requirements and your budget. Instead of being locked together in a rigid fashion, you place each component where you want and hook them together with cables. Each cable has a specific kind of plug that fits into a matching port on a component, so you can't plug a speaker wire into a video output. You can hook up your old turntable if you want. When you want to upgrade your system, you can replace one component at a time without trashing the entire system and starting over. Components provide more flexibility and permit you to obtain higher quality, if you want it and can afford it.

Software is similar. You can construct an application as a large, monolithic unit, but it will be rigid and difficult to modify as needs change. In addition, you can't take advantage of existing capabilities. Even if an existing system has much of the functionality you need, it may also have a lot of other parts that you don't want, and they are difficult or impossible to remove. The solution for software systems is the same as for electronics systems: Build them from well defined components that can be wired together flexibly and replaced individually as requirements change.

Terms and Concepts

Interfaces are discussed in Chapter 11; classes are discussed in Chapters 4 and 9.

An *interface* is a collection of operations that specify a service that is provided by or requested from a class or component.

A *component* is a replaceable part of a system that conforms to and provides the realization of a set of interfaces.

A *port* is a specific window into an encapsulated component accepting messages to and from the component conforming to specified interfaces.

Internal structure is the implementation of a component by means of a set of parts that are connected together in a specific way.

A *part* is the specification of a role that composes part of the implementation of a component. In an instance of the component, there is an instance corresponding to the part.

A *connector* is a communication relationship between two parts or ports within the context of a component.

Components and Interfaces

Interfaces are discussed in Chapter 11.

An interface is a collection of operations that are used to specify a service of a class or a component. The relationship between component and interface is important. All the most common component-based operating system facilities (such as COM+, CORBA, and Enterprise Java Beans) use interfaces as the glue that binds components together.

Modeling distributed systems is discussed in Chapter 24.

To construct a system based on components, you decompose your system by specifying interfaces that represent the major seams in the system. You then provide components that realize the interfaces, along with other components that access the services through their interfaces. This mechanism permits you to deploy a system whose services are somewhat location-independent and, as discussed in the next section, replaceable.

Realization is discussed in Chapter 10.

An interface that a component realizes is called a *provided interface*, meaning an interface that the component provides as a service to other components. A component may declare many provided interfaces. The interface that a component uses is called a *required interface*, meaning an interface that the component conforms to when requesting services from other components. A component may conform to many required interfaces. Also, a component may both provide and require interfaces.

As Figure 15-1 indicates, a component is shown as a rectangle with a small two-pronged icon in its upper right corner. The name of the component appears in the rectangle. A component can have attributes and operations, but these are often elided in diagrams. A component can show a network of internal structure, as described later in this chapter.

You can show the relationship between a component and its interfaces in one of two ways. The first (and most common) style renders the interface in its elided, iconic form. A provided interface is shown as a circle attached to the component by a line (a "lollipop"). A required interface is shown as a semicircle attached to the component by a line (a "socket"). In both cases, the name of the interface is placed next to the symbol. The second style renders the interface in its expanded form, perhaps revealing its operations. The component that realizes the interface is connected to the interface using a full realization

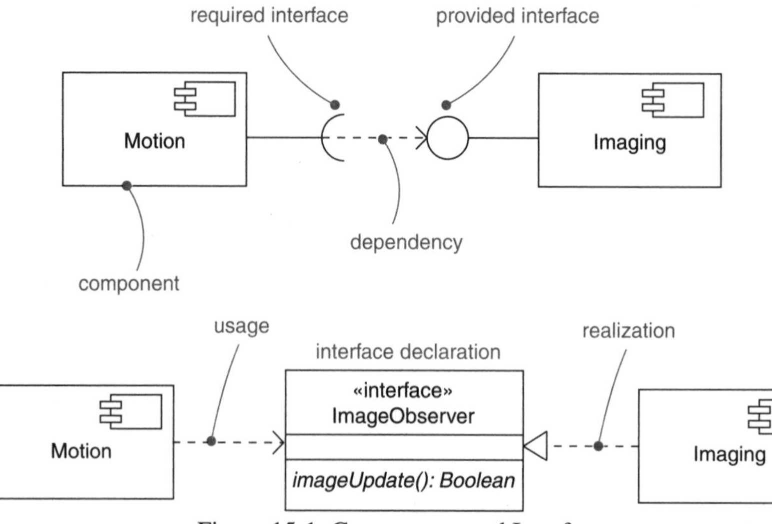

Figure 15-1: Components and Interfaces

relationship. The component that accesses the services of the other component through the interface is connected to the interface using a dependency relationship.

A given interface may be provided by one component and required by another. The fact that this interface lies between the two components breaks the direct dependency between the components. A component that uses a given interface will function properly no matter what component realizes that interface. Of course, a component can be used in a context if and only if all its required interfaces are realized as provided interfaces of other components.

Note: Interfaces apply at multiple levels just like other elements. The design-level interface you find used or realized by a component will map to an implementation-level interface used or realized by the artifact that implements the component.

Replaceability

Artifacts are discussed in Chapter 26.

The basic intent of every component-based operating system facility is to permit the assembly of systems from binary replaceable artifacts. This means that you can design a system using components and then implement those components using artifacts. You can then evolve that system by adding new components and replacing old ones, without rebuilding the system. Interfaces are the key to making this happen. In the executable system, you can use any artifacts that implement a component conforming to or providing that interface. You can extend the system by making the components provide new services through other interfaces, which, in turn, other components can discover and use. These semantics explain the intent behind the definition of components in the UML. A component conforms to and provides the realization of a set of interfaces and enables substitutability both in the logical design and in the physical implementation based on it.

A component is *replaceable*. A component is substitutable—it is possible to replace a component with another that conforms to the same interfaces. At design time, you choose a different component. Typically, the mechanism of inserting or replacing an artifact in a run time system is transparent to the component user and is enabled by object models (such as COM+ and Enterprise Java Beans) that require little or no intervening transformation or by tools that automate the mechanism.

Systems and subsystems are discussed in Chapter 32.

A component is *part of a system*. A component rarely stands alone. Rather, a given component collaborates with other components and in so doing exists in the architectural or technology context in which it is intended to be used. A component is logically and physically cohesive and thus denotes a meaningful structural and/or behavioral chunk of a larger system. A component may be reused across many systems. Therefore, a component represents a fundamental building block on which systems can be designed and composed. This definition is recursive—a system at one level of abstraction may simply be a component at a higher level of abstraction.

Finally, as discussed in the previous section, a component *conforms to and provides the realization of a set of interfaces.*

Organizing Components

Packages are discussed in Chapter 12.

You can organize components by grouping them in packages in the same manner in which you organize classes.

Relationships are discussed in Chapters 5 and 10.

You can also organize components by specifying dependency, generalization, association (including aggregation), and realization relationships among them.

Components can be built from other components. See the discussion on internal structure later in this chapter.

Ports

Interfaces are useful in declaring the overall behavior of a component, but they have no individual identity; the implementation of the component must merely ensure that all the operations in all of the provided interfaces are implemented. To have greater control over the implementation, ports can be used.

A *port* is an explicit window into an *encapsulated component*. In an encapsulated component, all of the interactions into and out of the component pass through ports. The externally visible behavior of the component is the sum of its ports, no more and no less. In addition, a port has identity. Another component can communicate with the component through a specific port. The communications are described completely by the interfaces that the port supports, even if the component supports other interfaces. In the implementation, the internal parts of the component may interact through a specific external port, so that each part can be independent of the requirements of the other parts. Ports permit the interfaces of a component to be divided into discrete packets and used independently. The encapsulation and independence provided by ports permit a much greater degree of encapsulation and substitutability.

A port is shown as a small square straddling the border of a component—it represents a hole through the encapsulation boundary of the component. Both provided and required interfaces may be attached to the port symbol. A provided interface represents a service that can be requested through that port. A required interface represents a service that the port needs to obtain from some other component. Each port has a name so that it can be uniquely identified given the component and the port name. The port name can be used by internal parts of the component to identify the port through which to send and receive messages. The component name and port name together uniquely identify a specific port in a specific component for use by other components.

Parts may also have multiplicity, therefore one part in a component may correspond to several instances in an instance of the component.

Ports are part of a component. Instances of ports are created and destroyed along with the instance of the component to which they belong. Ports may also have multiplicity; this indicates the possible number of instances of a particular port within an instance of the component. Each port on a component instance has an array of port instances. Although the port instances in an array all satisfy the same interface and accept the same kinds of requests, they may have different states and data values. For example, each instance in an array might have a different priority level, with the higher-priority port instances being served first.

Figure 15-2 shows the model of a `Ticket Seller` component with ports. Each port has a name and, optionally, a type to tell what kind of a port it is. The component has ports for ticket sales, attractions, and credit card charging.

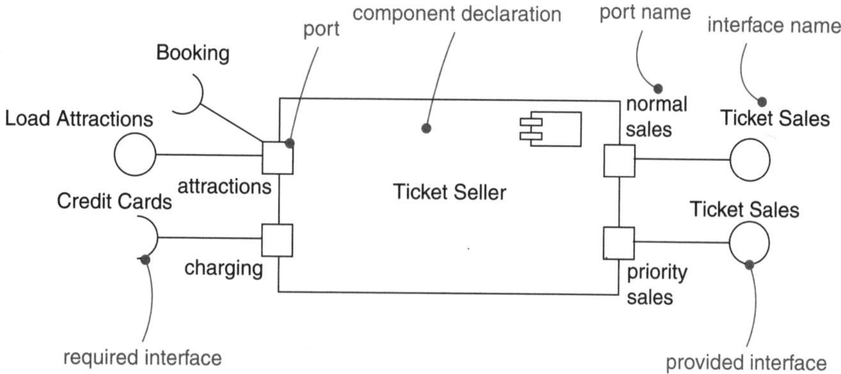

Figure 15-2: Ports on a Component

There are two ports for ticket sales, one for normal customers and one for priority customers. They both have the same provided interface of type `Ticket Sales`. The credit card processing port has a required interface; any component that provides the specified services can satisfy it. The attractions port has both provided and required interfaces. Using the `Load Attractions` interface, a theater can enter shows and other attractions into the ticket database for sale. Using the `Booking` interface, the ticket seller component can query the theaters for the availability of tickets and actually buy the tickets.

Internal Structure

A component can be implemented as a single piece of code, but in larger systems it is desirable to be able to build large components using smaller components as building blocks. The internal structure of a component is the parts that compose the implementation of the component together with the connections among them. In many cases, the internal parts can be instances of smaller components that are wired together statically through ports to provide the necessary behavior without the need for the modeler to specify extra logic.

A *part* is a unit of the implementation of a component. A part has a name and a type. In an instance of the component, there is one or more instance corresponding to each part having the type specified by the part. A part has a multiplicity within its component. If the multiplicity of the part is greater than one, there may be more than one part instance in a given component instance. If the multiplicity is something other than a single integer, the number of part instances may vary from one instance of the component to another. A component instance is created with the minimum number of parts; additional parts can be added later. An attribute of a class is a kind of part: it has a type and a

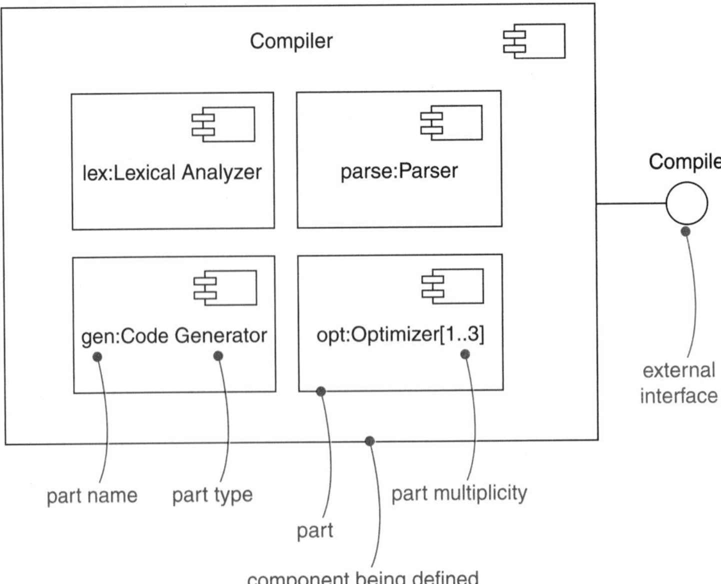

Figure 15-3: Parts Within a Component

multiplicity, and each instance of the class has one or more instance of the given type.

Figure 15-3 shows a compiler component built from four kinds of parts. There is a lexical analyzer, a parser, a code generator, and one to three optimizers. More complete versions of the compiler can be configured with different levels of optimization; within a given version, the appropriate optimizer can be selected at run time.

Note that a part is not the same as a class. Each part is potentially distinguishable by its name, just like each attribute in a class is distinguishable. There can be more than one part of the same type, but you can tell them apart by their names, and presumably they have distinct functions within the component. For example, in Figure 15-4 an `Air Ticket Sales` component might have separate `Sales` parts for frequent fliers and for regular customers; they both work the same, but the frequent-flier part is available only to special customers and involves less chance of waiting in line and may provide additional perks. Because these components have the same type, they must have names to distinguish them. The other two components of types `SeatAssignment` and `InventoryManagement` do not require names because there is only one of each type within the `Air Ticket Sales` component.

If the parts are components with ports, you can wire them together through their ports. The rule is simple: Two ports can be connected together if one pro-

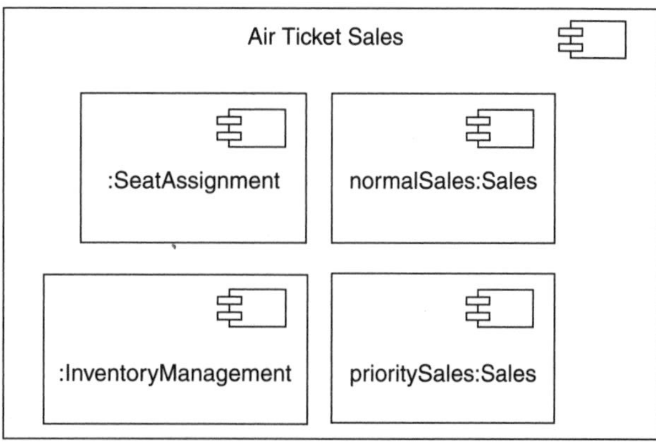

Figure 15-4: Parts of the Same Type

vides a given interface and the other requires the interface. Connecting the ports means that the requiring port will invoke the providing port to obtain services. The advantage of ports and interfaces is that nothing else needs to be known; if the interfaces are compatible, the ports can be connected. A tool could automatically generate calling code from one component to another. They can also be reconnected to other components that provide the same interfaces, if new components become available. A wire between two ports is called a *connector*. In an instance of the overall component, it represents a link or a transient link. A link is an instance of an ordinary association. A transient link represents a usage relationship between two components. Instead of an ordinary association, it might be supplied by a procedure parameter or a local variable that serves as the target of an operation. The advantage of ports and interfaces is that the two components don't have to know about each other at design time, as long as their interfaces are compatible.

You can show connectors in two ways (Figure 15-5). If two components are explicitly wired together, either directly or through ports, just draw a line between them or their ports. On the other hand, if two components are connected because they have compatible interfaces, you can use a ball-and-socket notation to show that there is no inherent relationship between the components, although they are connected inside this component. You could substitute some other component that satisfies the interface.

You can also wire internal ports to external ports of the overall component. This is called a delegation connector, because messages on the external port are delegated to the internal port. This is shown by an arrow from an internal port to an external port. You can think of this in two ways, whichever you prefer: In the first approach, the internal port *is* the same as the external port; it has been moved to the boundary and allowed to peek through. In the second

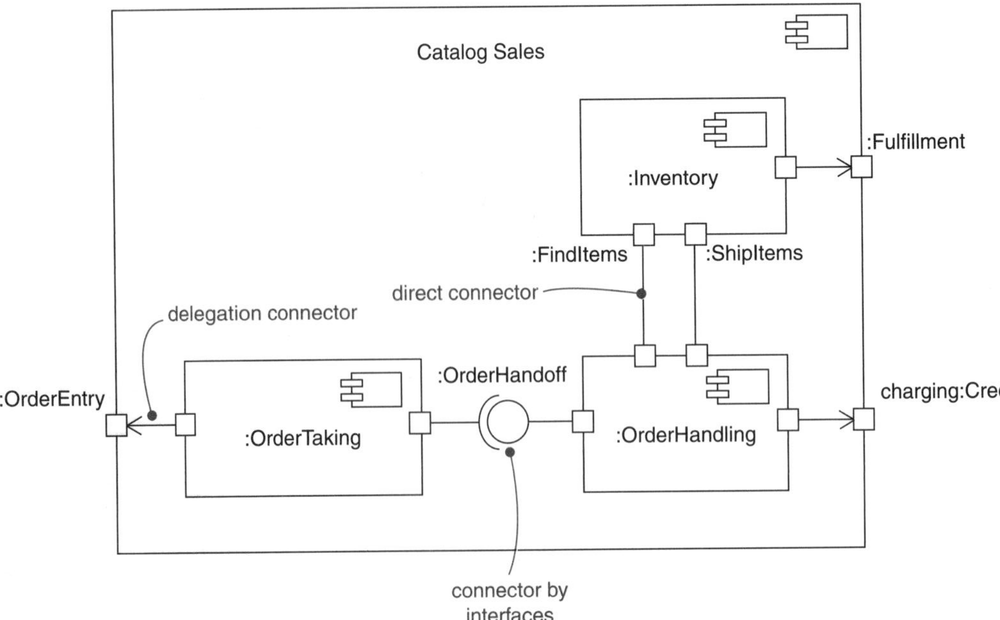

Figure 15-5: Connectors

approach, any message to the external port is transmitted immediately to the internal port, and vice versa. It really doesn't matter; the behavior is the same in either case.

Figure 15-5 shows an example with internal ports and different kinds of connectors. External requests on the `OrderEntry` port are delegated to the internal port of the `OrderTaking` subcomponent. This component in turn sends its output to its `OrderHandoff` port. This port is connected by a ball-and-socket symbol to the `OrderHandling` subcomponent. This kind of connection implies that there is no special knowledge between the two components; the output could be connected to any component that obeys the `OrderHandoff` interface. The `OrderHandling` component communicates with the Inventory component to find the items in stock. This is shown as a direct connector; because no interfaces are shown, this tends to suggest that the connection is more tightly coupled. Once the items are found in stock, the `OrderHandling` component accesses an external `Credit` service; this is shown by the delegation connector to the external port called `changing`. Once the external credit service responds, the `OrderHandling` component communicates with a different port `ShipItems` on the `Inventory` component to prepare the order for shipment. The `Inventory` component accesses an external `Fulfillment` service to actually perform the shipment.

Interaction diagrams are discussed in Chapter 19.

Note that the component diagram shows the structure and potential message paths of the component. The component diagram itself does not show the sequencing of messages through the component. Sequencing and other kinds of dynamic information can be shown using interaction diagrams.

Note: Internal structure, including ports, parts, and connectors, can be used as the implementation of any class, not just components. There really isn't much of a semantic distinction between classes and components. It is often useful, however, to use the convention that components are used for encapsulated concepts with internal structure, particularly those concepts that do not map directly to a single class in the implementation.

Common Modeling Techniques

Modeling Structured Classes

A structured class can be used to model data structures in which the parts have contextual connections that apply only within the class. Ordinary attributes or associations can define composite parts of a class, but the parts cannot be related to each other on a plain class diagram. A class whose internal structure is shown with parts and connectors avoids this problem.

To model a structured class,

- Identify the internal parts of the class and their types.
- Give each part a name that indicates its purpose in the structured class, not its generic type.
- Draw connectors between parts that communicate or have contextual relationships.
- Feel free to use other structured classes as the types of parts, but remember that you can't make connections to parts inside another structured class; connect to its external ports.

Figure 15-6 shows the design of the structured class `TicketOrder`. This class has four parts and one ordinary attribute, `price`. The `customer` is a `Person` object. The `customer` may or may not have a `priority` status, so the `priority` part is shown with multiplicity 0..1; the connector from `cus-`

`tomer` to `priority` also has the same multiplicity. There are one or more seats reserved; `seat` has a multiplicity value. It is unnecessary to show a connector from `customer` to `seats` because they are in the same structured class anyway. Notice that `Attraction` is drawn with a dashed border. This means that the part is a reference to an object that is not owned by the structured class. The reference is created and destroyed with an instance of the `TicketOrder` class, but instances of *Attraction* are independent of the `TicketOrder` class. The `seat` part is connected to the `attraction` reference because the order may include seats for more than one `attraction`, and each `seat` reservation must be connected to a specific `attraction`. We see from the multiplicity on the connector that each `Seat` reservation is connected to exactly one `Attraction` object.

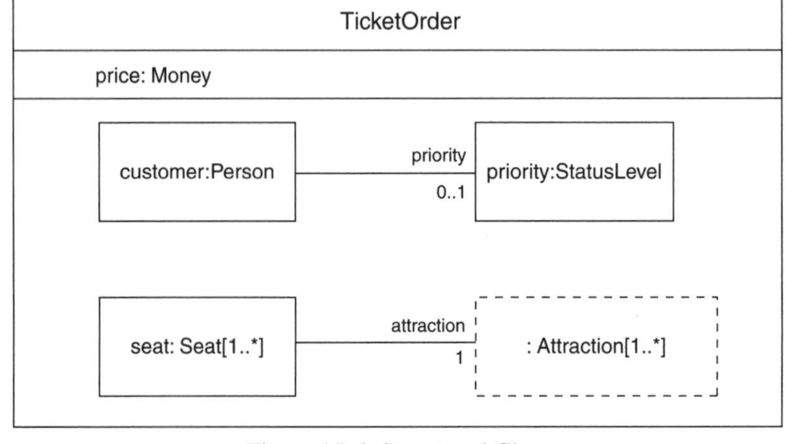

Figure 15-6: Structured Class

Modeling an API

If you are a developer who's assembling a system from component parts, you'll often want to see the application programming interfaces (APIs) that you use to glue these parts together. APIs represent the programmatic seams in your system, which you can model using interfaces and components.

An API is essentially an interface that is realized by one or more components. As a developer, you'll really care only about the interface itself; which component realizes an interface's operations is not relevant as long as *some* component realizes it. From a system configuration management perspective, though, these realizations are important because you need to ensure that when you publish an API, there's some realization available that carries out the API's obligations. Fortunately, with the UML, you can model both perspectives.

The operations associated with any semantically rich API will be fairly extensive, so most of the time you won't need to visualize all these operations at once. Instead, you'll tend to keep the operations in the backplane of your models and use interfaces as handles with which you can find these sets of operations. If you want to construct executable systems against these APIs, you will need to add enough detail so that your development tools can compile against the properties of your interfaces. Along with the signatures of each operation, you'll probably also want to include uses cases that explain how to use each interface.

To model an API,

- Identify the seams in your system and model each seam as an interface, collecting the attributes and operations that form this edge.
- Expose only those properties of the interface that are important to visualize in the given context; otherwise, hide these properties, keeping them in the interface's specification for reference, as necessary.
- Model the realization of each API only insofar as it is important to show the configuration of a specific implementation.

Figure 15-7 exposes the APIs of an animation component. You'll see four interfaces that form the API: `IApplication`, `IModels`, `IRendering`, and `IScripts`. Other components can use one or more of these interfaces as needed.

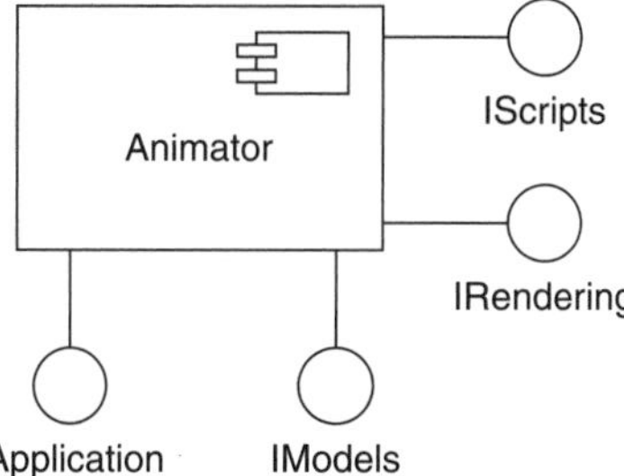

Figure 15-7: Modeling an API

Hints and Tips

Components allow you to encapsulate the parts of your system to reduce dependencies, make them explicit, and enhance replaceability and flexibility when the system must be changed in the future. A good component:

- Encapsulates a service that has a well-defined interface and boundary.
- Has enough internal structure to be worth describing.
- Does not combine unrelated functionality into a single unit.
- Organizes its external behavior using a few interfaces and ports.
- Interacts only through declared ports.

If you choose to show the implementation of a component using nested subcomponents:

- Use a moderate number of subcomponents. If there are too many to show comfortably on one page, use additional levels of decomposition in some of the subcomponents.
- Ensure that the subcomponents interact only through defined ports and connectors.
- Determine which subcomponents interact directly with the external world and model them with delegation connectors.

When you draw a component in the UML:

- Give it a name that clearly indicates its purpose. Name interfaces in the same way.
- Name subcomponents and ports if their meaning is not clear from their types or if there are multiple parts of the same type.
- Hide unnecessary detail. You don't have to show every detail of the implementation on the component diagram.
- Show the dynamics of a component using interaction diagrams.

Part 4
Basic Behavioral Modeling

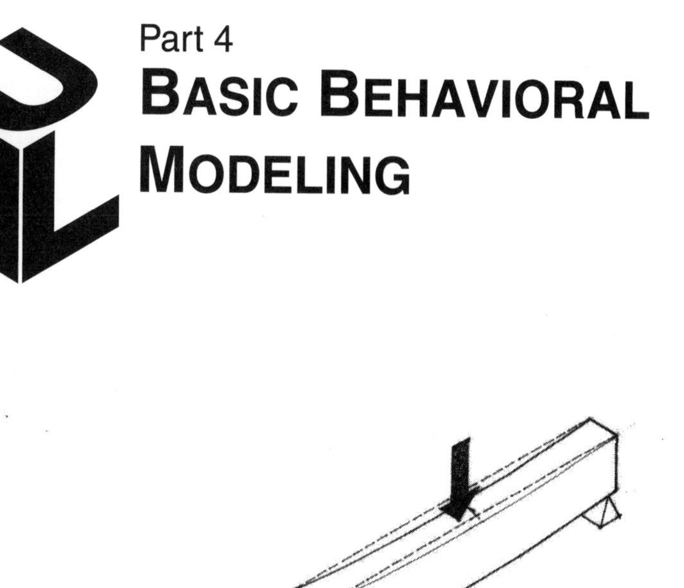

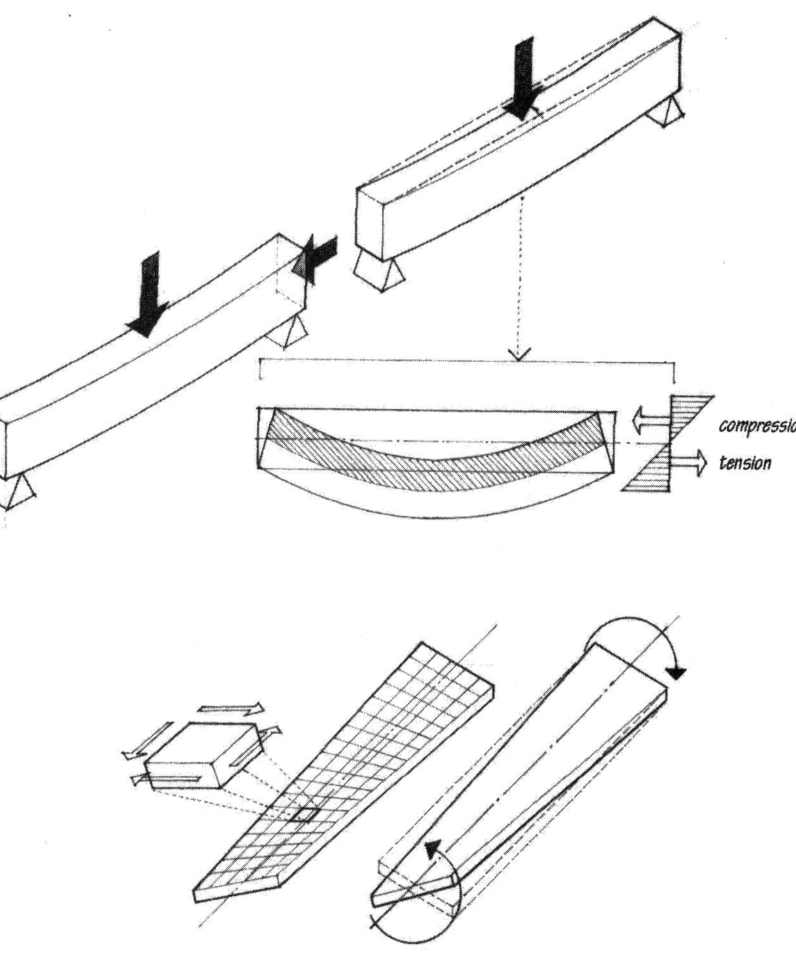

Chapter 16

INTERACTIONS

In this chapter

- Roles, links, messages, actions, and sequences
- Modeling flows of control
- Creating well-structured algorithms

In every interesting system, objects don't just sit idle; they interact with one another by passing messages. An interaction is a behavior that comprises a set of messages exchanged among a set of objects within a context to accomplish a purpose.

You use interactions to model the dynamic aspect of collaborations, representing societies of objects playing specific roles, all working together to carry out some behavior that's bigger than the sum of the elements. These roles represent prototypical instances of classes, interfaces, components, nodes, and use cases. Their dynamic aspects are visualized, specified, constructed, and documented as flows of control that may encompass simple, sequential threads through a system, as well as more-complex flows that involve branching, looping, recursion, and concurrency. You can model each interaction in two ways: by emphasizing its time ordering of messages or by emphasizing its sequencing of messages in the context of some structural organization of objects.

Well-structured interactions are like well-structured algorithms—efficient, simple, adaptable, and understandable.

Getting Started

The differences between building a dog house and building a high rise are discussed in Chapter 1.

A building is a living thing. Although every building is constructed of static stuff, such as bricks, mortar, lumber, plastic, glass, and steel, those things work together dynamically to carry out behavior that is useful to those who use the building. Doors and windows open and close. Lights turn on and off. A building's furnace, air conditioner, thermostat, and ventilation ducts work together to regulate the building's temperature. In intelligent buildings, sensors detect the presence or absence of activity and adjust lighting, heating, cooling, and music as conditions change. Buildings are laid out to facilitate the flow of people and materials from place to place. More subtly, buildings are designed to adapt to changes in temperature, expanding and contracting during the day and night and across the seasons. All well-structured buildings are designed to react to dynamic forces, such as wind, earthquakes, and the movement of its occupants, in ways that keep the building in equilibrium.

Modeling the structural aspects of a system is discussed in Parts 2 and 3; you can also model the dynamic aspects of a system by using state machines, as discussed in Chapter 22; object diagrams are discussed in Chapter 14; interaction diagrams are discussed in Chapter 19; collaborations are discussed in Chapter 28.

Software-intensive systems are the same way. An airline system might manage many terabytes of information that sit untouched on some disk most of the time, only to be brought to life by outside events, such as the booking of a reservation, the movement of an aircraft, or the scheduling of a flight. In reactive systems, such as those found on the computer in a microwave oven, objects spring to life and work gets carried out when the system is stimulated by such events as a user pushing a button or by the passage of time.

In the UML, you model the static aspects of a system by using such elements as class diagrams and object diagrams. These diagrams let you visualize, specify, construct, and document the things that live in your system, including classes, interfaces, components, nodes, and use cases and their instances, together with the way those things sit in relationship to one another.

In the UML, you model the dynamic aspects of a system by using interactions. Like an object diagram, an interaction statically sets the stage for its behavior by introducing all the objects that work together to carry out some action. Going beyond object diagrams, however, interactions also introduce messages that are dispatched from object to object. Most often, messages involve the invocation of an operation or the sending of a signal; messages may also encompass the creation and destruction of other objects.

You use interactions to model the flow of control within an operation, a class, a component, a use case, or the system as a whole. Using interaction diagrams, you can reason about these flows in two ways. First, you can focus on how messages are dispatched across time. Second, you can focus on the structural relationships among the objects in an interaction and then consider how messages are passed within the context of that structure.

The UML provides a graphical representation of messages, as Figure 16-1 shows. This notation permits you to visualize a message in a way that lets you emphasize its most important parts: its name, parameters (if any), and sequence. Graphically, a message is rendered as a directed line and almost always includes the name of its operation.

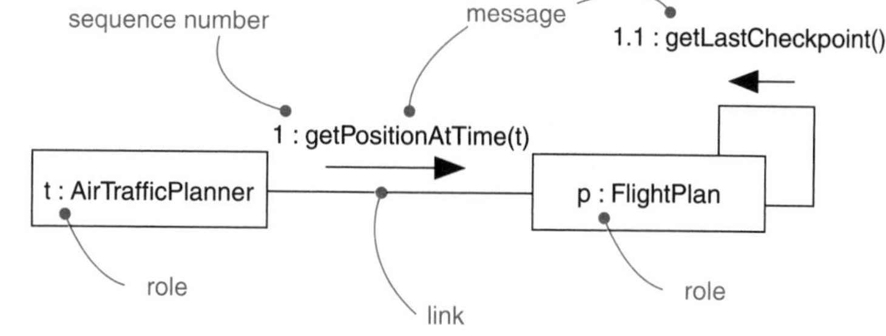

Figure 16-1: Messages, Links, and Sequencing

Terms and Concepts

Internal structure diagrams show the structural connection among roles, as discussed in Chapter 15; objects are discussed in Chapter 14; systems and subsystems are discussed in Chapter 32; collaborations are discussed in Chapter 28.

An *interaction* is a behavior that comprises a set of messages exchanged among objects in a set of roles within a context to accomplish a purpose. A *message* is a specification of a communication between objects that conveys information with the expectation that activity will ensue.

Context

You may find an interaction wherever objects are linked to one another. You'll find interactions in the collaboration of objects that exist in the context of your system or subsystem. You will also find interactions in the context of an operation. Finally, you'll find interactions in the context of a class.

Most often, you'll find interactions in the collaboration of objects that exist in the context of your system or subsystem as a whole. For example, in a system for Web commerce, you'll find objects on the client (such as instances of the classes `BookOrder` and `OrderForm`) interacting with one another. You'll also find objects on the client (again, such as instances of `BookOrder`) interacting with objects on the server (such as instances of `BackOrderManager`). These interactions therefore not only involve localized collaborations of objects (such as the interactions surrounding `OrderForm`), but they may also cut across many conceptual levels of your system (such as the interactions surrounding `BackOrderManager`).

Operations are discussed in Chapters 4 and 9; modeling an operation is discussed in Chapters 20 and 28.

You'll also find interactions among objects in the implementation of an operation. The parameters of an operation, any variables local to the operation, and any objects global to the operation (but still visible to the operation) may interact with one another to carry out the algorithm of that operation's implementation. For example, the operation `moveToPosition(p : Position)` defined for a class in a mobile robot will involve the interaction of a parameter (`p`), an object global to the operation (such as the object `currentPosition`), and possibly several local objects (such as local variables used by the operation to calculate intermediate points in a path to the new position).

Classes are discussed in Chapters 4 and 9.

Finally, you will find interactions in the context of a class. You can use interactions to visualize, specify, construct, and document the semantics of a class. For example, to understand the meaning of a class `RayTraceAgent`, you might create interactions that show how the attributes of that class collaborate with one another (and with objects global to instances of the class and with parameters defined in the class's operations).

Components are discussed in Chapter 15; nodes are discussed in Chapter 27; use cases are discussed in Chapter 17; modeling the realization of a use case is discussed in Chapter 28; classifiers are discussed in Chapter 9.

Note: An interaction may also be found in the representation of a component, node, or use case, each of which is really a kind of UML classifier. In the context of a use case, an interaction represents a scenario that, in turn, represents one thread through the action of the use case.

Objects and Roles

The objects that participate in an interaction are either concrete things or prototypical things. As a concrete thing, an object represents something in the real world. For example, `p`, an instance of the class `Person`, might denote a particular human. Alternately, as a prototypical thing, `p` might represent any instance of `Person`.

Note: In a collaboration, the interactors are usually prototypical things that play particular roles, not specific objects in the real world, although it is sometimes useful to describe collaborations among particular objects.

Abstract classes are discussed in Chapter 4; interfaces are discussed in Chapter 11.

In the context of an interaction, you may find instances of classes, components, nodes, and use cases. Although abstract classes and interfaces, by definition, may not have any direct instances, you may represent instances of these things in an interaction. Such instances do not represent direct instances of the abstract class or of the interface, but may represent, respectively, indirect (or prototypical) instances of any concrete children of the abstract class of some concrete class that realizes that interface.

Instances are discussed in Chapter 13; object diagrams are discussed in Chapter 14.

You can think of an object diagram as a representation of the static aspect of an interaction, setting the stage for the interaction by specifying all the objects that work together. An interaction goes further by introducing a dynamic sequence of messages that may pass along the links that connect these objects.

Links and Connectors

Associations are discussed in Chapters 5 and 10; connectors and roles are discussed in Chapter 15.

A link is a semantic connection among objects. In general, a link is an instance of an association. As Figure 16-2 shows, wherever a class has an association to another class, there may be a link between the instances of the two classes; wherever there is a link between two objects, one object can send a message to the other object.

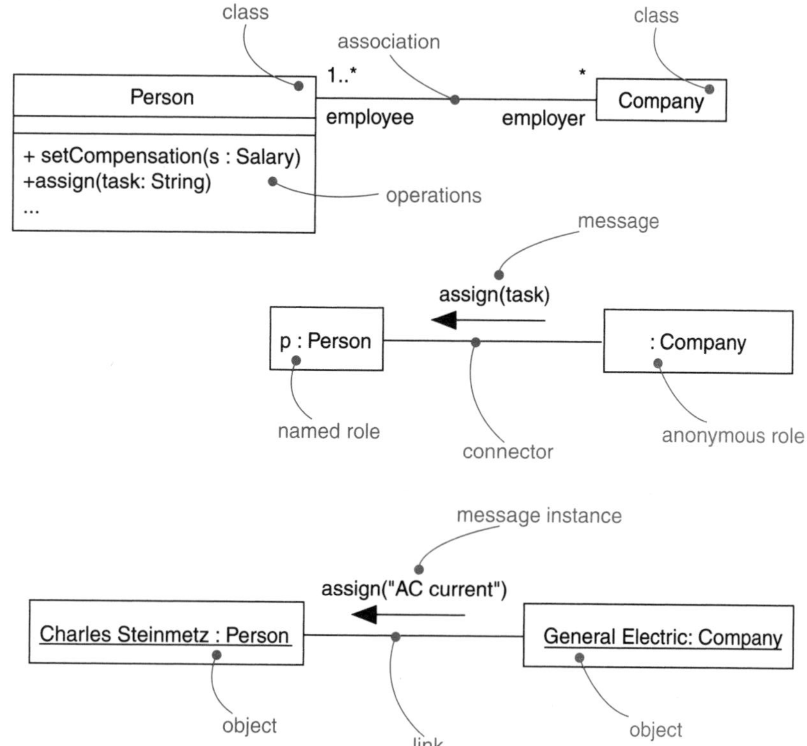

Figure 16-2: Associations, Links, and Connectors

A link specifies a path along which one object can dispatch a message to another (or the same) object. Most of the time it is sufficient to specify that such a path exists. If you need to be more precise about how that path exists, you can adorn the appropriate end of the link with one of the following constraints:

- `association` Specifies that the corresponding object is visible by association
- `self` Specifies that the corresponding object is visible because it is the dispatcher of the operation
- `global` Specifies that the corresponding object is visible because it is in an enclosing scope
- `local` Specifies that the corresponding object is visible because it is in a local scope
- `parameter` Specifies that the corresponding object is visible because it is a parameter

---

Note: As an instance of an association, a link may be rendered with most of the adornments appropriate to associations, such as a name, association role name, navigation, and aggregation. Multiplicity, however, does not apply to links, since they are instances of an association.

Roles, connectors, and internal structure are discussed in Chapter 15; collaborations are discussed in Chapter 28.

In most models, we are more interested in prototypical objects and links within some context rather than individual objects and links. A prototypical object is called a *role*; a prototypical link is called a *connector*; the context is a collaboration or the internal structure of a classifier. The multiplicity of roles and connectors are defined relative to their enclosing context. For example, a multiplicity of 1 on a role means one object represents the role for each object that represents the context. A collaboration or internal structure can be used many times, just like a class declaration; each use is bound to a separate set of objects and links for the context, roles, and links.

Figure 16-2 shows an example. The top of the figure shows a class diagram that declares classes `Person` and `Company` and the many-to-many `employee-employer` association between them. The middle shows the contents of a collaboration `WorkAssignment` that assigns an employee to a job. It has two roles and a connector between them. The bottom shows an instance of this collaboration, in which there are objects and links bound to the roles and connectors. A concrete message in the bottom represents the prototypical message declaration in the collaboration.

Messages

Object diagrams are discussed in Chapter 14.

Suppose you have a set of objects and a set of links that connect those objects. If that's all you have, then you have a completely static model that can be represented by an object diagram. Object diagrams model the state of a society of objects at a given moment in time and are useful when you want to visualize, specify, construct, or document a static object structure.

Operations are discussed in Chapters 4 and 9; events are discussed in Chapter 21; instances are discussed in Chapter 13.

Suppose you want to model the changing state of a society of objects over a period of time. Think of it as taking a motion picture of a set of objects, each frame representing a successive moment in time. If these objects are not totally idle, you'll see objects passing messages to other objects, sending events, and invoking operations. In addition, at each frame you can explicitly visualize the current state and role of individual instances.

A message is the specification of a communication among objects that conveys information with the expectation that activity will ensue. The receipt of a message instance may be considered an occurrence of an event. (An *occurrence* is the UML name for an instance of an event.)

When you pass a message, an action usually results on its receipt. An action may result in a change in state of the target object and objects accessible from it.

In the UML, you can model several kinds of messages.

Operations are discussed in Chapters 4 and 9; signals are discussed in Chapter 21.

- Call — Invokes an operation on an object; an object may send a message to itself, resulting in the local invocation of an operation
- Return — Returns a value to the caller
- Send — Sends a signal to an object
- Create — Creates an object
- Destroy — Destroys an object; an object may commit suicide by destroying itself

---

Note: You can model complex actions in the UML as well. In addition to the five basic kinds of messages listed above, you can include actions on individual objects. The UML does not specify the syntax or semantics of such actions; it is expected that tools will supply various actions languages or use the syntax of programming languages.

Create and destroy are visualized as stereotypes, which are discussed in Chapter 6; the distinction between synchronous and asynchronous messages is most relevant in the context of concurrency, as discussed in Chapter 23.

The UML provides a visual distinction among these kinds of messages, as Figure 16-3 shows.

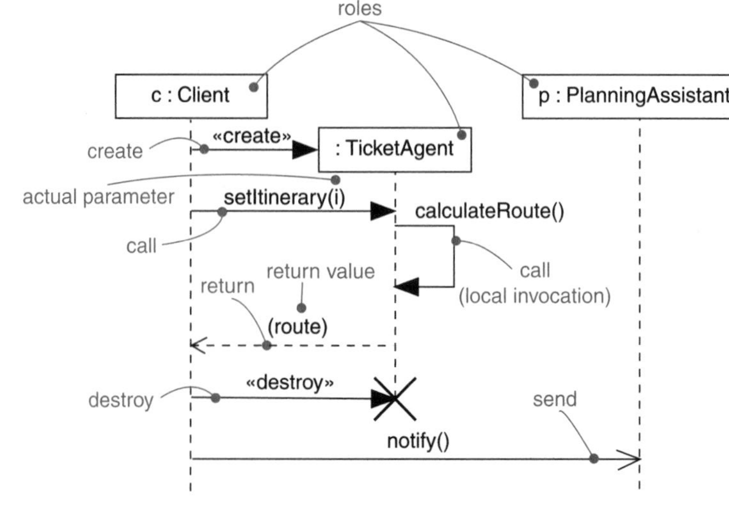

Figure 16-3: Messages

Classes are discussed in Chapters 4 and 9.

The most common kind of message you'll model is the call, in which one object invokes an operation of another (or the same) object. An object can't just call any random operation. If an object, such as `c` in the example above, calls the operation `setItinerary` on an instance of the class `TicketAgent`, the operation `setItinerary` must not only be defined for the class `TicketAgent` (that is, it must be declared in the class `TicketAgent` or one of its parents), it must also be visible to the caller `c`.

Note: Languages such as C++ are statically typed (although polymorphic), meaning that the legality of a call is checked at compilation time. Languages such as Smalltalk, however, are dynamically typed, meaning that you can't determine if an object can properly receive a message until execution time. In the UML, a well-formed model can in general be checked statically by a tool because, at modeling time, the developer typically knows the intent of the operation.

When an object calls an operation or sends a signal to another object, you can provide actual parameters to the message. Similarly, when an object returns control to another object, you can model the return value as well.

Interfaces are discussed in Chapter 11.

Messages can also correspond to the sending of signals. A signal is an object value communicated to a target object asynchronously. After sending a signal, the sending object continues its own execution. When the target object

Note: You can also qualify an operation by the class or interface in which it is declared. For example, invoking the operation `register` upon an instance of `Student` would polymorphically invoke whatever operation matches that name in the `Student` class hierarchy; invoking `IMember::register` would invoke the operation specified in the interface `IMember` (and realized by some suitable class, also in the `Student` class hierarchy).

receives the signal message, it independently decides what to do about it. Usually signals trigger transitions in the state machine of the target object. Firing a transition causes the target object to execute actions and change to a new state. In an asynchronous message-passing system, communicating objects execute concurrently and independently. They share values only by passing messages, so there is no danger of conflict over shared memory.

Sequencing

Processes and threads are discussed in Chapter 23.

When an object passes a message to another object (in effect, delegating some action to the receiver), the receiving object might in turn send a message to another object, which might send a message to yet a different object, and so on. This stream of messages forms a sequence. Any sequence must have a beginning; the start of every sequence is rooted in some process or thread. Furthermore, any sequence will continue as long as the process or thread that owns it lives. A nonstop system, such as you might find in real time device control, will continue to execute as long as the node it runs on is up.

Systems are discussed in Chapter 32.

Each process and thread within a system defines a distinct flow of control, and within each flow, messages are ordered in sequence by time. To better visualize the sequence of a message, you can explicitly model the order of the message relative to the start of the sequence by prefixing the message with a sequence number set apart by a colon separator.

A communication diagram shows message flow between roles within a collaboration. Messages flow along connections of the collaboration, as in Figure 16-4.

Most commonly, you can specify a procedural or nested flow of control, rendered using a filled solid arrowhead, as Figure 16-4 shows. In this case, the message `findAt` is specified as the first message nested in the second message of the sequence (`2.1`).

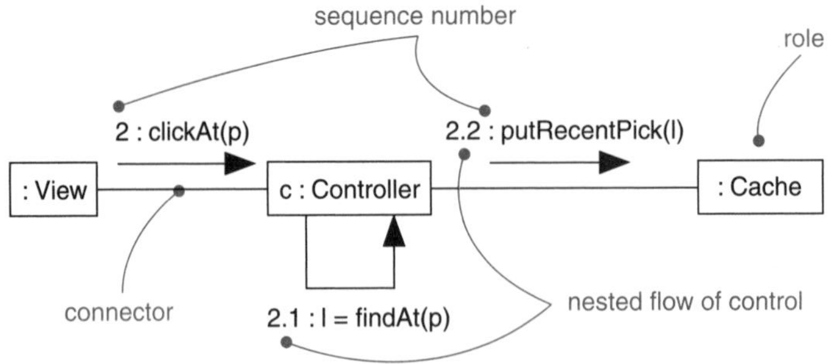

Figure 16-4: Procedural Sequence

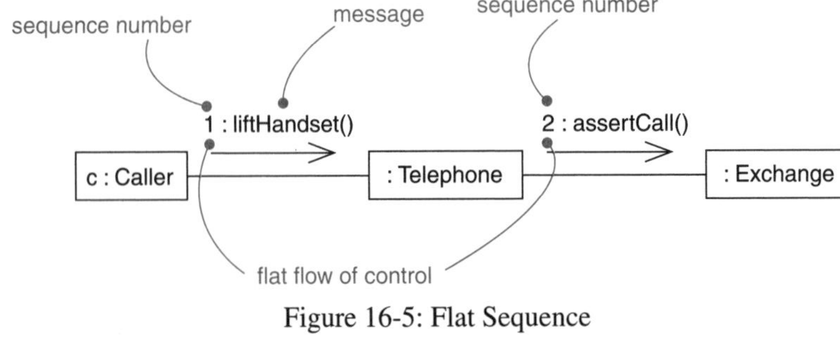

Figure 16-5: Flat Sequence

Less common but also possible, as Figure 16-5 shows, you can specify a flat flow of control, rendered using a stick arrowhead, to model the nonprocedural progression of control from step to step. In this case, the message `assertCall` is specified as the second message in the sequence.

Note: The distinction between asynchronous and procedural sequences is important in the modern concurrent computing world. To show the overall behavior of a system of concurrent objects, use asynchronous message passing. This is the most general case. When the calling object is able to make a request and wait for a respond, you can use procedural flow of control. Procedural flow of control is familiar from traditional programming languages, but keep in mind that a series of nested procedure calls results in a stack of blocked objects that are temporarily unable to do anything, so it is not very useful if they represent servers or shared resources.

Processes and threads are discussed in Chapter 23; you can also specify asynchronous flow of control, rendered using a half-stick arrowhead, as discussed in Chapter 23.

When you are modeling interactions that involve multiple flows of control, it's especially important to identify the process or thread that sent a particular message. In the UML, you can distinguish one flow of control from another by prefixing a message's sequence number with the name of the process or thread that sits at the root of the sequence. For example, the expression

```
D5 : ejectHatch(3)
```

specifies that the operation `ejectHatch` is dispatched (with the actual argument `3`) as the fifth message in the sequence rooted by the process or thread named `D`.

Not only can you show the actual arguments sent along with an operation or a signal in the context of an interaction, you can show the return values of a function as well. As the following expression shows, the value `p` is returned from the operation `find`, dispatched with the actual parameter `"Rachelle"`. This is a nested sequence, dispatched as the second message nested in the third message nested in the first message of the sequence. In the same diagram, `p` can then be used as an actual parameter in subsequent messages.

Iteration, branching, and guarded messages are discussed in Chapter 19; timing marks are discussed in Chapter 24; stereotypes and constraints are discussed in Chapter 6.

```
1.3.2 : p := find("Rachelle")
```

Note: In the UML, you can also model more-complex forms of sequencing, such as iteration, branching, and guarded messages. In addition, to model timing constraints such as you might find in real time systems, you can associate timing marks with a sequence. Other, more exotic forms of messaging, such as balking and time out, can be modeled by defining an appropriate message stereotype.

Creation, Modification, and Destruction

Most of the time the objects you show participating in an interaction exist for the entire duration of the interaction. However, in some interactions objects may be created (specified by a `create` message) and destroyed (specified by a `destroy` message). The same is true of links: The relationships among objects may come and go. To specify if an object or link enters and/or leaves during an interaction, you can attach a note to its role within a communication diagram.

Lifelines are discussed in Chapter 19.

During an interaction, an object typically changes the values of its attributes, its state, or its roles. You can represent the modification of an object in a sequence diagram by showing the state or the values on the lifeline.

Within a sequence diagram, the lifetime, creation, and destruction of objects or roles are explicitly shown by the vertical extent of their lifelines. Within a communication diagram, creation and destruction must be indicated using notes. Use sequence diagrams if object lifetimes are important to show.

Representation

When you model an interaction, you typically include both roles (each one representing objects that appear in an instance of the interaction) and messages (each one representing the communication between objects, with some resulting action).

Interaction diagrams are discussed in Chapter 19.

You can visualize those roles and messages involved in an interaction in two ways: by emphasizing the time ordering of its messages, and by emphasizing the structural organization of the roles that send and receive messages. In the UML, the first kind of representation is called a sequence diagram; the second kind of representation is called a communication diagram. Both sequence diagrams and communication diagrams are kinds of interaction diagrams. (UML also has a more specialized kind of interaction diagram called a *timing diagram*, which shows the exact times at which messages are exchanged by roles. This diagram is not covered in this book. See the *UML Reference Manual* for more information.)

Sequence diagrams and communication diagrams are similar, meaning that you can take one and transform it into the other, although they often show different information, so it may not be so useful to go back and forth. There are some visual differences. First, sequence diagrams permit you to model the lifeline of an object. An object's lifeline represents the existence of the object at a particular time, possibly covering the object's creation and destruction. Second, communication diagrams permit you to model the structural links that may exist among the objects in an interaction.

Common Modeling Techniques

Modeling a Flow of Control

Use cases are discussed in Chapter 17; patterns and frameworks are discussed in Chapter 29; classes and operations are discussed in Chapters 4 and 9; interfaces are discussed in Chapter 11; components are discussed in Chapter 15; nodes are discussed in Chapter 27; you can also model the dynamic aspects of a system by using state machines, as discussed in Chapter 22.

The most common purpose for which you'll use interactions is to model the flow of control that characterizes the behavior of a system as a whole, including use cases, patterns, mechanisms, and frameworks, or the behavior of a class or an individual operation. Whereas classes, interfaces, components, nodes, and their relationships model the static aspects of your system, interactions model its dynamic aspects.

When you model an interaction, you essentially build a storyboard of the actions that take place among a set of objects. Techniques such as CRC cards are particularly useful in helping you to discover and think about such interactions.

To model a flow of control,

- Set the context for the interaction, whether it is the system as a whole, a class, or an individual operation.
- Set the stage for the interaction by identifying which objects play a role; set their initial properties, including their attribute values, state, and role. Name the roles.
- If your model emphasizes the structural organization of these objects, identify the links that connect them, relevant to the paths of communication that take place in this interaction. Specify the nature of the links using the UML's standard stereotypes and constraints, as necessary.
- In time order, specify the messages that pass from object to object. As necessary, distinguish the different kinds of messages; include parameters and return values to convey the necessary detail of this interaction.
- Also to convey the necessary detail of this interaction, adorn each object at every moment in time with its state and role.

Sequence diagrams are discussed in Chapter 19.

For example, Figure 16-6 shows a set of roles that interact in the context of a publish and subscribe mechanism (an instance of the observer design pattern). This figure includes three roles: `p` (a `StockQuotePublisher`), `s1`, and `s2` (both instances of `StockQuoteSubscriber`). This figure is an example of a sequence diagram, which emphasizes the time order of messages.

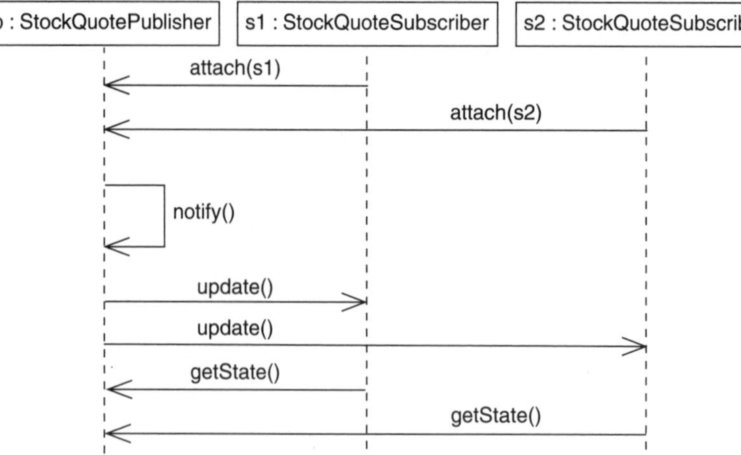

Figure 16-6: Flow of Control by Time

Communication diagrams are discussed in Chapter 19.

Figure 16-7 is semantically equivalent to the previous one, but it is drawn as a communication diagram, which emphasizes the structural organization of the objects. This figure shows the same flow of control, but it also provides a visualization of the links among these objects.

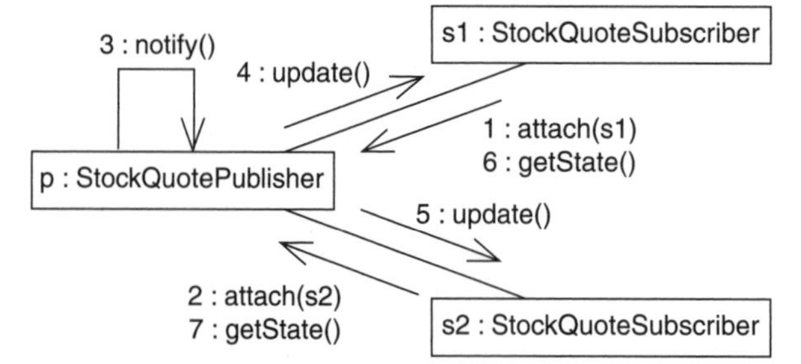

Figure 16-7: Flow of Control by Organization

Hints and Tips

When you model interactions in the UML, remember that every interaction represents the dynamic aspect of a society of objects. A well-structured interaction

- Is simple and should encompass only those objects that work together to carry out some behavior bigger than the sum of all these elements.

- Has a clear context and may represent the interaction of objects in the context of an operation, a class, or the system as a whole.
- Is efficient and should carry out its behavior with an optimal balance of time and resources.
- Is adaptable, and elements of an interaction that are likely to change should be isolated so that they can be easily modified.
- Is understandable and should be straightforward, involving no hacks, hidden side effects, or obscure semantics.

When you draw an interaction in the UML,

- Choose an emphasis for the interaction. You can emphasize either the ordering of messages over time or the sequencing of messages in the context of some structural organization of objects. You can't do both at the same time.
- Note that events in separate subsequences are only partially ordered. Each subsequence is ordered but the relative times of events in different subsequences is not fixed.
- Show only those properties of each object (such as attribute values, role, and state) that are important to understanding the interaction in its context.
- Show only those properties of each message (such as its parameters, concurrency semantics, and return value) that are important to understanding the interaction in its context.

Chapter 17
USE CASES

In this chapter

- Use cases, actors, include, and extend
- Modeling the behavior of an element
- Realizing use cases with collaborations

No system exists in isolation. Every interesting system interacts with human or automated actors that use that system for some purpose, and those actors expect that system to behave in predictable ways. A use case specifies the behavior of a subject—a system or a part of a system—it describes sequences of actions, including variants, that a subject performs to yield an observable result of value to an actor.

You apply use cases to capture the intended behavior of the system you are developing, without having to specify how that behavior is implemented. Use cases provide a way for your developers to come to a common understanding with your system's end users and domain experts. In addition, use cases serve to help validate your architecture and to verify your system as it evolves during development. As you implement your system, these use cases are realized by collaborations whose elements work together to carry out each use case.

Well-structured use cases denote essential subject behaviors only, and are neither overly general nor too specific.

Getting Started

A well-designed house is much more than a bunch of walls thrown together to hold up a roof that keeps out the weather. When you work with your architect to design your house, you'll give strong consideration to how you'll use that house. If you like entertaining, you'll want to think about the flow of people through your family room in a way that facilitates conversation and avoids dead ends that result in bunching. As you think about preparing meals for your family, you'll want to make sure your kitchen is designed for efficient placement of storage and appliances. Even plotting the path from your car to the kitchen in order to unload groceries will affect how you eventually connect rooms to one another. If you have a large family, you'll want to give thought to bathroom usage. Planning for the right number and right placement of bathrooms early on in the design will greatly reduce the risk of bottlenecks in the morning as your family heads to school and work. If you have teenagers, this issue has especially high risk, because the emotional cost of failure is high.

Reasoning about how you and your family will use your house is an example of use case–based analysis. You consider the various ways in which you'll use the house, and these use cases drive the architecture. Many families will have the same kinds of use cases—you use houses to eat, sleep, raise children, and hold memories. Every family will also have its own special use cases or variations of these basic ones. The needs of a large family, for example, are different from the needs of a single adult just out of college. It's these variations that have the greatest impact on the shape of your final home.

One key factor in creating use cases such as these is that you do so without specifying how the use cases are implemented. For example, you can specify how an ATM system should behave by stating in use cases how users interact with the system; you don't need to know anything about the inside of the ATM at all. Use cases specify externally visible behavior; they do not dictate how that behavior will be carried out internally. The great thing about this is that it lets you (as an end user and domain expert) communicate with your developers (who build systems that satisfy your requirements) without getting hung up on details. Those details will come, but use cases let you focus on the issues of highest risk to you.

In the UML, all such behaviors are modeled as use cases that may be specified independent of their realization. A use case is a description of a set of sequences of actions, including variants, that a subject performs to yield an observable result of value to an actor. There are a number of important parts to this definition.

Interactions are discussed in Chapter 16; requirements are discussed in Chapter 6.

At the system level, a use case describes a set of sequences, in which each sequence represents the interaction of the things outside the system (its actors) with the system itself (and its key abstractions). These behaviors are in effect system-level functions that you use to visualize, specify, construct, and document the intended behavior of your system during requirements capture and analysis. A use case represents a functional requirement of your system as a whole. For example, one central use case of a bank is to process loans.

A use case involves the interaction of actors and the system or other subject. An actor represents a coherent set of roles that users of use cases play when interacting with these use cases. Actors can be human or they can be automated systems. For example, in modeling a bank, processing a loan involves, among other things, the interaction between a customer and a loan officer.

A use case may have variants. In all interesting systems, you'll find use cases that are specialized versions of other use cases, use cases that are included as parts of other use cases, and use cases that extend the behavior of other core use cases. You can factor the common, reusable behavior of a set of use cases by organizing them according to these three kinds of relationships. For example, in modeling a bank, you'll find many variations among the basic use case of processing a loan, such as the difference in processing a jumbo mortgage versus a small business loan. In each case, however, these use cases share some degree of common behavior, such as the use case of qualifying the customer for the loan, a behavior that is part of processing every kind of loan.

A use case carries out some tangible amount of work. From the perspective of a given actor, a use case does something that's of value to an actor, such as calculate a result, generate a new object, or change the state of another object. For example, in modeling a bank, processing a loan results in the delivery of an approved loan, manifest in a pile of money handed to the customer.

Subsystems are discussed in Chapter 32; classes are discussed in Chapters 4 and 9; interfaces are discussed in Chapter 11.

You can apply use cases to your whole system. You can also apply use cases to part of your system, including subsystems and even individual classes and interfaces. In each case, these use cases not only represent the desired behavior of these elements, but they can also be used as the basis of test cases for these elements as they evolve during development. Use cases applied to subsystems are excellent sources of regression tests; use cases applied to the whole system are excellent sources of integration and system tests. The UML provides a graphical representation of a use case and an actor, as Figure 17-1 shows. This notation permits you to visualize a use case apart from its realization and in context with other use cases.

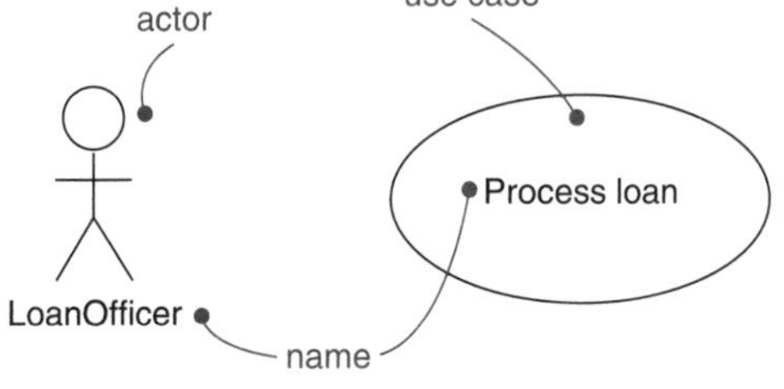

Figure 17-1: Actor and Use Case

Terms and Concepts

The notation for use cases is similar to that for collaborations, as discussed in Chapter 28.

A *use case* is a description of a set of sequences of actions, including variants, that a system performs to yield an observable result of value to an actor. Graphically, a use case is rendered as an ellipse.

Subject

The *subject* is a class described by a set of use cases. Usually the class is a system or subsystem. The use cases represent aspects of the behavior of the class. The actors represent aspects of other classes that interact with the subject. Taken together, the use cases describe the complete behavior of the subject.

Names

A use case name must be unique within its enclosing package, as discussed in Chapter 12.

Every use case must have a name that distinguishes it from other use cases. A *name* is a textual string. That name alone is known as a *simple name*; a *qualified name* is the use case name prefixed by the name of the package in which that use case lives. A use case is typically drawn showing only its name, as in Figure 17-2.

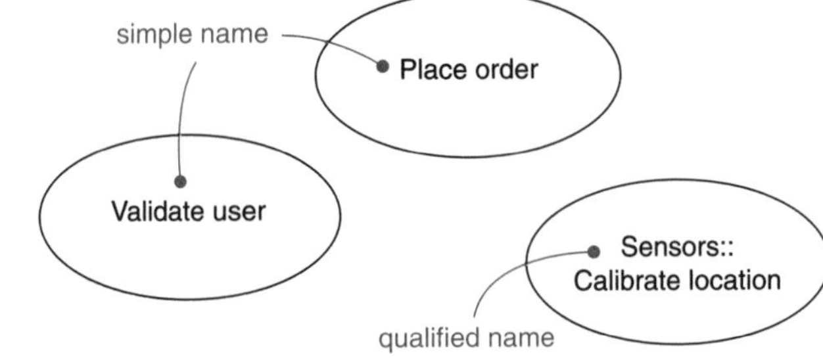

Figure 17-2: Simple and Qualified Names

Note: A use case name may be text consisting of any number of letters, numbers, and most punctuation marks (except for marks such as the colon, which is used to separate a class name and the name of its enclosing package) and may continue over several lines. In practice, use case names are short active verb phrases naming some behavior found in the vocabulary of the system you are modeling.

Use Cases and Actors

An actor represents a coherent set of roles that users of use cases play when interacting with these use cases. Typically, an actor represents a role that a human, a hardware device, or even another system plays with a system. For example, if you work for a bank, you might be a `LoanOfficer`. If you do your personal banking there, as well, you'll also play the role of `Customer`. An instance of an actor, therefore, represents an individual interacting with the system in a specific way. Although you'll use actors in your models, actors are not actually part of the software application. They live outside the application within the surrounding environment.

In an executing system, actors need not exist as separate entities. One object may play the part of multiple actors. For example, one `Person` may be both a `LoanOfficer` and a `Customer`. An actor represents one aspect of an object.

Generalization is discussed in Chapters 5 and 10.

As Figure 17-3 indicates, actors are rendered as stick figures. You can define general kinds of actors (such as `Customer`) and specialize them (such as `CommercialCustomer`) using generalization relationships.

Stereotypes are discussed in Chapter 6.

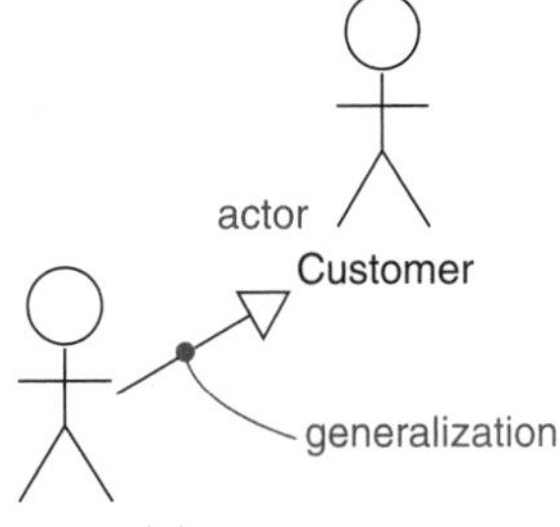

Figure 17-3: Actors

Association relationships are discussed in Chapters 5 and 10; messages are discussed in Chapter 16.

Note: You can use the UML's extensibility mechanisms to stereotype an actor in order to provide a different icon that might offer a better visual cue for your purposes.

Actors may be connected to use cases only by association. An association between an actor and a use case indicates that the actor and the use case communicate with one another, each one possibly sending and receiving messages.

Use Cases and Flow of Events

A use case describes *what* a system (or a subsystem, class, or interface) does but it does not specify *how* it does it. When you model, it's important that you keep clear the separation of concerns between this outside and inside view.

You can specify the behavior of a use case by describing a flow of events in text clearly enough for an outsider to understand it easily. When you write this flow of events, you should include how and when the use case starts and ends, when the use case interacts with the actors and what objects are exchanged, and the basic flow and alternative flows of the behavior.

For example, in the context of an ATM system, you might describe the use case `ValidateUser` in the following way:

> *Main flow of events*: The use case starts when the system prompts the *Customer* for a PIN number. The *Customer* can now enter a PIN number via the keypad. The *Customer* commits the entry by pressing the Enter button. The system then checks this PIN number to see if it is valid. If the PIN number is valid, the system acknowledges the entry, thus ending the use case.
>
> *Exceptional flow of events*: The *Customer* can cancel a transaction at any time by pressing the Cancel button, thus restarting the use case. No changes are made to the *Customer*'s account.
>
> *Exceptional flow of events*: The *Customer* can clear a PIN number anytime before committing it and reenter a new PIN number.
>
> *Exceptional flow of events*: If the *Customer* enters an invalid PIN number, the use case restarts. If this happens three times in a row, the system cancels the entire transaction, preventing the *Customer* from interacting with the ATM for 60 seconds.

Note: You can specify a use case's flow of events in a number of ways, including informal structured text (as in the example above), formal structured text (with pre- and postconditions), state machines (particularly for reactive systems), activity diagrams (particularly for workflows), and pseudocode.

Use Cases and Scenarios

Interaction diagrams, including sequence diagrams and collaboration diagrams, are discussed in Chapter 19.

Typically, you'll first describe the flow of events for a use case in text. As you refine your understanding of your system's requirements, however, you'll want to also use interaction diagrams to specify these flows graphically. Typically, you'll use one sequence diagram to specify a use case's main flow, and variations of that diagram to specify a use case's exceptional flows.

It is desirable to separate main versus alternative flows because a use case describes a set of sequences, not just a single sequence, and it would be impossible to express all the details of an interesting use case in just one sequence. For example, in a human resources system, you might find the use case `Hire employee`. This general business function might have many possible variations. You might hire a person from another company (the most common scenario); you might transfer a person from one division to another (common in international companies); or you might hire a foreign national (which involves its own special rules). Each of these variants can be expressed in a different sequence.

Instances are discussed in Chapter 13.

This one use case (`Hire employee`) actually describes a set of sequences in which each sequence in the set represents one possible flow through all these variations. Each sequence is called a scenario. A scenario is a specific sequence of actions that illustrates behavior. Scenarios are to use cases as instances are to classes, meaning that a scenario is basically one instance of a use case.

Note: There's an expansion factor from use cases to scenarios. A modestly complex system might have a few dozen use cases that capture its behavior, and each use case might expand out to several dozen scenarios. For each use case, you'll find primary scenarios (which define essential sequences) and secondary scenarios (which define alternative sequences).

Use Cases and Collaborations

Collaborations are discussed in Chapter 28.

A use case captures the intended behavior of the system (or subsystem, class, or interface) you are developing, without having to specify how that behavior is implemented. That's an important separation because the analysis of a system (which specifies behavior) should, as much as possible, not be influenced by implementation issues (which specify how that behavior is to be carried out). Ultimately, however, you have to implement your use cases, and you do so by creating a society of classes and other elements that work together to implement the behavior of this use case. This society of elements, including both its static and dynamic structure, is modeled in the UML as a collaboration.

Realization is discussed in Chapters 9 and 10.

As Figure 17-4 shows, you can explicitly specify the realization of a use case by a collaboration. Most of the time, though, a given use case is realized by exactly one collaboration, so you will not need to model this relationship explicitly.

Note: Although you may not visualize this relationship explicitly, the tools you use to manage your models will likely maintain this relationship.

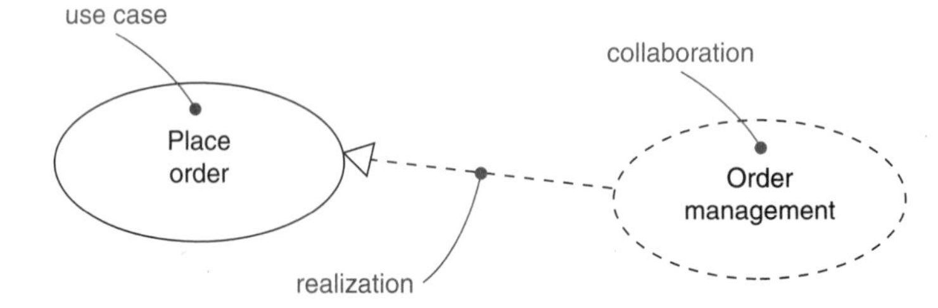

Figure 17-4: Use Cases and Collaborations

Architecture is discussed in Chapter 2.

Note: Finding the minimal set of well-structured collaborations that satisfy the flow of events specified in all the use cases of a system is the focus of a system's architecture.

Organizing Use Cases

Packages are discussed in Chapter 12.

You can organize use cases by grouping them in packages in the same manner in which you can organize classes.

You can also organize use cases by specifying generalization, include, and extend relationships among them. You apply these relationships in order to factor common behavior (by pulling such behavior from other use cases that it includes) and in order to factor variants (by pushing such behavior into other use cases that extend it).

Generalization is discussed in Chapters 5 and 10.

Generalization among use cases is just like generalization among classes. Here it means that the child use case inherits the behavior and meaning of the parent use case; the child may add to or override the behavior of its parent; and the child may be substituted any place the parent appears (both the parent and the child may have concrete instances). For example, in a banking system, you might have the use case `Validate User`, which is responsible for verifying the identity of the user. You might then have two specialized children of this use case (`Check password` and `Retinal scan`), both of which behave just like `Validate User` and may be applied anywhere `Validate User` appears, yet both of which add their own behavior (the former by checking a textual password, the latter by checking the unique retina patterns of the user). As shown in Figure 17-5, generalization among use cases is rendered as a solid directed line with a large triangular arrowhead, just like generalization among classes.

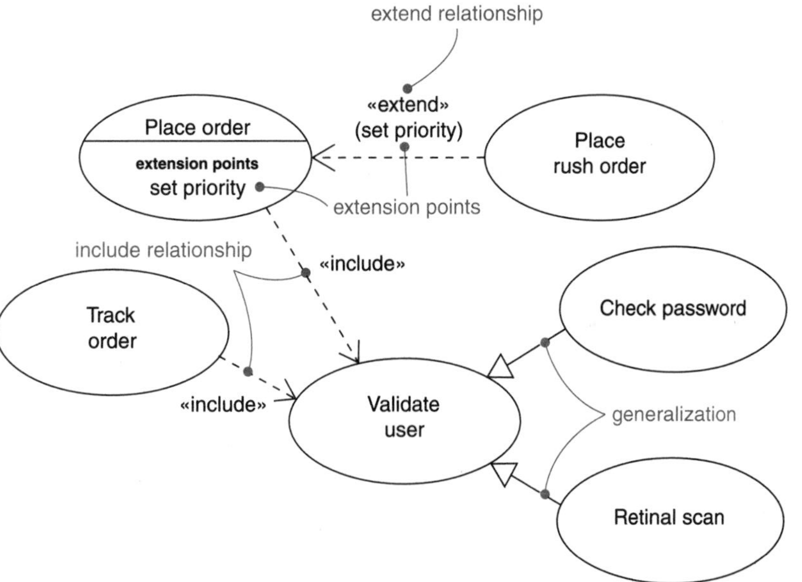

Figure 17-5: Generalization, Include, and Extend

An include relationship between use cases means that the base use case explicitly incorporates the behavior of another use case at a location specified in the base. The included use case never stands alone, but is only instantiated as part of some larger base that includes it. You can think of include as the base use case pulling behavior from the supplier use case.

You use an include relationship to avoid describing the same flow of events several times, by putting the common behavior in a use case of its own (the use case that is included by a base use case). The include relationship is essentially an example of delegation—you take a set of responsibilities of the system and capture it in one place (the included use case), then let all other parts of the system (other use cases) include the new aggregation of responsibilities whenever they need to use that functionality.

Dependency relationships are discussed in Chapters 5 and 10; stereotypes are discussed in Chapter 6.

You render an include relationship as a dependency, stereotyped as `include`. To specify the location in a flow of events in which the base use case includes the behavior of another, you simply write `include` followed by the name of the use case you want to include, as in the following flow for `Track order`:

```
Track order:
  obtain and verify the order number;
  include 'Validate user';
  for each part in the order,
    query the order status;
  report overall status to user.
```

Note: There is no predefined UML notation for expressing use case scenarios. The syntax used here is a kind of structured natural language. Several authors have suggested that an informal notation is best, because use cases should not be regarded as rigid specifications that generate code automatically; others have proposed formal notations.

An extend relationship between use cases means that the base use case implicitly incorporates the behavior of another use case at a location specified indirectly by the extending use case. The base use case may stand alone, but under certain conditions its behavior may be extended by the behavior of another use case. This base use case may be extended only at certain points called, not surprisingly, its extension points. You can think of extend as the extension use case pushing behavior to the base use case.

You use an extend relationship to model the part of a use case the user may see as optional system behavior. In this way, you separate optional behavior from mandatory behavior. You may also use an extend relationship to model a separate subflow that is executed only under given conditions. Finally, you may use an extend relationship to model several flows that may be inserted at a certain point, governed by explicit interaction with an actor. You may also use an extend relationship to distinguish configurable parts of an implementable system; the implication is that the system can exist with or without the various extensions.

Dependency relationships are discussed in Chapters 5 and 10; stereotypes and extra compartments are discussed in Chapter 6.

You render an extend relationship as a dependency, stereotyped as `extend`. You may list the extension points of the base use case in an extra compartment. These extension points are just labels that may appear in the flow of the base use case. For example, the flow for `Place order` might read as follows:

```
Place order:
  include 'Validate user';
  collect the user's order items;
  set priority: extension point;
  submit the order for processing.
```

In this example, `set priority` is an extension point. A use case may have more than one extension point (which may appear more than once), and these are always matched by name. Under normal circumstances, this base use case will execute without regard for the priority of the order. If, on the other hand, this is an instance of a priority order, the flow for this base case will carry out as above. But at the extension point `set priority`, the behavior of the extending use case `Place rush order` will be performed, then the flow will resume. If there are multiple extension points, the extending use case will simply fold in its flows in order.

Note: Organizing your use cases by extracting common behavior (through include relationships) and distinguishing variants (through extend relationships) is an important part of creating a simple, balanced, and understandable set of use cases for your system.

Other Features

Attributes and operations are discussed in Chapter 4; state machines are discussed in Chapter 22.

Use cases are classifiers, so they may have attributes and operations that you may render just as for classes. You can think of these attributes as the objects inside the use case that you need to describe its outside behavior. Similarly, you can think of these operations as the actions of the system you need to describe a flow of events. These objects and operations may be used in your interaction diagrams to specify the behavior of the use case.

As classifiers, you can also attach state machines to use cases. You can use state machines as yet another way to describe the behavior represented by a use case.

Common Modeling Techniques

Modeling the Behavior of an Element

Systems and subsystems are discussed in Chapter 32; classes are discussed in Chapters 4 and 9.

The most common thing for which you'll apply use cases is to model the behavior of an element, whether it is the system as a whole, a subsystem, or a class. When you model the behavior of these things, it's important that you focus on what that element does, not how it does it.

Applying use cases to elements in this way is important for three reasons. First, by modeling the behavior of an element with use cases, you provide a way for domain experts to specify its outside view to a degree sufficient for developers to construct its inside view. Use cases provide a forum for your domain experts, end users, and developers to communicate to one another. Second, use cases provide a way for developers to approach an element and understand it. A system, subsystem, or class may be complex and full of operations and other parts. By specifying an element's use cases, you help users of these elements to approach them in a direct way, according to how they are likely to use them. In the absence of such use cases, users have to discover on their own how to use those elements. Use cases let the author of an element communicate his or her intent about how that element should be used. Third, use cases serve as the basis for developing tests for each element as it evolves during development. By deriving tests from use cases and applying them repeatedly, you continuously validate the implementation. Not only do these use cases provide a source of regression tests, but every time you throw a new use case at an element, you are forced to reconsider your implementation to ensure that this element is resilient to change. If it is not, you must fix your architecture appropriately.

To model the behavior of an element,

- Identify the actors that interact with the element. Candidate actors include groups that require certain behavior to perform their tasks or that are needed directly or indirectly to perform the element's functions.
- Organize actors by identifying general and more specialized roles.
- For each actor, consider the primary ways in which that actor interacts with the element. Consider also interactions that change the state of the element or its environment or that involve a response to some event.
- Consider also the exceptional ways in which each actor interacts with the element.
- Organize these behaviors as use cases, applying include and extend relationships to factor common behavior and distinguish exceptional behavior.

For example, a retail system will interact with customers who place and track orders. In turn, the system will ship orders and bill the customer. As Figure 17-6 shows, you can model the behavior of such a system by declaring these behaviors as use cases (`Place order`, `Track order`, `Ship order`, and `Bill customer`). Common behavior can be factored out (`Validate customer`) and variants (`Ship partial order`) can be distinguished as well. For each of these use cases, you would include a specification of the behavior, either by text, state machine, or interactions.

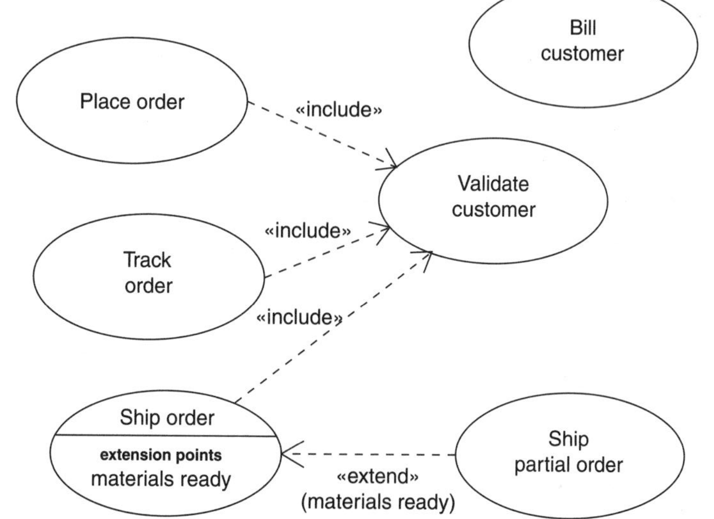

Figure 17-6: Modeling the Behavior of an Element

Packages are discussed in Chapter 12.

As your models get bigger, you will find that many use cases tend to cluster together in groups that are conceptually and semantically related. In the UML, you can use packages to model these clusters of classes.

Hints and Tips

When you model use cases in the UML, every use case should represent some distinct and identifiable behavior of the system or part of the system. A well-structured use case

- Names a single, identifiable, and reasonably atomic behavior of the system or part of the system.

- Factors common behavior by pulling such behavior from other use cases that it includes.
- Factors variants by pushing such behavior into other use cases that extend it.
- Describes the flow of events clearly enough for an outsider to easily understand it.
- Is described by a minimal set of scenarios that specify the normal and variant semantics of the use case.

When you draw a use case in the UML,

- Show only those use cases that are important to understand the behavior of the system or the part of the system in its context.
- Show only those actors that relate to these use cases.

Chapter 18
USE CASE DIAGRAMS

In this chapter

- Modeling the context of a system
- Modeling the requirements of a system
- Forward and reverse engineering

Activity diagrams are discussed in Chapter 20; state diagrams are discussed in Chapter 25; sequence and communication diagrams are discussed in Chapter 19.

Use case diagrams are one of the diagrams in the UML for modeling the dynamic aspects of systems. (Activity diagrams, state diagrams, sequence diagrams, and communication diagrams are four other kinds of diagrams in the UML for modeling the dynamic aspects of systems.) Use case diagrams are central to modeling the behavior of a system, a subsystem, or a class. Each one shows a set of use cases and actors and their relationships.

You apply use case diagrams to model the use case view of a system. For the most part, this involves modeling the context of a system, subsystem, or class, or modeling the requirements of the behavior of these elements.

Use case diagrams are important for visualizing, specifying, and documenting the behavior of an element. They make systems, subsystems, and classes approachable and understandable by presenting an outside view of how those elements may be used in context. Use case diagrams are also important for testing executable systems through forward engineering and for comprehending executable systems through reverse engineering.

Getting Started

Suppose someone hands you a box. On one side of that box, there are some buttons and a small LCD panel. Other than that, the box is nondescript; you aren't even given a hint about how to use it. You could randomly punch buttons and see what happens, but you'd be hard pressed to figure out what that box does or how to use it properly unless you spent a lot of trial-and-error time.

Software-intensive systems can be like that. If you are a user, you might be handed an application and told to use it. If the application follows normal conventions of the operating system you are used to, you might be able to get it to do something useful after a fashion, but you'd never come to understand its more complex and subtle behavior that way. Similarly, if you are a developer, you might be handed a legacy application or a set of components and told to use them. You'd be hard pressed to know how to use the elements until you formed a conceptual model for their use.

With the UML, you apply use case diagrams to visualize the behavior of a system, subsystem, or class so that users can comprehend how to use that element, and so that developers can implement that element. As Figure 18-1 shows, you can provide a use case diagram to model the behavior of that box—which most people would call a cellular phone.

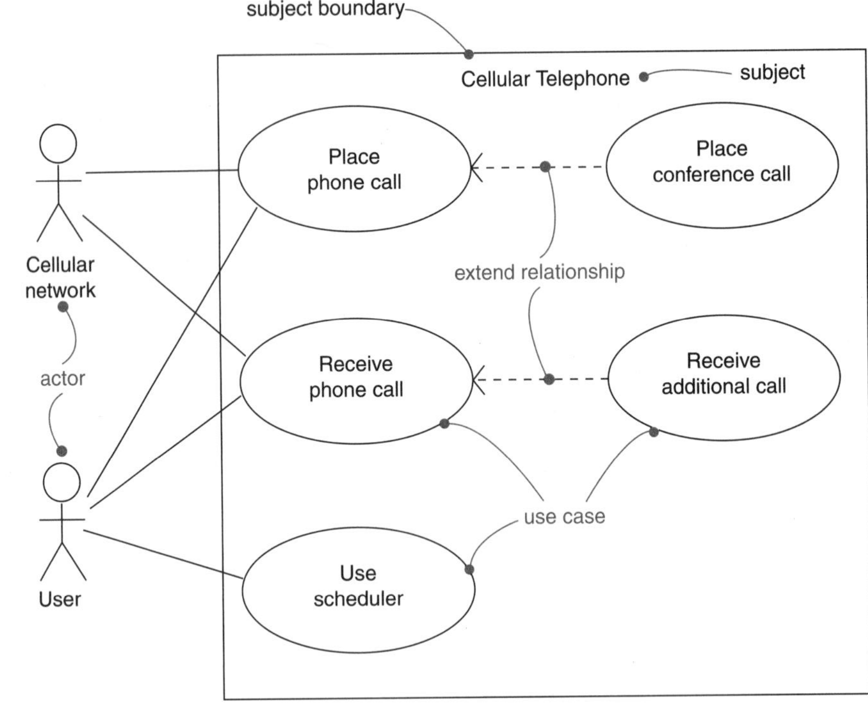

Figure 18-1: A Use Case Diagram

Terms and Concepts

A *use case diagram* is a diagram that shows a set of use cases and actors and their relationships.

Common Properties

The general properties of diagrams are discussed in Chapter 7.

A use case diagram is just a special kind of diagram and shares the same common properties as do all other diagrams—a name and graphical contents that are a projection into a model. What distinguishes a use case diagram from all other kinds of diagrams is its particular content.

Contents

Use cases and actors are discussed in Chapter 17; relationships are discussed in Chapters 5 and 10; packages are discussed in Chapter 12; instances are discussed in Chapter 13.

Use case diagrams commonly contain

- Subject
- Use cases
- Actors
- Dependency, generalization, and association relationships

Like all other diagrams, use case diagrams may contain notes and constraints.

Use case diagrams may also contain packages, which are used to group elements of your model into larger chunks. Occasionally, you'll want to place instances of use cases in your diagrams as well, especially when you want to visualize a specific executing system.

Notation

The subject is shown as a rectangle containing a set of use case ellipses. The name of the subject is placed within the rectangle. The actors are shown as stick figures placed outside the rectangle; their names are placed under them. Lines connect actor icons to the use case ellipses with which they communicate. Relationships among use cases (such as extend and include) are drawn inside the rectangle.

Common Uses

Use case views are discussed in Chapter 2.

You apply use case diagrams to model the use case view of a subject, such as a system. This view primarily models the external behavior of a subject—the outwardly visible services that the subject provides in the context of its environment.

When you model the use case view of a subject, you'll typically apply use case diagrams in one of two ways.

1. To model the context of a subject

Modeling the context of a subject involves drawing a line around the whole system and asserting which actors lie outside the subject and interact with it. Here, you'll apply use case diagrams to specify the actors and the meaning of their roles.

Requirements are discussed in Chapters 4 and 6.

2. To model the requirements of a subject

Modeling the requirements of a subject involves specifying what that subject should do (from a point of view of outside the subject) independent of how that subject should do it. Here, you'll apply use case diagrams to specify the desired behavior of the subject. In this manner, a use case diagram lets you view the whole subject as a black box; you can see what's outside the subject and you can see how that subject reacts to the things outside, but you can't see how that subject works on the inside.

Common Modeling Techniques

Modeling the Context of a System

Given a system—any system—some things will live inside the system, some things will live outside it. For example, in a credit card validation system, you'll find such things as accounts, transactions, and fraud detection agents inside the system. Similarly, you'll find such things as credit card customers and retail institutions outside the system. The things that live inside the system are responsible for carrying out the behavior that those on the outside expect the system to provide. All those things on the outside that interact with the system constitute the system's context. This context defines the environment in which that system lives.

Systems are discussed in Chapter 32.

In the UML, you can model the context of a system with a use case diagram, emphasizing the actors that surround the system. Deciding what to include as an actor is important because in doing so you specify a class of things that interact with the system. Deciding what not to include as an actor is equally, if not more, important because that constrains the system's environment to include only those actors that are necessary in the life of the system.

To model the context of a system,

- Identify the boundaries of the system by deciding which behaviors are part of it and which are performed by external entities. This defines the subject.
- Identify the actors that surround the system by considering which groups require help from the system to perform their tasks, which groups are needed to execute the system's functions, which groups interact with external hardware or other software systems, and which groups perform secondary functions for administration and maintenance.
- Organize actors that are similar to one another in a generalization-specialization hierarchy.
- Where it aids understandability, provide a stereotype for each such actor.

Populate a use case diagram with these actors and specify the paths of communication from each actor to the system's use cases.

For example, Figure 18-2 shows the context of a credit card validation system, with an emphasis on the actors that surround the system. You'll find `Customers`, of which there are two kinds (`Individual customer` and `Corporate customer`). These actors are the roles that humans play when interacting with the system. In this context, there are also actors that represent other institutions, such as `Retail institution` (with which a `Customer` performs a card transaction to buy an item or a service) and `Sponsoring financial institution` (which serves as the clearinghouse for the credit card account). In the real world, these latter two actors are likely software-intensive systems themselves.

Subsystems are discussed in Chapter 32.

This same technique applies to modeling the context of a subsystem. A system at one level of abstraction is often a subsystem of a larger system at a higher level of abstraction. Modeling the context of a subsystem is therefore useful when you are building systems of interconnected systems.

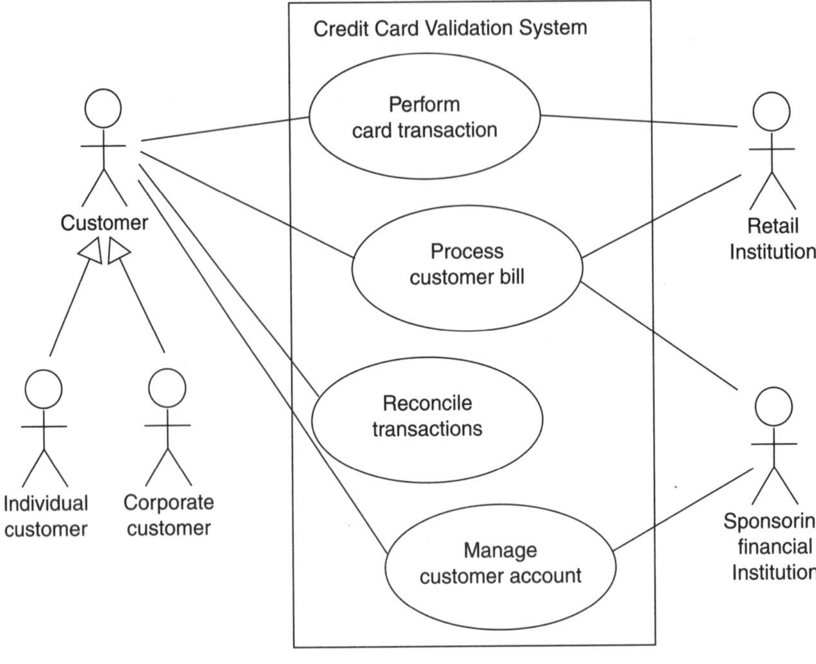

Figure 18-2: Modeling the Context of a System

Modeling the Requirements of a System

A requirement is a design feature, property, or behavior of a system. When you state a system's requirements, you are asserting a contract, established between those things that lie outside the system and the system itself, which declares what you expect that system to do. For the most part, you don't care how the system does it, you just care *that* it does it. A well-behaved system will carry out all its requirements faithfully, predictably, and reliably. When you build a system, it's important to start with agreement about what that system should do, although you will certainly evolve your understanding of those requirements as you iteratively and incrementally implement the system. Similarly, when you are handed a system to use, knowing how it behaves is essential to using it properly.

Notes can be used to state requirements, as discussed in Chapter 6.

Requirements can be expressed in various forms, from unstructured text to expressions in a formal language, and everything in between. Most, if not all, of a system's functional requirements can be expressed as use cases, and the UML's use case diagrams are essential for managing these requirements.

To model the requirements of a system,

- Establish the context of the system by identifying the actors that surround it.
- For each actor, consider the behavior that each expects or requires the system to provide.
- Name these common behaviors as use cases.
- Factor common behavior into new use cases that are used by others; factor variant behavior into new use cases that extend more main line flows.
- Model these use cases, actors, and their relationships in a use case diagram.
- Adorn these use cases with notes or constraints that assert nonfunctional requirements; you may have to attach some of these to the whole system.

Modeling dynamics for load balancing and network reconfiguration are discussed in Chapter 24.

Figure 18-3 expands on the previous use case diagram. Although it elides the relationships among the actors and the use cases, it adds additional use cases that are somewhat invisible to the average customer yet are essential behaviors of the system. This diagram is valuable because it offers a common starting place for end users, domain experts, and developers to visualize, specify, construct, and document their decisions about the functional requirements of this system. For example, `Detect card fraud` is a behavior important to both the `Retail institution` and the `Sponsoring financial institution`. Similarly, `Report on account status` is another behavior required of the system by the various institutions in its context.

The requirement modeled by the use case `Manage network outage` is a bit different from all the others because it represents a secondary behavior of the system necessary for its reliable and continuous operation.

Once the structure of the use case is determined, you must describe the behavior of each use case. Usually you should write one or more sequence diagrams for each mainline case. Then you should write sequence diagrams for variant cases. Finally, you should write at least one sequence diagram to illustrate each kind of error or exception condition; error handling is part of the use case and should be planned along with the normal behavior.

Subsystems are discussed in Chapter 32.

This same technique applies to modeling the requirements of a subsystem.

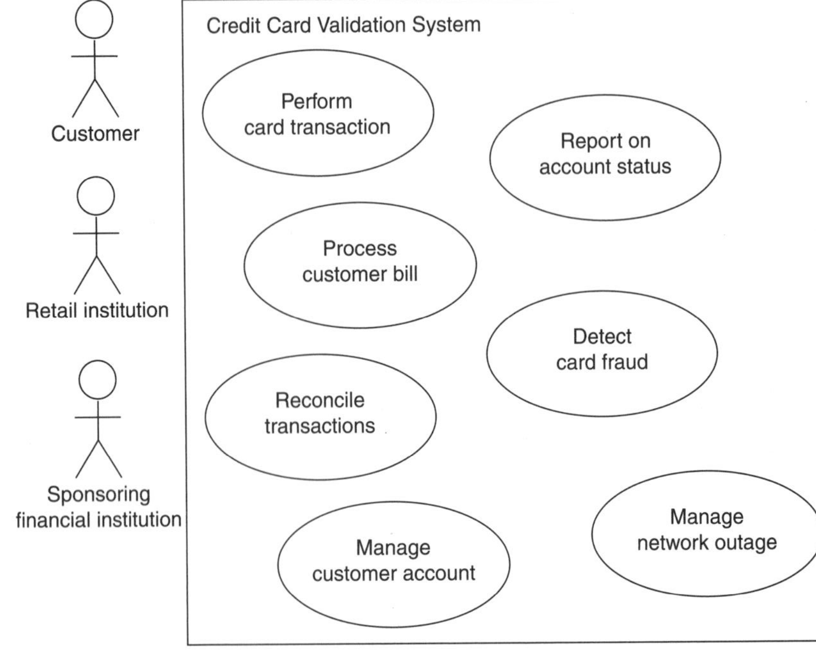

Figure 18-3: Modeling the Requirements of a System

Forward and Reverse Engineering

Diagrams are discussed in Chapter 7; use cases are discussed in Chapter 17.

Most of the UML's other diagrams, including class, component, and state diagrams, are clear candidates for forward and reverse engineering because each has an analog in the executable system. Use case diagrams are a bit different in that they reflect rather than specify the implementation of a system, subsystem, or class. Use cases describe how an element behaves, not how that behavior is implemented, so it cannot be directly forward or reverse engineered.

Forward engineering is the process of transforming a model into code through a mapping to an implementation language. A use case diagram can be forward engineered to form tests for the element to which it applies. Each use case in a use case diagram specifies a flow of events (and variants of those flows), and these flows specify how the element is expected to behave—that's something worthy of testing. A well-structured use case will even specify pre- and postconditions that can be used to define a test's initial state and its success criteria. For each use case in a use case diagram, you can create a test case that you can run every time you release a new version of that element, thereby confirming that it works as required before other elements rely on it.

To forward engineer a use case diagram,

- Identify the objects that interact with the system. Try to identify the various roles that each external object may play.
- Make up an actor to represent each distinct interaction role.
- For each use case in the diagram, identify its flow of events and its exceptional flow of events.
- Depending on how deeply you choose to test, generate a test script for each flow, using the flow's preconditions as the test's initial state and its postconditions as its success criteria.
- As necessary, generate test scaffolding to represent each actor that interacts with the use case. Actors that push information to the element or are acted on by the element may either be simulated or substituted by its real-world equivalent.
- Use tools to run these tests each time you release the element to which the use case diagram applies.

Reverse engineering is the process of transforming code into a model through a mapping from a specific implementation language. To automatically reverse engineer a use case diagram is currently beyond the state of the art, simply because there is a loss of information when moving from a specification of how an element behaves to how it is implemented. However, you can study an existing system and discern its intended behavior by hand, which you can then put in the form of a use case diagram. Indeed, this is pretty much what you have to do anytime you are handed an undocumented body of software. The UML's use case diagrams simply give you a standard and expressive language in which to state what you discover.

To reverse engineer a use case diagram,

- Identify each actor that interacts with the system.
- For each actor, consider the manner in which that actor interacts with the system, changes the state of the system or its environment, or responds to some event.
- Trace the flow of events in the executable system relative to each actor. Start with primary flows and only later consider alternative paths.
- Cluster related flows by declaring a corresponding use case. Consider modeling variants using extend relationships, and consider modeling common flows by applying include relationships.
- Render these actors and use cases in a use case diagram, and establish their relationships.

Hints and Tips

When you create use case diagrams in the UML, remember that every use case diagram is just a graphical presentation of the static use case view of a system. This means that no single use case diagram need capture everything about a system's use case view. Collectively, all the use case diagrams of a system represent the system's complete static use case view; individually, each represents just one aspect.

A well-structured use case diagram

- Is focused on communicating one aspect of a system's static use case view.
- Contains only those use cases and actors that are essential to understanding that aspect.
- Provides detail consistent with its level of abstraction; you should expose only those adornments (such as extension points) that are essential to understanding.
- Is not so minimalist as to misinform the reader about semantics that are important.

When you draw a use case diagram,

- Give it a name that communicates its purpose.
- Lay out its elements to minimize lines that cross.
- Organize its elements spatially so that behaviors and roles that are semantically close are laid out physically close.
- Use notes and color as visual cues to draw attention to important features of your diagram.
- Try not to show too many kinds of relationships. In general, if you have complicated include and extend relationships, take these elements to another diagram.

Chapter 19

INTERACTION DIAGRAMS

In this chapter

- Modeling flows of control by time ordering
- Modeling flows of control by organization
- Forward and reverse engineering

Activity diagrams, state diagrams, and use case diagrams are three other kinds of diagrams used in the UML for modeling the dynamic aspects of systems; activity diagrams are discussed in Chapter 20; state diagrams are discussed in Chapter 25; use case diagrams are discussed in Chapter 18.

Sequence diagrams and communication diagrams—which are collectively called interaction diagrams—are two of the diagrams used in the UML for modeling the dynamic aspects of systems. An interaction diagram shows an interaction, consisting of a set of objects and their relationships, including the messages that may be dispatched among them. A sequence diagram is an interaction diagram that emphasizes the time ordering of messages; a communication diagram is an interaction diagram that emphasizes the structural organization of the objects that send and receive messages.

You use interaction diagrams to model the dynamic aspects of a system. For the most part, this involves modeling concrete or prototypical instances of classes, interfaces, components, and nodes, along with the messages that are dispatched among them, all in the context of a scenario that illustrates a behavior. Interaction diagrams may stand alone to visualize, specify, construct, and document the dynamics of a particular society of objects, or they may be used to model one particular flow of control of a use case.

Interaction diagrams are not only important for modeling the dynamic aspects of a system, but also for constructing executable systems through forward and reverse engineering.

Getting Started

When you watch a movie projected from film or broadcast on television, your mind actually plays tricks on you. Instead of seeing continuous motion as you would in live action, you really see a series of static images played back to you fast enough to give the illusion of continuous motion.

When directors and animators plan a film, they use the same technique but at lower fidelity. By storyboarding key frames, they build up a model of each scene, sufficient in detail to communicate the intent to all the stakeholders on the production team. In fact, creating this storyboard is a major activity in the production process, helping the team visualize, specify, construct, and document a model of the movie as it evolves from inception through construction and finally deployment.

Modeling the structural aspects of a system is discussed in Parts 2 and 3.

In modeling software-intensive systems, you have a similar problem: How do you model its dynamic aspects? Imagine, for a moment, how you might visualize a running system. If you have an interactive debugger attached to the system, you might be able to watch a section of memory and observe how it changes its contents over time. With a bit more focus, you might even monitor several objects of interest. Over time, you'd see the creation of some objects, changes in the value of their attributes, and then the destruction of some of them.

The value of visualizing the dynamic aspects of a system this way is quite limited, especially if you are talking about a distributed system with multiple concurrent flows of control. You might as well try to understand the human circulatory system by looking at the blood that passes through one point in one artery over time. A better way to model the dynamic aspects of a system is by building up storyboards of scenarios, involving the interaction of certain interesting objects and the messages that may be dispatched among them.

In the UML, you model these storyboards by using interaction diagrams. As Figure 19-1 shows, you can build up these storyboards in two ways: by emphasizing the time ordering of messages and by emphasizing the structural relationships among the objects that interact. Either way, the diagrams are semantically equivalent; you can convert one to the other without loss of information.

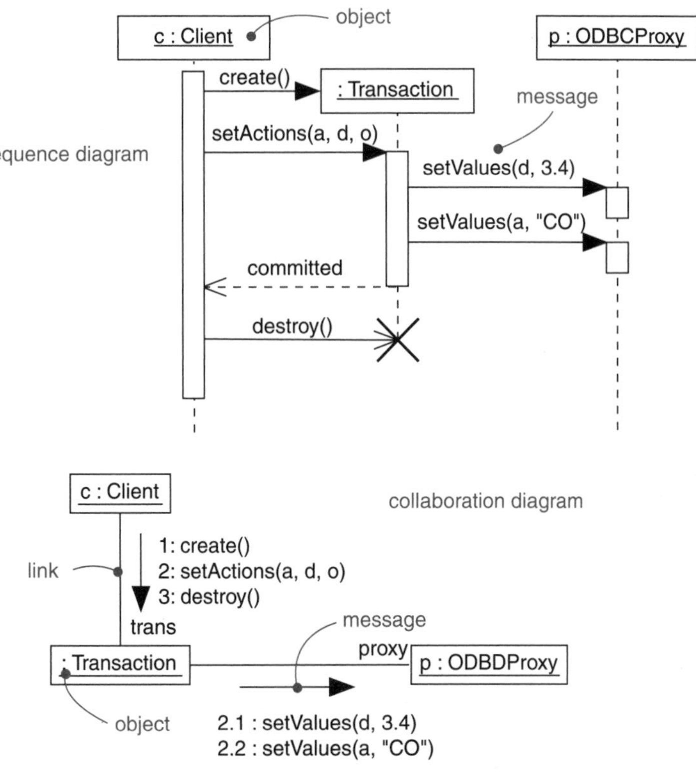

Figure 19-1: Interaction Diagrams

Terms and Concepts

An *interaction diagram* shows an interaction, consisting of a set of objects and their relationships, including the messages that may be dispatched among them. A *sequence diagram* is an interaction diagram that emphasizes the time ordering of messages. Graphically, a sequence diagram is a table that shows objects arranged along the X axis and messages, ordered in increasing time, along the Y axis. A *communication diagram* is an interaction diagram that emphasizes the structural organization of the objects that send and receive messages. Graphically, a communication diagram is a collection of vertices and arcs.

Common Properties

The general properties of diagrams are discussed in Chapter 7.

An interaction diagram is just a special kind of diagram and shares the same common properties as do all other diagrams—a name and graphical contents that are a projection into a model. What distinguishes an interaction diagram from all other kinds of diagrams is its particular content.

Contents

Objects are discussed in Chapter 13; links are discussed in Chapters 14 and 16; messages and interactions are discussed in Chapter 16; internal structure is discussed in Chapter 15; collaborations are discussed in Chapter 28.

Interaction diagrams commonly contain

- Roles or objects
- Communications or links
- Messages

Note: An interaction diagram is basically a projection of the elements found in an interaction. The semantics of an interaction's context, objects and roles, links and connectors, messages, and sequencing apply to interaction diagrams.

Like all other diagrams, interaction diagrams may contain notes and constraints.

Sequence Diagrams

A sequence diagram emphasizes the time ordering of messages. As Figure 19-2 shows, you form a sequence diagram by first placing the objects or roles that participate in the interaction at the top of your diagram, across the horizontal axis. Typically, you place the object or role that initiates the interaction at the left, and increasingly more subordinate objects or roles to the right. Next, you arrange the messages that these objects send and receive along the vertical axis in order of increasing time from top to bottom. This gives the reader a clear visual cue to the flow of control over time.

Sequence diagrams have two features that distinguish them from communication diagrams. First, there is the lifeline. An object lifeline is the vertical dashed line that represents the existence of an object over a period of time. Most objects that appear in an interaction diagram will be in existence for the duration of the interaction, so these objects are all aligned at the top of the diagram, with their lifelines drawn from the top of the diagram to the bottom.

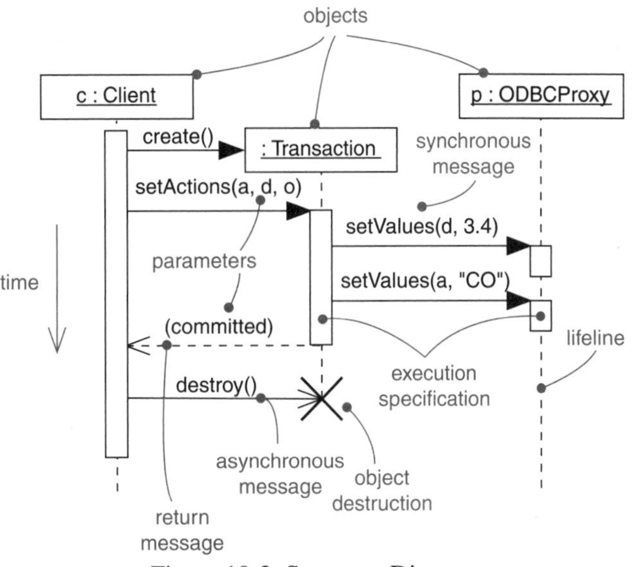

Figure 19-2: Sequence Diagram

Objects may be created during the interaction. Their lifelines start with the receipt of the message `create` (drawn to box at the head of the lifeline). Objects may be destroyed during the interaction. Their lifelines end with the receipt of the message `destroy` (and are given the visual cue of a large `X`, marking the end of their lives).

If the interaction represents the history of specific, individual objects, then object symbols with underlined names are placed at the head of the lifelines. Most of the time, however, you will be showing prototypical interactions. The lifelines do not represent specific objects; they represent prototypical roles that represent different objects in each instance of the interaction. In that normal case, you do not underline the names, as they are not specific objects.

Note: If an object changes the values of its attributes, its state, or its roles, you can place a state icon on its lifeline at the point that the change occurs, showing those modifications.

Second, there is the focus of control. The focus of control is a tall, thin rectangle that shows the period of time during which an object is performing an action, either directly or through a subordinate procedure. The top of the rectangle is aligned with the start of the action; the bottom is aligned with its completion (and can be marked by a return message). You can show the nesting of a focus of control (caused by recursion, a call to a self-operation, or by a callback from another object) by stacking another focus of control slightly to the right of its parent (and can do so to an arbitrary depth). If you want to be especially precise about where the focus of control lies, you can also shade the region of the rectangle during which the object's method is actually computing and control has not passed to another object, but this is rather fussy.

The main content in a sequence diagram is the messages. A message is shown by an arrow from one lifeline to another. The arrowhead points to the receiver. If the message is asynchronous, the line has a stick arrowhead. If the message is synchronous (a call), the line has a filled triangular arrowhead. A reply to a synchronous message (a return from a call) is shown by a dashed arrow with a stick arrowhead. The return message may be omitted, as there is an implicit return after any call, but it is often useful for showing return values.

The ordering of time along a single lifeline is significant. Usually the exact distance does not matter; lifelines only show relative sequences, so the lifeline is not a scale diagram of time. Usually the positions of messages on separate pairs of lifelines do not imply any sequencing information; the messages could occur in any order. The entire set of messages on separate lifelines forms a partial ordering. A series of messages establishes a chain of causality, however, so that any point on another lifeline at the end of the chain must always follow the point on the original lifeline at the start of the chain.

Structured Control in Sequence Diagrams

A sequence of messages is fine for showing a single, linear sequence, but often we need to show conditionals and loops. Sometimes we want to show concurrent execution of multiple sequences. This kind of high-level control can be shown using structured control operators in sequence diagrams.

A control operator is shown as a rectangular region within the sequence diagram. It has a tag—a text label inside a small pentagon in the upper left corner—to tell what kind of a control operator it is. The operator applies to the lifelines that cross it. This is considered the body of the operator. If a lifeline does not apply to the operator, it may be interrupted at the top of the control operator and resumed at the bottom. The following kinds of control are the most common:

Optional execution. The tag is `opt`. The body of the control operator is executed if a guard condition is true when the operator is entered. The guard condition is a Boolean expression that may appear in square brackets at the top of any one lifeline within the body and may reference attributes of that object.

Conditional execution. The tag is `alt`. The body of the control operator is divided into multiple subregions by horizontal dashed lines. Each subregion represents one branch of a conditional. Each subregion has a guard condition. If the guard condition for a subregion is true, the subregion is executed. However, at most one subregion may be executed; if more than one guard condition is true, the choice of subregion is nondeterministic and could vary from execution to execution. If no guard condition is true, then control continues past the control operator. One subregion may have a the special guard condition `[else]`; this subregion is executed if none of the other guard conditions are true.

Parallel execution. The tag is `par`. The body of the control operator is divided into multiple subregions by horizontal dashed lines. Each subregion represents a parallel (concurrent) computation. In most cases, each subregion involves different lifelines. When the control operator is entered, all of the subregions execute concurrently. The execution of the messages in each subregion is sequential, but the relative order of messages in parallel subregions is completely arbitrary. This construct should not be used if the different computations interact. There are very many real-world situations that decompose into independent, parallel activities, however, so this is a very useful operator.

Loop (iterative) execution. The tag is `loop`. A guard condition appears at the top of one lifeline within the body. The body of the loop is executed repeatedly as long as the guard condition is true before each iteration. When the guard condition is false at the top of the body, control passes out of the control operator.

There are many other kinds of operators, but these are the most useful.

To provide a clear indication of the boundary, a sequence diagram may be enclosed in a rectangle, with a tag in the upper left corner. The tag is `sd`, which may be followed by the name of the diagram.

Figure 19-3 shows a simplified example that illustrates some control operators. The user initiates the sequence. The first operator is a loop operator. The numbers in parentheses (1,3) indicate the minimum and maximum number of times the loop body must be executed. Since the minimum is one, the body is always executed at least once before the condition is tested. In the loop, the user enters the password and the system verifies it. The loop continues as long as the password is incorrect. However, after three tries, the loop terminates in any case.

The next operator is an optional operator. The optional body is executed if the password is valid; otherwise the rest of the sequence diagram is skipped. The optional body contains a parallel operator. Operators can be nested as shown.

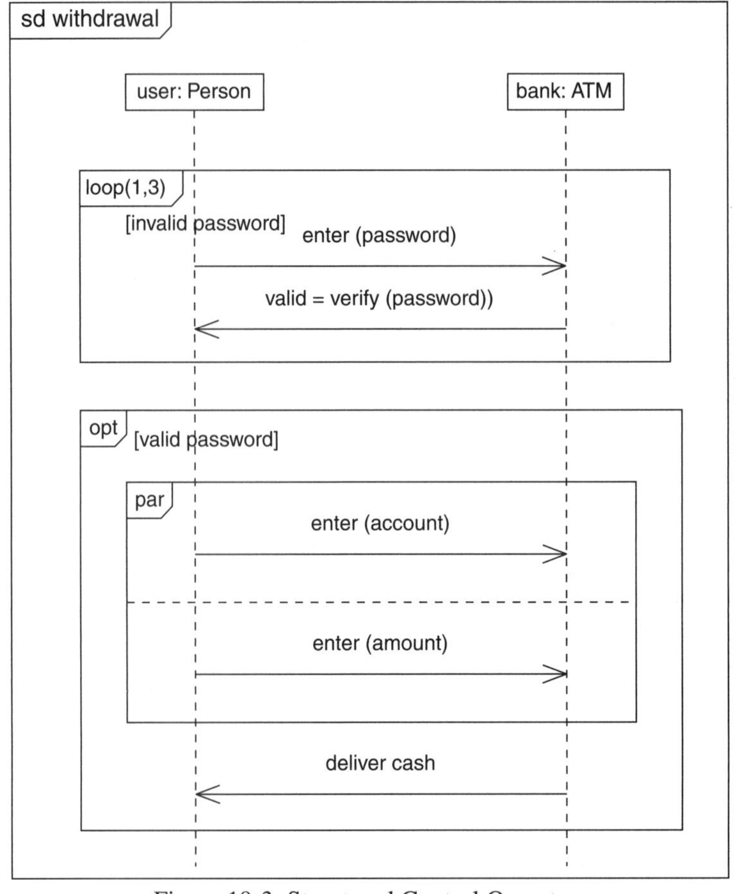

Figure 19-3: Structured Control Operators

The parallel operator has two subregions: one allows the user to enter an account and the other allows the user to enter an amount. Because they are parallel, there is no required order for making the two entries; they can occur in either order. This emphasizes that concurrency does not always imply physically simultaneous execution. Concurrency really means that two actions are uncoordinated and can happen in any order. If they are truly independent actions, they can overlap; if they are sequential actions, they can occur in any order.

Once both actions have been performed, the parallel operator is complete. In the next action within the optional operator, the bank delivers cash to the user. The sequence diagram is now complete.

Nested Activity Diagrams

Activity diagrams that are too large can be difficult to understand. Structured sections of an activity can be organized into a subordinate activity, especially if the subordinate activity is used more than once within the main activity. The main activity and the subordinate activities are shown on separate diagrams. Within the main activity diagram, a use of a subordinate activity is shown by a rectangle with the tag ref in its upper left corner; the name of the subordinate behavior is shown in the box. The subordinate behavior is not restricted to an activity diagram; it could also be a state machine, sequence diagram, or other behavioral specification. Figure 19-4 shows the diagram from Figure 19-3 rearranged by moving two sections into separate activity diagrams and referencing them from the main diagram.

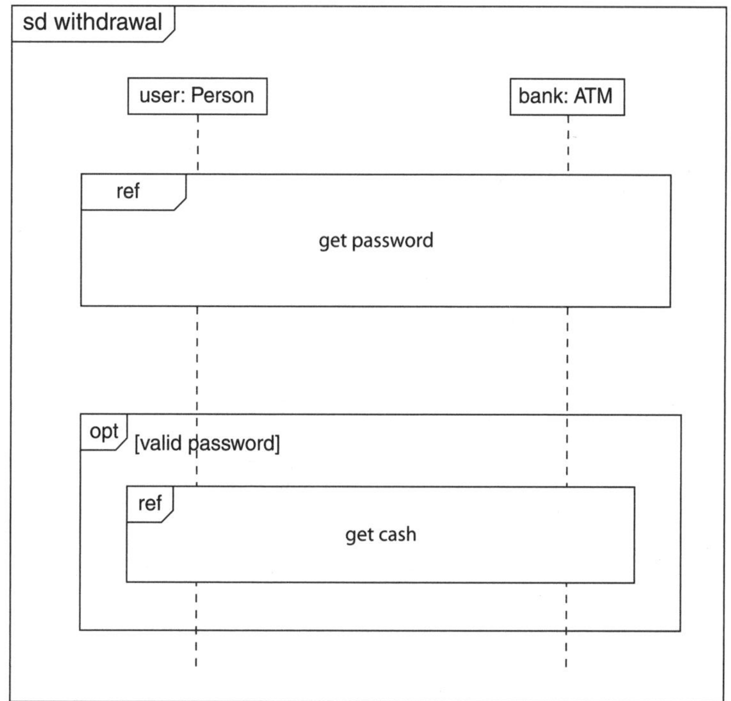

Figure 19-4: Nested activity diagram

Communication Diagrams

A communication diagram emphasizes the organization of the objects that participate in an interaction. As Figure 19-5 shows, you form a communication diagram by first placing the objects that participate in the interaction as the vertices in a graph. Next, you render the links that connect these objects as the arcs of this graph. The links may have rolenames to identify them. Finally, you adorn these links with the messages that objects send and receive. This gives the reader a clear visual cue to the flow of control in the context of the structural organization of objects that collaborate.

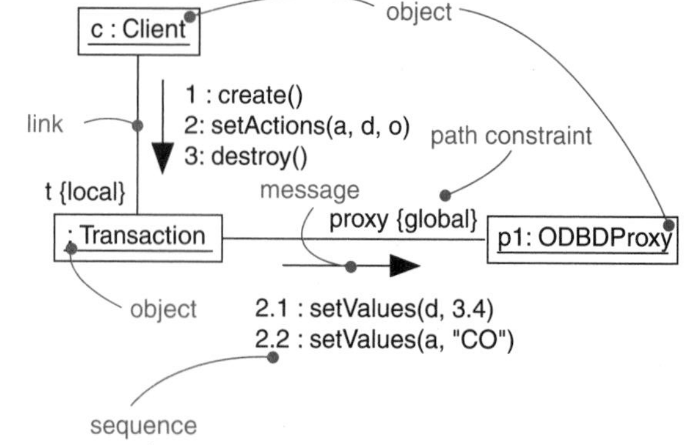

Figure 19-5: Communication Diagram

Note: Unlike a sequence diagram, you don't show the lifeline of an object explicitly in a communication diagram, although you can show both `create` and `destroy` messages. In addition, you don't show the focus of control explicitly in a communication diagram, although the sequence number on each message can indicate nesting.

Communication diagrams have two features that distinguish them from sequence diagrams. First, there is the path. You render a path corresponding to an association. You also render paths corresponding to local variables, parameters, global variables, and self access. A path represents a source of knowledge to an object.

You can use an advanced form of sequence numbers to distinguish concurrent flows of control, as discussed in Chapter 23; path stereotypes are discussed in Chapter 18; complex branching and iteration can be more easily specified in activity diagrams, as discussed in Chapter 20.

Second, there is the sequence number. To indicate the time order of a message, you prefix the message with a number (starting with the message numbered `1`), increasing monotonically for each new message in the flow of control (`2`, `3`, and so on). To show nesting, you use Dewey decimal numbering (`1` is the first message, which contains message `1.1 and` message `1.2`, and so on). You can show nesting to an arbitrary depth. Note also that, along the same link, you can show many messages (possibly being sent from different directions), and each will have a unique sequence number.

Most of the time you'll model straight, sequential flows of control. However, you can also model more-complex flows involving iteration and branching. An iteration represents a repeated sequence of messages. To model an iteration, you prefix the sequence number of a message with an iteration expression such as `*[i := 1..n]` (or just `*` if you want to indicate iteration but don't want to specify its details). An iteration indicates that the message (and any nested messages) will be repeated in accordance with the given expression. Similarly, a condition represents a message whose execution is contingent on the evaluation of a Boolean condition. To model a condition, you prefix the sequence number of a message with a condition clause, such as `[x > 0]`. The alternate paths of a branch will have the same sequence number, but each path must be uniquely distinguishable by a nonoverlapping condition.

For both iteration and branching, the UML does not prescribe the format of the expression inside the brackets; you can use pseudocode or the syntax of a specific programming language.

Note: You don't show the links among objects explicitly in a sequence diagram. You don't show the sequence number of a message in a sequence diagram explicitly either: It is implicit in the physical ordering of messages from top to bottom of the diagram. You can show iteration and branching, however, using sequence diagram control structures.

Semantic Equivalence

Because they both derive from the same information in the UML's metamodel, sequence diagrams and communication diagrams are semantically equivalent. As a result, you can take a diagram in one form and convert it to the other without any loss of information, as you can see in the previous two figures, which are semantically equivalent. However, this does not mean that both diagrams will explicitly visualize the same information. For example, in the previous two figures, the communication diagram shows how the objects are linked (note the `{local}` and `{global}` annotations); the corresponding sequence diagram does not. Similarly, the sequence diagram shows message return (note the return value `committed`), but the corresponding communication diagram does not. In both cases, the two diagrams share the same underlying model, but each may render some things the other does not. However, a model entered in one format may lack some of the information shown on the other format, so although the underlying model can include both kinds of information, the two kinds of diagrams may lead to different models.

The five views of an architecture are discussed in Chapter 2; instances are discussed in Chapter 13; classes are discussed in Chapters 4 and 9; active classes are discussed in Chapter 23; interfaces are discussed in Chapter 11; components are discussed in Chapter 15; nodes are discussed in Chapter 27; systems and subsystems are discussed in Chapter 32; operations are discussed in Chapters 4 and 9; use cases are discussed in Chapter 17; collaborations are discussed in Chapter 28.

Common Uses

You use interaction diagrams to model the dynamic aspects of a system. These dynamic aspects may involve the interaction of any kind of instance in any view of a system's architecture, including instances of classes (including active classes), interfaces, components, and nodes.

When you use an interaction diagram to model some dynamic aspect of a system, you do so in the context of the system as a whole, a subsystem, an operation, or a class. You can also attach interaction diagrams to use cases (to model a scenario) and to collaborations (to model the dynamic aspects of a society of objects).

When you model the dynamic aspects of a system, you typically use interaction diagrams in two ways.

1. To model flows of control by time ordering

Here you'll use sequence diagrams. Modeling a flow of control by time ordering emphasizes the passing of messages as they unfold over time, which is a particularly useful way to visualize dynamic behavior in the context of a use case scenario. Sequence diagrams do a better job of visualizing simple iteration and branching than do communication diagrams.

2. To model flows of control by organization

Here you'll use communication diagrams. Modeling a flow of control by organization emphasizes the structural relationships among the instances in the interaction, along which messages may be passed.

Common Modeling Techniques

Modeling Flows of Control by Time Ordering

Systems and subsystems are discussed in Chapter 32; operations and classes are discussed in Chapters 4 and 9; use cases are discussed in Chapter 17; collaborations are discussed in Chapter 28.

Consider the objects that live in the context of a system, subsystem, operation or class. Consider also the objects and roles that participate in a use case or collaboration. To model a flow of control that winds through these objects and roles, you use an interaction diagram; to emphasize the passing of messages as they unfold over time, you use a sequence diagram, a kind of interaction diagram.

To model a flow of control by time ordering,

- Set the context for the interaction, whether it is a system, subsystem, operation, or class, or one scenario of a use case or collaboration.
- Set the stage for the interaction by identifying which objects play a role in the interaction. Lay them out on the sequence diagram from left to right, placing the more important objects to the left and their neighboring objects to the right.
- Set the lifeline for each object. In most cases, objects will persist through the entire interaction. For those objects that are created and destroyed during the interaction, set their lifelines, as appropriate, and explicitly indicate their birth and death with appropriately stereotyped messages.
- Starting with the message that initiates this interaction, lay out each subsequent message from top to bottom between the lifelines, showing each message's properties (such as its parameters), as necessary to explain the semantics of the interaction.
- If you need to visualize the nesting of messages or the points in time when actual computation is taking place, adorn each object's lifeline with its focus of control.
- If you need to specify time or space constraints, adorn each message with a timing mark and attach suitable time or space constraints.
- If you need to specify this flow of control more formally, attach pre- and postconditions to each message.

Timing marks are discussed in Chapter 24; pre- and postconditions are discussed in Chapter 4; packages are discussed in Chapter 12.

A single sequence diagram can show only one thread of control (although you can show structured concurrency by using the structured control constructs). Typically, you'll have a number of interaction diagrams, some of which are primary and others that show alternative paths or exceptional conditions. You can use packages to organize these collections of sequence diagrams, giving each diagram a suitable name to distinguish it from its siblings.

Signals are discussed in Chapter 21; timing marks are discussed in Chapter 24; constraints are discussed in Chapter 6; responsibilities are discussed in Chapter 4; notes are discussed in Chapter 6.

For example, Figure 19-6 shows a sequence diagram that specifies the flow of control involved in initiating a simple, two-party phone call. At this level of abstraction, there are four roles involved: two `Callers` (`s` and `r`); an unnamed telephone `Switch`; and `c`, the reification of the `Conversation` between the two parties. Note that the diagram models the four roles; each instance of the diagram has particular objects bound to each of the roles. The same pattern of interaction applies to every instance of the diagram.

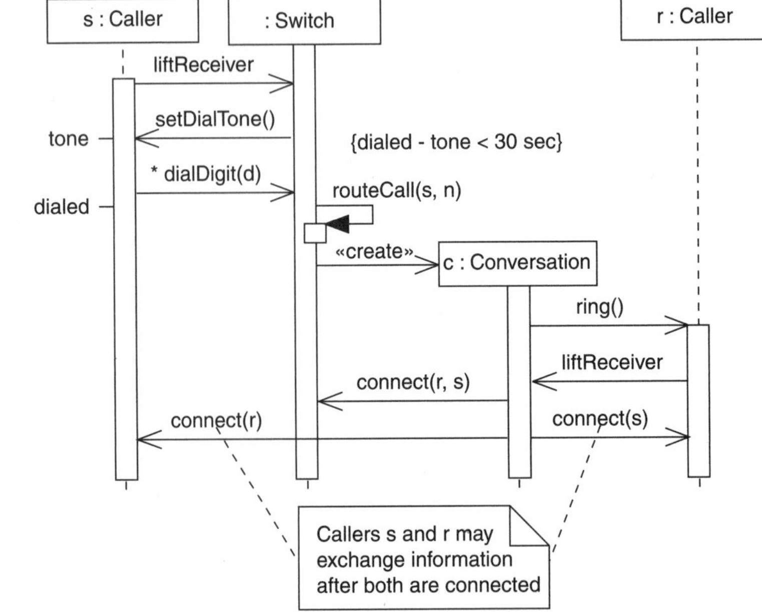

Figure 19-6: Modeling Flows of Control by Time Ordering

The sequence begins with one `Caller` (`s`) dispatching a signal (`liftReceiver`) to the `Switch` object. In turn, the `Switch` sends `setDialTone` to the `Caller`, and the `Caller` iterates on the message `dialDigit`. Note that this sequence must be less than 30 seconds, as specified by the constraint. This diagram does not indicate what happens if this time constraint is violated. To show that, you could include a branch or a completely separate sequence diagram. The `Switch` object then calls itself to perform the `routeCall` operation. It then creates a `Conversation` object (`c`), to which it delegates the rest of the work. Although not shown in this interaction, `c` would have the additional responsibility of being a party in the switch's billing mechanism (which would be expressed in another interaction diagram). The `Conversation` object (`c`) rings the `Caller` (`r`), who asynchronously sends the message `liftReceiver`. The `Conversation` object then tells the `Switch` to `connect` the call, then tells both `Caller` objects to `connect`, after which they may exchange information, as indicated by the attached note.

An interaction diagram can begin or end at any point of a sequence. A complete trace of the flow of control would be incredibly complex, so it's reasonable to break up parts of a larger flow into separate diagrams.

Modeling Flows of Control by Organization

Systems and subsystems are discussed in Chapter 32; operations and classes are discussed in Chapters 4 and 9; use cases are discussed in Chapter 17; collaborations are discussed in Chapter 28.

Consider the objects that live in the context of a system, subsystem, operation, or class. Consider also the objects and roles that participate in a use case or collaboration. To model a flow of control that winds through these objects and roles, you use an interaction diagram; to show the passing of messages in the context of that structure, you use a communication diagram, a kind of interaction diagram.

To model a flow of control by organization,

- Set the context for the interaction, whether it is a system, subsystem, operation, or class, or one scenario of a use case or collaboration.
- Set the stage for the interaction by identifying which objects play a role in the interaction. Lay them out on the communication diagram as vertices in a graph, placing the more important objects in the center of the diagram and their neighboring objects to the outside.
- Specify the links among these objects, along which messages may pass.
  1. Lay out the association links first; these are the most important ones, because they represent structural connections.
  2. Lay out other links next, and adorn them with suitable path annotations (such as `global` and `local`) to explicitly specify how these objects are related to one another.
- Starting with the message that initiates this interaction, attach each subsequent message to the appropriate link, setting its sequence number, as appropriate. Show nesting by using Dewey decimal numbering.
- If you need to specify time or space constraints, adorn each message with a timing mark and attach suitable time or space constraints.
- If you need to specify this flow of control more formally, attach pre- and postconditions to each message.

Dependency relationships are discussed in Chapters 5 and 10; path constraints are discussed in Chapter 16.

Timing marks are discussed in Chapter 24; pre- and postconditions are discussed in Chapter 4; packages are discussed in Chapter 12.

As with sequence diagrams, a single communication diagram can show only one flow of control (although you can show simple variations by using the UML's notation for interaction and branching). Typically, you'll have a number of such interaction diagrams, some of which are primary and others that show alternative paths or exceptional conditions. You can use packages to organize these collections of communication diagrams, giving each diagram a suitable name to distinguish it from its siblings.

For example, Figure 19-7 shows a communication diagram that specifies the flow of control involved in registering a new student at a school, with an emphasis on the structural relationships among these objects. You see four roles: a `RegistrarAgent` (`r`), a `Student` (`s`), a `Course` (`c`), and an unnamed `School` role. The flow of control is numbered explicitly. Action begins with the `RegistrarAgent` creating a `Student` object, adding the student to the school (the message `addStudent`), then telling the `Student` object to register itself. The `Student` object then invokes `getSchedule` on itself, obtaining a set of `Course` objects for which it must register. For each course object in the set, the `Student` object then adds itself to each `Course` object.

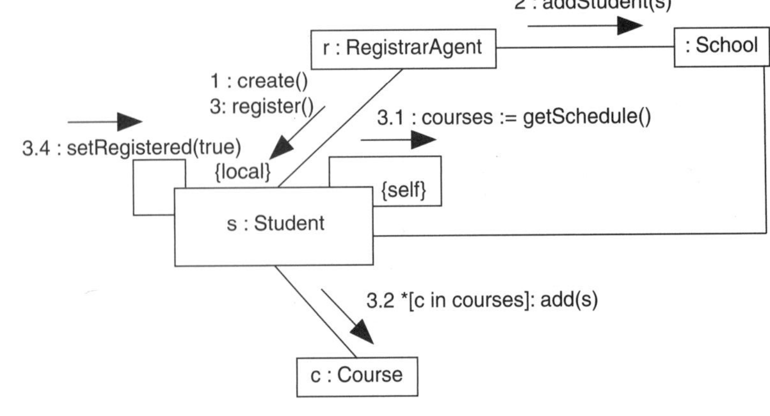

Figure 19-7: Modeling Flows of Control by Organization

Forward and Reverse Engineering

Forward engineering (the creation of code from a model) is possible for both sequence and communication diagrams, especially if the context of the diagram is an operation. For example, using the previous communication diagram, a reasonably clever forward engineering tool could generate the following Java code for the operation `register`, attached to the `Student` class.

```
public void register() {
  CourseCollection courses = getSchedule();
  for (int i = 0; i < courses.size(); i++)
    courses.item(i).add(this);
  this.registered = true;
}
```

"Reasonably clever" means the tool would have to realize that `getSchedule` returns a `CourseCollection` object, which it could determine by looking at the operation's signature. By walking across the contents of this object using a standard iteration idiom (which the tool could know about implicitly), the code could then generalize to any number of course offerings.

Reverse engineering (the creation of a model from code) is also possible for both sequence and communication diagrams, especially if the context of the code is the body of an operation. Segments of the previous diagram could have been produced by a tool from a prototypical execution of the `register` operation.

Note: Forward engineering is straightforward; reverse engineering is hard. It's easy to get too much information from simple reverse engineering, so the hard part is being clever about what details to keep.

However, more interesting than the reverse engineering of a model from code is the animation of a model against the execution of a deployed system. For example, given the previous diagram, a tool could animate the messages in the diagram as they were dispatched in a running system. Even better, with this tool under the control of a debugger, you could control the speed of execution, possibly setting breakpoints to stop the action at interesting points to examine the attribute values of individual objects.

Hints and Tips

When you create interaction diagrams in the UML, remember that sequence diagrams and communication diagrams are both projections on the same model of a system's dynamic aspects. No single interaction diagram can capture everything about a system's dynamic aspects. Rather, you'll want to use many interaction diagrams to model the dynamics of the system as a whole, as well as its subsystems, operations, classes, use cases, and collaborations.

A well-structured interaction diagram

- Is focused on communicating one aspect of a system's dynamics.
- Contains only those elements that are essential to understanding that aspect.
- Provides detail consistent with its level of abstraction and should expose only those adornments that are essential to understanding.

- Is not so minimalist that it misinforms the reader about semantics that are important.

When you draw an interaction diagram,

- Give it a name that communicates its purpose.
- Use a sequence diagram if you want to emphasize the time ordering of messages. Use a communication diagram if you want to emphasize the organization of the objects involved in the interaction.
- Lay out its elements to minimize lines that cross.
- Use notes and color as visual cues to draw attention to important features of your diagram.
- Use branching sparingly; you can represent complex branching much better using activity diagrams.

Chapter 20
ACTIVITY DIAGRAMS

In this chapter

- Modeling a workflow
- Modeling an operation
- Forward and reverse engineering

Sequence diagrams, communication diagrams, state diagrams, and use case diagrams also model the dynamic aspects of systems. Sequence and communication diagrams are discussed in Chapter 19; state diagrams are discussed in Chapter 25; use case diagrams are discussed in Chapter 18; actions are discussed in Chapter 16.

Activity diagrams are one of the five diagrams in the UML for modeling the dynamic aspects of systems. An activity diagram is essentially a flowchart, showing flow of control from activity to activity. Unlike a traditional flowchart, an activity diagram shows concurrency as well as branches of control.

You use activity diagrams to model the dynamic aspects of a system. For the most part, this involves modeling the sequential (and possibly concurrent) steps in a computational process. With an activity diagram, you can also model the flow of values among steps. Activity diagrams may stand alone to visualize, specify, construct, and document the dynamics of a society of objects, or they may be used to model the flow of control of an operation. Whereas interaction diagrams emphasize the flow of control from object to object, activity diagrams emphasize the flow of control from step to step. An activity is an ongoing structured execution of a behavior. The execution of an activity ultimately expands into the execution of individual actions, each of which may change the state of the system or communicate messages.

Activity diagrams are not only important for modeling the dynamic aspects of a system, but also for constructing executable systems through forward and reverse engineering.

Getting Started

Consider the workflow associated with building a house. First, you select a site. Next, you commission an architect to design your house. After you've settled on the plan, your developer asks for bids to price the house. Once you agree on a price and a plan, construction can begin. Permits are secured, ground is broken, the foundation is poured, the framing is erected, and so on, until everything is done. You're then handed the keys and a certificate of occupancy, and you take possession of the house.

Although that's a tremendous simplification of what really goes on in a construction process, it does capture the critical path of the workflow. In a real project, there are lots of parallel activities among various trades. Electricians can be working at the same time as plumbers and carpenters, for example. You'll also encounter conditions and branches. For example, depending on the result of soils tests, you might have to blast, dig, or float. There might even be iterations. For example, a building inspection might reveal code violations that result in scrap and rework.

In the construction industry, such techniques as Gantt charts and Pert charts are commonly used for visualizing, specifying, constructing, and documenting the workflow of the project.

Modeling the structural aspects of a system is discussed in Parts 2 and 3; interaction diagrams are discussed in Chapter 19.

In modeling software-intensive systems, you have a similar problem. How do you best model a workflow or an operation, both of which are aspects of the system's dynamics? The answer is that you have two basic choices, similar to the use of Gantt charts and Pert charts.

On the one hand, you can build up storyboards of scenarios, involving the interaction of certain interesting objects and the messages that may be dispatched among them. In the UML, you can model these storyboards in two ways: by emphasizing the time ordering of messages (using sequence diagrams) or by emphasizing the structural relationships among the objects that interact (using collaboration diagrams). Interaction diagrams such as these are akin to Gantt charts, which focus on the objects (resources) that carry out some activity over time.

Actions are discussed in Chapter 16.

On the other hand, you can model these dynamic aspects using activity diagrams, which focus first on the activities that take place among objects, as Figure 20-1 shows. In that regard, activity diagrams are akin to Pert charts. An activity diagram is essentially a flowchart that emphasizes the activity that takes place over time. You can think of an activity diagram as an interaction diagram turned inside out. An interaction diagram looks at the objects that pass messages; an activity diagram looks at the operations that are passed among objects. The semantic difference is subtle, but it results in a very different way of looking at the world.

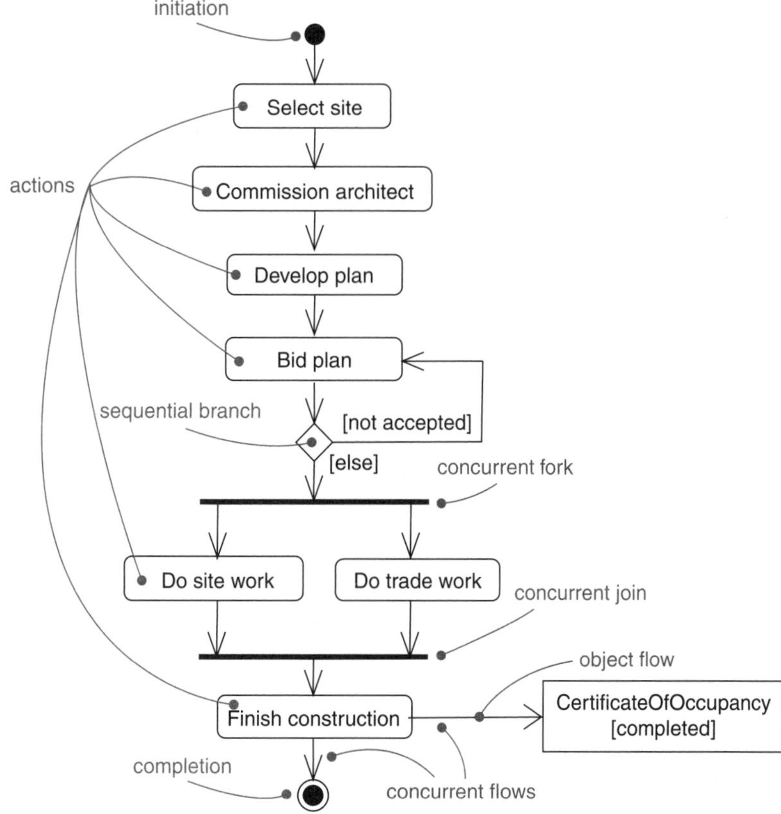

Figure 20-1: Activity Diagram

Terms and Concepts

An *activity diagram* shows the flow from activity to activity. An *activity* is an ongoing nonatomic execution within a state machine. The execution of an activity ultimately expands into the execution of individual *actions*, each of which may change the state of the system or communicate messages. Actions encompass calling another operation, sending a signal, creating or destroying an object, or some pure computation such as evaluating an expression. Graphically, an activity diagram is a collection of nodes and arcs.

Common Properties

The general properties of diagrams are discussed in Chapter 7.

An activity diagram is a kind of diagram and shares the same common properties as do all other diagrams—a name and graphical contents that are a projection into a model. What distinguishes an interaction diagram from other kinds of diagrams is its content.

Contents

States, transitions, and state machines are discussed in Chapter 22; objects are discussed in Chapter 13.

Activity diagrams commonly contain

- Actions
- Activity nodes
- Flows
- Object values

Like all other diagrams, activity diagrams may contain notes and constraints.

Actions and Activity Nodes

Attributes and operations are discussed in Chapters 4 and 9; signals are discussed in Chapter 21; creation and destruction of objects are discussed in Chapter 16; states and state machines are discussed in Chapter 22.

In the flow of control modeled by an activity diagram, things happen. You might evaluate some expression that sets the value of an attribute or that returns some value. Alternately, you might call an operation on an object, send a signal to an object, or even create or destroy an object. These executable, atomic computations are called actions. As Figure 20-2 shows, you represent an action using a rounded box. Inside that shape, you may write an expression.

Note: The UML does not prescribe the language of these expressions. Abstractly, you might just use structured text; more concretely, you might use the syntax and semantics of a specific programming language.

Actions can't be decomposed. Furthermore, actions are atomic, meaning that events may occur, but the internal behavior of the action state is not visible. You can't execute part of an action; either it executes completely or not at all. Finally, the work of an action state is often considered to take insignificant execution time, but some actions may have substantial duration.

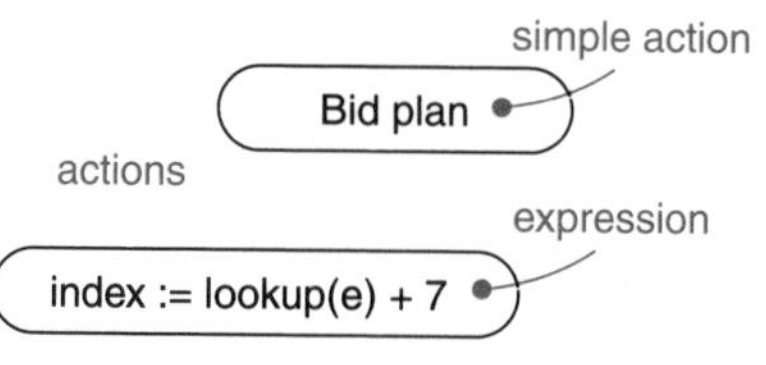

Figure 20-2: Actions

Modeling time and space is discussed in Chapter 24.

Note: In the real world, of course, every computation takes some amount of time and space. Especially for hard real time systems, it's important that you model these properties.

An *activity node* is an organizational unit within an activity. In general, activity nodes are nested groupings of actions or other nested activity nodes. Furthermore, activity nodes have visible substructure; in general, they are considered to take some duration to complete. You can think of an action as a special case of an activity node. An action is an activity node that cannot be further decomposed. Similarly, you can think of an activity node as a composite whose flow of control is made up of other activity nodes and actions. Zoom into the details of an activity node and you'll find another activity diagram. As Figure 20-3 shows, there's no notational distinction between actions and activity nodes, except that an activity node may have additional parts, which will usually be maintained in the background by an editing tool.

Figure 20-3: Activity Nodes

Control Flows

When an action or activity node completes execution, flow of control passes immediately to the next action or activity node. You specify this flow by using flow arrows to show the path of control from one action or activity node to the next action or activity node. In the UML, you represent a flow as a simple arrow from the predecessor action to its successor, without an event label, as Figure 20-4 shows.

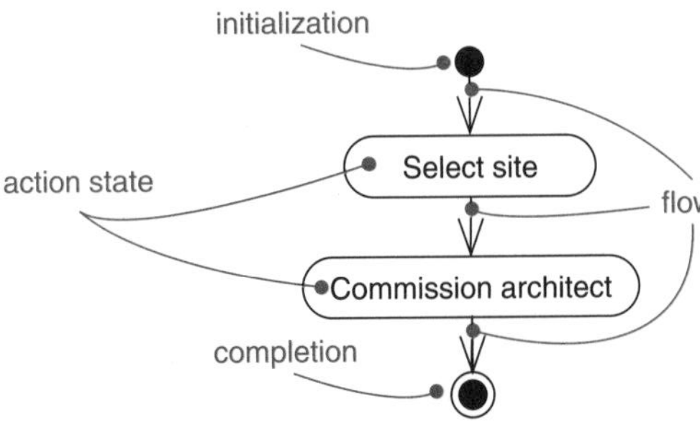

Figure 20-4: Completion Transitions

Indeed, a flow of control has to start and end someplace (unless, of course, it's an infinite flow, in which case it will have a beginning but no end). Therefore, as the figure shows, you may specify initialization (a solid ball) and completion (a solid ball inside a circle) as special symbols.

Branching

Branches are a notational convenience, semantically equivalent to multiple transitions with guards, as discussed in Chapter 22.

Simple, sequential flows are common, but they aren't the only kind of path you'll need to model a flow of control. As in a flowchart, you can include a branch, which specifies alternate paths taken based on some Boolean expression. As Figure 20-5 shows, you represent a branch as a diamond. A branch may have one incoming and two or more outgoing flows. On each outgoing flow, you place a Boolean expression, which is evaluated on entering the branch. The guards on the outgoing flows should not overlap (otherwise, the flow of control would be ambiguous), but they should cover all possibilities (otherwise, the flow of control would freeze).

As a convenience, you can use the keyword `else` to mark one outgoing transition, representing the path taken if no other guard expression evaluates to true.

Branching and iteration are possible in interaction diagrams, as discussed in Chapter 19.

When two paths of control merge back together, you can also use a diamond symbol with two input arrows and one output arrow. No guards are necessary on merge.

You can achieve the effect of iteration by using one action that sets the value of an iterator, another action that increments the iterator, and a branch that evaluates if the iteration is finished. The UML includes node types for loops, but these may often be expressed more easily in text than in graphics.

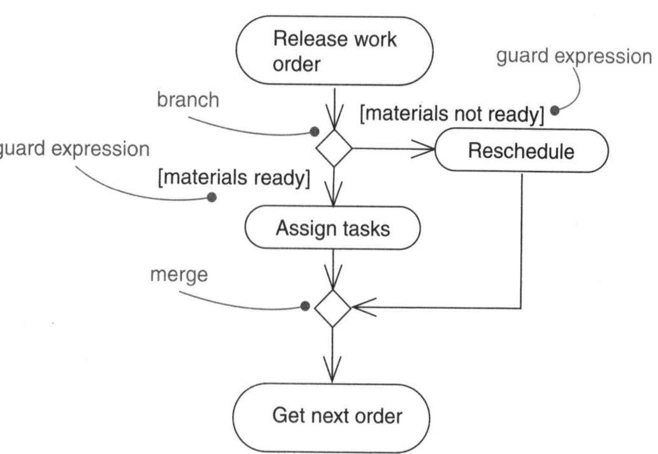

Figure 20-5: Branching

Note: The UML does not prescribe the language of these expressions. Abstractly, you might just use structured text; more concretely, you might use the syntax and semantics of a specific programming language.

Forking and Joining

A concurrent flow of control often lives in the context of an independent active object, which is typically modeled as either a process or a thread, as discussed in Chapter 23; nodes are discussed in Chapter 27.

Simple and branching sequential transitions are the most common paths you'll find in activity diagrams. However—especially when you are modeling workflows of business processes—you might encounter flows that are concurrent. In the UML, you use a synchronization bar to specify the forking and joining of these parallel flows of control. A synchronization bar is rendered as a thick horizontal or vertical line.

For example, consider the concurrent flows involved in controlling an audio-animatronic device that mimics human speech and gestures. As Figure 20-6 shows, a fork represents the splitting of a single flow of control into two or more concurrent flows of control. A fork may have one incoming transition and two or more outgoing transitions, each of which represents an independent flow of control. Below the fork, the activities associated with each of these paths continues in parallel. Conceptually, the activities of each of these flows are truly parallel, although, in a running system, these flows may be either truly concurrent (in the case of a system deployed across multiple nodes) or sequential yet interleaved (in the case of a system deployed across one node), thus giving only the illusion of true concurrency.

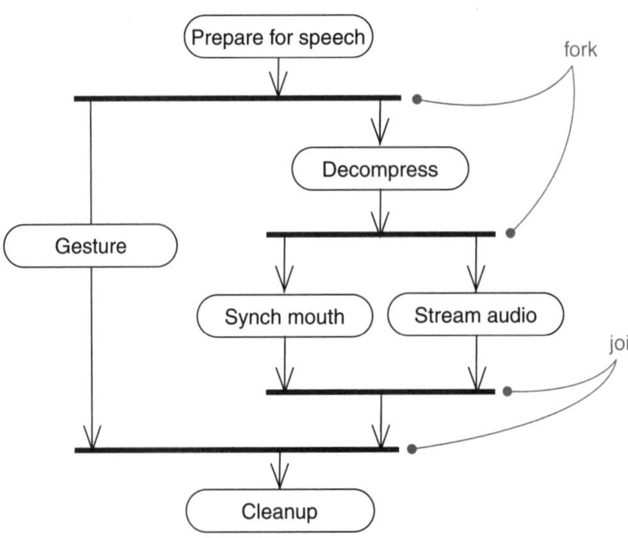

Figure 20-6: Forking and Joining

As the figure also shows, a join represents the synchronization of two or more concurrent flows of control. A join may have two or more incoming transitions and one outgoing transition. Above the join, the activities associated with each of these paths continues in parallel. At the join, the concurrent flows synchronize, meaning that each waits until all incoming flows have reached the join, at which point one flow of control continues on below the join.

Active objects are discussed in Chapter 23; signals are discussed in Chapter 21.

Note: Joins and forks should balance, meaning that the number of flows that leave a fork should match the number of flows that enter its corresponding join. Also, activities that are in parallel flows of control may communicate with one another by sending signals. This style of communicating sequential processes is called a coroutine. Most of the time you model this style of communication using active objects.

Swimlanes

You'll find it useful, especially when you are modeling workflows of business processes, to partition the activity states on an activity diagram into groups, each group representing the business organization responsible for those activities. In the UML, each group is called a swimlane because, visually, each group is divided from its neighbor by a vertical solid line, as shown in Figure 20-7. A swimlane specifies a set of activities that share some organizational property.

A swimlane is a kind of package. Packages are discussed in Chapter 12; classes are discussed in Chapters 4 and 9; processes and threads are discussed in Chapter 23.

Each swimlane has a name unique within its diagram. A swimlane really has no deep semantics, except that it may represent some real-world entity, such as an organizational unit of a company. Each swimlane represents a high-level responsibility for part of the overall activity of an activity diagram, and each swimlane may eventually be implemented by one or more classes. In an activity diagram partitioned into swimlanes, every activity belongs to exactly one swimlane, but transitions may cross lanes.

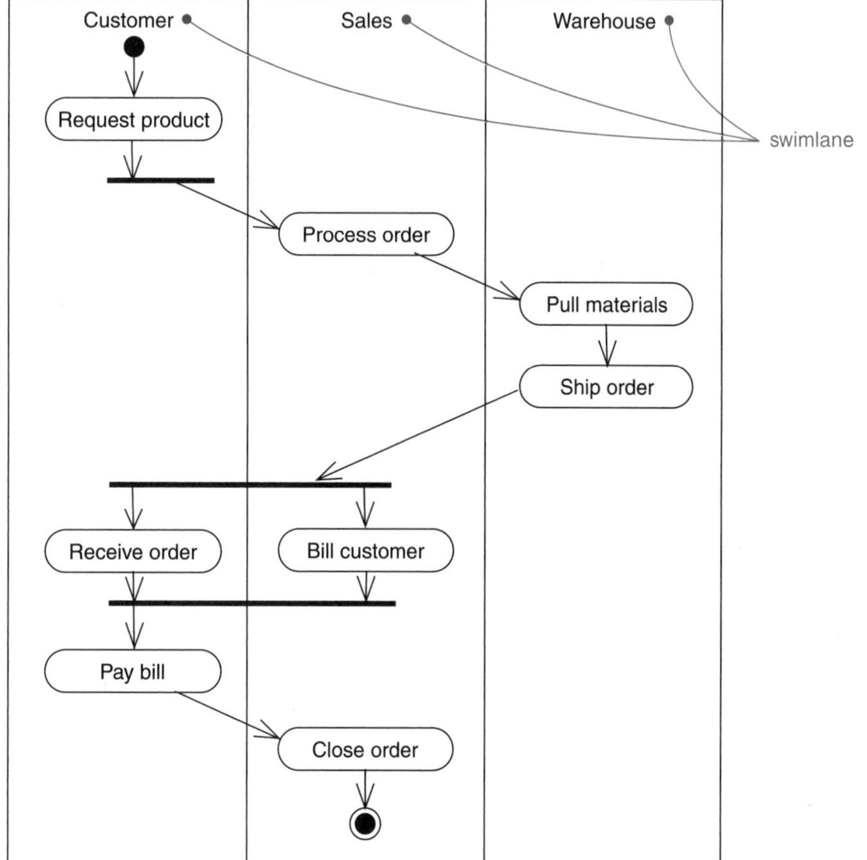

Figure 20-7: Swimlanes

Note: There's a loose connection between swimlanes and concurrent flows of control. Conceptually, the activities of each swimlane are generally—but not always—considered separate from the activities of neighboring swimlanes. That makes sense because, in the real world, the business organizations that generally map to these swimlanes are independent and concurrent.

Object Flow

Objects are discussed in Chapter 13; modeling the vocabulary of a system is discussed in Chapter 4.

Objects may be involved in the flow of control associated with an activity diagram. For example, in the workflow of processing an order as in the previous figure, the vocabulary of your problem space will also include such classes as `Order` and `Bill`. Instances of these two classes will be produced by certain activities (`Process order` will create an `Order` object, for example); other activities may use or modify these objects (for example, `Ship order` will change the state of the `Order` object to `filled`).

Dependency relationships are discussed in Chapters 5 and 10.

As Figure 20-8 shows, you can specify the things that are involved in an activity diagram by placing these objects in the diagram, connected by arrows to the actions that produce or consume them.

This called an object flow because it represents the flow of an object value from one action to another. An object flow inherently implies control flow (you can't execute an action that requires a value without the value!), so it is unnecessary to draw a control flow between actions connected by object flows.

The values and state of an object are discussed in Chapter 13; attributes are discussed in Chapters 4 and 9.

In addition to showing the flow of an object through an activity diagram, you can also show how its state changes. As shown in the figure, you represent the state of an object by naming its state in brackets below the object's name.

Expansion Regions

Often the same operation must be performed on the elements of a set. For example, if an order comprises a set of line items, the order handler must perform the same operation for each line item: check availability, look up the cost, check if this kind of item is taxable, and so on. Operations on lists are often modeled as loops, but then the modeler must iterate over the items, extract them one at a time, perform the operation, assemble the results into an output array, increment the index, and check for completion. The mechanics of executing the loop obscure the actual significance of the operation. This extremely common pattern can be modeled directly using an *expansion region*.

An expansion region represents a activity model fragment that is performed on the elements of a list or set. It is shown in an activity diagram by drawing a dashed line around a region in the diagram. The inputs to the region and the outputs from the region are collections of values, such as the line items in an order. Collection inputs and outputs are shown as a row of small squares joined together (to suggest an array of values). When an array value arrives at a collection input on an expansion region from the rest of the activity model, it is broken apart into the individual values. The execution region is executed

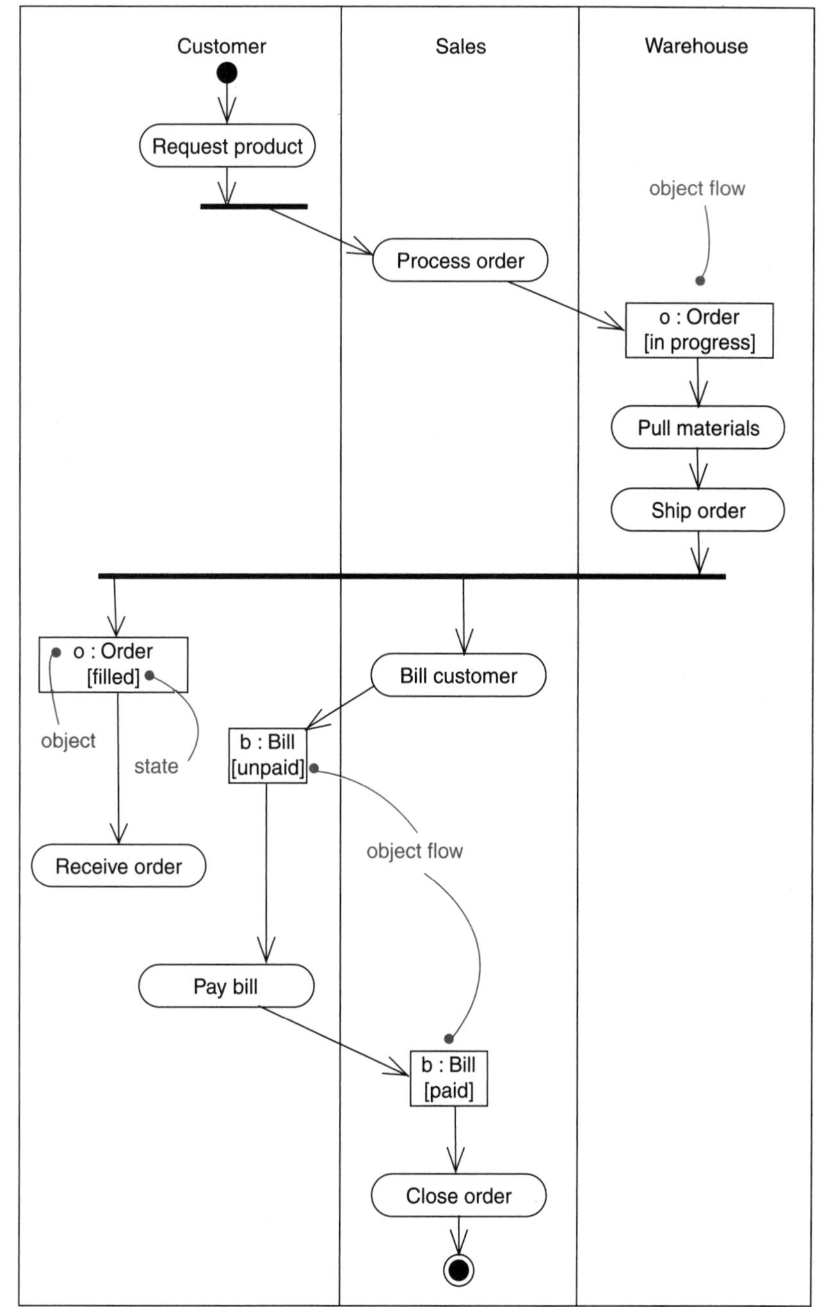

Figure 20-8: Object Flow

once for each element in the array. It is unnecessary to model the iteration; it is implicit in the expansion region. The different executions can be performed concurrently, if possible. When each execution of the expansion region completes, its output value (if any) is placed into an output array in the same order as the corresponding input. In other words, an expansion region performs a "forall" operation on the elements of an array to create a new array.

In the simplest case, an expansion region has one array input and one array output, but it can have one or more input array and zero or more output arrays. All of the arrays must be the same size, but they need not contain the same type of value. Values from corresponding positions execute together to produce output values at the same position. The region could have zero outputs if all the operations are performed as side effects directly on array elements.

Expansion regions allow operations on collections and operations on individual elements of the collections to be shown on the same diagram, without the need to show all of the detailed but straightforward iteration machinery.

Figure 20-9 shows an example of an expansion region. In the main body of the diagram, an order is received. This produces a value of type `Order`, which consists of an array of `LineItem` values. The `Order` value is the input to an

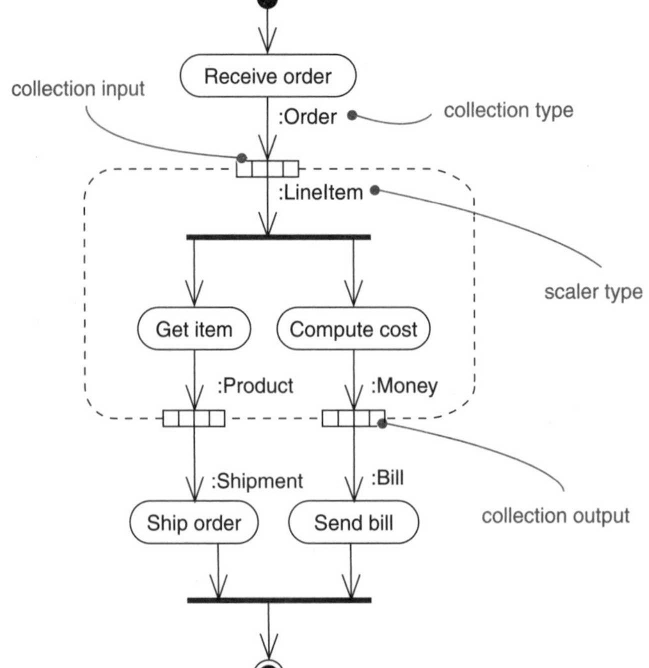

Figure 20-9: Expansion region

expansion region. Each execution of the expansion region works on one element from the `Order` collection. Therefore, inside the region the type of input value corresponds to one element of the `Order` array, namely a `LineItem`. The expansion region activity forks into two actions: one action finds the `Product` and adds it to the shipment, and the other action computes the cost of that item. It is not necessary that the `LineItems` be taken in order; the different executions of the expansion region can proceed concurrently. When all executions of the expansion region are complete, the Items are formed into a `Shipment` (a collection of `Products`) and the charges are formed into a `Bill` (a collection of `Money` values). The `Shipment` value is the input to the `ShipOrder` action and the `Bill` value is the input to the `SendBill` action.

Common Uses

The five views of an architecture are discussed in Chapter 2; classes are discussed in Chapters 4 and 9; active classes are discussed in Chapter 23; interfaces are discussed in Chapter 11; operations are discussed in Chapters 4 and 9; use cases and actors are discussed in Chapter 17; components are discussed in Chapter 15; nodes are discussed in Chapter 27; systems and subsystems are discussed in Chapter 32.

You use activity diagrams to model the dynamic aspects of a system. These dynamic aspects may involve the activity of any kind of abstraction in any view of a system's architecture, including classes (which includes active classes), interfaces, components, and nodes.

When you use an activity diagram to model some dynamic aspect of a system, you can do so in the context of virtually any modeling element. Typically, however, you'll use activity diagrams in the context of the system as a whole, a subsystem, an operation, or a class. You can also attach activity diagrams to use cases (to model a scenario) and to collaborations (to model the dynamic aspects of a society of objects).

When you model the dynamic aspects of a system, you'll typically use activity diagrams in two ways.

1. To model a workflow

Here you'll focus on activities as viewed by the actors that collaborate with the system. Workflows often lie on the fringe of software-intensive systems and are used to visualize, specify, construct, and document business processes that involve the system you are developing. In this use of activity diagrams, modeling object flow is particularly important.

2. To model an operation

Here you'll use activity diagrams as flowcharts to model the details of a computation. In this use of activity diagrams, the modeling of branch, fork, and join states is particularly important. The context of an activity diagram used in this way involves the parameters of the operation and its local objects.

Common Modeling Techniques

Modeling a Workflow

Modeling the context of a system is discussed in Chapter 18.

No software-intensive system exists in isolation; there's always some context in which a system lives, and that context always encompasses actors that interact with the system. Especially for mission-critical enterprise software, you'll find automated systems working in the context of higher-level business processes. These business processes are kinds of workflows because they represent the flow of work and objects through the business. For example, in a retail business, you'll have some automated systems (for example, point-of-sale systems that interact with marketing and warehouse systems), as well as human systems (the people that work at each retail outlet, as well as the telesales, marketing, buying, and shipping departments). You can model the business processes for the way these various automated and human systems collaborate by using activity diagrams.

To model a workflow,

Modeling the vocabulary of a system is discussed in Chapter 4; preconditions and postconditions are discussed in Chapter 9.

- Establish a focus for the workflow. For nontrivial systems, it's impossible to show all interesting workflows in one diagram.
- Select the business objects that have the high-level responsibilities for parts of the overall workflow. These may be real things from the vocabulary of the system, or they may be more abstract. In either case, create a swimlane for each important business object or organization.
- Identify the preconditions of the workflow's initial state and the postconditions of the workflow's final state. This is important in helping you model the boundaries of the workflow.
- Beginning at the workflow's initial state, specify the actions that take place over time and render them in the activity diagram.
- For complicated actions or for sets of actions that appear multiple times, collapse these into calls to a separate activity diagram.
- Render the flows that connect these actions and activity nodes. Start with the sequential flows in the workflow first, next consider branching, and only then consider forking and joining.
- If there are important object values that are involved in the workflow, render them in the activity diagram as well. Show their changing values and state as necessary to communicate the intent of the object flow.

For example, Figure 20-10 shows an activity diagram for a retail business, which specifies the workflow involved when a customer returns an item from a mail order. Work starts with the `Customer` action `Request return` and then flows through `Telesales` (`Get return number`), back to the `Customer` (`Ship item`), then to the `Warehouse` (`Receive item` then `Restock item`), finally ending in `Accounting` (`Credit account`). As the diagram indicates, one significant object (an instance of `Item`) also flows the process, changing from the `returned` to the `available` state.

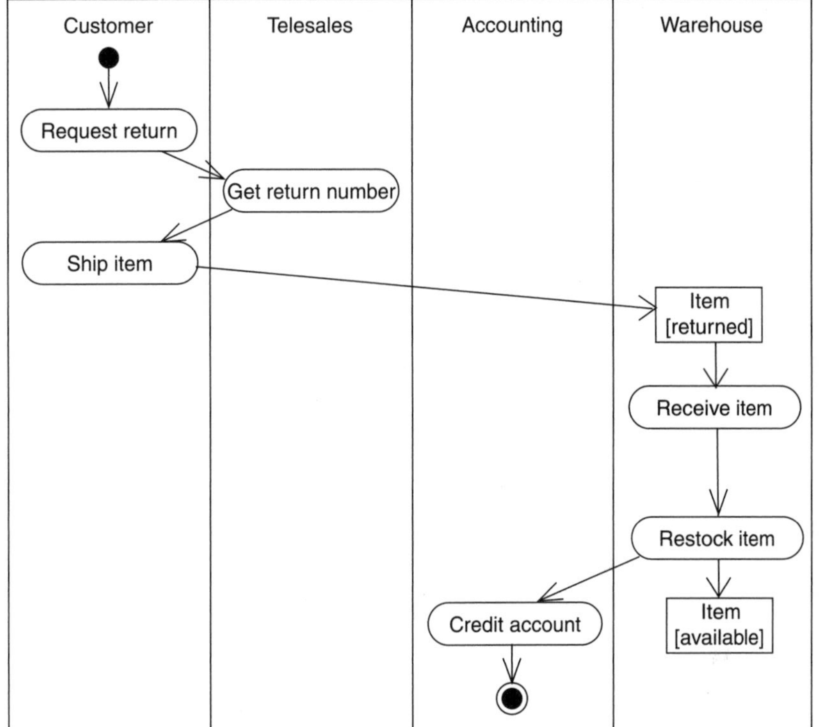

Figure 20-10: Modeling a Workflow

Note: Workflows are most often business processes, but not always. For example, you can also use activity diagrams to specify software development processes, such as your process for configuration management. Furthermore, you can use activity diagrams to model nonsoftware systems, such as the flow of patients through a healthcare system.

In this example, there are no branches, forks, or joins. You'll encounter these features in more complex workflows.

Modeling an Operation

Classes and operations are discussed in Chapters 4 and 9; interfaces are discussed in Chapter 11; components are discussed in Chapter 15; nodes are discussed in Chapter 27; use cases are discussed in Chapter 17; collaborations are discussed in Chapter 28; preconditions, postconditions, and invariants are discussed in Chapter 9; active classes are discussed in Chapter 23.

An activity diagram can be attached to any modeling element for the purpose of visualizing, specifying, constructing, and documenting that element's behavior. You can attach activity diagrams to classes, interfaces, components, nodes, use cases, and collaborations. The most common element to which you'll attach an activity diagram is an operation.

Used in this manner, an activity diagram is simply a flowchart of an operation's actions. An activity diagram's primary advantage is that all the elements in the diagram are semantically tied to a rich underlying model. For example, any other operation or signal that an action state references can be type-checked against the class of the target object.

To model an operation,

- Collect the abstractions that are involved in this operation. This includes the operation's parameters (including its return type, if any), the attributes of the enclosing class, and certain neighboring classes.
- Identify the preconditions at the operation's initial state and the postconditions at the operation's final state. Also identify any invariants of the enclosing class that must hold during the execution of the operation.
- Beginning at the operation's initial state, specify the activities and actions that take place over time and render them in the activity diagram as either activity states or action states.
- Use branching as necessary to specify conditional paths and iteration.
- Only if this operation is owned by an active class, use forking and joining as necessary to specify parallel flows of control.

If an operation involves the interaction of a society of objects, you can also model the realization of that operation using collaborations, as discussed in Chapter 28.

For example, in the context of the class `Line`, Figure 20-11 shows an activity diagram that specifies the algorithm of the operation `intersection`, whose signature includes one parameter (`line`, of the class `Line`) and one return value (of the class `Point`). The class `Line` has two attributes of interest: `slope` (which holds the slope of the line) and `delta` (which holds the offset of the line relative to the origin).

The algorithm of this operation is simple, as shown in the following activity diagram. First, there's a guard that tests whether the `slope` of the current line is the same as the `slope` of parameter `line`. If so, the lines do not intersect, and a `Point` at `(0,0)` is returned. Otherwise, the operation first calculates an `x` value for the point of intersection, then a `y` value; `x` and `y` are both objects local to the operation. Finally, a `Point` at `(x,y)` is returned.

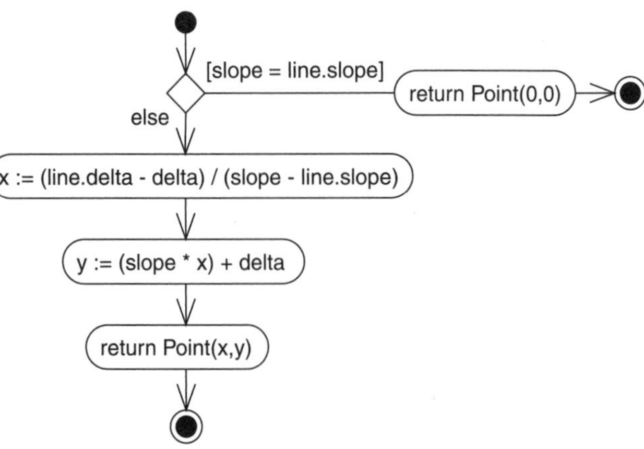

Figure 20-11: Modeling an Operation

Note: Using activity diagrams to flowchart an operation lies on the edge of making the UML a visual programming language. You *can* flowchart every operation, but pragmatically, you won't want to. Writing the body of an operation in a specific programming language is usually more direct. You will want to use activity diagrams to model an operation when the behavior of that operation is complex and therefore difficult to understand just by staring at code. Looking at a flowchart will reveal things about the algorithm you could not have seen just by looking at the code.

Forward and Reverse Engineering

Forward engineering (the creation of code from a model) is possible for activity diagrams, especially if the context of the diagram is an operation. For example, using the previous activity diagram, a forward engineering tool could generate the following C++ code for the operation `intersection`.

```
Point Line::intersection (line : Line) {
  if (slope == line.slope) return Point(0,0);
  int x = (line.delta - delta) /
                  (slope - line.slope);
  int y = (slope * x) + delta;
  return Point(x, y);
}
```

There's a bit of cleverness here, involving the declaration of the two local variables. A less-sophisticated tool might have first declared the two variables and then set their values.

Reverse engineering (the creation of a model from code) is also possible for activity diagrams, especially if the context of the code is the body of an operation. In particular, the previous diagram could have been generated from the implementation of the class `Line`.

More interesting than the reverse engineering of a model from code is the animation of a model against the execution of a deployed system. For example, given the previous diagram, a tool could animate the action states in the diagram as they were dispatched in a running system. Even better, with this tool also under the control of a debugger, you could control the speed of execution, possibly setting breakpoints to stop the action at interesting points in time to examine the attribute values of individual objects.

Hints and Tips

When you create activity diagrams in the UML, remember that activity diagrams are just projections on the same model of a system's dynamic aspects. No single activity diagram can capture everything about a system's dynamic aspects. Rather, you'll want to use many activity diagrams to model the dynamics of a workflow or an operation.

A well-structured activity diagram

- Is focused on communicating one aspect of a system's dynamics.
- Contains only those elements that are essential to understanding that aspect.
- Provides detail consistent with its level of abstraction; you expose only those adornments that are essential to understanding.
- Is not so minimalist that it misinforms the reader about important semantics.

When you draw an activity diagram,

- Give it a name that communicates its purpose.
- Start with modeling the primary flow. Address branching, concurrency, and object flow as secondary considerations, possibly in separate diagrams.
- Lay out its elements to minimize lines that cross.
- Use notes and color as visual cues to draw attention to important features of your diagram.

UNIFIED
MODELING
LANGUAGE

Part 5

Advanced Behavioral Modeling

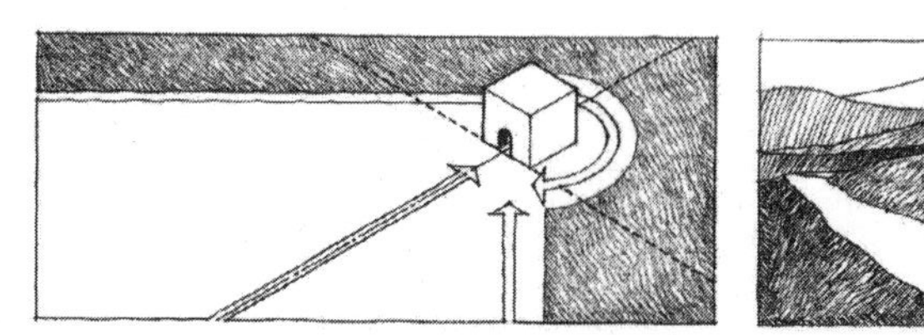

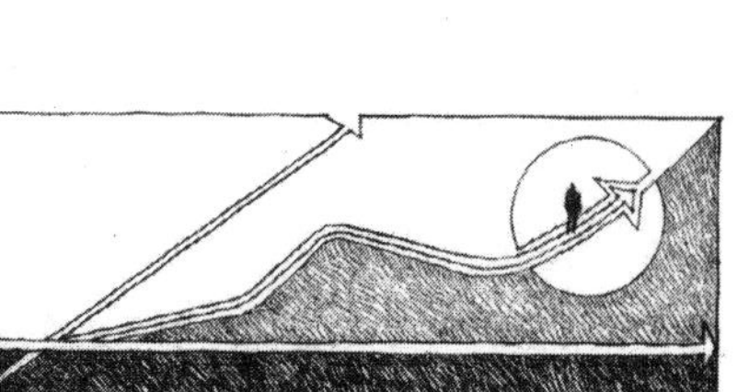

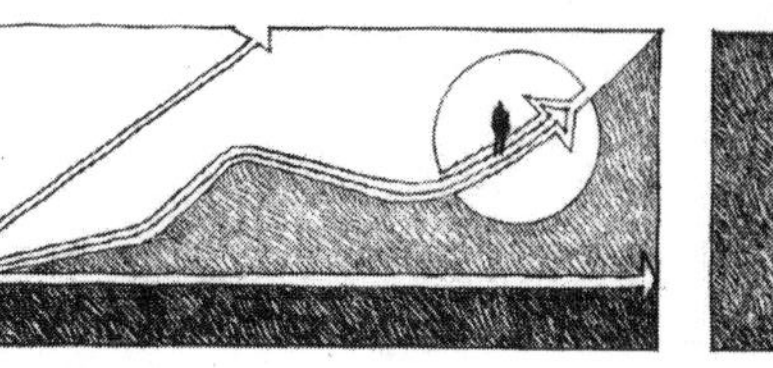

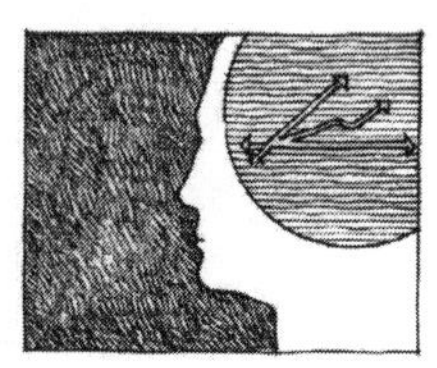

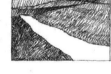

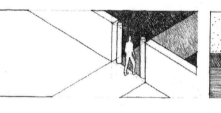

Chapter 21

EVENTS AND SIGNALS

In this chapter

- Signal events, call events, time events, and change events
- Modeling a family of signals
- Modeling exceptions
- Handling events in active and passive objects

In the real world, things happen. Not only do things happen, but lots of things may happen at the same time, and at the most unexpected times. "Things that happen" are called events, and each one represents the specification of a significant occurrence that has a location in time and space.

In the context of state machines, you use events to model the occurrence of a stimulus that can trigger a state transition. Events may include signals, calls, the passing of time, or a change in state.

Events may be synchronous or asynchronous, so modeling events is wrapped up in the modeling of processes and threads.

Getting Started

A perfectly static system is intensely uninteresting because nothing ever happens. All real systems have some dynamic dimension to them, and these dynamics are triggered by things that happen externally or internally. At an ATM machine, action is initiated by a user pressing a button to start a transaction. In an autonomous robot, action is initiated by the robot bumping into an object. In a network router, action is initiated by the detection of an overflow of message buffers. In a chemical plant, action is initiated by the passage of time sufficient for a chemical reaction.

In the UML, each thing that happens is modeled as an event. An event is the specification of a significant occurrence that has a location in time and space. A signal, the passing of time, and a change of state are asynchronous events, representing events that can happen at arbitrary times. Calls are generally synchronous events, representing the invocation of an operation.

The UML provides a graphical representation of an event, as Figure 21-1 shows. This notation permits you to visualize the declaration of events (such as the signal `OffHook`) as well as the use of events to trigger a state transition (such as the signal `OffHook`, which causes a transition from the `Active` to the `Idle` state as well as the execution of the `dropConnection` action).

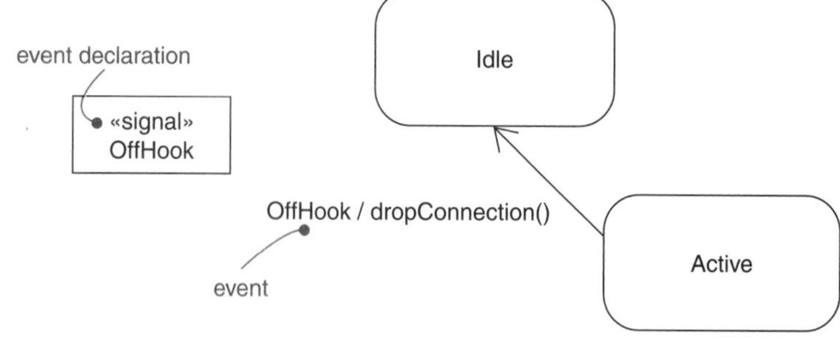

Figure 21-1: Events

Terms and Concepts

An *event* is the specification of a significant occurrence that has a location in time and space. In the context of state machines, an event is an occurrence of a stimulus that can trigger a state transition. A *signal* is a kind of event that represents the specification of an asynchronous message communicated between instances.

Kinds of Events

Actors are discussed in Chapter 17; systems are discussed in Chapter 32.

Events may be external or internal. External events are those that pass between the system and its actors. For example, the pushing of a button and an interrupt from a collision sensor are both examples of external events. Internal events are those that pass among the objects that live inside the system. An overflow exception is an example of an internal event.

The creation and destruction of objects are also kinds of signals, as discussed in Chapter 16.

In the UML, you can model four kinds of events: signals, calls, the passing of time, and a change in state.

Signals

A message is a named object that is sent asynchronously by one object and then received by another. A signal is a classifier for messages; it is a message type.

Classes are discussed in Chapters 4 and 9; generalization is discussed in Chapters 5 and 10.

Signals have a lot in common with plain classes. For example, signals may have instances, although you don't generally need to model them explicitly. Signals may also be involved in generalization relationships, permitting you to model hierarchies of events, some of which are general (for example, the signal `NetworkFailure`) and some of which are specific (for example, a specialization of `NetworkFailure` called `WarehouseServerFailure`). Also as for classes, signals may have attributes and operations. Before it has been sent by one object or after it is received by another, a signal is just an ordinary data object.

Note: The attributes of a signal serve as its parameters. For example, when you send a signal such as `Collision`, you can also specify a value for its attributes as parameters, such as `Collision(5.3)`.

State machines are discussed in Chapter 22; interactions are discussed in Chapter 16; interfaces are discussed in Chapter 11; dependencies are discussed in Chapter 5; stereotypes are discussed in Chapter 6.

A signal may be sent by the action of a transition in a state machine. It may be modeled as a message between two roles in an interaction. The execution of a method can also send signals. In fact, when you model a class or an interface, an important part of specifying the behavior of that element is specifying the signals that its operations can send.

In the UML, as Figure 21-2 shows, you model signals as stereotyped classes. You can use a dependency, stereotyped as `send`, to indicate that an operation sends a particular signal.

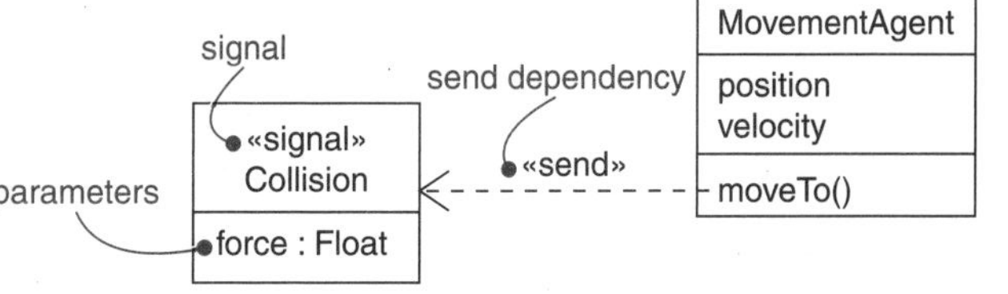

Figure 21-2: Signals

Call Events

State machines are discussed in Chapter 22.

Just as a signal event represents the occurrence of a signal, a call event represents the receipt by an object of a call request for an operation on the object. A call event may trigger a state transition in a state machine or it may invoke a method on the target object. The choice is specified in the class definition for the operation.

Whereas a signal is an asynchronous event, a call event is usually synchronous. This means that when an object invokes an operation on another object that has a state machine, control passes from the sender to the receiver, the transition is triggered by the event, the operation is completed, the receiver transitions to a new state, and control returns to the sender. In those cases where the caller does not need to wait for a response, a call can be specified as asynchronous.

As Figure 21-3 shows, modeling a call event is indistinguishable from modeling a signal event. In both cases, you show the event, along with its parameters, as the trigger for a state transition.

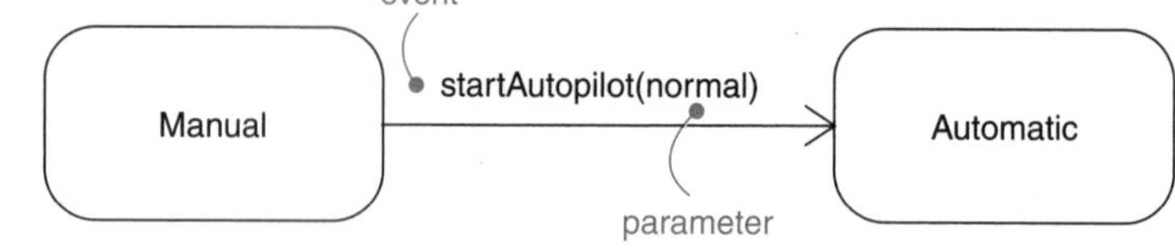

Figure 21-3: Call Events

Note: Although there are no visual cues to distinguish a signal event from a call event, the difference is clear in the backplane of your model. The receiver of an event will know the difference, of course (by declaring the operation in its operation list). Typically, a signal will be handled by its state machine, and a call event will be handled by a method. You can use your tools to navigate from the event to the signal or the operation.

Time and Change Events

A time event is an event that represents the passage of time. As Figure 21-4 shows, in the UML you model a time event by using the keyword `after` followed by some expression that evaluates to a period of time. Such expressions can be simple (for example, `after 2 seconds`) or complex (for example, `after 1 ms since exiting Idle`). Unless you specify it explicitly, the starting time of such an expression is the time since entering the current state. To indicate a time event that occurs at an absolute time, use the keyword `at`. For example, the time event `at (1 Jan 2005, 1200 UT)` specifies an event that occurs on noon Universal Time on New Year's Day 2005.

A change event is an event that represents a change in state or the satisfaction of some condition. As Figure 21-4 shows, in the UML you model a change event by using the keyword `when` followed by some Boolean expression. You can use such expressions for the continuous test of an expression (for example, `when altitude < 1000`).

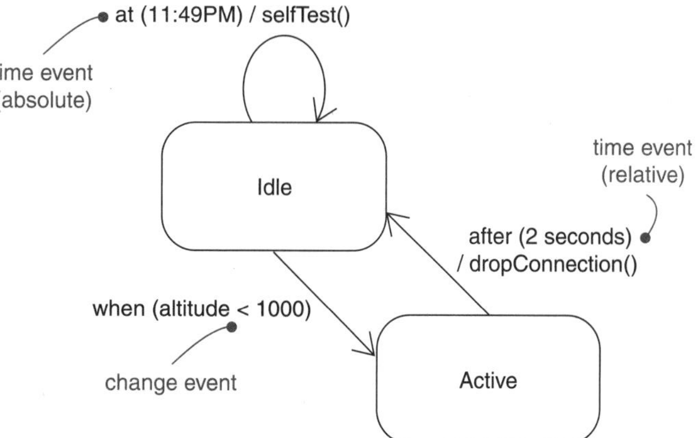

Figure 21-4: Time and Change Events

A change event occurs once when the value of the condition changes from false to true. It does not occur when the value of the condition changes from true to false. The event does not recur while the event remains true.

Note: Although a change event models a condition that is tested continuously, you can typically analyze the situation to see when to test the condition at discrete points in time.

Sending and Receiving Events

Processes and threads are discussed in Chapter 23.

Signal events and call events involve at least two objects: the object that sends the signal or invokes the operation and the object to which the event is directed. Because signals are asynchronous, and because asynchronous calls are themselves signals, the semantics of events interact with the semantics of active objects and passive objects.

Instances are discussed in Chapter 13.

Any instance of any class can send a signal to or invoke an operation of a receiving object. When an object sends a signal, the sender dispatches the signal and then continues along its flow of control, not waiting for any return from the receiver. For example, if an actor interacting with an ATM system sends the signal `pushButton`, the actor may continue along its way independent of the system to which the signal was sent. In contrast, when an object calls an operation, the sender dispatches the operation and then waits for the receiver to reply. For example, in a trading system, an instance of the class `Trader` might invoke the operation `confirmTransaction` on some instance of the class `Trade`, thereby affecting the state of the `Trade` object. If this is a synchronous call, the `Trader` object will wait until the operation is finished.

Note: In some situations, you may want to show one object sending a signal to a set of objects (multicasting) or to any object in the system that might be listening (broadcasting). To model multicasting, you'd show an object sending a signal to a collection containing a set of receivers. To model broadcasting, you'd show an object sending a signal to another object that represents the system as a whole.

State machines are discussed in Chapter 22; active objects are discussed in Chapter 23.

Any instance of any class can receive a call event or a signal. If this is a synchronous call event, then the sender and the receiver are in a rendezvous for the duration of the operation. This means that the flow of control of the sender suspends until the execution of the operation completes. If this is a signal, then the sender and receiver do not rendezvous: The sender dispatches the signal but does not wait for a response from the receiver. In either case, this event may be lost (if no response to the event is specified), it may trigger the receiver's state machine (if there is one), or it may just invoke a normal method call.

Note: A call may be asynchronous. In this case, the caller continues immediately after issuing the call. The transmission of the message to the receiver and its execution by the receiver occur concurrently with the subsequent execution of the caller. When the execution of the method is complete, it just ends. If the method attempts to return values, they are ignored.

Operations are discussed in Chapter 4; extra class compartments are discussed in Chapter 4.

In the UML, you model the call events that an object may receive as operations on the class of the object. In the UML, you model the named signals that an object may receive by naming them in an extra compartment of the class, as shown in Figure 21-5.

Interfaces are discussed in Chapter 11; asynchronous operations are discussed in Chapter 23.

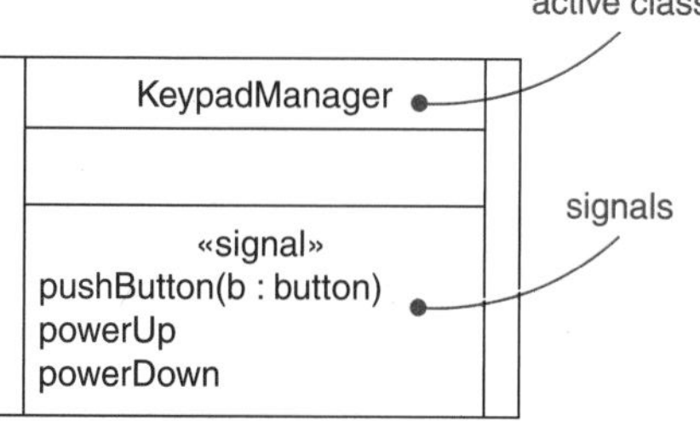

Figure 21-5: Signals and Active Classes

Note: You can also attach named signals to an interface in this same manner. In either case, the signals you list in this extra compartment are not the declarations of a signal, but only the use of a signal.

Common Modeling Techniques

Modeling a Family of Signals

Generalization is discussed in Chapters 5 and 10.

In most event-driven systems, signal events are hierarchical. For example, an autonomous robot might distinguish between external signals, such as a `Collision`, and internal ones, such as a `HardwareFault`. External and internal signals need not be disjoint, however. Even within these two broad classifications, you might find specializations. For example, `HardwareFault` signals might be further specialized as `BatteryFault` and `MovementFault`. Even these might be further specialized, such as `MotorStall`, a kind of `MovementFault`.

State machines are discussed in Chapter 22.

By modeling hierarchies of signals in this manner, you can specify polymorphic events. For example, consider a state machine with a transition triggered only by the receipt of a `MotorStall`. As a leaf signal in this hierarchy, the transition can be triggered only by that signal, so it is not polymorphic. In contrast, suppose you modeled the state machine with a transition triggered by the receipt of a `HardwareFault`. In this case, the transition is polymorphic and can be triggered by a `HardwareFault` or any of its specializations, including `BatteryFault`, `MovementFault`, and `MotorStall`.

To model a family of signals,

- Consider all the different kinds of signals to which a given set of active objects may respond.
- Look for the common kinds of signals and place them in a generalization/specialization hierarchy using inheritance. Elevate more general ones and lower more specialized ones.
- Look for the opportunity for polymorphism in the state machines of these active objects. Where you find polymorphism, adjust the hierarchy as necessary by introducing intermediate abstract signals.

Abstract classes are discussed in Chapters 5 and 9.

Figure 21-6 models a family of signals that may be handled by an autonomous robot. Note that the root signal (`RobotSignal`) is abstract, which means that there may be no direct instances. This signal has two immediate concrete specializations (`Collision` and `HardwareFault`), one of which (`HardwareFault`) is further specialized. Note that the `Collision` signal has one parameter.

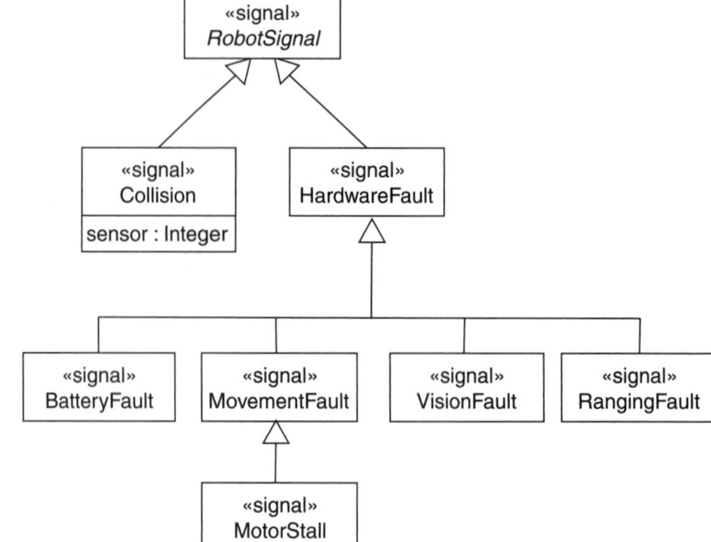

Figure 21-6: Modeling Families of Signals

Modeling Abnormal Occurrences

Classes are discussed in Chapters 4 and 9; interfaces are discussed in Chapter 11; stereotypes are discussed in Chapter 6.

An important part of visualizing, specifying, and documenting the behavior of a class or an interface is specifying the abnormal occurrences that its operations can produce. If you are handed a class or an interface, the operations you can invoke will be clear, but the abnormal occurrences that each operation may raise will not be clear unless you model them explicitly.

In the UML, abnormal occurrences are just additional kinds of events that can be modeled as signals. Error events may be attached to specification operations. Modeling exceptions is somewhat the inverse of modeling a general family of signals. You model a family of signals primarily to specify the kinds of signals an active object may receive; you model abnormal occurrences primarily to specify the kinds of abnormal occurrences that an object may produce.

To model abnormal occurrences

- For each class and interface, and for each operation of such elements, consider the normal things that happen. Then think of things that can go wrong and model them as signals among objects.
- Arrange the signals in a hierarchy. Elevate general ones, lower specialized ones, and introduce intermediate exceptions as necessary.
- For each operation, specify the abnormal occurrence signals that it may raise. You can do so explicitly (by showing `send` dependencies from an operation to its signals) or you can use sequence diagrams illustrating various scenarios.

Template classes are discussed in Chapter 9.

Figure 21-7 models a hierarchy of abnormal occurrences that may be produced by a standard library of container classes, such as the template class `Set`. This hierarchy is headed by the abstract signal `Error` and includes three specialized kinds of errors: `Duplicate`, `Overflow`, and `Underflow`. As shown, the `add` operation may produce `Duplicate` and `Overflow` signals, and the `remove` operation produces only the `Underflow` signal. Alternatively, you could have put these dependencies in the background by naming them in each operation's specification. Either way, by knowing which signals each operation may send, you can create clients that use the `Set` class correctly.

Note: Signals, including abnormal occurrence signals, are asynchronous events between objects. UML also includes exceptions such as those found in Ada or C++. Exceptions are conditions that cause the mainline execution path to be abandoned and a secondary execution path executed instead. Exceptions are not signals; instead, they are a convenient mechanism for specifying an alternate flow of control within a single synchronous thread of execution.

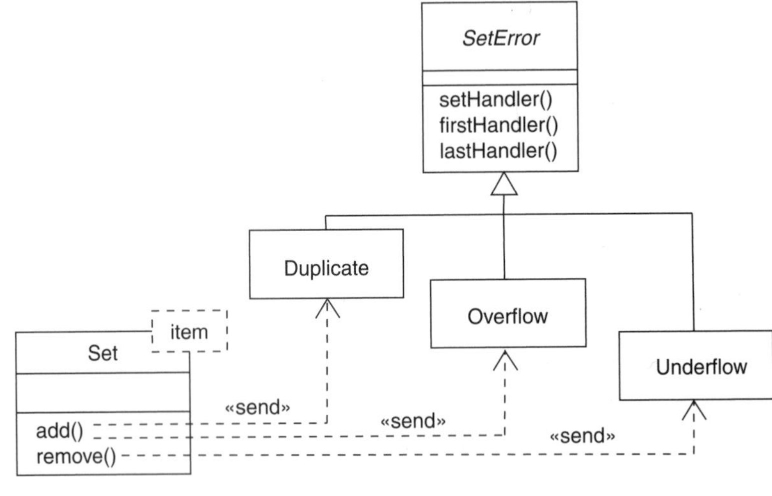

Figure 21-7: Modeling Error Conditions

Hints and Tips

When you model an event,

- Build hierarchies of signals so that you exploit the common properties of related signals.
- Be sure you have a suitable state machine behind each element that may receive the event.
- Be sure to model not only those elements that may receive events, but also those elements that may send them.

When you draw an event in the UML,

- In general, model hierarchies of events explicitly, but model their use in the backplane of each class that sends or receives such an event.

Chapter 22
STATE MACHINES

In this chapter

- States, transitions, and activities
- Modeling the lifetime of an object
- Creating well-structured algorithms

Interactions are discussed in Chapter 16; objects are discussed in Chapter 13.

Using an interaction, you can model the behavior of a society of objects that work together. Using a state machine, you can model the behavior of an individual object. A state machine is a behavior that specifies the sequences of states an object goes through during its lifetime in response to events, together with its responses to those events.

Classes are discussed in Chapters 4 and 9; use cases are discussed in Chapter 17; systems are discussed in Chapter 32; activity diagrams are discussed in Chapter 20; state diagrams are discussed in Chapter 25.

You use state machines to model the dynamic aspects of a system. For the most part, this involves specifying the lifetime of the instances of a class, a use case, or an entire system. These instances may respond to such events as signals, operations, or the passing of time. When an event occurs, some effect will take place, depending on the current state of the object. An *effect* is the specification of a behavior execution within a state machine. Effects ultimately resolve into in the execution of actions that change the state of an object or return values. A *state* of an object is a period of time during which it satisfies some condition, performs some activity, or waits for some event.

You can visualize the dynamics of execution in two ways: by emphasizing the flow of control from activity to activity (using activity diagrams) or by emphasizing the potential states of the objects and the transitions among those states (using state diagrams).

Well-structured state machines are like well-structured algorithms: They are efficient, simple, adaptable, and understandable.

Getting Started

Consider the life of your home's thermostat on one crisp fall day. In the wee hours of the morning, things are pretty quiet for the humble thermostat. The temperature of the house is stable and, save for a rogue gust of wind or a passing storm, the temperature outside the house is stable, too. Toward dawn, however, things get more interesting. The sun starts to peek over the horizon, raising the ambient temperature slightly. Family members start to wake; someone might tumble out of bed and twist the thermostat's dial. Both of these events are significant to the home's heating and cooling system. The thermostat starts behaving like all good thermostats should, by commanding the home's heater to raise the inside temperature or the air conditioner to lower the inside temperature.

Once everyone has left for work or school, things get quiet, and the temperature of the house stabilizes once again. However, an automatic program might then cut in, commanding the thermostat to lower the temperature to save on electricity and gas. The thermostat goes back to work. Later in the day, the program comes alive again, this time commanding the thermostat to raise the temperature so that the family can come home to a cozy house.

In the evening, with the home filled with warm bodies and heat from cooking, the thermostat has a lot of work to do to keep the temperature even while it runs the heater and cooler efficiently. Finally, at night, things return to a quiet state.

A number of software-intensive systems behave just like that thermostat. A pacemaker runs continuously but adapts to changes in activity or heartbeat pattern. A network router runs continuously as well, silently guiding asynchronous streams of bits, sometimes adapting its behavior in response to commands from the network administrator. A cell phone works on demand, responding to input from the user and to messages from the local cells.

Modeling the structural aspects of a system is discussed in Parts 2 and 3.

In the UML, you model the static aspects of a system by using such elements as class diagrams and object diagrams. These diagrams let you visualize, specify, construct, and document the things that live in your system, including classes, interfaces, components, nodes, and use cases and their instances, together with the way those things sit in relationship to one another.

You can also model the dynamic aspects of a system by using interactions, as discussed in Chapter 16; events are discussed in Chapter 21.

In the UML, you model the dynamic aspects of a system by using state machines. Whereas an interaction models a society of objects that work together to carry out some action, a state machine models the lifetime of a single object, whether it is an instance of a class, a use case, or even an entire system. In the life of an object, it may be exposed to a variety of events, such as a signal, the invocation of an operation, the creation or destruction of the object, the passing of time, or the change in some condition. In response to these events, the object performs some action, which is a computation, and then it changes its state to a new value. The behavior of such an object is therefore affected by the past, at least as the past is reflected in the current state. An object may receive an event, respond with an action, then change its state. An object may receive another event and its response may be different, depending on its current state in response to the previous event.

Activity diagrams are discussed in Chapter 20; state diagrams are discussed in Chapter 25.

You use state machines to model the behavior of any modeling element, most commonly a class, a use case, or an entire system. State machines may be visualized using state diagrams. You can focus on the event-ordered behavior of an object, which is especially useful in modeling reactive systems.

The UML provides a graphical representation of states, transitions, events, and effects, as Figure 22-1 shows. This notation permits you to visualize the behavior of an object in a way that lets you emphasize the important elements in the life of that object.

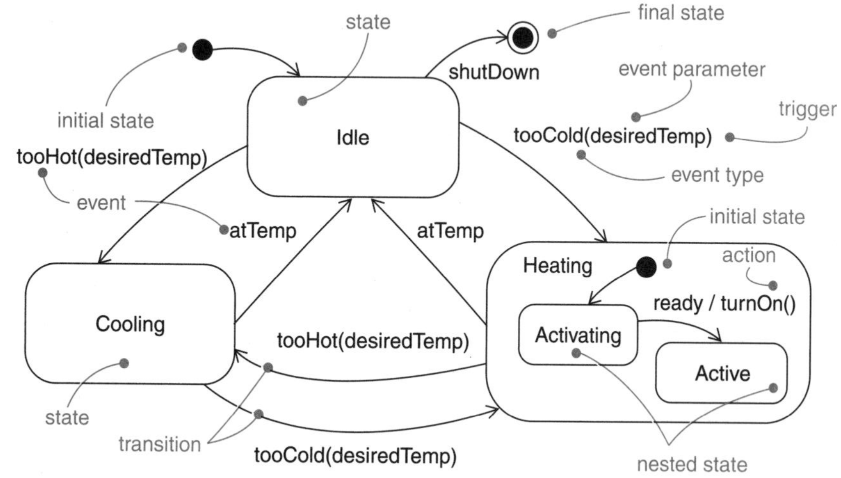

Figure 22-1: State Machines

Terms and Concepts

A *state machine* is a behavior that specifies the sequences of states an object goes through during its lifetime in response to events, together with its responses to those events. A *state* is a condition or situation during the life of an object during which it satisfies some condition, performs some activity, or waits for events. An *event* is the specification of a significant occurrence that has a location in time and space. In the context of state machines, an event is an occurrence of a stimulus that can trigger a state transition. A *transition* is a relationship between two states indicating that an object in the first state will perform certain actions and enter the second state when a specified event occurs and specified conditions are satisfied. An *activity* is ongoing nonatomic execution within a state machine. An *action* is an executable computation that results in a change in state of the model or the return of a value. Graphically, a state is rendered as a rectangle with rounded corners. A transition is rendered as a solid directed line or path from the original state to the new state.

Context

Objects are discussed in Chapter 13; messages are discussed in Chapter 16.

Every object has a lifetime. On creation, an object is born; on destruction, an object ceases to exist. In between, an object may act on other objects (by sending them messages) as well as be acted on (by being the target of a message). In many cases, these messages will be simple, synchronous operation calls. For example, an instance of the class `Customer` might invoke the operation `getAccountBalance` on an instance of the class `BankAccount`. Objects such as these don't need a state machine to specify their behavior because their current behavior does not depend on their past.

Signals are discussed in Chapter 21.

In other kinds of systems, you'll encounter objects that must respond to signals, which are asynchronous messages communicated between instances. For example, a cellular phone must respond to random phone calls (from other phones), keypad events (from the customer initiating a phone call), and to events from the network (when the phone moves from one call to another). Similarly, you'll encounter objects whose current behavior depends on their past behavior. For example, the behavior of an air-to-air missile guidance system will depend on its current state, such as `NotFlying` (it's not a good idea to launch a missile while it's attached to an aircraft that's still sitting on the ground) or `Searching` (you shouldn't arm the missile until you have a good idea what it's going to hit).

Active objects are discussed in Chapter 23; modeling reactive systems is discussed in Chapter 25; use cases and actors are discussed in Chapter 17; interactions are discussed in Chapter 16; interfaces are discussed in Chapter 11.

The behavior of an object that must respond to asynchronous messages or whose current behavior depends on its past is best specified by using a state machine. This encompasses instances of classes that can receive signals, including many active objects. In fact, an object that receives a signal but has no transition for that signal in its current state and does not defer the signal in that state will simply ignore that signal. In other words, the absence of a transition for a signal is not an error; it means that the signal is not of interest at that point. You'll also use state machines to model the behavior of entire systems, especially reactive systems, which must respond to signals from actors outside the system.

Note: Most of the time, you'll use interactions to model the behavior of a use case, but you can also use state machines for the same purpose. Similarly, you can use state machines to model the behavior of an interface. Although an interface may not have any direct instances, a class that realizes such an interface may. Such a class must conform to the behavior specified by the state machine of this interface.

States

A state is a condition or situation during the life of an object during which it satisfies some condition, performs some activity, or waits for some event. An object remains in a state for a finite amount of time. For example, a `Heater` in a home might be in any of four states: `Idle` (waiting for a command to start heating the house), `Activating` (its gas is on, but it's waiting to come up to temperature), `Active` (its gas and blower are both on), and `ShuttingDown` (its gas is off but its blower is on, flushing residual heat from the system).

You can visualize the state of an object in an interaction, as discussed in Chapter 13; the last four parts of a state are discussed in later sections of this chapter.

When an object's state machine is in a given state, the object is said to be in that state. For example, an instance of `Heater` might be `Idle` or perhaps `ShuttingDown`.

A state has several parts:

1. Name — A textual string that distinguishes the state from other states; a state may be anonymous, meaning that it has no name
2. Entry/exit effects — Actions executed on entering and exiting the state, respectively
3. Internal transitions — Transitions that are handled without causing a change in state

4. Substates	The nested structure of a state, involving nonorthogonal (sequentially active) or orthogonal (concurrently active) substates
5. Deferred events	A list of events that are not handled in that state but, rather, are postponed and queued for handling by the object in another state

Note: A state name may be text consisting of any number of letters, numbers, and certain punctuation marks (except for marks such as the colon) and may continue over several lines. In practice, state names are short nouns or noun phrases drawn from the vocabulary of the system you are modeling. Typically, you capitalize the first letter of every word in a state name, as in `Idle` or `ShuttingDown`.

As Figure 22-2 shows, you represent a state as a rectangle with rounded corners.

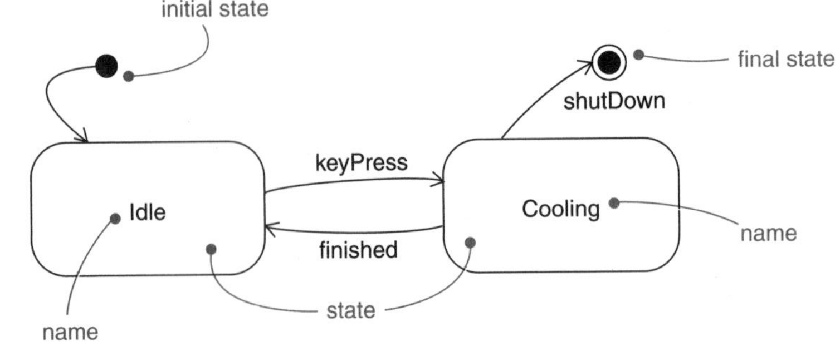

Figure 22-2: States

Initial and Final States As the figure shows, there are two special states that may be defined for an object's state machine. First, there's the initial state, which indicates the default starting place for the state machine or substate. An initial state is represented as a filled black circle. Second, there's the final state, which indicates that the execution of the state machine or the enclosing state has been completed. A final state is represented as a filled black circle surrounded by an unfilled circle (a bull's eye).

Note: Initial and final states are really pseudostates. Neither may have the usual parts of a normal state, except for a name. A transition from an initial state to an ordinary state may have the full complement of features, including a guard condition and action (but not a trigger event).

Transitions

A transition is a relationship between two states indicating that an object in the first state will perform certain actions and enter the second state when a specified event occurs and specified conditions are satisfied. On such a change of state, the transition is said to fire. Until the transition fires, the object is said to be in the source state; after it fires, it is said to be in the target state. For example, a `Heater` might transition from the `Idle` to the `Activating` state when an event such as `tooCold` (with the parameter `desiredTemp`) occurs.

Events are discussed in Chapter 21.

A transition has five parts.

1. Source state — The state affected by the transition; if an object is in the source state, an outgoing transition may fire when the object receives the trigger event of the transition and if the guard condition, if any, is satisfied
2. Event trigger — The event whose recognition by the object in the source state makes the transition eligible to fire, providing its guard condition is satisfied
3. Guard condition — A Boolean expression that is evaluated when the transition is triggered by the reception of the event trigger; if the expression evaluates true, the transition is eligible to fire; if the expression evaluates false, the transition does not fire, and if there is no other transition that could be triggered by that same event, the event is lost
4. Effect — An executable behavior, such as an action, that may act on the object that owns the state machine and indirectly on other objects that are visible to the object
5. Target state — The state that is active after the completion of the transition

As Figure 22-3 shows, a transition is rendered as a solid directed line from the source to the target state. A self-transition is a transition whose source and target states are the same.

Note: A transition may have multiple sources (in which case, it represents a join from multiple concurrent states) as well as multiple targets (in which case, it represents a fork to multiple concurrent states). See later discussion under orthogonal substates.

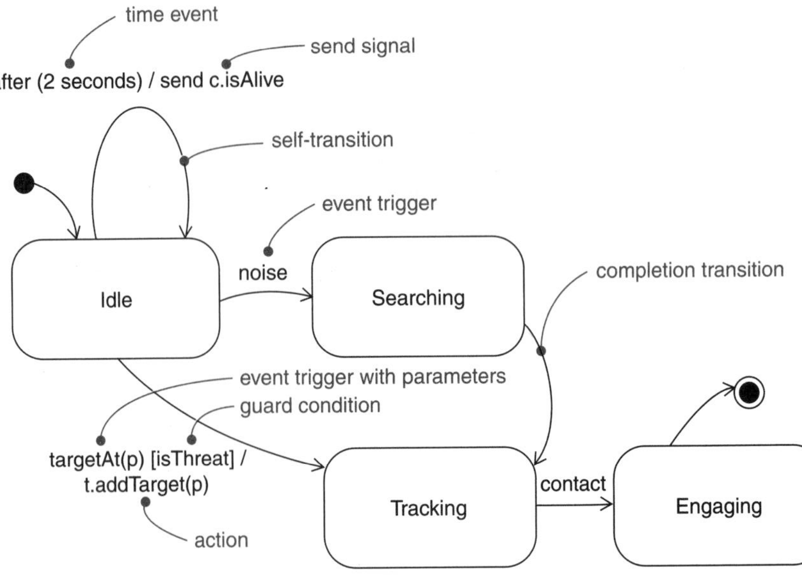

Figure 22-3: Transitions

Events are discussed in Chapter 21.

Event Trigger An event is the specification of a significant occurrence that has a location in time and space. In the context of state machines, an event is an occurrence of a stimulus that can trigger a state transition. As shown in the previous figure, events may include signals, calls, the passing of time, or a change in state. A signal or a call may have parameters whose values are available to the transition, including expressions for the guard condition and action.

Specifying a family of signals is discussed in Chapter 21; multiple, nonoverlapping guard conditions form a branch, as discussed in Chapter 20.

It is also possible to have a completion transition, represented by a transition with no event trigger. A completion transition is triggered implicitly when its source state has completed its behavior, if any.

Note: An event trigger may be polymorphic. For example, if you've specified a family of signals, then a transition whose trigger event is `S` can be triggered by `S`, as well as by any children of `S`.

Guard Condition As the previous figure shows, a guard condition is rendered as a Boolean expression enclosed in square brackets and placed after the trigger event. A guard condition is evaluated only after the trigger event for its transition occurs. Therefore, it's possible to have multiple transitions from the same source state and with the same event trigger, as long as those conditions don't overlap.

A guard condition is evaluated just once for each transition at the time the event occurs, but it may be evaluated again if the transition is retriggered. Within the Boolean expression, you can include conditions about the state of an object (for example, the expression `aHeater in Idle`, which evaluates true if the `Heater` object is currently in the `Idle` state). If the condition is not true when it is tested, the event does not occur later when the condition becomes true. Use a change event to model that kind of behavior.

Change events are discussed in Chapter 21.

Note: Although a guard condition is evaluated only once each time its transition triggers, a change event is potentially evaluated continuously.

Effect An effect is a behavior that is executed when a transition fires. Effects may include inline computation, operation calls (to the object that owns the state machine as well as to other visible objects), the creation or destruction of another object, or the sending of a signal to an object. To indicate sending a signal you can prefix the signal name with the keyword `send` as a visual cue.

Activities are discussed in a later section of this chapter; dependencies are discussed in Chapters 5 and 10.

Transitions only occur when the state machine is quiescent, that is, when it is not executing an effect from a previous transition. The execution of the effect of a transition and any associated entry and exit effects run to completion before any additional events are allowed to cause additional transitions. This is in contrast to a do-activity (described later in this chapter), which may be interrupted by events.

Note: You can explicitly show the object to which a signal is sent by using a dependency stereotyped as `send`, whose source is the state and whose target is the object.

Advanced States and Transitions

You can model a wide variety of behavior using only the basic features of states and transitions in the UML. Using these features, you'll end up with flat state machines, which means that your behavioral models will consist of nothing more than arcs (transitions) and vertices (states).

UML state machines have a number of features that help you to manage complex behavioral models. These features often reduce the number of states and transitions you'll need, and they codify a number of common and somewhat complex idioms you'd otherwise encounter using flat state machines. Some of these advanced features include entry and exit effects, internal transitions, do-activities, and deferred events. These features are shown as text strings within a text compartment of the state symbol, as shown in Figure 22-4.

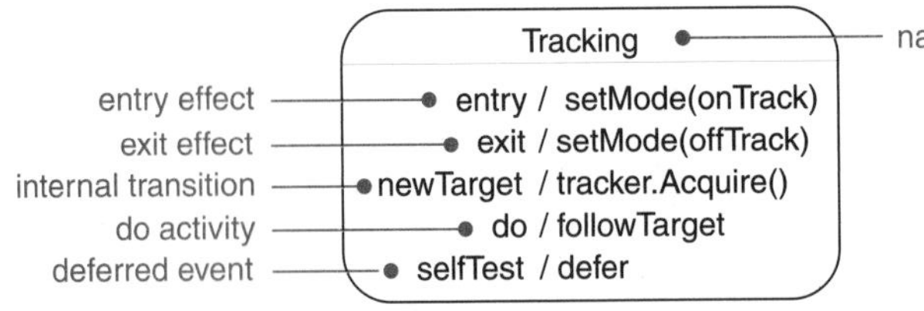

Figure 22-4: Advanced States and Transitions

Entry and Exit Effects In a number of modeling situations, you'll want to perform some setup action whenever you enter a state, no matter which transition led you there. Similarly, when you leave a state, you'll want to perform some cleanup action no matter which transition led you away. For example, in a missile guidance system, you might want to explicitly announce the system is `onTrack` whenever it's in the `Tracking` state, and `offTrack` whenever it's out of the state. Using flat state machines, you can achieve this effect by putting those actions on every entering and exiting transition, as appropriate. However, that's somewhat error prone; you have to remember to add these actions every time you add a new transition. Furthermore, modifying this action means that you have to touch every neighboring transition.

As Figure 22-4 shows, the UML provides a shorthand for this idiom. In the symbol for the state, you can include an entry effect (marked by the keyword `entry`) and an exit effect (marked by the keyword `exit`), each with its appropriate action. Whenever you enter the state, its entry action is dispatched; whenever you leave the state, its exit action is dispatched.

Entry and exit effects may not have arguments or guard conditions, but the entry effect at the top level of a state machine for a class may have parameters for the arguments that the machine receives when the object is created.

Internal Transitions Once inside a state, you'll encounter events you'll want to handle without leaving the state. These are called internal transitions, and they are subtly different from self-transitions. In a self-transition, such as you see in Figure 21-3, an event triggers the transition, you leave the state, an action (if any) is performed, and then you reenter the same state. Because this transition exits and then enters the state, a self-transition executes the state's exit action, then it executes the action of the self-transition, and finally, it executes the state's entry action.

However, suppose you want to handle the event but don't want to execute the state's entry and exit actions. The UML provides a shorthand for this idiom using an internal transition. An *internal transition* is a transition that responds to an event by performing an effect but does not change state. In Figure 21-4, the event `newTarget` labels an internal transition; if this event occurs while the object is in the `Tracking` state, action `tracker.acquire` is executed but the state remains the same, and no entry or exit actions are executed. You indicate an internal transition by including a transition string (including an event name, optional guard condition, and effect) inside the symbol for a state instead of on a transition arrow. Note that the keywords `entry`, `exit`, and `do` are reserved words that may not be used as event names. Whenever you are in the state and an event labeling an internal transition occurs, the corresponding effect is performed without leaving and then reentering the state. Therefore, the event is handled without invoking the state's exit and then entry actions.

Note: Internal transitions may have events with parameters and guard conditions.

Do-Activities When an object is in a state, it generally sits idle, waiting for an event to occur. Sometimes, however, you may wish to model an ongoing activity. While in a state, the object does some work that will continue until it is interrupted by an event. For example, if an object is in the `Tracking` state, it might `followTarget` as long as it is in that state. As Figure 21-4 shows, in the UML you use the special `do` transition to specify the work that's to be done inside a state after the entry action is dispatched. You can also specify a behavior, such as a sequence of actions—for example, do / op1(a); op2(b); op3(c). If the occurrence of an event causes a transition that forces an exit from the state, any ongoing do-activity of the state is immediately terminated.

Note: A do-activity is equivalent to an entry effect that starts the activity when the state is entered and an exit effect that stops the activity when the state is exited.

Events are discussed in Chapter 21.

Deferred Events Consider a state such as `Tracking`. As illustrated in Figure 21-3, suppose there's only one transition leading out of this state, triggered by the event `contact`. While in the state `Tracking`, any events other than `contact` and other than those handled by its substates will be lost. That means that the event may occur, but it will be ignored and no action will result because of the presence of that event.

In every modeling situation, you'll want to recognize some events and ignore others. You include those you want to recognize as the event triggers of transitions; those you want to ignore you just leave out. However, in some modeling situations, you'll want to accept some events but postpone a response to them until later. For example, while in the `Tracking` state, you may want to postpone a response to signals such as `selfTest`, perhaps sent by some maintenance agent in the system.

In the UML, you can specify this behavior by using deferred events. A deferred event is an event whose processing in the state is postponed until another state becomes active; if the event is not deferred in that state, the event is handled and may trigger transitions as if it had just occurred. If the state machine passes through a sequence of states in which the event is deferred, it is preserved until a state is finally encountered in which the event is not deferred. Other nondeferred events may occur during the interval. As you can see in Figure 21-4, you can specify a deferred event by listing the event with the special action `defer`. In this example, `selfTest` events may happen while in the `Tracking` state, but they are held until the object is in the `Engaging` state, at which time it appears as if they just occurred.

Note: The implementation of deferred events requires the presence of an internal queue of events. If an event happens but is listed as deferred, it is queued. Events are taken off this queue as soon as the object enters a state that does not defer these events.

Submachines A state machine may be referenced within another state machine. Such a referenced state machine is called a *submachine*. They are useful in building large state models in a structured manner. See the *UML Reference Manual* for details.

Substates

These advanced features of states and transitions solve a number of common state machine modeling problems. However, there's one more feature of the UML's state machines—substates—that does even more to help you simplify the modeling of complex behaviors. A substate is a state that's nested inside another one. For example, a `Heater` might be in the `Heating` state, but also while in the `Heating` state, there might be a nested state called `Activating`. In this case, it's proper to say that the object is both `Heating` and `Activating`.

Composite states have a nested structure similar to composition, as discussed in Chapters 5 and 10.

A simple state is a state that has no substructure. A state that has substates—that is, nested states—is called a composite state. A composite state may contain either concurrent (orthogonal) or sequential (nonorthogonal) substates. In the UML, you render a composite state just as you do a simple state, but with an optional graphic compartment that shows a nested state machine. Substates may be nested to any level.

Nonorthogonal Substates Consider the problem of modeling the behavior of an ATM. This system might be in one of three basic states: `Idle` (waiting for customer interaction), `Active` (handling a customer's transaction), and `Maintenance` (perhaps having its cash store replenished). While `Active`, the behavior of the ATM follows a simple path: Validate the customer, select a transaction, process the transaction, and then print a receipt. After printing, the ATM returns to the `Idle` state. You might represent these stages of behavior as the states `Validating`, `Selecting`, `Processing`, and `Printing`. It would even be desirable to let the customer select and process multiple transactions after `Validating` the account and before `Printing` a final receipt.

The problem here is that, at any stage in this behavior, the customer might decide to cancel the transaction, returning the ATM to its `Idle` state. Using flat state machines, you can achieve that effect, but it's quite messy. Because the customer might cancel the transaction at any point, you'd have to include a suitable transition from every state in the `Active` sequence. That's messy because it's easy to forget to include these transitions in all the right places, and many such interrupting events means you end up with a multitude of transitions zeroing in on the same target state from various sources, but with the same event trigger, guard condition, and action.

Using nested substates, there's a simpler way to model this problem, as Figure 22-5 shows. Here, the `Active` state has a substructure, containing the substates `Validating`, `Selecting`, `Processing`, and `Printing`. The state of the ATM changes from `Idle` to `Active` when the customer enters a credit card in the machine. On entering the `Active` state, the entry action `readCard` is performed. Starting with the initial state of the substructure, control passes to the `Validating` state, then to the `Selecting` state, and then to the `Processing` state. After `Processing`, control may return to `Selecting` (if the customer has selected another transaction) or it may move on to `Printing`. After `Printing`, there's a completion transition back to the `Idle` state. Notice that the `Active` state has an exit action, which ejects the customer's credit card.

Notice also the transition from the `Active` state to the `Idle` state, triggered by the event `cancel`. In any substate of `Active`, the customer might cancel

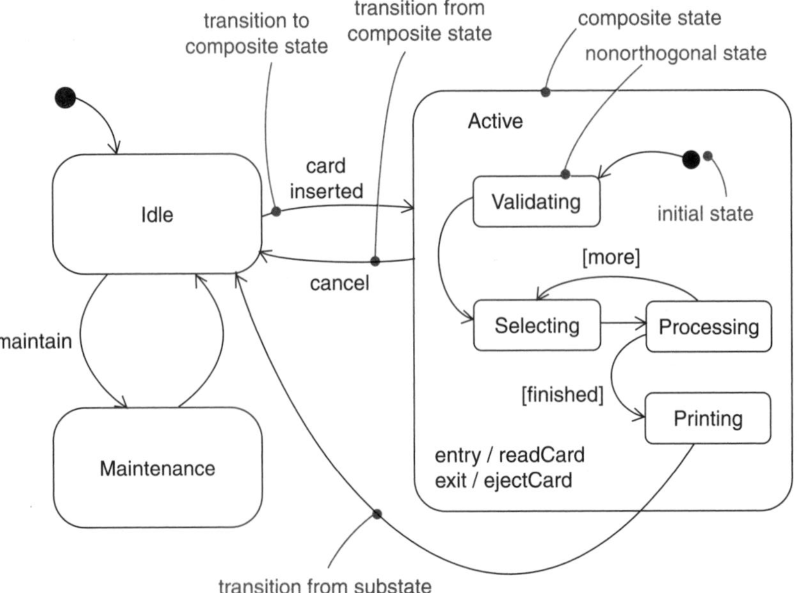

Figure 22-5: Sequential Substates

the transaction, and that returns the ATM to the `Idle` state (but only after ejecting the customer's credit card, which is the exit action dispatched on leaving the `Active` state, no matter what caused a transition out of that state). Without substates, you'd need a transition triggered by `cancel` on every substructure state.

Substates such as `Validating` and `Processing` are called nonorthogonal, or disjoint, substates. Given a set of nonorthogonal substates in the context of an enclosing composite state, the object is said to be in the composite state and in only one of those substates (or the final state) at a time. Therefore, nonorthogonal substates partition the state space of the composite state into disjoint states.

From a source outside an enclosing composite state, a transition may target the composite state or it may target a substate. If its target is the composite state, the nested state machine must include an initial state, to which control passes after entering the composite state and after performing its entry action, if any. If its target is the nested state, control passes to the nested state after performing the entry action (if any) of the composite state and then the entry action (if any) of the substate.

A transition leading out of a composite state may have as its source the composite state or a substate. In either case, control first leaves the nested state (and its exit action, if any, is executed), then it leaves the composite state (and its exit action, if any, is executed). A transition whose source is the composite state essentially cuts short (interrupts) the activity of the nested state machine. The completion transition of a composite state is taken when control reaches the final substate within the composite state.

Note: A nested nonorthogonal state machine may have at most one initial substate and one final substate.

History States A state machine describes the dynamic aspects of an object whose current behavior depends on its past. A state machine in effect specifies the legal ordering of states an object may go through during its lifetime.

Unless otherwise specified, when a transition enters a composite state, the action of the nested state machine starts over again at its initial state (unless, of course, the transition targets a substate directly). However, there are times you'd like to model an object so that it remembers the last substate that was active prior to leaving the composite state. For example, in modeling the behavior of an agent that does an unattended backup of computers across a network, you'd like it to remember where it was in the process if it ever gets interrupted by, for example, a query from the operator.

Using flat state machines, you can model this, but it's messy. For each sequential substate, you'd need to have its exit action post a value to some variable local to the composite state. Then the initial state to this composite state would need a transition to every substate with a guard condition, querying the variable. In this way, leaving the composite state would cause the last substate to be remembered; entering the composite state would transition to the proper substate. That's messy because it requires you to remember to touch every substate and to set an appropriate exit action. It leaves you with a multitude of transitions fanning out from the same initial state to different target substates with very similar (but different) guard conditions.

In the UML, a simpler way to model this idiom is by using history states. A history state allows a composite state that contains nonorthogonal substates to remember the last substate that was active in it prior to the transition from the composite state. As Figure 22-6 shows, you represent a shallow history state as a small circle containing the symbol `H`.

If you want a transition to activate the last substate, you show a transition from outside the composite state directly to the history state. The first time you enter a composite state, it has no history. This is the meaning of the single transition

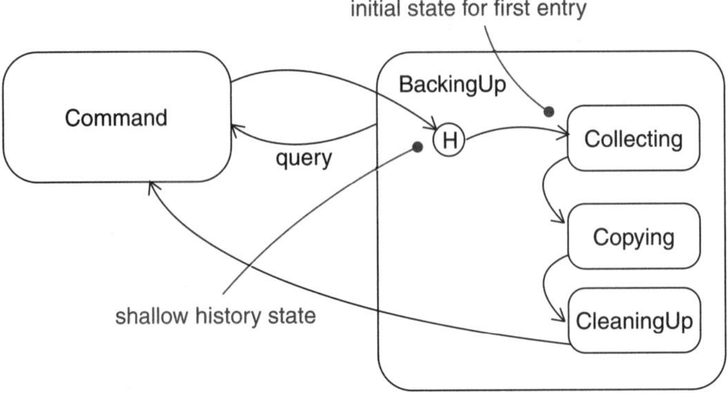

Figure 22-6: History State

from the history state to a sequential substate such as `Collecting`. The target of this transition specifies the initial state of the nested state machine the first time it is entered. Continuing, suppose that while in the `BackingUp` state and the `Copying` state, the `query` event is posted. Control leaves `Copying` and `BackingUp` (dispatching their exit actions as necessary) and returns to the `Command` state. When the action of `Command` completes, the completion transition returns to the history state of the composite state `BackingUp`. This time, because there is a history to the nested state machine, control passes back to the `Copying` state—thus bypassing the `Collecting` state—because `Copying` was the last substate active prior to the transition from the state `BackingUp`.

Note: The symbol `H` designates a shallow history, which remembers only the history of the immediate nested state machine. You can also specify deep history, shown as a small circle containing the symbol `H*`. Deep history remembers down to the innermost nested state at any depth. If you have only one level of nesting, shallow and deep history states are semantically equivalent. If you have more than one level of nesting, shallow history remembers only the outermost nested state; deep history remembers the innermost nested state at any depth.

In either case, if a nested state machine reaches a final state, it loses its stored history and behaves as if it had not yet been entered for the first time.

Orthogonal Substates Nonorthogonal substates are the most common kind of nested state machine you'll encounter. In certain modeling situations, however, you'll want to specify orthogonal regions. These regions let you specify two or more state machines that execute in parallel in the context of the enclosing object.

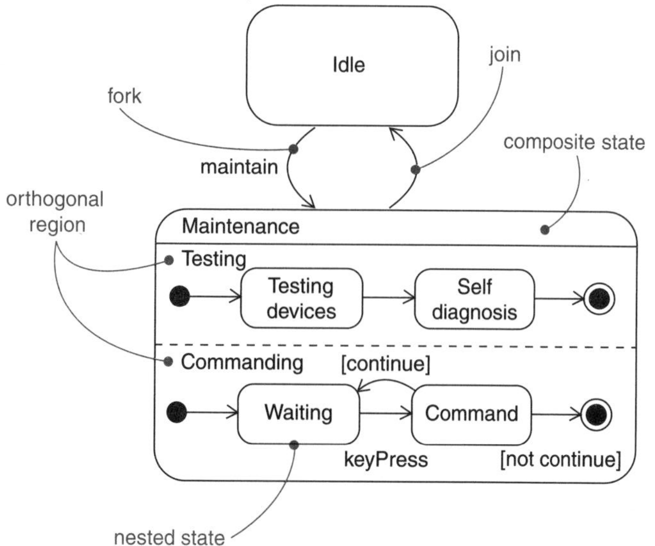

Figure 22-7: Concurrent Substates

For example, Figure 22-7 shows an expansion of the `Maintenance` state from Figure 21-5. `Maintenance` is decomposed into two orthogonal regions, `Testing` and `Commanding`, shown by nesting them in the `Maintenance` state but separating them from one another with a dashed line. Each of these orthogonal regions is further decomposed into substates. When control passes from the `Idle` to the `Maintenance` state, control then forks to two concurrent flows—the enclosing object will be in both the `Testing` region and the `Commanding` region. Furthermore, while in the `Commanding` region, the enclosing object will be in the `Waiting` or the `Command` state.

Note: This is what distinguishes nonorthogonal substates and orthogonal substates. Given two or more nonorthogonal substates at the same level, an object will be in one of those substates or the other. Given two or more orthogonal regions at the same level, an object will be in a state from each of the orthogonal regions.

Execution of these two orthogonal regions continues in parallel. Eventually, each nested state machine reaches its final state. If one orthogonal region reaches its final state before the other, control in that region waits at its final state. When both nested state machines reach their final states, control from the two orthogonal regions joins back into one flow.

Whenever there's a transition to a composite state decomposed into orthogonal regions, control forks into as many concurrent flows as there are orthogonal regions. Similarly, whenever there's a transition from a composite substate decomposed into orthogonal regions, control joins back into one flow. This holds true in all cases. If all orthogonal regions reach their final states, or if there is an explicit transition out of the enclosing composite state, control joins back into one flow.

Note: Each orthogonal region may have an initial, final, and history state.

Fork and Join Usually, entry to a composite state with orthogonal regions goes to the initial state of each orthogonal region. It is also possible to transition from an external state directly to one or more orthogonal states. This is called a fork, because control passes from a single state to several orthogonal states. It is shown as a heavy black line with one incoming arrow and several outgoing arrows, each to one of the orthogonal states. There must be at most one target state in each orthogonal region. If one or more orthogonal regions have no target states, then the initial state of those regions is implicitly chosen. A transition to a single orthogonal state within a composite state is also an implicit fork; the initial states of all the other orthogonal regions are implicitly part of the fork.

Similarly, a transition from any state within a composite state with orthogonal regions forces an exit from all the orthogonal regions. Such a transition often represents an error condition that forces termination of parallel computations.

A join is a transition with two or more incoming arrows and one outgoing arrow. Each incoming arrow must come from a state in a different orthogonal region of the same composite state. The join may have a trigger event. The join transition is effective only if all of the source states are active; the status of other orthogonal regions in the composite state is irrelevant. If the event occurs, control leaves all of the orthogonal regions in the composite state, not just the ones with arrows from them.

Figure 22-8 shows a variation on the previous example with explicit fork and join transitions. The transition `maintain` to the composite state `Maintenance` is still an implicit fork into the default initial states of the orthogonal regions. In this example, however, there is also an explicit fork from `Idle` into the two nested states `Self diagnose` and the final state of the `Commanding` region. (A final state is a real state and can be the target of a transition.) If an error event occurs while the `Self diagnose` state is active, the implicit join transition to `Repair` fires: Both the `Self diagnose` state and whatever state is active in the `Commanding` region are exited. There is also an

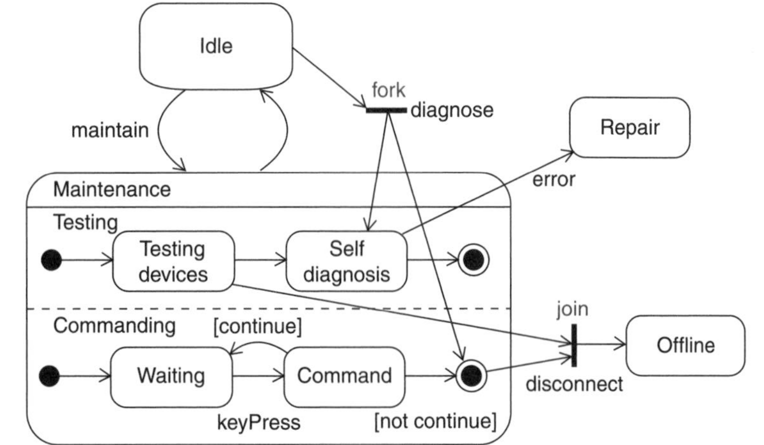

Figure 22-8: Fork and join transitions

explicit join transition to the `Offline` state. This transition fires only if the `disconnect` event occurs while the `Testing devices` state and the final state of the `Commanding` region are both active; if both states are not active, the event has no effect.

Active objects are discussed in Chapter 23.

Active Objects Another way to model concurrency is by using active objects. Thus, rather than partitioning one object's state machine into two (or more) concurrent regions, you could define two active objects, each of which is responsible for the behavior of one of the concurrent regions. If the behavior of one of these concurrent flows is affected by the state of the other, you'll want to model this using orthogonal regions. If the behavior of one of these concurrent flows is affected by messages sent to and from the other, you'll want to model this using active objects. If there's little or no communication between the concurrent flows, then the approach you choose is a matter of taste, although most of the time, using active objects makes your design decisions more obvious.

Common Modeling Techniques

Modeling the Lifetime of an Object

The most common purpose for which you'll use state machines is to model the lifetime of an object, especially instances of classes, use cases, and the system as a whole. Whereas interactions model the behavior of a society of objects working together, a state machine models the behavior of a single object over its lifetime, such as you'll find with user interfaces, controllers, and devices.

When you model the lifetime of an object, you essentially specify three things: the events to which the object can respond, the response to those events, and the impact of the past on current behavior. Modeling the lifetime of an object also involves deciding on the order in which the object can meaningfully respond to events, starting at the time of the object's creation and continuing until its destruction.

Objects are discussed in Chapter 13; classes are discussed in Chapters 4 and 9; use cases are discussed in Chapter 17; systems are discussed in Chapter 32; interactions are discussed in Chapter 16; collaborations are discussed in Chapter 28; pre- and post-conditions are discussed in Chapter 10; interfaces are discussed in Chapter 11.

To model the lifetime of an object,

- Set the context for the state machine, whether it is a class, a use case, or the system as a whole.
  - If the context is a class or a use case, find the neighboring classes, including any parents of the class and any classes reachable by associations or dependences. These neighbors are candidate targets for actions and are candidates for including in guard conditions.
  - If the context is the system as a whole, narrow your focus to one behavior of the system. Theoretically, every object in the system may be a participant in a model of the system's lifetime, and except for the most trivial systems, a complete model would be intractable.
- Establish the initial and final states for the object. To guide the rest of your model, possibly state the pre- and postconditions of the initial and final states, respectively.
- Decide on the events to which this object may respond. If already specified, you'll find these in the object's interfaces; if not already specified, you'll have to consider which objects may interact with the object in your context, and then which events they may possibly dispatch.
- Starting from the initial state to the final state, lay out the top-level states the object may be in. Connect these states with transitions triggered by the appropriate events. Continue by adding actions to these transitions.
- Identify any entry or exit actions (especially if you find that the idiom they cover is used in the state machine).
- Expand these states as necessary by using substates.
- Check that all events mentioned in the state machine match events expected by the interface of the object. Similarly, check that all events expected by the interface of the object are handled by the state machine. Finally, look to places where you explicitly want to ignore events.
- Check that all actions mentioned in the state machine are sustained by the relationships, methods, and operations of the enclosing object.

- Trace through the state machine, either manually or by using tools, to check it against expected sequences of events and their responses. Be especially diligent in looking for unreachable states and states in which the machine may get stuck.
- After rearranging your state machine, check it against expected sequences again to ensure that you have not changed the object's semantics.

For example, Figure 22-9 shows the state machine for the controller in a home security system, which is responsible for monitoring various sensors around the perimeter of the house.

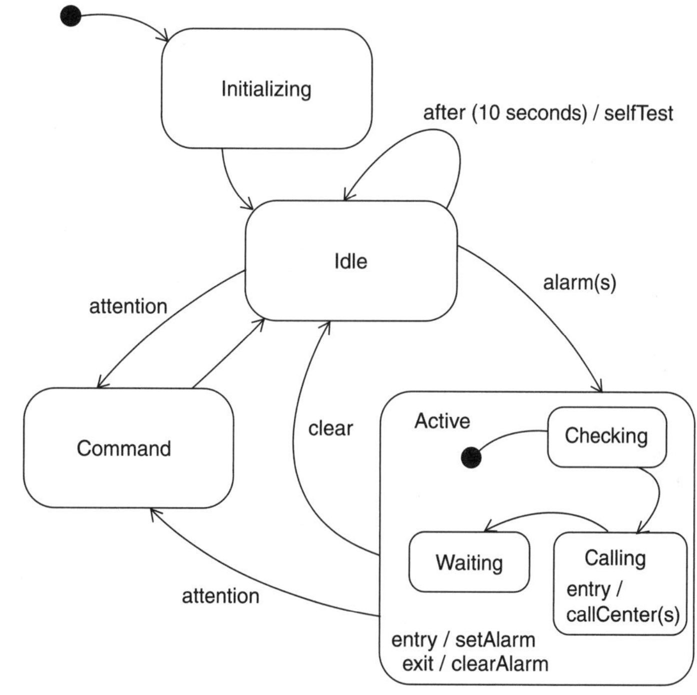

Figure 22-9: Modeling the Lifetime of An Object

In the lifetime of this controller class, there are four main states: `Initializing` (the controller is starting up), `Idle` (the controller is ready and waiting for alarms or commands from the user), `Command` (the controller is processing commands from the user), and `Active` (the controller is processing an alarm condition). When the controller object is first created, it moves first to the `Initializing` state and then unconditionally to the `Idle` state. The details of these two states are not shown, other than the self-transition with the time event in the `Idle` state. This kind of time event is commonly found in embedded systems, which often have a heartbeat timer that causes a periodic check of the system's health.

Control passes from the `Idle` state to the `Active` state on receipt of an `alarm` event (which includes the parameter `s`, identifying the sensor that was tripped). On entering the `Active` state, `setAlarm` is performed as the entry action, and control then passes first to the `Checking` state (validating the alarm), then to the `Calling` state (calling the alarm company to register the alarm), and finally to the `Waiting` state. The `Active` and `Waiting` states are exited only upon `clearing` the alarm or by the user signaling the controller for `attention`, presumably to issue a command.

Notice that there is no final state. That, too, is common in embedded systems, which are intended to run indefinitely.

Hints and Tips

When you model state machines in the UML, remember that every state machine represents the dynamic aspects of an individual object, typically representing an instance of a class, a use case, or the system as a whole. A well-structured state machine

- Is simple and therefore should not contain any superfluous states or transitions.
- Has a clear context and therefore may have access to all the objects visible to its enclosing object (these neighbors should be used only as necessary to carry out the behavior specified by the state machine).
- Is efficient and therefore should carry out its behavior with an optimal balance of time and resources as required by the actions it dispatches.
- Is understandable and therefore should name its states and transitions from the vocabulary of the system.
- Is not nested too deeply (nesting substates at one or two levels will handle most complex behaviors).
- Uses orthogonal regions sparingly because using active classes is often a better alternative.

Modeling the vocabulary of a system is discussed in Chapter 4.

When you draw a state machine in the UML,

- Avoid transitions that cross.
- Expand composite states in place only as necessary to make the diagram understandable.

Chapter 23

Processes and Threads

In this chapter

- Active objects, processes, and threads
- Modeling multiple flows of control
- Modeling interprocess communication
- Building thread-safe abstractions

Interaction views in the context of software architecture are discussed in Chapter 2.

Not only is the real world a harsh and unforgiving place, but it is a very busy place as well. Events happen and things take place all at the same time. Therefore, when you model a system of the real world, you must take into account its process view, which encompasses the threads and processes that form the system's concurrency and synchronization mechanisms.

In the UML, you model each independent flow of control as an active object that represents a process or thread that can initiate control activity. A process is a heavyweight flow that can execute concurrently with other processes; a thread is a lightweight flow that can execute concurrently with other threads within the same process.

Building abstractions so that they work safely in the presence of multiple flows of control is hard. In particular, you have to consider approaches to communication and synchronization that are more complex than for sequential systems. You also have to be careful to neither over-engineer your process view (too many concurrent flows and your system ends up thrashing) nor under-engineer it (insufficient concurrency does not optimize the system's throughput.

Getting Started

Modeling doghouses and high rises is discussed in Chapter 1.

In the life of a dog and his doghouse, the world is a pretty simple and sequential place. Eat. Sleep. Chase a cat. Eat some more. Dream about chasing cats. Using the doghouse to sleep in or for shelter from the rain is never a problem because the dog, and only the dog, needs to go in and out through the doghouse door. There's never any contention for resources.

In the life of a family and its house, the world is not so simple. Without getting too metaphysical, each family member lives his or her own life, yet still interacts with other members of the family (for dinner, watching television, playing games, cleaning). Family members will share certain resources. Children might share a bedroom; the whole family might share one phone or one computer. Family members will also share chores. Dad does the laundry and the grocery shopping; mom does the bills and the yard work; the children help with the cleaning and cooking. Contention among these shared resources and coordination among these independent chores can be challenging. Sharing one bathroom when everyone is getting ready to go to school or to work can be problematic; dinner won't be served if dad didn't first get the groceries.

In the life of a high rise and its tenants, the world is really complex. Hundreds, if not thousands, of people might work in the same building, each following his or her own agenda. All must pass through a limited set of entrances. All must jockey for the same bank of elevators. All must share the same heating, cooling, water, electrical, sanitation, and parking facilities. If they are to work together optimally, they have to communicate and synchronize their interactions properly.

Objects are discussed in Chapter 13.

In the UML, each independent flow of control is modeled as an active object. An active object is a process or thread that can initiate control activity. As for every kind of object, an active object is an instance of a class. In this case, an active object is an instance of an active class. Also, as for every kind of object, active objects can communicate with one another by passing messages, although here, message passing must be extended with certain concurrency semantics to help you to synchronize the interactions among independent flows.

In software, many programming languages directly support the concept of an active object. Java, Smalltalk, and Ada all have concurrency built in. C++ supports concurrency through various libraries that build on a host operating system's concurrency mechanisms. Using the UML to visualize, specify, construct, and document these abstractions is important because without doing so, it's nearly impossible to reason about issues of concurrency, communication, and synchronization.

Classes are discussed in Chapters 4 and 9; signals are discussed in Chapter 21.

The UML provides a graphical representation of an active class, as Figure 23-1 shows. Active classes are kinds of classes, so they have all the usual compartments for class name, attributes, and operations. Active classes often receive signals, which you typically enumerate in an extra compartment.

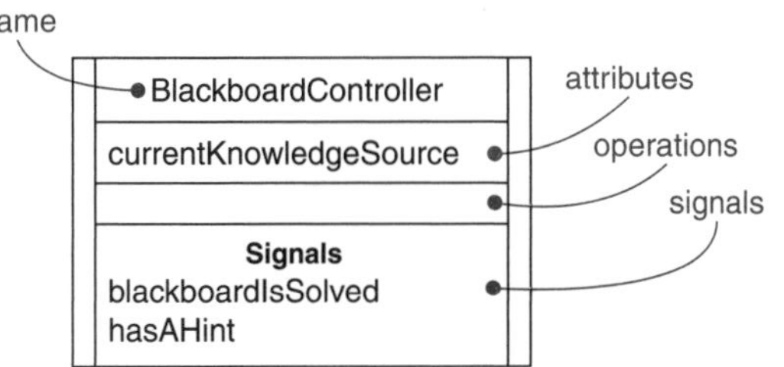

Figure 23-1: Active Class

Terms and Concepts

Interaction diagrams are discussed in Chapter 19.

An *active object* is an object that owns a process or thread and can initiate control activity. An *active class* is a class whose instances are active objects. A *process* is a heavyweight flow that can execute concurrently with other processes. A *thread* is a lightweight flow that can execute concurrently with other threads within the same process. Graphically, an active class is rendered as a rectangle with double lines for left and right sides. Processes and threads are rendered as stereotyped active classes (and also appear as sequences in interaction diagrams).

Flow of Control

Actors are discussed in Chapter 17.

In a purely sequential system, there is one flow of control. This means that one thing, and one thing only, can take place at a time. When a sequential program starts, control is rooted at the beginning of the program and operations are dispatched one after another. Even if there are concurrent things happening among the actors outside the system, a sequential program will process only one event at a time, queuing or discarding any concurrent external events.

Actions are discussed in Chapter 16.

This is why it's called a flow of control. If you trace the execution of a sequential program, you'll see the locus of execution flow from one statement to another, in sequential order. You might see actions that branch, loop, and jump about, and if there is any recursion or iteration, you see the flow circle back on itself. Nonetheless, in a sequential system, there would be a single flow of execution.

In a concurrent system, there is more than one flow of control—that is, more than one thing can take place at a time. In a concurrent system, there are multiple simultaneous flows of control, each rooted at the head of an independent process or a thread. If you take a snapshot of a concurrent system while it's running, you'll logically see multiple loci of execution.

Nodes are discussed in Chapter 27.

In the UML, you use an active class to represent a process or thread that is the root of an independent flow of control and that is concurrent with all peer flows of control.

Note: You can achieve true concurrency in one of three ways: first, by distributing active objects across multiple nodes; second, by placing active objects on nodes with multiple processors; and third, by a combination of both methods.

Classes and Events

Classes are discussed in Chapters 4 and 9.

Active classes are just classes, albeit ones with a very special property. An active class represents an independent flow of control, whereas a plain class embodies no such flow. In contrast to active classes, plain classes are implicitly called passive because they cannot independently initiate control activity.

Objects are discussed in Chapter 13; attributes and operations are discussed in Chapter 4; relationships are discussed in Chapters 4 and 10; extensibility mechanisms are discussed in Chapter 6; interfaces are discussed in Chapter 11.

You use active classes to model common families of processes or threads. In technical terms, this means that an active object—an instance of an active class—reifies (is a manifestation of) a process or thread. By modeling concurrent systems with active objects, you give a name to each independent flow of control. When an active object is created, the associated flow of control is started; when the active object is destroyed, the associated flow of control is terminated.

Active classes share the same properties as all other classes. Active classes may have instances. Active classes may have attributes and operations. Active classes may participate in dependency, generalization, and association (including aggregation) relationships. Active classes may use any of the UML's extensibility mechanisms, including stereotypes, tagged values, and constraints. Active classes may be the realization of interfaces. Active classes may be realized by collaborations, and the behavior of an active class may be specified by using state machines. Active classes may participate in collaborations.

State machines are discussed in Chapter 22; events are discussed in Chapter 21.

In your diagrams, active objects may appear wherever passive objects appear. You can model the collaboration of active and passive objects by using interaction diagrams (including sequence and collaboration diagrams). An active object may appear as the target of an event in a state machine.

Speaking of state machines, both passive and active objects may send and receive signal events and call events.

Note: The use of active classes is optional. They don't actually add much to the semantics.

Communication

Interactions are discussed in Chapter 16.

When objects collaborate with one another, they interact by passing messages from one to the other. In a system with both active and passive objects, there are four possible combinations of interaction that you must consider.

First, a message may be passed from one passive object to another. Assuming there is only one flow of control passing through these objects at a time, such an interaction is nothing more than the simple invocation of an operation.

Signal events and call events are discussed in Chapter 21.

Second, a message may be passed from one active object to another. When that happens, you have interprocess communication, and there are two possible styles of communication. First, one active object might synchronously call an operation of another. That kind of communication has rendezvous semantics, which means that the caller calls the operation; the caller waits for the receiver to accept the call; the operation is invoked; a method is chosen for execution based on the operation and the class of the receiver object; the method is executed; a return object (if any) is passed back to the caller; and then the two objects continue on their independent paths. For the duration of the call, the two flows of control are in lock step. Second, one active object might asynchronously send a signal or call an operation of another object. That kind of communication has mailbox semantics, which means that the caller sends the signal or calls the operation and then continues on its independent way. In the meantime, the receiver accepts the signal or call whenever it is ready (with intervening events or calls queued) and continues on its way after it is done. This is called a mailbox because the two objects are not synchronized; rather, one object drops off a message for the other.

In the UML, you render a synchronous message with a solid (filled) arrowhead and an asynchronous message as a stick arrowhead, as in Figure 23-2.

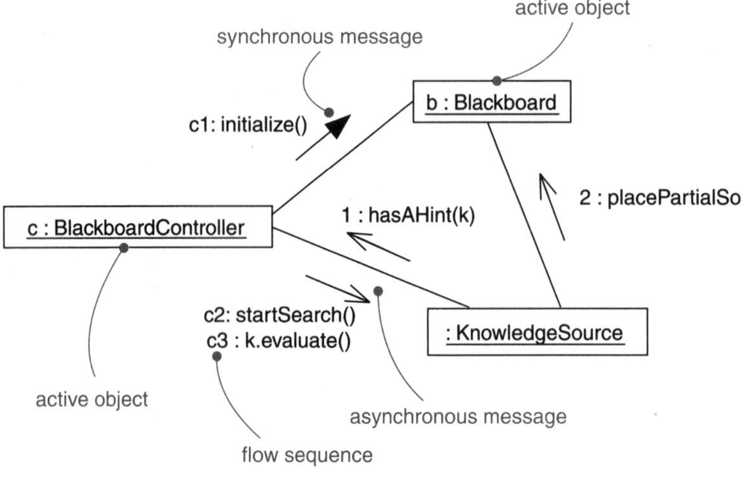

Figure 23-2: Communication

Third, a message may be passed from an active object to a passive object. A potential conflict arises if more than one active object at a time passes its flow of control through one passive object. It is an actual conflict if more than one object writes or reads and writes the same attributes. In that situation, you have to model the synchronization of these two flows very carefully, as discussed in the next section.

Constraints are discussed in Chapter 6.

Fourth, a message may be passed from a passive object to an active one. At first glance, this may seem illegal, but if you remember that every flow of control is rooted in some active object, you'll understand that a passive object passing a message to an active object has the same semantics as an active object passing a message to an active object.

Note: It is possible to model variations of synchronous and asynchronous message passing by using constraints. For example, to model a balking rendezvous as found in Ada, you'd use a synchronous message with a constraint such as `{wait = 0}`, saying that the caller will not wait for the receiver. Similarly, you can model a time out by using a constraint such as `{wait = 1 ms}`, saying that the caller will wait no more than one millisecond for the receiver to accept the message.

Synchronization

Visualize for a moment the multiple flows of control that weave through a concurrent system. When a flow passes through an operation, we say that at a given moment, the locus of control is in the operation. If that operation is defined for some class, we can also say that at a given moment, the locus of control is in a specific instance of that class. You can have multiple flows of control in one operation (and therefore in one object), and you can have different flows of control in different operations (but still result in multiple flows of control in the one object).

The problem arises when more than one flow of control is in one object at the same time. If you are not careful, more than one flow might modify the same attribute, corrupting the state of the object or losing information. This is the classical problem of mutual exclusion. A failure to deal with it properly yields all sorts of race conditions and interference that cause concurrent systems to fail in mysterious and unrepeatable ways.

The key to this problem is serialization of access to the critical object. There are three approaches, each of which involves attaching certain synchronization properties to the operations defined in a class. In the UML, you can model all three approaches.

1. Sequential — Callers must coordinate outside the object so that only one flow is in the object at a time. In the presence of multiple flows of control, the semantics and integrity of the object cannot be guaranteed.
2. Guarded — The semantics and integrity of the object are guaranteed in the presence of multiple flows of control by sequentializing all calls to all of the object's guarded operations. In effect, exactly one operation at a time can execute on the object, reducing this to sequential semantics. There is a danger of deadlock if care is not taken.
3. Concurrent — The semantics and integrity of the object are guaranteed in the presence of multiple flows of control because multiple flows of control access disjoint sets of data or only read data. This situation can be arranged by careful design rules.

Some programming languages support these constructs directly. Java, for example, has the `synchronized` property, which is equivalent to the UML's `concurrent` property. In every language that supports concurrency, you can build support for all these properties by constructing them out of semaphores.

Constraints are discussed in Chapter 6.

As Figure 23-3 shows, you can attach these properties to an operation, which you can render in the UML by using constraint notation. Note that concurrency must be asserted separately for each operation and for the entire object. Asserting concurrency for an operation means that multiple invocations of that operation can execute concurrently without danger. Asserting concurrency for an object means that invocations of different operations can execute concurrently without danger; this is a more stringent condition.

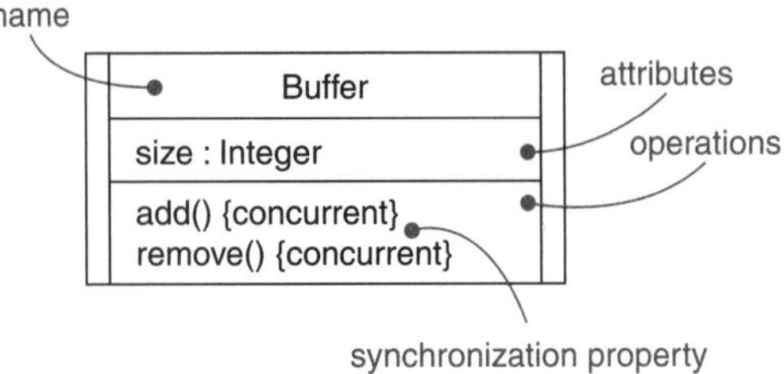

Figure 23-3: Synchronization

Note: It is possible to model variations of these synchronization primitives by using constraints. For example, you might modify the `concurrent` property by allowing multiple simultaneous readers but only a single writer.

Common Modeling Techniques

Modeling Multiple Flows of Control

Mechanisms are discussed in Chapter 29; class diagrams are discussed in Chapter 8; interaction diagrams are discussed in Chapter 19.

Building a system that encompasses multiple flows of control is hard. Not only do you have to decide how best to divide work across concurrent active objects, but once you've done that, you also have to devise the right mechanisms for communication and synchronization among your system's active and passive objects to ensure that they behave properly in the presence of these multiple flows. For that reason, it helps to visualize the way these flows interact with one another. You can do that in the UML by applying class diagrams (to capture their static semantics) and interaction diagrams (to capture their dynamic semantics) containing active classes and objects.

To model multiple flows of control,

Process views are discussed in Chapter 19; classes are discussed in Chapters 4 and 9; relationships are discussed in Chapters 5 and 10.

- Identify the opportunities for concurrent execution and reify each flow as an active class. Generalize common sets of active objects into an active class. Be careful not to over-engineer your system by introducing unnecessary concurrency.
- Consider a balanced distribution of responsibilities among these active classes, then examine the other active and passive classes with which each collaborates statically. Ensure that each active class is both tightly cohesive and loosely coupled relative to these neighboring classes and that each has the right set of attributes, operations, and signals.
- Capture these static decisions in class diagrams, explicitly highlighting each active class.
- Consider how each group of classes collaborates with one another dynamically. Capture those decisions in interaction diagrams. Explicitly show active objects as the root of such flows. Identify each related sequence by identifying it with the name of the active object.
- Pay close attention to communication among active objects. Apply synchronous and asynchronous messaging, as appropriate.
- Pay close attention to synchronization among these active objects and the passive objects with which they collaborate. Apply sequential, guarded, or concurrent operation semantics, as appropriate.

For example, Figure 23-4 shows part of the process view of a trading system. You'll find three objects that push information into the system concurrently: a `StockTicker`, an `IndexWatcher`, and a `CNNNewsFeed` (named `s`, `i`, and `c`, respectively). Two of these objects (`s` and `i`) communicate with their own `Analyst` instances (`a1` and `a2`). At least as far as this model goes, the `Analyst` can be designed under the simplifying assumption that only one flow of control will be active in its instances at a time. Both `Analyst` instances, however, communicate simultaneously with an `AlertManager` (named `m`). Therefore, `m` must be designed to preserve its semantics in the presence of multiple flows. Both `m` and `c` communicate simultaneously with `t`, a `TradingManager`. Each flow is given a sequence number that is distinguished by the flow of control that owns it.

Note: Interaction diagrams such as these are useful in helping you to visualize where two flows of control might cross paths and, therefore, where you must pay particular attention to the problems of communication and synchronization. Tools are permitted to offer even more distinct visual cues, such as by coloring each flow in a distinct way.

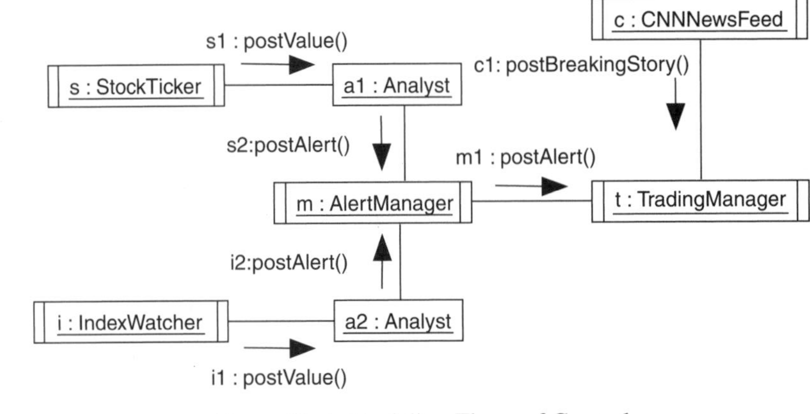

Figure 23-4: Modeling Flows of Control

State machines are discussed in Chapter 22.

In diagrams such as this, it's also common to attach corresponding state machines, with orthogonal states showing the detailed behavior of each active object.

Modeling Interprocess Communication

Signals and call events are discussed in Chapter 21.

As part of incorporating multiple flows of control in your system, you also have to consider the mechanisms by which objects that live in separate flows communicate with one another. Across threads (which live in the same address space), objects may communicate via signals or call events, the latter of which may exhibit either asynchronous or synchronous semantics. Across processes (which live in separate address spaces), you usually have to use different mechanisms.

Modeling location is discussed in Chapter 24.

The problem of interprocess communication is compounded by the fact that, in distributed systems, processes may live on separate nodes. Classically, there are two approaches to interprocess communication: message passing and remote procedure calls. In the UML, you still model these as asynchronous or synchronous events, respectively. But because these are no longer simple in-process calls, you need to adorn your designs with further information.

To model interprocess communication,

Stereotypes are discussed in Chapter 6; notes are discussed in Chapter 6; collaborations are discussed in Chapter 28; nodes are discussed in Chapter 27.

- Model the multiple flows of control.
- Model messaging using asynchronous communication; model remote procedure calls using synchronous communication.
- Informally specify the underlying mechanism for communication by using notes, or more formally by using collaborations.

Figure 23-5 shows a distributed reservation system with processes spread across four nodes. Each object is marked using the `process` stereotype. Each object is marked with a `location` attribute, specifying its physical location. Communication among the `ReservationAgent`, `TicketingManager`, and `HotelAgent` is asynchronous. Communication is described in a note as building on a Java Beans messaging service. Communication between the `TripPlanner` and the `ReservationSystem` is synchronous. The semantics of their interaction is found in the collaboration named `CORBA ORB`. The `TripPlanner` acts as a `client`, and the `ReservationAgent` acts as a `server`. By zooming into the collaboration, you'll find the details of how this server and client collaborate.

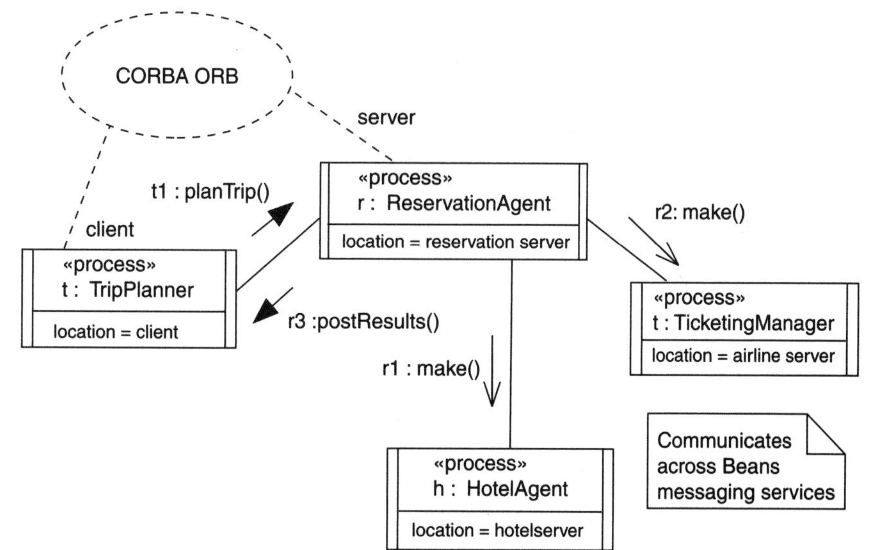

Figure 23-5: Modeling Interprocess Communication

Hints and Tips

A well-structured active class and active object

- Represents an independent flow of control that maximizes the potential for true concurrency in the system.
- Is not so fine-grained that it requires a multitude of other active elements that might result in an over-engineered and fragile process architecture.
- Carefully manages communication among peer active elements, choosing between asynchronous and synchronous messaging.
- Carefully treats each object as a critical region, using suitable synchronization properties to preserve its semantics in the presence of multiple flows of control.

When you draw an active class or an active object in the UML,

- Mark those attributes, operations, and signals that are important in understanding the abstraction in its context and hide the others using a filtering capability, if your modeling tool allows.
- Explicitly show all operation synchronization properties.

Chapter 24

Time and Space

In this chapter

- Time, duration, and location
- Modeling timing constraints
- Modeling the distribution of objects
- Modeling objects that migrate
- Dealing with real time and distributed systems

The real world is a harsh and unforgiving place. Events may happen at unpredictable times yet demand specific responses at specific times. A system's resources may have to be distributed around the world—some of those resources might even move about—raising issues of latency, synchronization, security, and quality of service.

Modeling time and space is an essential element of any real time and/or distributed system. You use a number of the UML's features, including timing marks, time expressions, constraints, and tagged values, to visualize, specify, construct, and document these systems.

Dealing with real time and distributed systems is hard. Good models reveal the properties of a system's time and space characteristics.

Getting Started

When you start to model most software systems, you can usually assume a frictionless environment—messages are sent in zero time, networks never go down, workstations never fail, the load across your network is always evenly balanced. Unfortunately, the real world does not work that way—messages do take time to deliver (and, sometimes, never get delivered), networks do go down, workstations do fail, and a network's load is often unbalanced. Therefore, when you encounter systems that must operate in the real world, you have to take into account the issues of time and space.

A real-time system is one in which certain behavior must be carried out at a precise absolute or relative time and within a predictable, often constrained, duration. At one extreme, such systems may be hard real time and require complete and repeatable behavior within nanoseconds or milliseconds. At the other extreme, models may be near real time and also require predictable behavior, but on the order of seconds or longer.

Components are discussed in Chapter 26; nodes are discussed in Chapter 27.

A distributed system is one in which components may be physically distributed across nodes. These nodes may represent different processors physically located in the same box, or they may even represent computers that are located half a world away from one another.

To represent the modeling needs of real time and distributed systems, the UML provides a graphic representation for timing marks, time expressions, timing constraints, and location, as Figure 24-1 shows.

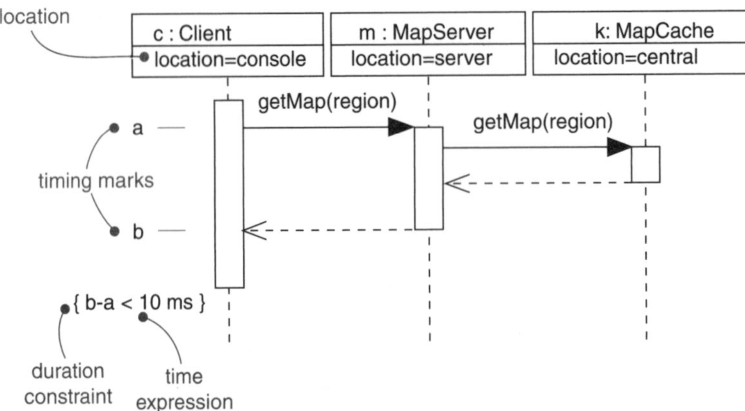

Figure 24-1: Timing Constraints and Location

Terms and Concepts

A *timing mark* is a denotation for the time at which an event occurs. Graphically, a timing mark is depicted as a small hash mark (horizontal line) on the border of a sequence diagram. A *time expression* is an expression that evaluates to an absolute or relative value of time. A time expression can also be formed using the name of a message and an indication of a stage in its processing, for example, `request.sendTime` or `request.receiveTime`. A *timing constraint* is a semantic statement about the relative or absolute value of time. Graphically, a timing constraint is rendered as for any constraint—that is, a string enclosed by brackets and generally connected to an element by a dependency relationship. *Location* is the placement of a component on a node. Location is an attribute of an object.

Time

Events, including time events, are discussed in Chapter 21; messages and interactions are discussed in Chapter 16; constraints are discussed in Chapter 6.

Real time systems are, by their very name, time-critical systems. Events may happen at regular or irregular times; the response to an event must happen at predictable absolute times or at predictable times relative to the event itself.

The passing of messages represents the dynamic aspect of any system, so when you model the time-critical nature of a system with the UML, you can give a name to each message in an interaction to be used in time expressions. Messages in an interaction are usually not given names. They are mainly rendered with the name of an event, such as a signal or a call. However, you can give them names to write a time expression because the same event may trigger different messages. If the designated message is ambiguous, use the explicit name of the message in an expression to designate the message you want to mention in a time expression. Given a message name, you can refer to any of three functions of that message—that is, `sendTime`, `receiveTime`, and `transmissionTime`. (These are our suggested functions, not official UML functions. A real-time system might have even more functions.) For synchronous calls, you can also reference the round-trip message time with `executionTime` (again our suggestion). You can then use these functions to specify arbitrarily complex time expressions, perhaps even using weights or offsets that are either constants or variables (as long as those variables can be bound at execution time). Finally, as shown in Figure 24-2, you can place these time expressions in a timing constraint to specify the timing behavior of the system. As constraints, you can render them by placing them adjacent to the appropriate message, or you can explicitly attach them using dependency relationships.

Note: Especially for complex systems, it's a good idea to write expressions with named constants instead of writing explicit times. You can define those constants in one part of your model and then refer to those constants in multiple places. In that way, it's easier to update your model if the timing requirements of your system change.

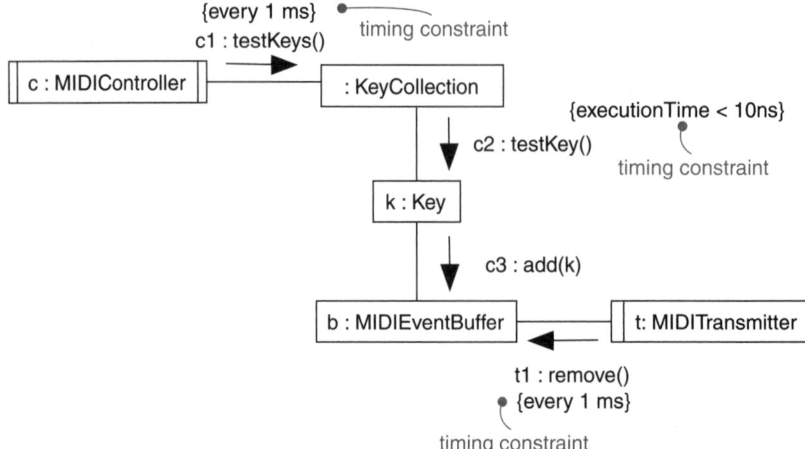

Figure 24-2: Time

Location

Components are discussed in Chapter 15; nodes are discussed in Chapter 27; deployment diagrams are discussed in Chapter 31; the class/object dichotomy is discussed in Chapters 2 and 13; classes are discussed in Chapters 4 and 9.

Distributed systems, by their nature, encompass components that are physically scattered among the nodes of a system. For many systems, components are fixed in place at the time they are loaded on the system; in other systems, components may migrate from node to node.

In the UML, you model the deployment view of a system by using deployment diagrams that represent the topology of the processors and devices on which your system executes. Artifacts such as executables, libraries, and tables reside on these nodes. Each instance of a node will own instances of certain artifacts, and each instance of an artifact will be owned by exactly one instance of a node (although instances of the same kind of artifact may be spread across different nodes).

Components and classes may be manifested as artifacts. For example, as Figure 24-3 shows, class `LoadAgent` is manifested by the artifact `initializer.exe` that lives on the node of type `Router`.

As the figure illustrates, you can model the location of an artifact in two ways in the UML. First, as shown for the `Router`, you can physically nest the element (textually or graphically) in a extra compartment in its enclosing node. Second, you can use a dependency with the keyword «`deploy`» from the artifact to the node that contains it.

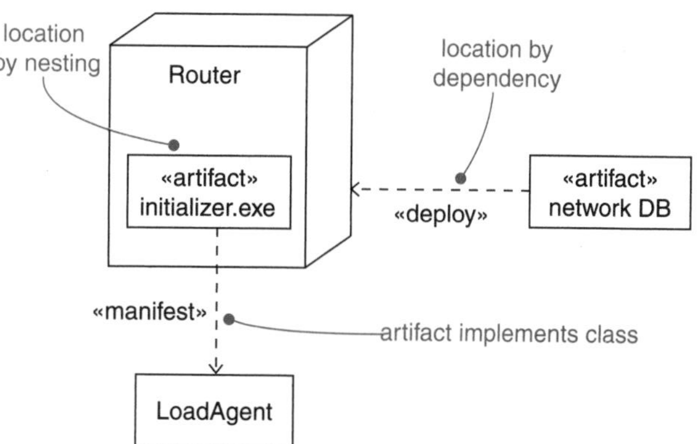

Figure 24-3: Location

Common Modeling Techniques

Modeling Timing Constraints

Constraints, one of the UML's extensibility mechanisms, are discussed in Chapter 6.

Modeling the absolute time of an event and modeling the relative time between events are the primary time-critical properties of real time systems for which you'll use timing constraints.

To model timing constraints,

- For each event in an interaction, consider whether it must start at some absolute time. Model that real time property as a timing constraint on the message.
- For each interesting sequence of messages in an interaction, consider whether there is an associated maximum relative time for that sequence. Model that real time property as a timing constraint on the sequence.

For example, as shown in Figure 24-4, the left-most constraint specifies the repeating start time for the call event `refresh`. Similarly, the right timing constraint specifies the maximum duration for calls to `getImage`.

Often, you'll choose short names for messages so that you don't confuse them with operation names.

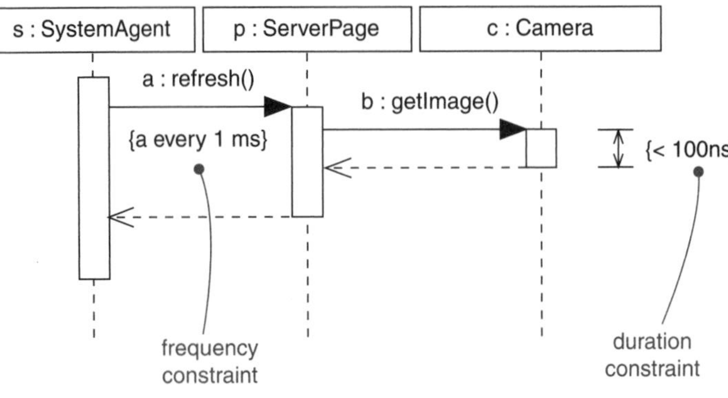

Figure 24-4: Modeling Timing Constraint

Modeling the Distribution of Objects

Modeling the distribution of a component is discussed in Chapter 15.

When you model the topology of a distributed system, you'll want to consider the physical placement of both nodes and artifacts. If your focus is the configuration management of the deployed system, modeling the distribution of nodes is especially important in order to visualize, specify, construct, and document the placement of physical things such as executables, libraries, and tables. If your focus is the functionality, scalability, and throughput of the system, modeling the distribution of objects is what's important.

Modeling processes and threads is discussed in Chapter 23.

Deciding how to distribute the objects in a system is a difficult problem, and not just because the problems of distribution interact with the problems of concurrency. Naive solutions tend to yield profoundly poor performance, and over-engineered solutions aren't much better. In fact, they are probably worse because they usually end up being brittle.

To model the distribution of objects,

- For each interesting class of objects in your system, consider its locality of reference. In other words, consider all its neighbors and their locations. A tightly coupled locality will have neighboring objects close by; a loosely coupled one will have distant objects (and thus there will be latency in communicating with them). Tentatively allocate objects closest to the actors that manipulate them.

- Next consider patterns of interaction among related sets of objects. Colocate sets of objects that have high degrees of interaction, to reduce the cost of communication. Partition sets of objects that have low degrees of interaction.
- Next consider the distribution of responsibilities across the system. Redistribute your objects to balance the load of each node.
- Consider also issues of security, volatility, and quality of service, and redistribute your objects as appropriate.
- Assign objects to artifacts so that tightly coupled objects are on the same artifact.
- Assign artifacts to nodes so that the computation needs of each node are within capacity. Add additional nodes if necessary.
- Balance performance and communication costs by assigning tightly coupled artifacts to the same node.

Object diagrams are discussed in Chapter 14.

Figure 24-5 provides an object diagram that models the distribution of certain objects in a retail system. The value of this diagram is that it lets you visualize the physical distribution of certain key objects. As the diagram shows, two objects reside on a `Workstation` (the `Order` and `Sales` objects), two objects reside on a `Server` (the `ObserverAgent` and the `Product` objects), and one object resides on a `DataWarehouse` (the `Product-Table` object).

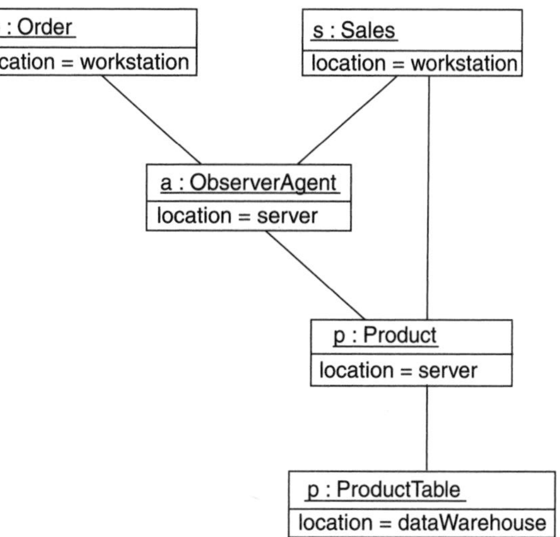

Figure 24-5: Modeling the Distribution of Objects

Hints and Tips

A well-structured model with time and space properties

- Exposes only those time and space properties that are necessary and sufficient to capture the desired behavior of the system.
- Centralizes the use of those properties so that they are easy to find and easy to modify.

When you draw a time or space property in the UML,

- Give your timing marks (the names of messages) meaningful names.
- Clearly distinguish between relative and absolute time expressions.
- Show space properties only when it's important to visualize the placement of elements across a deployed system.
- For more advanced needs, consider the *UML Profile for Schedulability, Performance, and Time*. This OMG specification addresses the needs of real-time and high-performance reactive systems.

Chapter 25
STATE DIAGRAMS

In this chapter

- Modeling reactive objects
- Forward and reverse engineering

Sequence diagrams, communication diagrams, activity diagrams, and use case diagrams also model the dynamic aspects of systems. Sequence diagrams and communication diagrams are discussed in Chapter 19; activity diagrams are discussed in Chapter 20; use case diagrams are discussed in Chapter 18.

State diagrams are one of the five diagrams in the UML for modeling the dynamic aspects of systems. A state diagram shows a state machine. Both activity and state diagrams are useful in modeling the lifetime of an object. However, whereas an activity diagram shows flow of control from activity to activity across various objects, a state diagram shows flow of control from state to state within a single object.

You use state diagrams to model the dynamic aspects of a system. For the most part, this involves modeling the behavior of reactive objects. A reactive object is one whose behavior is best characterized by its response to events dispatched from outside its context. A reactive object has a clear lifetime whose current behavior is affected by its past. State diagrams may be attached to classes, use cases, or entire systems in order to visualize, specify, construct, and document the dynamics of an individual object.

State diagrams are not only important for modeling the dynamic aspects of a system, but also for constructing executable systems through forward and reverse engineering.

Getting Started

The differences between building a dog house and building a high rise are discussed in Chapter 1.

Consider the investor who finances the building of a new high rise. She is unlikely to be interested in the details of the building process. The selection of materials, the scheduling of the trades, and the many meetings about engineering details are activities that are important to the builder, but far less so to the person bankrolling the project.

The investor is interested in getting a good return on the investment, and that also means protecting the investment against risk. A very trusting investor will give a builder a pile of money, walk away for a while, and return only when the builder is ready to hand over the keys to the building. Such an investor is really interested in the final state of the building.

A more pragmatic investor will still trust the builder, but will also want to verify that the project is on track before releasing money. So, rather than give the builder an unattended pile of money to dip into, the prudent investor will set up clear milestones for the project, each of which is tied to the completion of certain activities, and only after meeting each one will money be released to the builder for the next phase of the project. For example, a modest amount of funds might be released at the project's inception to fund the architectural work. After the architectural vision has been approved, then more funds may be released to pay for the engineering work. After that work is completed to the project stakeholders' satisfaction, a larger pile of money may be released so that the builder can proceed with breaking ground.

Gantt charts and Pert charts are discussed in Chapter 20.

Along the way, from ground breaking to issuance of the certificate of occupancy, there are other milestones. Each of these milestones names a stable state of the project: architecture complete, engineering done, ground broken, infrastructure completed, building sealed, and so on. For the investor, following the changing state of the building is more important than following the flow of activities, which is what the builder might be doing by using Pert charts to model the workflow of the project.

Activity diagrams as flowcharts are discussed in Chapter 20; state machines are discussed in Chapter 22.

In modeling software-intensive systems as well, you'll find that the most natural way to visualize, specify, construct, and document the behavior of certain kinds of objects is by focusing on the flow of control from state to state rather than from activity to activity. You would do the latter with a flowchart (and in the UML, with an activity diagram). Imagine, for a moment, modeling the behavior of an embedded home security system. Such a system runs continuously, reacting to events from the outside, such as the breaking of a window. In addition, the order of events changes the way the system behaves. For example, the detection of a broken window will only trigger an alarm if the system is first armed. The behavior of such a system is best specified by modeling its stable states (for example, `Idle`, `Armed`, `Active`, `Checking`, and so on), the events that trigger a change from state to state, and the actions that occur on each state change.

In the UML, you model the event-ordered behavior of an object by using state diagrams. As Figure 25-1 shows, a state diagram is simply a presentation of a state machine, emphasizing the flow of control from state to state.

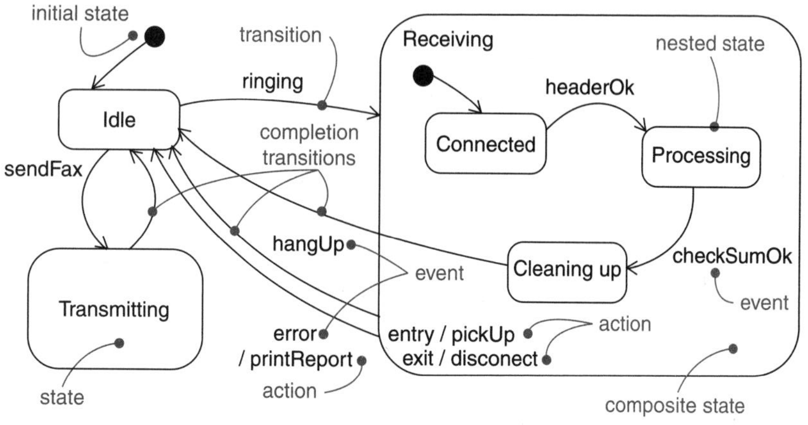

Figure 25-1: State Diagram

Terms and Concepts

A *state diagram* shows a state machine, emphasizing the flow of control from state to state. A *state machine* is a behavior that specifies the sequences of states an object goes through during its lifetime in response to events, together with its responses to those events. A *state* is a condition or situation in the life of an object during which it satisfies some condition, performs some activity, or waits for some event. An *event* is the specification of a significant occurrence that has a location in time and space. In the context of state machines, an event is an occurrence of a stimulus that can trigger a state transition. A *transition* is a relationship between two states indicating that an object in the first state will perform certain actions and enter the second state when a specified event occurs and specified conditions are satisfied. An *activity* specifies an ongoing execution within a state machine. An *action* specifies a primitive executable computation that results in a change in state of the model or the return of a value. Graphically, a state diagram is a collection of nodes and arcs.

Note: The state diagrams used in UML are based on the statechart notation invented by David Harel. In particular, the concepts of nested states and orthogonal states were developed by Harel into a precise, formal system. The concepts in UML are somewhat less formal than Harel's notation and differ in some details, in particular, by being focused on object-oriented systems.

Common Properties

The general properties of diagrams are discussed in Chapter 7.

A state diagram is just a special kind of diagram and shares the same common properties as do all other diagrams—that is, a name and graphical contents that are a projection into a model. What distinguishes a state diagram from all other kinds of diagrams is its content.

Contents

Simple states, composite states, transitions, events, and actions are discussed in Chapter 22; activity diagrams are discussed in Chapter 20; notes and constraints are discussed in Chapter 6.

State diagrams commonly contain

- Simple states and composite states
- Transitions, events, and actions

Like all other diagrams, state diagrams may contain notes and constraints.

Note: A state diagram is basically a projection of the elements found in a state machine. This means that state diagrams may contain branches, forks, joins, action states, activity states, objects, initial states, final states, history states, and so on. Indeed, a state diagram may contain any and all features of a state machine.

Common Uses

The five views of an architecture are discussed in Chapter 2; instances are discussed in Chapter 13; classes are discussed in Chapters 4 and 9.

You use state diagrams to model the dynamic aspects of a system. These dynamic aspects may involve the event-ordered behavior of any kind of object in any view of a system's architecture, including classes (which includes active classes), interfaces, components, and nodes.

When you use a state diagram to model some dynamic aspect of a system, you do so in the context of virtually any modeling element. Typically, however, you'll use state diagrams in the context of the system as a whole, a subsystem, or a class. You can also attach state diagrams to use cases (to model a scenario).

Active classes are discussed in Chapter 23; interfaces are discussed in Chapter 11; components are discussed in Chapter 15; nodes are discussed in Chapter 27; use cases are discussed in Chapter 17; systems are discussed in Chapter 32.

When you model the dynamic aspects of a system, a class, or a use case, you'll typically use state diagrams to model reactive objects.

A reactive—or event-driven—object is one whose behavior is best characterized by its response to events dispatched from outside its context. A reactive object is typically idle until it receives an event. When it receives an event, its response usually depends on previous events. After the object responds to an event, it becomes idle again, waiting for the next event. For these kinds of objects, you'll focus on the stable states of that object, the events that trigger a transition from state to state, and the actions that occur on each state change.

Note: In contrast, you'll use activity diagrams to model a workflow or to model an operation. Activity diagrams are better suited to modeling the flow of activities over time, such as you would represent in a flowchart.

Common Modeling Techniques

Modeling Reactive Objects

Interactions are discussed in Chapter 16; activity diagrams are discussed in Chapter 20.

The most common purpose for which you'll use state diagrams is to model the behavior of reactive objects, especially instances of classes, use cases, and the system as a whole. Whereas interactions model the behavior of a society of objects working together, a state diagram models the behavior of a single object over its lifetime. Whereas an activity diagram models the flow of control from activity to activity, a state diagram models the flow of control from event to event.

Modeling the lifetime of an object is discussed in Chapter 22.

When you model the behavior of a reactive object, you essentially specify three things: the stable states in which that object may live, the events that trigger a transition from state to state, and the actions that occur on each state change. Modeling the behavior of a reactive object also involves modeling the lifetime of an object, starting at the time of the object's creation and continuing until its destruction, highlighting the stable states in which the object may be found.

Time and space are discussed in Chapter 24.

A stable state represents a condition in which an object may exist for some identifiable period of time. When an event occurs, the object may transition from state to state. These events may also trigger self- and internal transitions, in which the source and the target of the transition are the same state. In reaction to an event or a state change, the object may respond by dispatching an action.

Note: When you model the behavior of a reactive object, you can specify its action by tying it to a transition or to a state change. In technical terms, a state machine whose actions are all attached to transitions is called a Mealy machine; a state machine whose actions are all attached to states is called a Moore machine. Mathematically, the two styles have equivalent power. In practice, you'll typically develop state diagrams that use a combination of Mealy and Moore machines.

To model a reactive object,

Pre- and postconditions are discussed in Chapter 10; interfaces are discussed in Chapter 11.

- Choose the context for the state machine, whether it is a class, a use case, or the system as a whole.
- Choose the initial and final states for the object. To guide the rest of your model, possibly state the pre- and postconditions of the initial and final states, respectively.
- Decide on the stable states of the object by considering the conditions in which the object may exist for some identifiable period of time. Start with the high-level states of the object and only then consider its possible substates.
- Decide on the meaningful partial ordering of stable states over the lifetime of the object.
- Decide on the events that may trigger a transition from state to state. Model these events as triggers to transitions that move from one legal ordering of states to another.
- Attach actions to these transitions (as in a Mealy machine) and/or to these states (as in a Moore machine).
- Consider ways to simplify your machine by using substates, branches, forks, joins, and history states.
- Check that all states are reachable under some combination of events.
- Check that no state is a dead end from which no combination of events will transition the object out of that state.
- Trace through the state machine, either manually or by using tools, to check it against expected sequences of events and their responses.

For example, Figure 25-2 shows the state diagram for parsing a simple context-free language, such as you might find in systems that stream in or stream

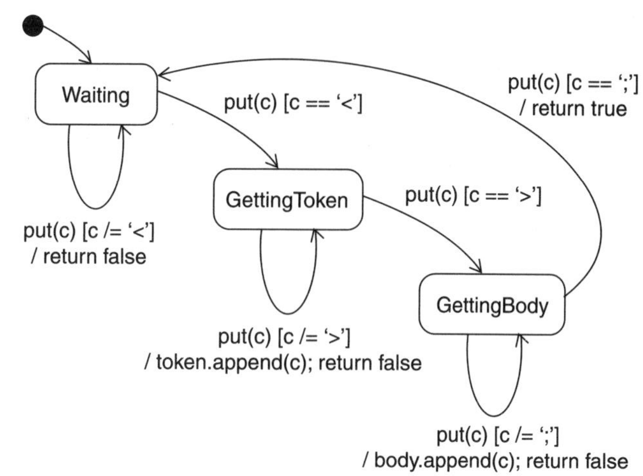

Figure 25-2: Modeling Reactive Objects

out messages to XML. In this case, the machine is designed to parse a stream of characters that match the syntax

```
message : '<' string '>' string ';'
```

The first string represents a tag; the second string represents the body of the message. Given a stream of characters, only well-formed messages that follow this syntax may be accepted.

Events are discussed in Chapter 21.

As the figure shows, there are only three stable states for this state machine: `Waiting`, `GettingToken`, and `GettingBody`. This state is designed as a Mealy machine, with actions tied to transitions. In fact, there is only one event of interest in this state machine, the invocation of `put` with the actual parameter `c` (a character). While `Waiting`, this machine throws away any character that does not designate the start of a token (as specified by the guard condition). When the start of a token is received, the state of the object changes to `GettingToken`. While in that state, the machine saves any character that does not designate the end of a token (as specified by the guard condition). When the end of a token is received, the state of the object changes to `GettingBody`. While in that state, the machine saves any character that does not designate the end of a message body (as specified by the guard condition). When the end of a message is received, the state of the object changes to `Waiting`, and a value is returned indicating that the message has been parsed (and the machine is ready to receive another message).

Note that this state specifies a machine that runs continuously; there is no final state.

Forward and Reverse Engineering

Forward engineering (the creation of code from a model) is possible for state diagrams, especially if the context of the diagram is a class. For example, using the previous state diagram, a forward engineering tool could generate the following Java code for the class `MessageParser`.

```
class MessageParser {
public
  boolean put(char c) {
    switch (state) {
      case Waiting:
        if (c == '<') {
          state = GettingToken;
          token = new StringBuffer();
          body = new StringBuffer();
        }
        break;
      case GettingToken :
        if (c == '>')
          state = GettingBody;
        else
          token.append(c);
        break;
      case GettingBody :
        if (c == ';')
          state = Waiting;
        else
          body.append(c);
        return true;
    }
    return false;
  }
  StringBuffer getToken() {
    return token;
  }
  StringBuffer getBody() {
    return body;
  }
private
  final static int Waiting = 0;
  final static int GettingToken = 1;
  final static int GettingBody = 2;
  int state = Waiting;
  StringBuffer token, body;
}
```

This requires a little cleverness. The forward engineering tool must generate the necessary private attributes and final static constants.

Reverse engineering (the creation of a model from code) is theoretically possible but practically not very useful. The choice of what constitutes a meaningful state is in the eye of the designer. Reverse engineering tools have no capacity for abstraction and therefore cannot automatically produce meaningful state diagrams. More interesting than the reverse engineering of a model from code is the animation of a model against the execution of a deployed system. For example, given the previous diagram, a tool could animate the states in the diagram as they were reached in the running system. Similarly, the firing of transitions could be animated, showing the receipt of events and the resulting dispatch of actions. Under the control of a debugger, you could control the speed of execution, setting breakpoints to stop the action at interesting states to examine the attribute values of individual objects.

Hints and Tips

When you create state diagrams in the UML, remember that every state diagram is just a projection on the same model of a system's dynamic aspects. A single state diagram can capture the semantics of a single reactive object, but no one state diagram can capture the semantics of an entire nontrivial system.

A well-structured state diagram

- Is focused on communicating one aspect of a system's dynamics.
- Contains only those elements essential to understanding that aspect.
- Provides detail consistent with its level of abstraction (expose only those features that are essential to understanding).
- Uses a balance between the styles of Mealy and Moore machines.

When you draw a state diagram,

- Give it a name that communicates its purpose.
- Start with modeling the stable states of the object, then follow with modeling the legal transitions from state to state. Address branching, concurrency, and object flow as secondary considerations, possibly in separate diagrams.
- Lay out its elements to minimize lines that cross.
- For large state diagrams, consider advanced features such as submachines that are included in the full UML specification.

UNIFIED
MODELING
LANGUAGE

Part 6
Architectural Modeling

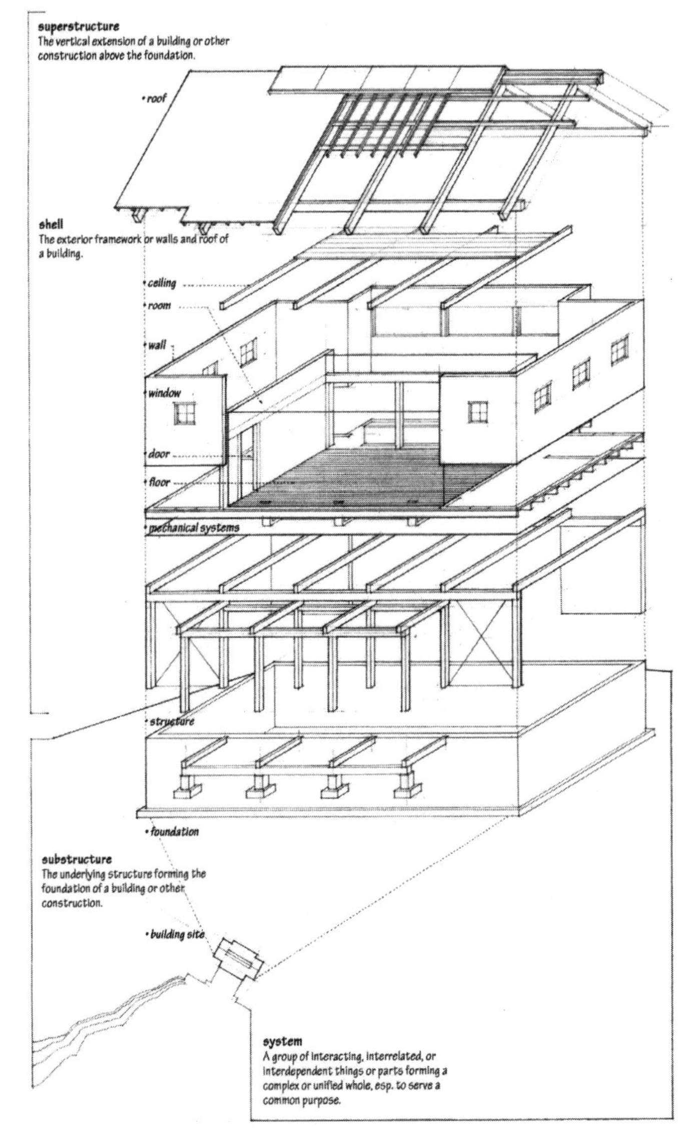
superstructure
The vertical extension of a building or other construction above the foundation.
roof
shell
The exterior framework or walls and roof of a building.
ceiling
room
wall
window
door
floor
mechanical systems
structure
foundation
substructure
The underlying structure forming the foundation of a building or other construction.
building site
system
A group of interacting, interrelated, or interdependent things or parts forming a complex or unified whole, esp. to serve a common purpose.

Chapter 26
ARTIFACTS

In this chapter

- Artifacts, classes, and manifestation
- Modeling executables and libraries
- Modeling tables, files, and documents
- Modeling source code

Artifacts live in the material world of bits and therefore are an important building block in modeling the physical aspects of a system. An artifact is a physical and replaceable part of a system.

You use artifacts to model the physical things that may reside on a node, such as executables, libraries, tables, files, and documents. An artifact typically represents the physical packaging of otherwise logical elements, such as classes, interfaces, and collaborations.

Getting Started

The end product of a construction company's work is a physical building that exists in the real world. You build logical models to visualize, specify, and document your decisions about the building envelope; the placement of walls, doors, and windows; the routing of electrical and plumbing systems; and the overall architectural style. When you actually construct the building, these walls, doors, windows, and other conceptual things get turned into real, physical things.

The differences between building a dog house and building a high rise are discussed in Chapter 1.

These logical and physical views are both necessary. If you are building a disposable building for which the cost of scrap and rework is essentially zero (for example, if you are building a doghouse), you can probably go straight to the physical building without doing any logical modeling. If, on the other hand, you are building something enduring for which the cost of change or failure is high, then building both logical and physical models is the pragmatic thing to do to manage risk.

It's the same thing when building a software-intensive system. You do logical modeling to visualize, specify, and document your decisions about the vocabulary of your domain and the structural and behavioral way those things collaborate. You do physical modeling to construct the executable system. Whereas these logical things live in the conceptual world, the physical things live in the world of bits—that is, they ultimately reside on physical nodes and can be executed directly or can, in some indirect manner, participate in an executing system.

In the UML, all these physical things are modeled as artifacts. An artifact is a physical thing at the level of the implementation platform.

In software, many operating systems and programming languages directly support the concept of an artifact. Object libraries, executables, .NET components, and Enterprise Java Beans are all examples of artifacts that may be represented directly in the UML. Not only can artifacts be used to model these kinds of things, they can also be used to represent other things that participate in an executing system, such as tables, files, and documents.

Stereotypes are discussed in Chapter 6.

The UML provides a graphical representation of an artifact, as Figure 26-1 shows. This canonical notation permits you to visualize an artifact apart from any operating system or programming language. Using stereotypes, one of the UML's extensibility mechanisms, you can tailor this notation to represent specific kinds of artifacts.

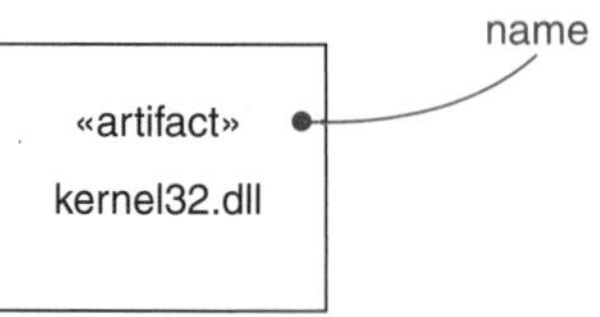

Figure 26-1: Artifacts

Terms and Concepts

A *artifact* is a physical part of a system that exists at the level of the implementation platform. Graphically, an artifact is rendered as a rectangle with the keyword «artifact».

Names

An artifact name must be unique within its enclosing node.

Every artifact must have a name that distinguishes it from other artifacts. A *name* is a textual string. That name alone is known as a *simple name*; a *qualified name* is the artifact name prefixed by the name of the package in which that artifact lives. An artifact is typically drawn showing only its name, as in Figure 26-2. Just as with classes, you may draw artifacts adorned with tagged values or with additional compartments to expose their details, as you see in the figure.

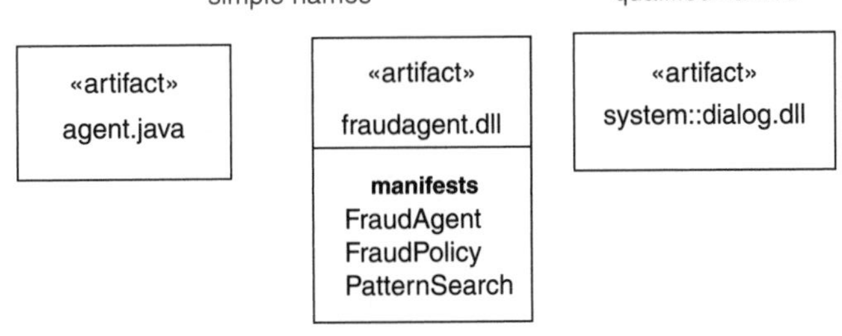

Figure 26-2: Simple and Qualified Artifact Names

Note: An artifact name may be text consisting of any number of letters, numbers, and certain punctuation marks (except for marks such as the colon, which is used to separate an artifact name and the name of its enclosing package) and may continue over several lines. In practice, artifact names are short nouns or noun phrases drawn from the vocabulary of the implementation and, depending on your target operating system, include extensions (such as `java` and `dll`).

Artifacts and Classes

Classes are discussed in Chapters 4 and 9; interactions are discussed in Chapter 16.

Classes and artifacts are both classifiers. However, there are some significant differences between artifacts and classes.

- Classes represent logical abstractions; artifacts represent physical things that live in the world of bits. In short, artifacts may live on nodes, classes may not.
- Artifacts represent the physical packaging of bits on the implementation platform.
- Classes may have attributes and operations. Artifacts may implement classes and methods, but they do not have attributes or operations themselves.

Nodes are discussed in Chapter 27.

The first difference is the most important. When modeling a system, deciding whether you should use a class or an artifact involves a simple decision—if the thing you are modeling lives directly on a node, use an artifact; otherwise, use a class. The second difference also makes this clear.

The third difference suggests a relationship between classes and artifacts. In particular, an artifact is the physical implementation of a set of logical elements, such as classes and collaborations. As Figure 26-3 shows, the relationship between an artifact and the classes it implements can be shown explicitly by using a manifestation relationship.

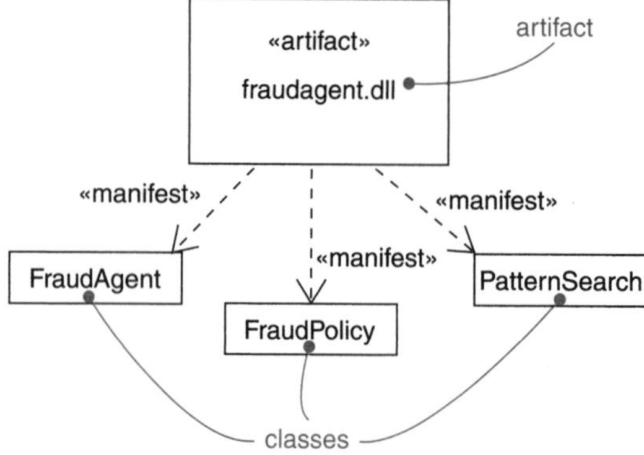

Figure 26-3: Artifacts and Classes

Kinds of Artifacts

Three kinds of artifacts may be distinguished.

First, there are *deployment artifacts*. These are the artifacts necessary and sufficient to form an executable system, such as dynamic libraries (DLLs) and executables (EXEs). The UML's definition of artifact is broad enough to address classic object models, such as .NET, CORBA, and Enterprise Java Beans, as well as alternative object models, perhaps involving dynamic Web pages, database tables, and executables using proprietary communication mechanisms.

Second, there are *work product artifacts*. These artifacts are essentially the residue of the development process, consisting of things such as source code files and data files from which deployment artifacts are created. These artifacts do not directly participate in an executable system but are the work products of development that are used to create the executable system.

Third are *execution artifacts*. These artifacts are created as a consequence of an executing system, such as a .NET object, which is instantiated from a DLL.

Standard Elements

The UML's extensibility mechanisms are discussed in Chapter 6.

UML's extensibility mechanisms apply to artifacts. Most often, you'll use tagged values to extend artifact properties (such as specifying the version of a development artifact) and stereotypes to specify new kinds of artifacts (such as operating system-specific artifacts).

The UML predefines standard stereotypes that apply to artifacts:

1. `executable` Specifies an artifact that may be executed on a node
2. `library` Specifies a static or dynamic object library
3. `file` Specifies an artifact that represents a document containing source code or data
4. `document` Specifies an artifact that represents a document

Others can be defined for specific platforms and systems.

Common Modeling Techniques

Modeling Executables and Libraries

The most common purpose for which you'll use artifacts is to model the deployment artifacts that make up your implementation. If you are deploying a trivial system whose implementation consists of exactly one executable file, you will not need to do any artifact modeling. If, on the other hand, the system you are deploying is made up of several executables and associated object libraries, doing artifact modeling will help you to visualize, specify, construct, and document the decisions you've made about the physical system. Artifact modeling is even more important if you want to control the versioning and configuration management of these parts as your system evolves.

These decisions are also affected by the topology of your target system, as discussed in Chapter 27.

For most systems, these deployment artifacts are drawn from the decisions you make about how to segment the physical implementation of your system. These decisions will be affected by a number of technical issues (such as your choice of artifact-based operating system facilities), configuration management issues (such as your decisions about which parts will likely change over time), and reuse issues (that is, deciding which artifacts you can reuse in or from other systems).

To model executables and libraries,

- Identify the partitioning of your physical system. Consider the impact of technical, configuration management, and reuse issues.
- Model any executables and libraries as artifacts, using the appropriate standard elements. If your implementation introduces new kinds of artifacts, introduce a new appropriate stereotype.
- If it's important for you to manage the seams in your system, model the significant interfaces that some artifacts use and others realize.
- As necessary to communicate your intent, model the relationships among these executables, libraries, and interfaces. Most often, you'll want to model the dependencies among these parts to visualize the impact of change.

For example, Figure 26-4 shows a set of artifacts drawn from a personal productivity tool that runs on a single personal computer. This figure includes one executable (`animator.exe`) and four libraries (`dlog.dll`, `wrfrme.dll`, `render.dll`, and `raytrce.dll`), all of which use the UML's standard elements for executables and libraries, respectively. This diagram also presents the dependencies among these artifacts.

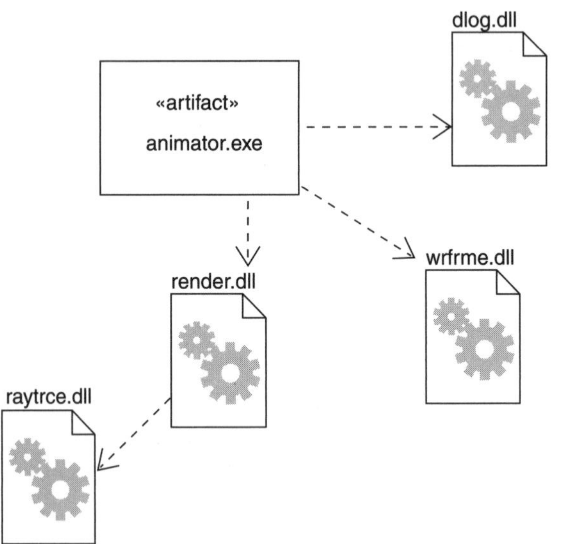

Figure 26-4: Modeling Executables and Libraries

Packages are discussed in Chapter 12.

As your models get bigger, you will find that many artifacts tend to cluster together in groups that are conceptually and semantically related. In the UML, you can use packages to model these clusters of artifacts.

Modeling deployment is discussed in Chapter 27.

For larger systems that are deployed across several computers, you'll want to model the way your artifacts are distributed by asserting the nodes on which they are located.

Modeling Tables, Files, and Documents

Modeling the executables and libraries that make up the physical implementation of your system is useful, but often you'll find there are a host of ancillary deployment artifacts that are neither executables nor libraries and yet are critical to the physical deployment of your system. For example, your implementation might include data files, help documents, scripts, log files, initialization files, and installation/removal files. Modeling these artifacts is an important part of controlling the configuration of your system. Fortunately, you can use UML artifacts to model all of these artifacts.

To model tables, files, and documents,

- Identify the ancillary artifacts that are part of the physical implementation of your system.
- Model these things as artifacts. If your implementation introduces new kinds of artifacts, introduce a new appropriate stereotype.
- As necessary to communicate your intent, model the relationships among these ancillary artifacts and the other executables, libraries, and interfaces in your system. Most often, you'll want to model the dependencies among these parts in order to visualize the impact of change.

Modeling logical and physical databases are discussed in Chapters 8 and 30, respectively.

For example, Figure 26-5 builds on the previous figure and shows the tables, files, and documents that are part of the deployed system surrounding the executable `animator.exe`. This figure includes one document (`animator.hlp`), one simple file (`animator.ini`), and one database table (`shapes.tbl`). This example illustrates some user-defined stereotypes and icons for artifacts.

Modeling databases can get complicated when you start dealing with multiple tables, triggers, and stored procedures. To visualize, specify, construct, and document these features, you'll need to model the logical schema as well as the physical databases.

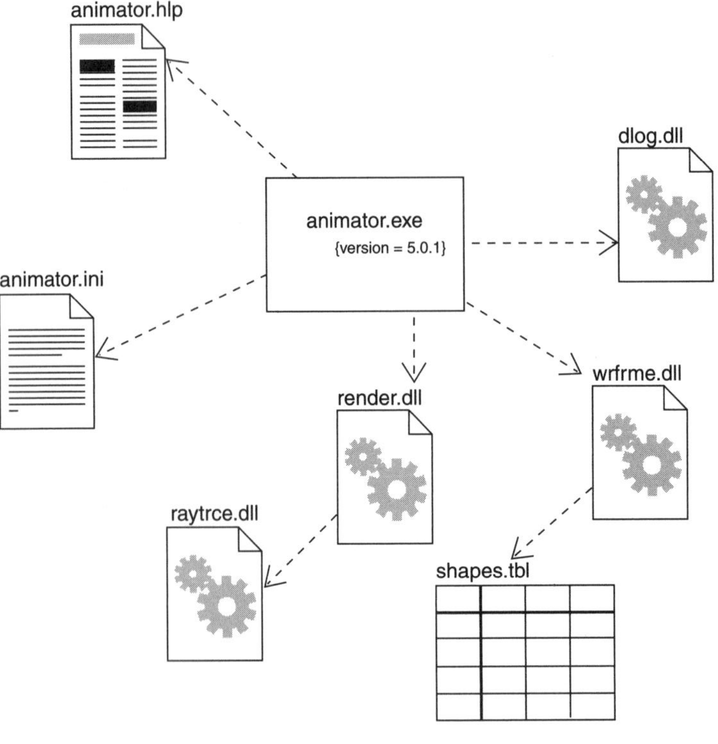

Figure 26-5: Modeling Tables, Files, and Documents

Modeling Source Code

The most common purpose for which you'll use artifacts is to model the physical parts that make up your implementation. The second most common purpose for which you'll use artifacts is to model the configuration of all the source code files that your development tools use to create these artifacts. These represent the work product artifacts of your development process.

Modeling source code graphically is particularly useful for visualizing the compilation dependencies among your source code files and for managing the splitting and merging of groups of these files when you fork and join development paths. In this manner, UML artifacts can be the graphical interface to your configuration management and version control tools.

For most systems, source code files are drawn from the decisions you make about how to segment the files your development environment needs. These files are used to store the details of your classes, interfaces, collaborations, and other logical elements as an intermediate step to creating the physical, binary artifacts that are derived from these elements by your tools. Most of the time these tools will impose a style of organization (one or two files per class is common), but you'll still want to visualize the relationships among these files. How you organize groups of these files using packages and how you manage versions of these files is driven by your decisions about how to manage change.

To model source code,

- Depending on the constraints imposed by your development tools, model the files used to store the details of all your logical elements, along with their compilation dependencies.
- If it's important for you to bolt these models to your configuration management and version control tools, you'll want to include tagged values, such as version, author, and check-in/check-out information, for each file that's under configuration management.
- As far as possible, let your development tools manage the relationships among these files, and use the UML only to visualize and document these relationships.

For example, Figure 26-6 shows some source code files that are used to build the library `render.dll` from the previous examples. This figure includes four header files (`render.h`, `rengine.h`, `poly.h`, and `colortab.h`) that represent the source code for the specification of certain classes. There is also one implementation file (`render.cpp`) that represents the implementation of one of these headers.

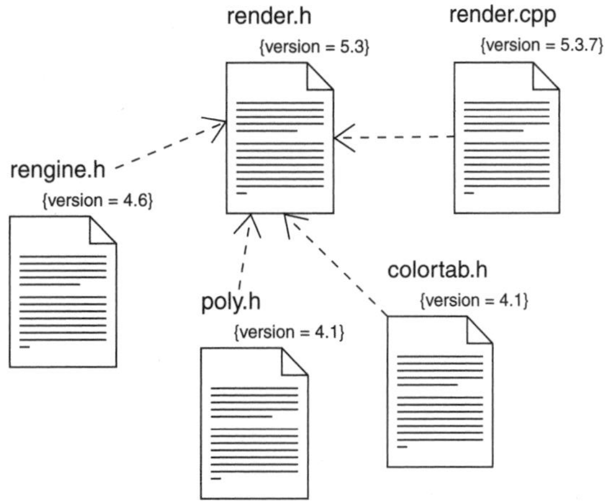

Figure 26-6: Modeling Source Code

Packages are discussed in Chapter 12; `trace` *relationships, a kind of dependency, are discussed in Chapters 5 and 10.*

As your models get bigger, you will find that many source code files tend to cluster together in groups that are conceptually and semantically related. Most of the time, your development tools will place these groups in separate directories. In the UML, you can use packages to model these clusters of source code files.

In the UML, it is possible to visualize the relationship of a class to its source code file and, in turn, the relationship of a source code file to its executable or library by using trace relationships. However, you'll rarely need to go to this detail of modeling.

Hints and Tips

When you model artifacts in the UML, remember that you are modeling in the physical dimension. A well-structured artifact

- Directly implements a set of classes that work together to carry out the semantics of these interfaces with economy and elegance.
- Is loosely coupled to other artifacts.

Chapter 27
DEPLOYMENT

In this chapter

- Nodes and connections
- Modeling processors and devices
- Modeling the distribution of artifacts
- Systems engineering

Nodes, just like artifacts, live in the material world and are an important building block in modeling the physical aspects of a system. A node is a physical element that exists at run time and represents a computational resource, generally having at least some memory and, often, processing capability.

You use nodes to model the topology of the hardware on which your system executes. A node typically represents a processor or a device on which artifacts may be deployed. Good nodes crisply represent the vocabulary of the hardware in your solution domain.

Getting Started

Modeling non-software things is discussed in Chapter 4; the five views of an architecture are discussed in Chapter 2.

The artifacts you develop or reuse as part of a software-intensive system must be deployed on some set of hardware in order to execute. This is in effect what a software-intensive *system* is all about—such a system encompasses both software and hardware.

When you architect a software-intensive system, you have to consider both its logical and physical dimensions. On the logical side, you'll find things such as classes, interfaces, collaborations, interactions, and state machines. On the physical side, you'll find artifacts (which represent the physical packaging of these logical things) and nodes (which represent the hardware on which these artifacts are deployed and execute).

Stereotypes are discussed in Chapter 6.

The UML provides a graphical representation of node, as Figure 27-1 shows. This canonical notation permits you to visualize a node apart from any specific hardware. Using stereotypes—one of the UML's extensibility mechanisms—you can (and often will) tailor this notation to represent specific kinds of processors and devices.

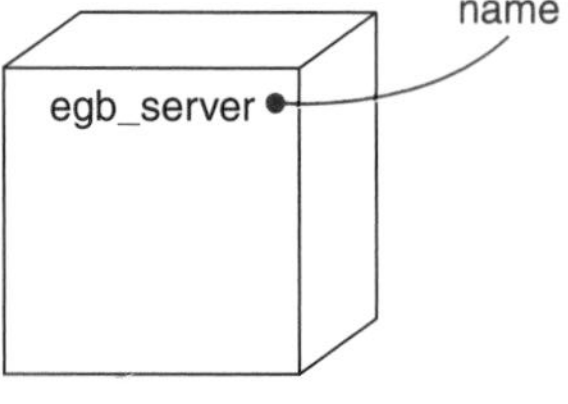

Figure 27-1: Nodes

Note: The UML is mainly intended for modeling software-intensive systems, although the UML, in conjunction with textual hardware modeling languages, such as VHDL, can be quite expressive for modeling hardware systems. The UML is also sufficiently expressive for modeling the topologies of stand-alone, embedded, client/server, and distributed systems.

Terms and Concepts

A *node* is a physical element that exists at run time and represents a computational resource, generally having at least some memory and, often, processing capability. Graphically, a node is rendered as a cube.

Names

A node name must be unique within its enclosing package, as discussed in Chapter 12.

Every node must have a name that distinguishes it from other nodes. A *name* is a textual string. That name alone is known as a *simple name*; a *qualified name* is the node name prefixed by the name of the package in which that node lives.

A node is typically drawn showing only its name, as in Figure 27-2. Just as with classes, you may draw nodes adorned with tagged values or with additional compartments to expose their details.

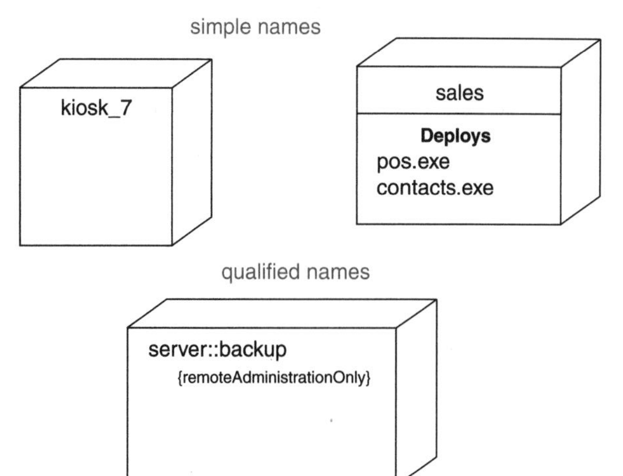

Figure 27-2: Nodes with Simple and Qualified Names

Note: A node name may be text consisting of any number of letters, numbers, and certain punctuation marks (except for marks such as the colon, which is used to separate a node name and the name of its enclosing package) and may continue over several lines. In practice, node names are short nouns or noun phrases drawn from the vocabulary of the implementation.

Nodes and Artifacts

Artifacts are discussed in Chapter 26.

In many ways, nodes are a lot like artifacts: Both have names; both may participate in dependency, generalization, and association relationships; both may be nested; both may have instances; both may be participants in interactions. However, there are some significant differences between nodes and artifacts.

- Artifacts are things that participate in the execution of a system; nodes are things that execute artifacts.
- Artifacts represent the physical packaging of otherwise logical elements; nodes represent the physical deployment of artifacts.

This first difference is the most important. Simply put, nodes execute artifacts; artifacts are things that are executed by nodes.

Dependency relationships are discussed in Chapters 5 and 10.

The second difference suggests a relationship among classes, artifacts, and nodes. In particular, an artifact is the manifestation of a set of logical elements, such as classes and collaborations, and a node is the location upon which artifacts are deployed. A class may be manifested by one or more artifacts, and, in turn, an artifact may be deployed on one or more nodes. As Figure 27-3 shows, the relationship between a node and the artifacts it deploys can be shown explicitly by using nesting. Most of the time, you won't need to visualize these relationships graphically but will indicate them as a part of the node's specification, for example, using a table.

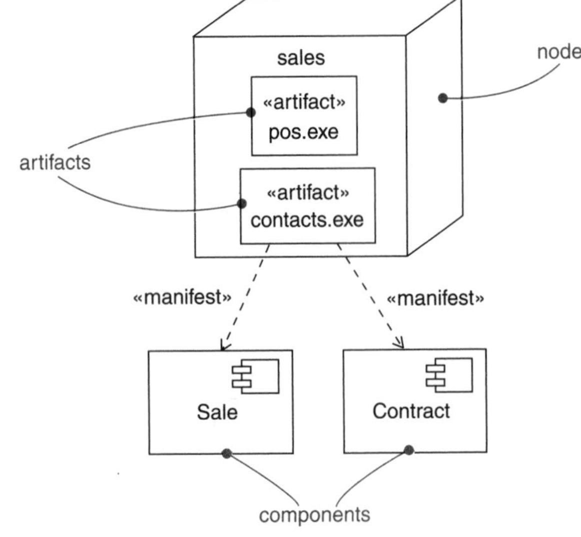

Figure 27-3: Nodes and Artifacts

A set of objects or artifacts that are allocated to a node as a group is called a *distribution unit*.

Note: Nodes are also class-like in that you can specify attributes and operations for them. For example, you might specify that a node provides the attributes `processorSpeed` and `memory`, as well as the operations `turnOn`, `turnOff`, and `suspend`.

Organizing Nodes

Packages are discussed in Chapter 12.

You can organize nodes by grouping them in packages in the same manner in which you can organize classes and artifacts.

Relationships are discussed in Chapters 5 and 10.

You can also organize nodes by specifying dependency, generalization, and association (including aggregation) relationships among them.

Connections

The most common kind of relationship you'll use among nodes is an association. In this context, an association represents a physical connection among nodes, such as an Ethernet connection, a serial line, or a shared bus, as Figure 27-4 shows. You can even use associations to model indirect connections, such as a satellite link between distant processors.

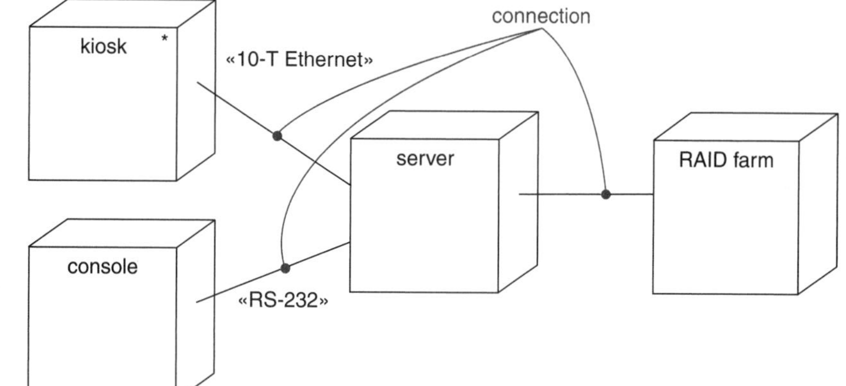

Figure 27-4: Connections

Because nodes are class-like, you have the full power of associations at your disposal. This means that you can include roles, multiplicity, and constraints. As in the previous figure, you should stereotype these associations if you want to model new kinds of connections—for example, to distinguish between a 10-T Ethernet connection and an RS-232 serial connection.

Common Modeling Techniques

Modeling Processors and Devices

Modeling the processors and devices that form the topology of a stand-alone, embedded, client/server, or distributed system is the most common use of nodes.

The UML's extensibility mechanisms are discussed in Chapter 6.

Because all of the UML's extensibility mechanisms apply to nodes, you will often use stereotypes to specify new kinds of nodes that you can use to represent specific kinds of processors and devices. A *processor* is a node that has processing capability, meaning that it can execute a artifact. A *device* is a node that has no processing capability (at least, none that are modeled at this level of abstraction) and, in general, represents something that interfaces to the real world.

To model processors and devices,

- Identify the computational elements of your system's deployment view and model each as a node.
- If these elements represent generic processors and devices, then stereotype them as such. If they are kinds of processors and devices that are part of the vocabulary of your domain, then specify an appropriate stereotype with an icon for each.
- As with class modeling, consider the attributes and operations that might apply to each node.

For example, Figure 27-5 takes the previous diagram and stereotypes each node. The `server` is a node stereotyped as a generic processor; the `kiosk` and the `console` are nodes stereotyped as special kinds of processors; and the `RAID farm` is a node stereotyped as a special kind of device.

Note: Nodes are probably the most stereotyped building block in the UML. When, as part of systems engineering, you model the deployment view of a software-intensive system, there's great value in providing visual cues that speak to your intended audience. If you are modeling a processor that's a common kind of computer, render it with an icon that looks like that computer. If you are modeling a common device, such as a cellular phone, fax, modem, or camera, render it with an icon that looks like that device.

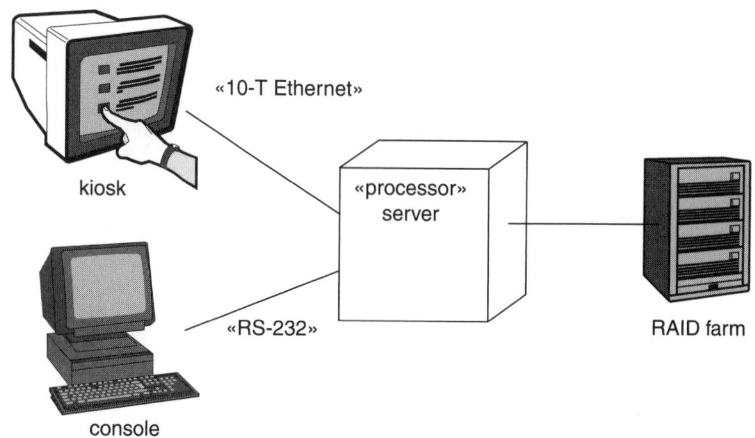

Figure 27-5: Processors and Devices

Modeling the Distribution of Artifacts

The semantics of location are discussed in Chapter 24.

When you model the topology of a system, it's often useful to visualize or specify the physical distribution of its artifacts across the processors and devices that make up the system.

To model the distribution of artifacts,

- For each significant artifact in your system, allocate it to a given node.
- Consider duplicate locations for artifacts. It's not uncommon for the same kind of artifact (such as specific executables and libraries) to reside on multiple nodes simultaneously.
- Render this allocation in one of three ways.
  1. Don't make the allocation visible, but leave it as part of the backplane of your model—that is, in each node's specification.
  2. Using dependency relationships, connect each node with the artifacts it deploys.
  3. List the artifacts deployed on a node in an additional compartment.

Instances are discussed in Chapter 13; object diagrams are discussed in Chapter 14.

Using the third approach, Figure 27-6 takes the earlier diagrams and specifies the executable artifacts that reside on each node. This diagram is a bit different from the previous ones in that it is an object diagram, visualizing specific instances of each node. In this case, the `RAID farm` and `kiosk` instances are both anonymous and the other two instances are named (`c` for the `console` and `s` for the `server`). Each processor in this figure is rendered with an additional compartment showing the artifact it deploys. The `server` object is also rendered with its attributes (`processorSpeed` and `memory`) and their values visible. The deployment compartment can show a text list of artifact names, or it can show nested artifact symbols.

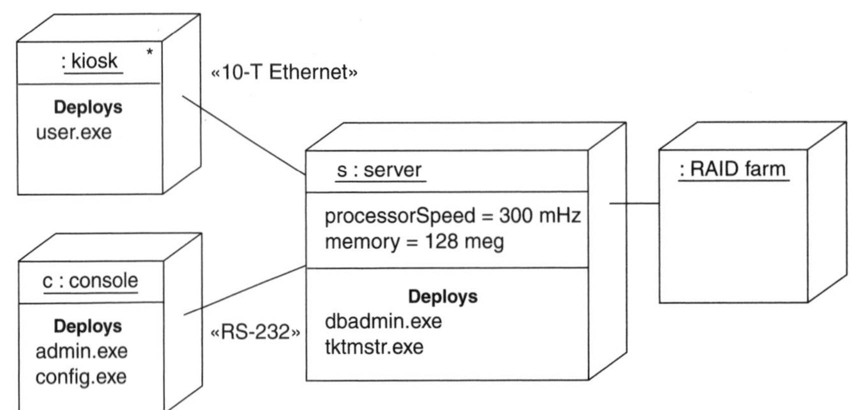

Figure 27-6: Modeling the Distribution of Artifacts

Hints and Tips

A well-structured node

- Provides a crisp abstraction of something drawn from the vocabulary of the hardware in your solution domain.
- Is decomposed only to the level necessary to communicate your intent to the reader.
- Exposes only those attributes and operations that are relevant to the domain you are modeling.
- Directly deploys a set of artifacts that reside on the node.
- Is connected to other nodes in a manner that reflects the topology of the real world system.

When you draw a node in the UML,

- For your project or organization as a whole, define a set of stereotypes with appropriate icons to provide meaningful visual cues to your readers.
- Show only the attributes and operations (if any) that are necessary to understand the meaning of that node in the given context.

Chapter 28 COLLABORATIONS

In this chapter

- Collaborations, realizations, and interactions
- Modeling the realization of a use case
- Modeling the realization of an operation
- Modeling a mechanism
- Reifying interactions

In the context of a system's architecture, a collaboration allows you to name a conceptual chunk that encompasses both static and dynamic aspects. A collaboration names a society of classes, interfaces, and other elements that work together to provide some cooperative behavior that's bigger than the sum of all its parts.

You use collaborations to specify the realization of use cases and operations, and to model the architecturally significant mechanisms of your system.

Getting Started

Think about the most beautiful building you've even seen—perhaps the Taj Mahal or Notre Dame. Both structures exhibit a quality that's hard to name. In many ways, both structures are architecturally simple, yet they are also profoundly deep. In each, you can immediately recognize a consistent symmetry. Look harder, and you'll see details that are themselves beautiful and that work together to produce a beauty and functionality that's greater than the individual parts.

Now think about the ugliest building you've even seen—perhaps your local fast food outlet. You'll find a visual cacophony of architectural styles—a touch of modernism combined with a Georgian roof line, all decorated in a jarring fashion, with bold colors that assault the eye. Usually these buildings are pure manipulation, with narrow function and hardly any form.

What's the difference between these two kinds of civil architecture? First, in buildings of quality, you'll find a harmony of design that's lacking in the others. Quality architecture uses a small set of architectural styles applied in a consistent fashion. For example, the Taj Mahal uses complex, symmetrical, and balanced geometric elements throughout. Second, in buildings of quality, you'll find common patterns that transcend the building's individual elements. For example, in Notre Dame, certain walls are load bearing and serve to support the cathedral's dome. Yet some of these same walls, along with other architectural details, serve as part of the building's system for diverting water and waste.

The five views of an architecture are discussed in Chapter 2.

So it is with software. A quality software-intensive system is not only functionally sound, but it also exhibits a harmony and balance of design that makes it resilient to change. This harmony and balance most often come from the fact that all well-structured object-oriented systems are full of patterns. Look at any quality object-oriented system and you'll see elements that work together in common ways to provide some cooperative behavior that's bigger than the sum of all its parts. In a well-structured system, many of the elements, in various combinations, will participate in different mechanisms.

Patterns and frameworks are discussed in Chapter 29.

Note: A pattern provides a good solution to a common problem in some context. In any well-structured system, you'll find a spectrum of patterns, including idioms (representing common ways of programming), mechanisms (design patterns that represent conceptual chunks of a system's architecture), and frameworks (architectural patterns that provide extensible templates for applications within a domain).

Structural modeling is discussed in Parts 2 and 3; behavioral modeling is discussed in Parts 4 and 5; interactions are discussed in Chapter 16.

In the UML, you model mechanisms using collaborations. A collaboration gives a name to the interacting building blocks of your system, encompassing both structural and behavioral elements. For example, you might have a distributed management information system whose databases are spread across several nodes. From the user's perspective, updating information looks atomic; from the inside perspective, it's not so simple, because such an action has to touch multiple machines. To give the illusion of simplicity, you'd want to devise a transaction mechanism with which a client could name what looks like a single, atomic transaction, even across various databases. Such a mechanism would span multiple classes working together to carry out a transaction. Many of these classes would be involved in other mechanisms as well, such as mechanisms for making information persistent. This collection of classes (the structural part), together with their interactions (the behavioral part), forms a mechanism, which, in the UML, you can represent as a collaboration.

Use cases are discussed in Chapter 17; operations are discussed in Chapters 4 and 9.

Collaborations not only name a system's mechanisms, they also serve as the realization of use cases and operations.

The UML provides a graphical representation for collaborations, as Figure 28-1 shows. This notation permits you to visualize the structural and behavioral building blocks of a system, especially as they may overlap the classes, interfaces, and other elements of the system.

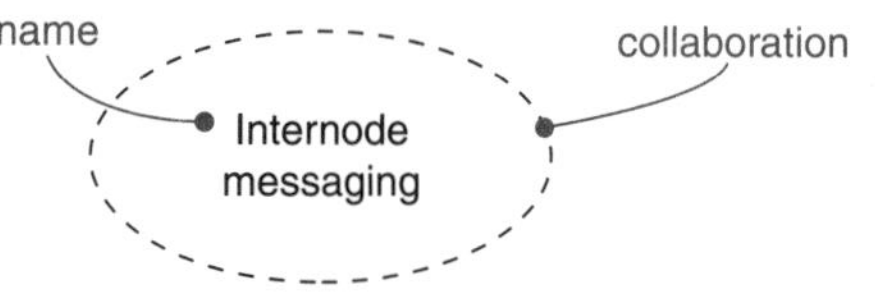

Figure 28-1: Collaborations

Class diagrams are discussed in Chapter 8; interaction diagrams are discussed in Chapter 19.

Note: This notation lets you visualize a collaboration from the outside as one chunk. What's often more interesting is what's inside this notation. Zoom into a collaboration and you'll be led to other diagrams—most notably, class diagrams (for the collaboration's structural part) and interaction diagrams (for the collaboration's behavioral part).

Terms and Concepts

The notation for collaborations is intentionally similar to that for use cases, as discussed in Chapter 17.

A *collaboration* is a society of classes, interfaces, and other elements that work together to provide some cooperative behavior that's bigger than the sum of all its parts. A collaboration is also the specification of how an element, such as a classifier (including a class, interface, component, node, or use case) or an operation, is realized by a set of classifiers and associations playing specific roles used in a specific way. Graphically, a collaboration is rendered as an ellipse with dashed lines.

Names

A collaboration name must be unique within its enclosing package, as discussed in Chapter 12.

Every collaboration must have a name that distinguishes it from other collaborations. A *name* is a textual string. That name alone is known as a *simple name*; a *qualified name* is the collaboration name prefixed by the name of the package in which that collaboration lives. Typically, a collaboration is drawn showing only its name, as in the previous figure.

Note: A collaboration name may be text consisting of any number of letters, numbers, and certain punctuation marks (except for marks such as the colon, which is used to separate a collaboration name and the name of its enclosing package) and may continue over several lines. In practice, collaboration names are short nouns or noun phrases drawn from the vocabulary of the system you are modeling. Typically, you capitalize the first letter of a collaboration name, as in `Transaction` or `Chain of responsibility`.

Structure

Structural elements are discussed in Parts 2 and 3.

Collaborations have two aspects: a structural part that specifies the classes, interfaces, and other elements that work together to carry out the named collaboration; and a behavioral part that specifies the dynamics of how those elements interact.

Classifiers are discussed in Chapter 9; relationships are discussed in Chapters 5 and 10; internal structure is discussed in Chapter 15; packages are discussed in Chapter 12; subsystems are discussed in Chapter 32; use cases are discussed in Chapter 17.

The structural part of a collaboration is an internal (composite) structure that may include any combination of classifiers, such as classes, interfaces, components, and nodes. Within a collaboration, these classifiers may be organized using all the usual UML relationships, including associations, generalizations, and dependencies. In fact, the structural aspects of a collaboration may use the full range of the UML's structural modeling facilities.

However, unlike a structured class, a collaboration does not own its structural elements. Rather, a collaboration simply references or uses the classes, interfaces, components, nodes, and other structural elements that are declared elsewhere. That's why a collaboration names a conceptual chunk—not a physical chunk—of a system's architecture. A collaboration may cut across many levels of a system. Furthermore, the same element may appear in more than one collaboration (and some elements will not be named as part of any collaboration at all).

For example, given a Web-based retail system described by a dozen or so use cases (such as `Purchase Items`, `Return Items`, and `Query Order`), each use case will be realized by a single collaboration. In addition, each of these collaborations will share some of the same structural elements (such as the classes `Customer` and `Order`), but they will be organized in different ways. You'll also find collaborations deeper inside the system, which represent architecturally significant mechanisms. For example, in this same retail system, you might have a collaboration called `Internode messaging` that specifies the details of secure messaging among nodes.

Class diagrams are discussed in Chapter 8.

Given a collaboration that names a conceptual chunk of a system, you can zoom inside that collaboration to expose the structural details of its parts. For example, Figure 28-2 illustrates how zooming inside the collaboration `Internode messaging` might reveal the following set of classes, rendered in a class diagram.

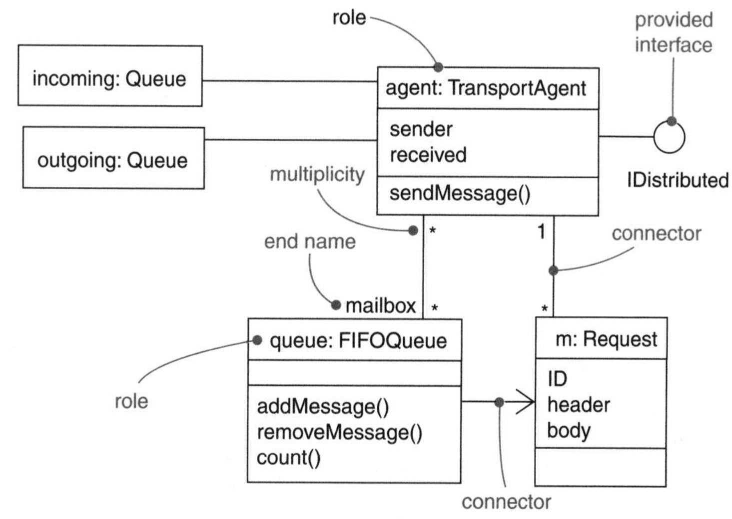

Figure 28-2: Structural Aspects of a Collaboration

Behavior

Interaction diagrams are discussed in Chapter 19; instances are discussed in Chapter 13; composite structure is discussed in Chapter 15.

Whereas the structural part of a collaboration is typically rendered using a composite structure diagram, the behavioral part of a collaboration is typically rendered using an interaction diagram. An interaction diagram specifies an interaction that represents a behavior comprised of a set of messages that are exchanged among a set of objects within a context to accomplish a specific purpose. An interaction's context is provided by its enclosing collaboration, which establishes the classes, interfaces, components, nodes, and other structural elements whose instances may participate in that interaction.

The behavioral part of a collaboration may be specified by one or more interaction diagrams. If you want to emphasize the time ordering of messages, use a sequence diagram. If you want to emphasize the structural relationships among these objects as they collaborate, use a collaboration diagram. Either diagram is appropriate because, for most purposes, they are semantically equivalent.

This means that when you model a society of classes by naming their interaction as a collaboration, you can zoom inside that collaboration to expose the details of their behavior. For example, zooming inside the collaboration named `Internode messaging` might reveal the interaction diagram shown in Figure 28-3.

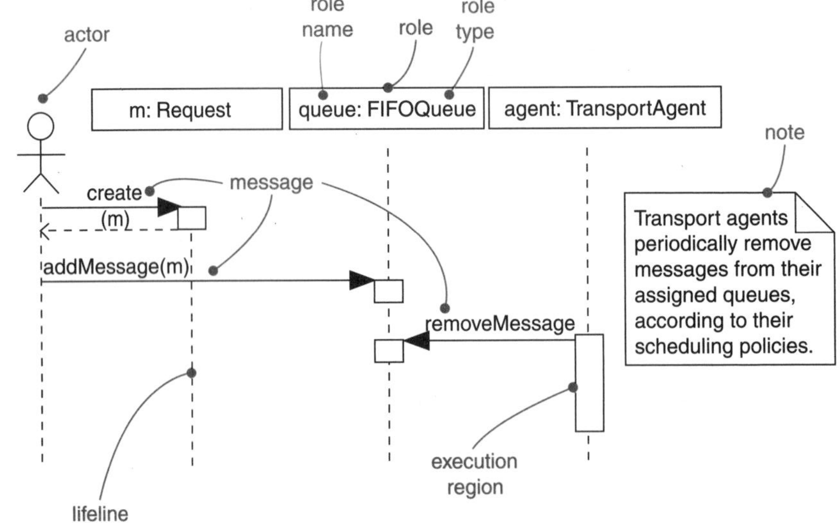

Figure 28-3: Behavioral Aspects of a Collaboration

Note: The behavioral parts of a collaboration must be consistent with its structural parts. This means that the roles found in a collaboration's interactions must match the roles found in its internal structure. Similarly, the messages named in an interaction must relate to operations visible in the collaboration's structural part. You can have more than one interaction associated with a collaboration, each of which may show a different—but consistent—aspect of its behavior.

Organizing Collaborations

The heart of a system's architecture is found in its collaborations, because the mechanisms that shape a system represent significant design decisions. All well-structured object-oriented systems are composed of a modestly sized and regular set of such collaborations, so it's important for you to organize your collaborations well. There are two kinds of relationships concerning collaborations that you'll need to consider.

Use cases are discussed in Chapter 17; operations are discussed in Chapters 4 and 9; realization relationships are discussed in Chapter 10.

First, there is the relationship between a collaboration and the thing it realizes. A collaboration may realize either a classifier or an operation, which means that the collaboration specifies the structural and behavioral realization of that classifier or operation. For example, a use case (which names a set of sequences of actions that a system performs) may be realized by a collaboration. That use case, including its associated actors and neighboring use cases, provides a context for the collaboration. Similarly, an operation (which names the implementation of a service) may be realized by a collaboration. That operation, including its parameters and possible return value, also provides a context for the collaboration. The relationship between a use case or an operation and the collaboration that realizes it is modeled as a realization relationship.

Classifiers are discussed in Chapter 9.

Note: A collaboration may realize any kind of classifier, including classes, use cases, interfaces, and components. A collaboration that models a mechanism of the system may also stand alone, therefore its context is the system as a whole.

Second, there is the relationship among collaborations. Collaborations may refine other collaborations, and you also model this relationship as a refinement. The refinement relationships among collaborations typically mirror the refinement relationships among the use cases they represent.

Figure 28-4 illustrates these two kinds of relationships.

Packages are discussed in Chapter 12.

Note: Collaborations, like any other modeling element in the UML, may be grouped into larger packages. Typically, you'll only need to do this for very large systems.

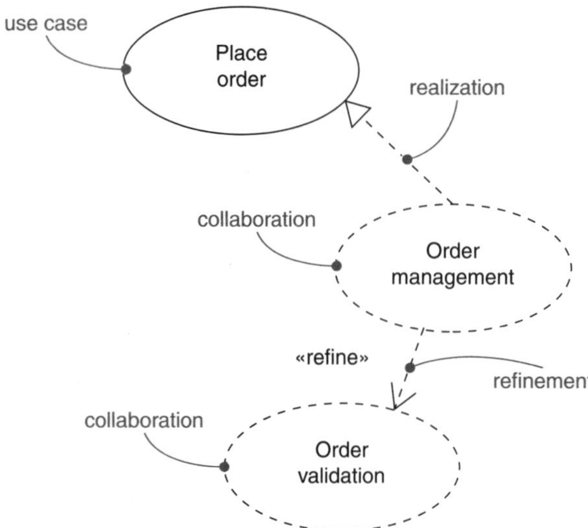

Figure 28-4: Organizing Collaborations

Common Modeling Techniques

Modeling Roles

Interactions are discussed in Chapters 16 and 19; internal structure is discussed in Chapter 15.

Objects represent single individuals in a situation or execution. They are useful within concrete examples, but most of the time we want to show general parts within some context. A part within a context is called a *role*. Perhaps the most important thing for which you'll use roles is to model the dynamic interactions. When you model such interactions, you are generally not modeling concrete instances that exist in the real world. Instead, you are modeling roles within a reusable pattern, within which the roles are essentially proxies or stand-ins for objects that will appear within individual instances of the pattern. For example, if you want to model the ways objects in a windowing application react to a mouse event, you'd draw an interaction diagram containing roles whose types include windows, events, and handlers.

To model roles,

- Identify a context within which several objects interact.
- Identify those roles necessary and sufficient to visualize, specify, construct, or document the context you are modeling.

- Render these roles in the UML as roles in a structured context. Where possible, give each role a name. If there is no meaningful name for the role, render it as an anonymous role.
- Expose the properties of each role necessary and sufficient to model your context.
- Render these roles and their relationships in an interaction diagram or a class diagram.

Note: The semantic difference between concrete objects and roles is subtle but not difficult. To be precise, a UML role is a predefined part of a structured classifier, such as a structured class or a collaboration. A role is not an object, but a description; a role is bound to a value within each instance of a structured classifier. A role therefore corresponds to many possible values, just as an attribute does. Concrete objects appear in specific examples, such as object diagrams, component diagrams, and deployment diagrams. Roles appear in generic descriptions as interaction diagrams and activity diagrams.

Interaction diagrams are discussed in Chapter 19; activity diagrams are discussed in Chapter 20.

Figure 28-5 shows an interaction diagram illustrating a partial scenario for initiating a phone call in the context of a switch. There are four roles: `a` (a `CallingAgent`), `c` (a `Connection`), and `t1` and `t2` (both instances of `Terminal`). All four of these roles represent conceptual proxies for concrete objects that may exist in the real world.

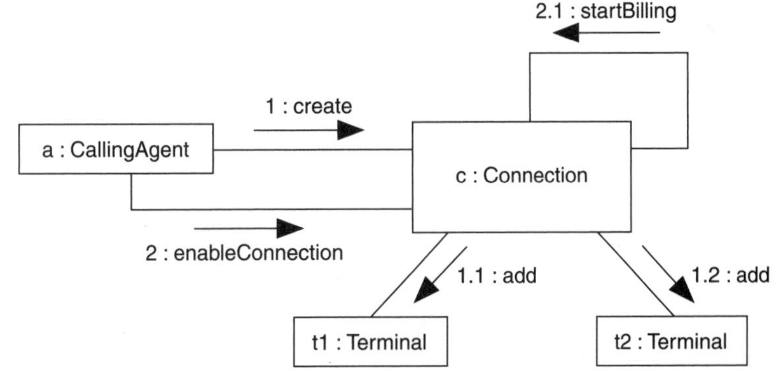

Figure 28-5: Modeling Roles

Note: This example is a collaboration, which represents a society of objects and other elements that work together to provide some cooperative behavior that's bigger than the sum of all the elements. Collaborations have two aspects—one structural (representing the classifier roles and their relationships) and one dynamic (representing the interactions among those prototypical instances).

Modeling the Realization of a Use Case

Use cases are discussed in Chapter 17.

One of the purposes for which you'll use collaborations is to model the realization of a use case. You'll typically drive the analysis of your system by identifying your system's use cases, but when you finally turn to implementation, you'll need to realize these use cases with concrete structures and behaviors. In general, every use case should be realized by one or more collaborations. For the system as a whole, the classifiers involved in a given collaboration that is linked to a use case will participate in other collaborations as well. In this way, the structural contents of collaborations tend to overlap one another.

To model the realization of a use case,

- Identify those structural elements necessary and sufficient to carry out the semantics of the use case.
- Capture the organization of these structural elements in class diagrams.
- Consider the individual scenarios that represent this use case. Each scenario represents a specific path through the use case.
- Capture the dynamics of these scenarios in interaction diagrams. Use sequence diagrams if you want to emphasize the time ordering of messages. Use communication diagrams if you want to emphasize the structural relationships among these objects as they collaborate.
- Organize these structural and behavioral elements as a collaboration that you can connect to the use case via realization.

For example, Figure 28-6 shows a set of use cases drawn from a credit card validation system, including the primary use cases `Place order` and `Generate bill`, together with two other subordinate use cases, `Detect card fraud` and `Validate transaction`. Although most of the time you won't need to model this relationship explicitly (but will leave it up to your tools), this figure explicitly models the realization of `Place order` by the collaboration `Order management`. In turn, this collaboration can be further expanded into its structural and behavioral aspects, leading you to class diagrams and interaction diagrams. It is through the realization relationship that you connect a use case to its scenarios.

In most cases, you won't need to model the relationship between a use case and the collaboration that realizes it explicitly. Instead, you'll tend to leave that in the backplane of your model. Then let tools use that connection to help you navigate between a use case and its realization.

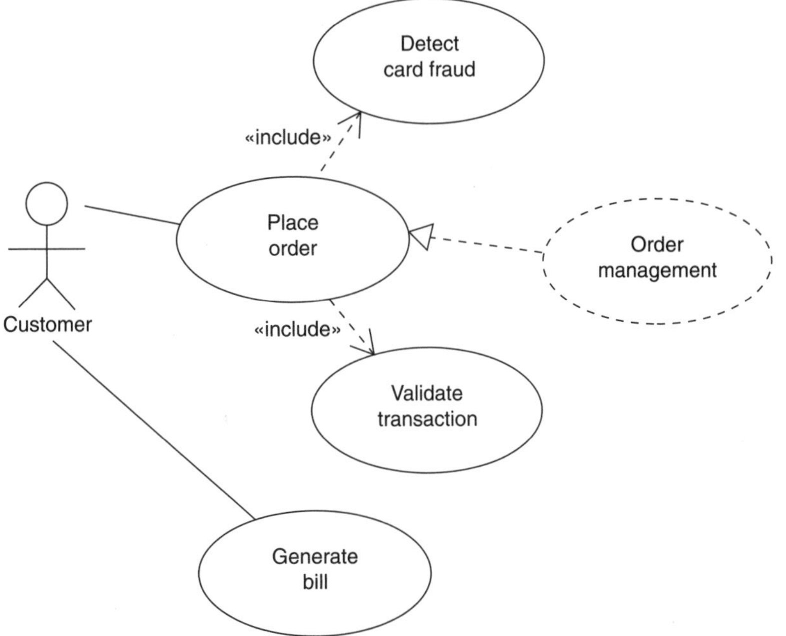

Figure 28-6: Modeling the Realization of a Use Case

Modeling the Realization of an Operation

Operations are discussed in Chapters 4 and 9.

Another purpose for which you'll use collaborations is to model the realization of an operation. In many cases, you can specify the realization of an operation by going straight to code. However, for those operations that require the collaboration of a number of objects, it's better to model their implementation via collaborations before you dive into code.

The parameters, return value, and objects local to an operation provide the context for its realization. Therefore, these elements are visible to the structural aspect of the collaboration that realizes the operation, just as actors are visible to the structural aspect of a collaboration that realizes a use case. You can model the relationship among these parts using a composite structure diagram that specifies the structural part of a collaboration.

To model the implementation of an operation,

Notes are discussed in Chapter 6.

- Identify the parameters, return value, and other objects visible to the operation. These become roles of the collaboration.
- If the operation is trivial, represent its implementation directly in code, which you can keep in the backplane of your model, or explicitly visualize it in a note.
- If the operation is algorithmically intensive, model its realization using an activity diagram.
- If the operation is complex or otherwise requires some detailed design work, represent its implementation as a collaboration. You can further expand the structural and behavioral parts of this collaboration using class and interaction diagrams, respectively.

Active classes are discussed in Chapter 23.

For example, Figure 28-7 shows the active class `RenderFrame` with three of its operations exposed. The function `progress` is simple enough to be implemented directly in code, as specified in the attached note. However, the operation `render` is much more complicated, so its implementation is realized by the collaboration `Ray trace`. Although not shown here, you could zoom inside the collaboration to see its structural and behavioral aspects.

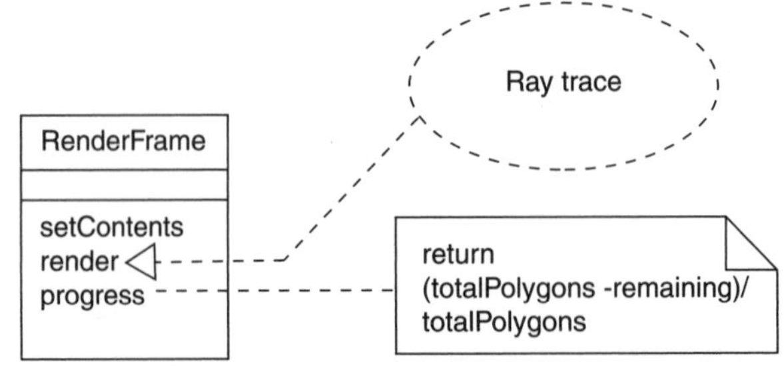

Figure 28-7: Modeling the Realization of an Operation

Activity diagrams are discussed in Chapter 20.

Note: You can also model an operation using activity diagrams. Activity diagrams are essentially flowcharts. So for those algorithmically intensive operations that you want to model explicitly, activity diagrams are usually the best choice. However, if your operation requires the participation of many objects, you'll want to use collaborations, because they let you model the structural, as well as behavioral, aspects of an operation.

Modeling a Mechanism

Patterns and frameworks are discussed in Chapter 29; an example of modeling a mechanism is discussed in the same chapter.

In all well-structured object-oriented systems, you'll find a spectrum of patterns. At one end, you'll find idioms that represent patterns of use of the implementation language. At the other end, you'll find architectural patterns and frameworks that shape the system as a whole and impose a particular style. In the middle, you'll find mechanisms that represent common design patterns by which the things in the system interact with one another in common ways. You can represent a mechanism in the UML as a collaboration.

Mechanisms are collaborations that stand alone; their context is not a single use case or an operation but, rather, the system as a whole. Any element visible in that part of the system is a candidate for participation in a mechanism.

Mechanisms such as these represent architecturally significant design decisions and should not be treated lightly. Typically, your system's architect will devise its mechanisms, and you'll evolve these mechanisms with each new release. At the end, you'll find your system simple (because these mechanisms reify common interactions), understandable (because you can approach the system from its mechanisms), and resilient (by tuning each mechanism, you tune the system as a whole).

To model a mechanism,

- Identify the major mechanisms that shape your system's architecture. These mechanisms are driven by the overall architectural style you choose to impose on your implementation, along with the style appropriate to your problem domain.
- Represent each of these mechanisms as a collaboration.
- Expand on the structural and behavioral part of each collaboration. Look for sharing, where possible.
- Validate these mechanisms early in the development lifecycle (they are of strategic importance), but evolve them with each new release, as you learn more about the details of your implementation.

Hints and Tips

When you model collaborations in the UML, remember that every collaboration should represent either the realization of a use case or operation or should stand alone as a mechanism of the system. A well-structured collaboration

- Consists of both structural and behavioral aspects.
- Provides a crisp abstraction of some identifiable interaction in the system.
- Is rarely completely independent, but will overlap with the structural elements of other collaborations.
- Is understandable and simple.

When you draw a collaboration in the UML,

- Explicitly render a collaboration only when it's necessary to understand its relationship to other collaborations, classifiers, operations, or the system as a whole. Otherwise, use collaborations, but keep them in the backplane.
- Organize collaborations according to the classifier or operation they represent, or in packages associated with the system as a whole.

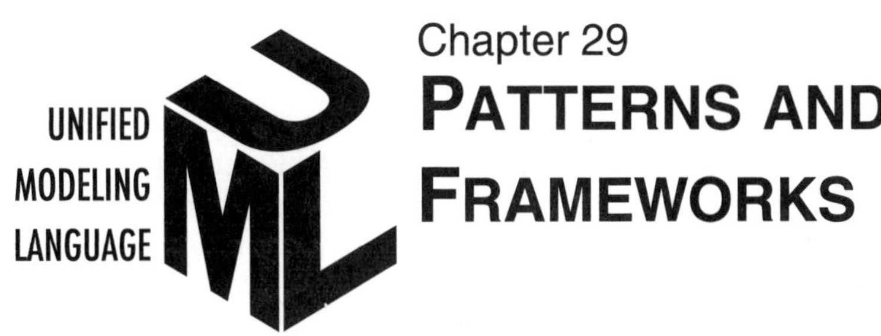

Chapter 29

Patterns and Frameworks

In this chapter

- Patterns and frameworks
- Modeling design patterns
- Modeling architectural patterns
- Making patterns approachable

All well-structured systems are full of patterns. A pattern provides a good solution to a common problem in a given context. A mechanism is a design pattern that applies to a society of classes; a framework is typically an architectural pattern that provides an extensible template for applications within a domain.

You use patterns to specify mechanisms and frameworks that shape the architecture of your system. You make a pattern approachable by clearly identifying the slots, tabs, knobs, and dials that a user of that pattern may adjust to apply the pattern in a particular context.

Getting Started

It's amazing to think of the various ways you can assemble a pile of lumber to build a house. In the hands of a master builder in San Francisco, you might see that pile transformed into a Victorian-style house, complete with a gabled roof line and brightly colored, storybook siding. In the hands of a master builder in Maine, you might see that same pile transformed into saltbox house, with clapboard siding and rectangular shapes throughout.

From the outside, these two houses represent clearly different architectural styles. Every builder, drawing from experience, must choose a style that best meets the needs of his or her customer, and then adapt that style to the customer's wishes and the constraints of the building site and local covenants.

For the inside, each builder must also design the house to solve some common problems. There are only so many proven ways to engineer trusses to support a roof; there are only so many proven ways to design a load-bearing wall that must also handle openings for doors and windows. Every builder must select the appropriate mechanisms that solve these common problems, adapted to an overall architectural style and the constraints of local building codes.

Building a software-intensive system is just like that. Every time you raise your eyes above individual lines of code, you'll find common mechanisms that shape the way you organize your classes and other abstractions. For example, in an event-driven system, using the chain of responsibility design pattern is a common way to organize event handlers. Raise your eyes above the level of these mechanisms and you'll find common frameworks that shape your system's entire architecture. For example, in information systems, using a three-tier architecture is a common way to achieve a clear separation of concerns among the system's user interface, its persistent information, and its business objects and rules.

Collaborations are discussed in Chapter 28; packages are discussed in Chapter 12.

In the UML, you will typically model design patterns—also called mechanisms—which you can represent as collaborations. Similarly, you will typically model architectural patterns as frameworks, which you can represent as stereotyped packages.

The UML provides a graphical representation for both kinds of patterns, as Figure 29-1 shows.

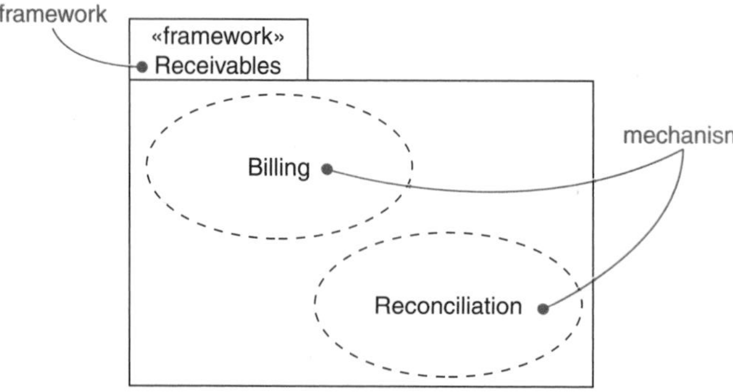

Figure 29-1: Mechanisms and Frameworks

Terms and Concepts

A *pattern* is a common solution to a common problem in a given context. A *mechanism* is a design pattern that applies to a society of classes. A *framework* is an architectural pattern that provides an extensible template for applications within a domain.

Patterns and Architecture

Software architecture is discussed in Chapter 2.

Whether you're architecting a new system or evolving an existing one, you never really start from scratch. Rather, experience and convention will lead you to apply common ways to solve common problems. For example, if you are building a user-intensive system, one proven way to organize your abstractions is to use a model-view-controller pattern, in which you clearly separate objects (the model) from their presentation (the view) and the agents that keep the two in sync (the controller). Similarly, if you are building a system for solving cryptograms, one proven way to organize your system is to use a blackboard architecture, which is well-suited to attacking intractable problems in opportunistic ways.

Both of these are examples of patterns—common solutions to common problems in a given context. In all well-structured systems, you'll find lots of patterns at various levels of abstraction. Design patterns specify the structure and behavior of a society of classes, whereas architectural patterns specify the structure and behavior of an entire system.

Patterns are part of the UML simply because patterns are important parts of a developer's vocabulary. By making the patterns in your system explicit, you make your system far more understandable and easier to evolve and maintain. For example, if you are handed a new, raw body of code to extend, you'll struggle for a while trying to figure out how it all fits together. On the other hand, if you are handed that same body of code and told, "These classes collaborate using a publish-and-subscribe mechanism," you will be a lot further down the path of understanding how it works. The same idea applies to a system as a whole. Saying "This system is organized as a set of pipes and filters" explains a great deal about the system's architecture that would otherwise be difficult to comprehend just by starting at individual classes.

Patterns help you to visualize, specify, construct, and document the artifacts of a software-intensive system. You can forward engineer a system by selecting an appropriate set of patterns and applying them to the abstractions specific to your domain. You can also reverse engineer a system by discovering the patterns it embodies, although that's hardly a perfect process. Even better, when you deliver a system, you can specify the patterns it embodies so that when someone later tries to reuse or adapt that system, its patterns will be clearly manifest.

In practice, there are two kinds of patterns of interest—design patterns and frameworks—and the UML provides a means of modeling both. When you model either pattern, you'll find that it typically stands alone in the context of some larger package, except for dependency relationships that bind them to other parts of your system.

Mechanisms

A mechanism is just another name for a design pattern that applies to a society of classes. For example, one common design problem you'll encounter in Java is adapting a class that knows how to respond to a certain set of events so that it responds to a slightly different set without altering the original class. A common solution to this problem is the adaptor pattern, a structural design pattern that converts one interface to another. This pattern is so common that it makes sense to name it and then model it so that you can use it anytime you encounter a similar problem.

In modeling, these mechanisms show up in two ways.

Collaborations are discussed in Chapter 28.

First, as shown in the previous figure, a mechanism simply names a set of abstractions that work together to carry out some common and interesting behavior. You model these mechanisms as plain collaborations because they just name a society of classes. Zoom into that collaboration and you'll see its structural aspects (typically rendered as class diagrams) as well as its behavioral aspects (typically rendered as interaction diagrams). Collaborations such as these cut across individual abstractions in the system; a given class will likely be a member of many collaborations.

Template classes are discussed in Chapter 9.

Second, as shown in Figure 29-2, a mechanism names a template for a set of abstractions that work together to carry out some common and interesting behavior. You model these mechanisms as parameterized collaborations, which are rendered in the UML similar to the way template classes are rendered. Zoom into that collaboration and you'll see its structural and behavioral aspects. Zoom out of the collaboration and you'll see how that pattern applies to your system by binding the template parts of the collaboration to existing abstractions in your system. When you model a mechanism as a parameterized collaboration, you identify the slots, tabs, knobs, and dials you use to adapt that pattern by means of its template parameters. Collaborations such as these may appear repeatedly in your system, bound to different sets of abstractions.

In this example, the `Subject` and the `Observer` classes of the pattern are bound to the concrete classes `TaskQueue` and `SliderBar`, respectively.

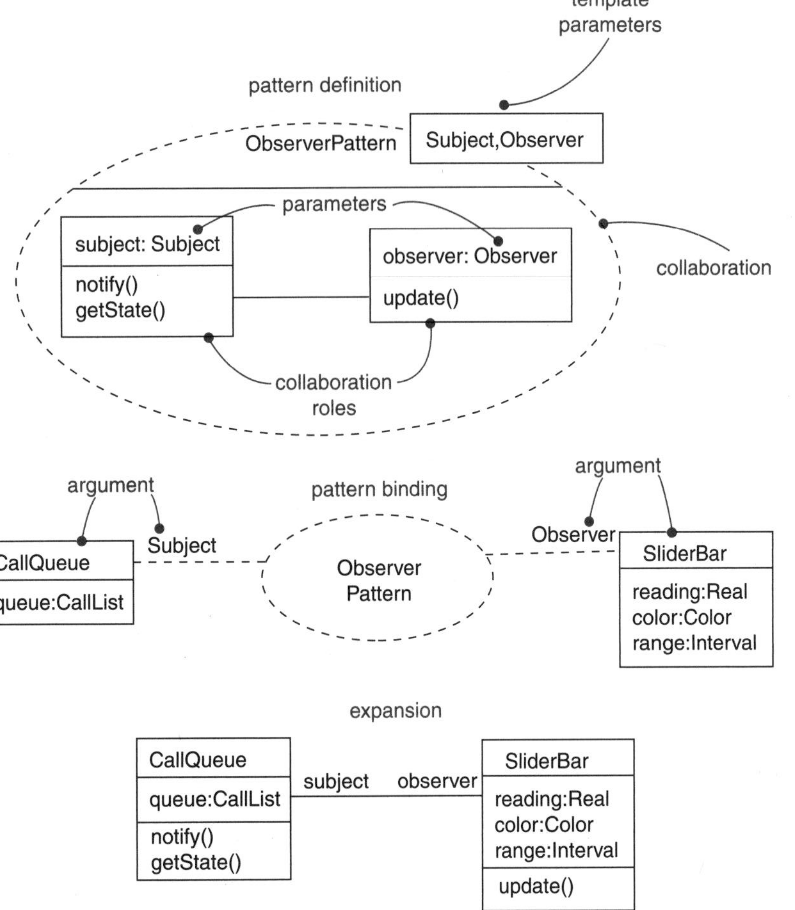

Figure 29-2: Mechanisms

Note: Deciding to model a mechanism as a plain collaboration versus a parameterized one is straightforward. Use a plain collaboration if all you are doing is naming a specific society of classes in your system that work together; use a template collaboration if you can abstract the essential structural and behavioral aspects of the mechanism in a completely domain-independent way, which you can then bind to your abstractions in a given context.

Frameworks

A framework is an architectural pattern that provides an extensible template for applications within a domain. For example, one common architectural pattern you'll encounter in real time systems is a cyclic executive, which divides time into frames and subframes, during which processing takes place under strict deadlines. Choosing this pattern versus its alternative (an event-driven architecture) colors your entire system. Because this pattern (and its alternative) is so common, it makes sense to name it as a framework.

The five views of an architecture are discussed in Chapter 2.

A framework is bigger than a mechanism. In fact, you can think of a framework as a kind of micro-architecture that encompasses a set of mechanisms that work together to solve a common problem for a common domain. When you specify a framework, you specify the skeleton of an architecture, together with the slots, tabs, knobs, and dials that you expose to users who want to adapt that framework to their own context.

Packages are discussed in Chapter 12; stereotypes are discussed in Chapter 6.

In the UML, you model a framework as a stereotyped package. Zoom inside that package and you'll see mechanisms that live in any of various views of a system's architecture. For example, not only might you find parameterized collaborations, you might also find use cases (which explain how to use the framework) as well as plain collaborations (which provide sets of abstractions that you can build upon—for instance, by subclassing).

Events are discussed in Chapter 21.

Figure 29-3 illustrates such a framework, named `CyclicExecutive`. Among other things, this framework includes a collaboration (`CommonEvents`) encompassing a set of event classes, along with a mechanism (`EventHandler`) for processing these events in a cyclic fashion. A client that builds on this framework (such as `Pacemaker`) could build on the abstractions in `CommonEvents` via subclassing and could also apply an instance of the `EventHandler` mechanism.

Note: Frameworks can be distinguished from plain class libraries. A class library contains abstractions that your abstractions instantiate or invoke; a framework contains abstractions that may instantiate or invoke your abstractions. Both of these kinds of connections constitute the framework's slots, tabs, knobs, and dials that you must adjust to adapt the framework to your context.

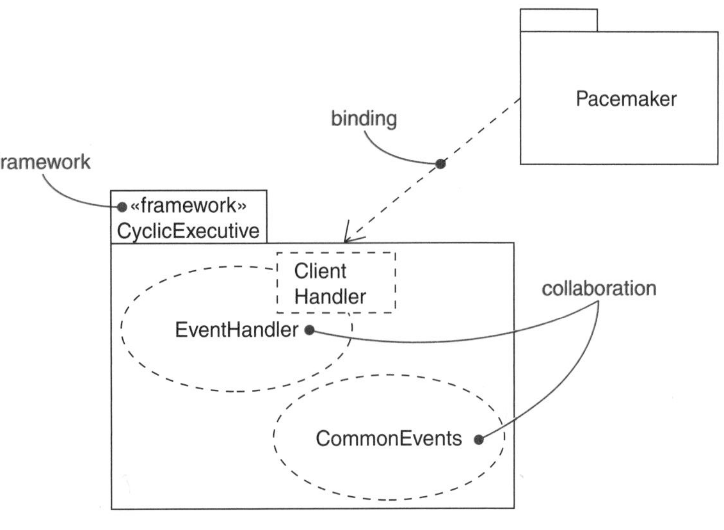

Figure 29-3: Frameworks

Common Modeling Techniques

Modeling Design Patterns

One thing for which you'll use patterns is to model a design pattern. When you model a mechanism such as this, you have to take into account its inside as well as its outside view.

When viewed from the outside, a design pattern is rendered as a parameterized collaboration. As a collaboration, a pattern provides a set of abstractions whose structure and behavior work together to carry out some useful function. The collaboration's parameters name the elements that a user of this pattern must bind. This makes the design pattern a template that you use in a particular context by supplying elements that match the template parameters.

When viewed from the inside, a design pattern is simply a collaboration and is rendered with its structural and behavioral parts. Typically, you'll model the inside of this collaboration with a set of class diagrams (for the structural aspect) and a set of interactions (for the behavioral aspect). The collaboration's parameters name certain of these structural elements, which, when the design pattern is bound in a particular context, are instantiated using abstractions from that context.

Using collaborations to model a mechanism is discussed in Chapter 28.

To model a design pattern,

- Identify the common solution to the common problem and reify it as a mechanism.
- Model the mechanism as a collaboration, providing its structural as well as its behavioral aspects.
- Identify the elements of the design pattern that must be bound to elements in a specific context and render them as parameters to the collaboration.

For example, Figure 29-4 shows a use of the `Command` design pattern (as discussed in Gamma et al., *Design Patterns*, Reading, Massachusetts: Addison-Wesley, 1995). As its documentation states, this pattern "encapsulates a request as an object, thereby letting you parameterize clients with different requests, queue or log requests, and support undoable operations." As the model indicates, this design pattern has three parameters that, when you apply the pattern, must be bound to elements in a given context. This model shows two such bindings, in which `PasteCommand` and `OpenCommand` are bound to separate bindings of the pattern.

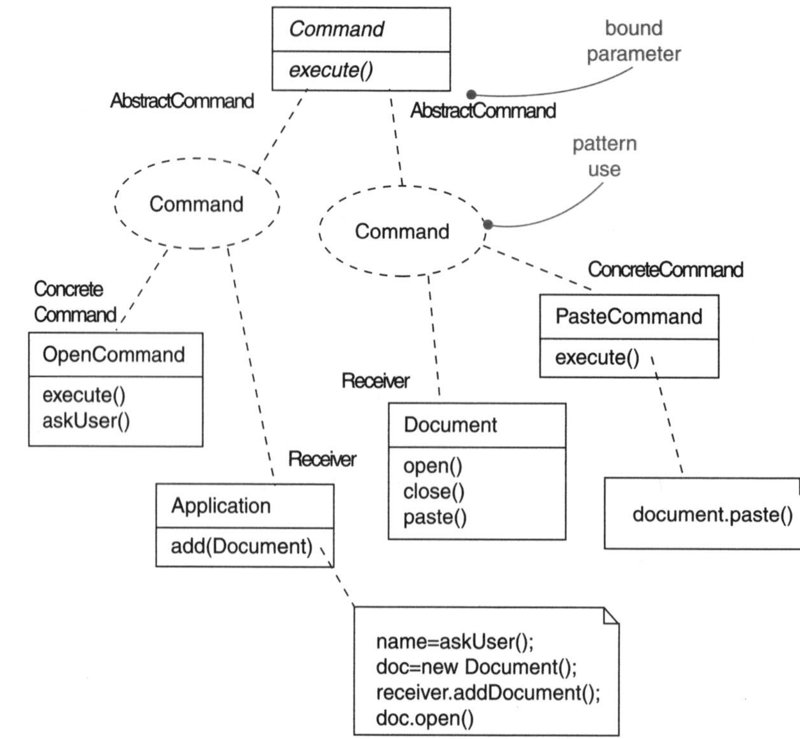

Figure 29-4: Modeling a Design Pattern

The parameters are the `AbstractCommand`, which must be bound to the same abstract superclass in every case; the `ConcreteCommand`, which is bound to the various specific classes in various bindings; and the `Receiver`, which is bound to the class on which the command acts. The `Command` class could be created by the pattern, but making it a parameter permits multiple command hierarchies to be created.

Note that `PasteCommand` and `OpenCommand` are both subclasses of the `Command` class. Very likely, your system will use this pattern a number of times, perhaps with different bindings. The ability to reuse a design pattern like this as a first-class modeling element is what makes developing with patterns so powerful.

To complete your model of a design pattern, you must specify its structural as well as its behavioral parts, which represent the inside of the collaboration.

Collaborations are discussed in Chapter 28; class diagrams are discussed in Chapter 8; interaction diagrams are discussed in Chapter 19.

For example, Figure 29-5 shows a class diagram that represents the structure of this design pattern. Notice how this diagram uses classes that are named as parameters to the pattern. Figure 29-6 shows a sequence diagram that represents the behavior of this design pattern. Note that the diagram is only suggestive of the possibilities; a design pattern is not a rigid thing.

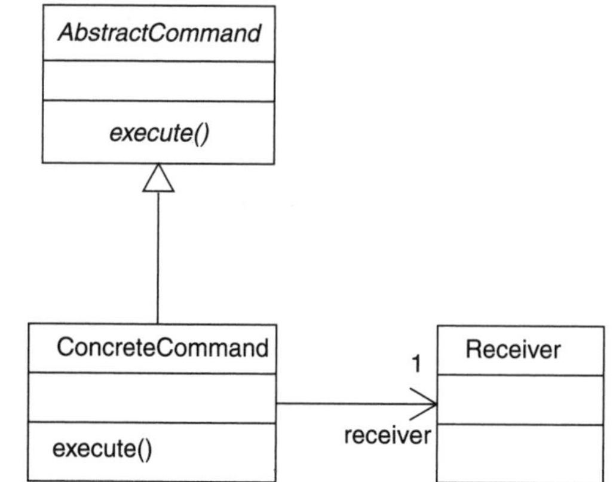

Figure 29-5: Modeling the Structural Aspect of a Design Pattern

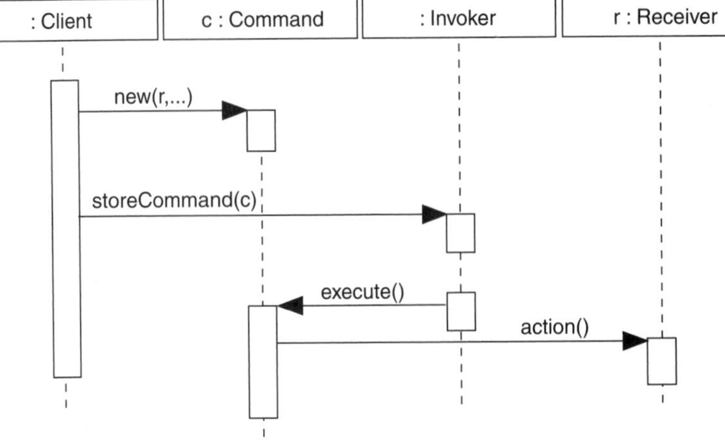

Figure 29-6: Modeling the Behavioral Aspect of a Design Pattern

Modeling Architectural Patterns

Packages are discussed in Chapter 12.

The other thing for which you'll use patterns is to model architectural patterns. When you model such a framework, you are, in effect, modeling the infrastructure of an entire architecture that you plan to reuse and adapt to some context.

A framework is rendered as a stereotyped package. As a package, a framework provides a set of elements, including—but certainly not limited to—classes, interfaces, use cases, components, nodes, collaborations, and even other frameworks. In fact, you'll place in a framework all the abstractions that work together to provide an extensible template for applications within a domain. Some of these elements will be public and represent resources that clients can build on. These are parts of the framework that you can connect to the abstractions in your context. Some of these public elements will be design patterns and represent resources to which clients bind. These are the parts of the framework that you fill in when you bind to the design pattern. Finally, some of these elements will be protected or private and represent encapsulated elements of the framework that are hidden from the outside view.

Software architecture is discussed in Chapter 2.

When you model an architectural pattern, remember that a framework is, in fact, a description of an architecture, albeit one that is incomplete and possibly parameterized. As such, everything you know about modeling a well-structured architecture applies to modeling well-structured frameworks. The best frameworks are not designed in isolation; to do so is an guaranteed way to fail. Rather, the best frameworks are harvested from existing architectures that are proven to work, and the frameworks evolve to find the slots, tabs, knobs, and dials that are necessary and sufficient to make that framework adaptable to other domains.

To model an architectural pattern,

- Harvest the framework from an existing, proven architecture.
- Model the framework as a stereotyped package, containing all the elements (and especially the design patterns) that are necessary and sufficient to describe the various views of that framework.
- Expose the plug-ins, interfaces, and parameters necessary to adapt the framework in the form of design patterns and collaborations. For the most part, this means making it clear to the user of the pattern which classes must be extended, which operations must be implemented, and which signals must be handled.

For example, Figure 29-7 shows a specification of the `Blackboard` architectural pattern (as discussed in Buschmann et al., *Pattern-Oriented Software Architecture*, New York, NY: Wiley, 1996). As its documentation states, this pattern "tackles problems that do not have a feasible deterministic solution for the transformation of raw data into high-level data structures." The heart of this architecture is the `Blackboard` design pattern, which dictates how `KnowledgeSources`, a `Blackboard`, and a `Controller` collaborate. This framework also includes the design pattern `Reasoning engine`, which specifies a general mechanism for how each `KnowledgeSource` is driven. Finally, as the figure shows, this framework exposes one use case, `Apply new knowledge sources`, which explains to a client how to adapt the framework itself.

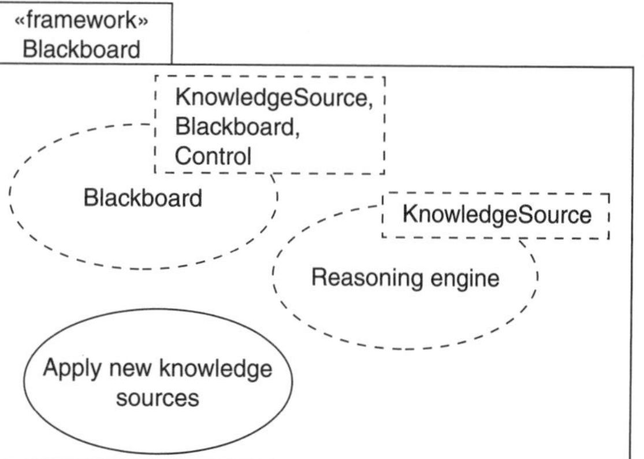

Figure 29-7: Modeling an Architectural Pattern

Note: In practice, modeling a framework completely is no less a task than modeling a system's architecture completely. In some ways, the task is even harder because to make the framework approachable, you must also expose the slots, tabs, knobs, and dials of the framework, and perhaps even provide meta-use cases (such as `Apply new knowledge sources`) that explain how to adapt the framework, as well as plain use cases that explain how the framework behaves.

Hints and Tips

When you model patterns in the UML, remember that they work at many levels of abstraction, from individual classes to the shape of the system as a whole. The most interesting kinds of patterns are mechanisms and frameworks. A well-structured pattern

- Solves a common problem in a common way.
- Consists of both structural and behavioral aspects.
- Exposes the slots, tabs, knobs, and dials by which you adapt those aspects to apply them to some context.
- Is atomic, meaning that it is not easily broken into smaller patterns.
- Tends to cut across individual abstractions in the system.

When you draw a pattern in the UML,

- Expose the elements of the pattern that you must adapt in context.
- Supply use cases for using, as well as adapting, the pattern.

Chapter 30
ARTIFACT DIAGRAMS

In this chapter

- Modeling source code
- Modeling executable releases
- Modeling physical databases
- Modeling adaptable systems
- Forward and reverse engineering

Deployment diagrams, the second kind of diagram used in modeling the physical aspects of an object-oriented system, are discussed in Chapter 31.

Artifact diagrams are one of the two kinds of diagrams found in modeling the physical aspects of object-oriented systems. An artifact diagram shows the organization and dependencies among a set of artifacts.

You use artifact diagrams to model the static implementation view of a system. This involves modeling the physical things that reside on a node, such as executables, libraries, tables, files, and documents. Artifact diagrams are essentially class diagrams that focus on a system's artifacts.

Artifact diagrams are not only important for visualizing, specifying, and documenting artifact-based systems, but also for constructing executable systems through forward and reverse engineering.

Getting Started

When you build a house, you must do more than create blueprints. Mind you, blueprints are important because they help you visualize, specify, and document the kind of house you want to build so that you'll build the right house at the right time at the right price. Eventually, however, you've got to turn your floor plans and elevation drawings into real walls, floors, and ceilings made of wood, stone, or metal. Not only will you build your house out of these raw materials, you'll also incorporate pre-built artifacts, such as cabinets, windows, doors, and vents. If you are renovating a house, you'll reuse even larger artifacts, such as whole rooms and frameworks.

It's the same with software. You create use case diagrams to reason about the desired behavior of your system. You specify the vocabulary of your domain with class diagrams. You create sequence diagrams, collaboration diagrams, state diagrams, and activity diagrams to specify the way the things in your vocabulary work together to carry out this behavior. Eventually, you will turn these logical blueprints into things that live in the world of bits, such as executables, libraries, tables, files, and documents. You'll find that you must build some of these artifacts from scratch, but you'll also end up reusing older artifacts in new ways.

With the UML, you use artifact diagrams to visualize the static aspect of these physical artifacts and their relationships and to specify their details for construction, as in Figure 30-1.

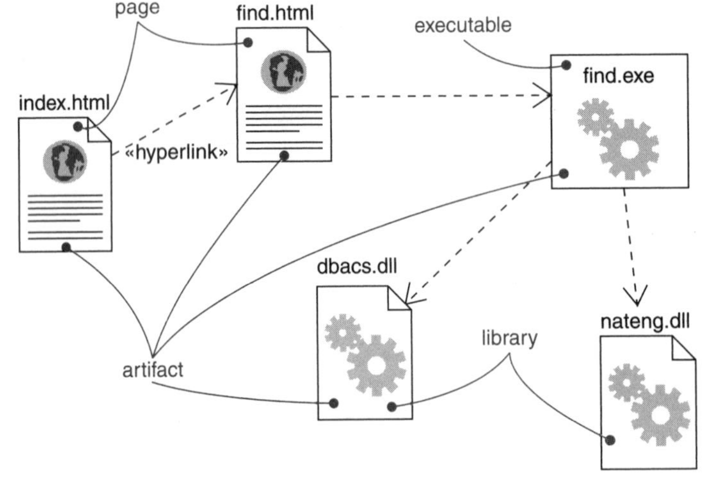

Figure 30-1: An Artifact Diagram

Terms and Concepts

A *artifact diagram* shows a set of artifacts and their relationships. Graphically, a artifact diagram is a collection of vertices and arcs.

Common Properties

The general properties of diagrams are discussed in Chapter 7.

An artifact diagram is just a special usage of diagram that shares the same common properties as do all other diagrams—a name and graphical contents that are a projection into a model. What distinguishes an artifact diagram from all other kinds of diagrams is its particular content.

Contents

Artifacts are discussed in Chapter 26; interfaces are discussed in Chapter 11; relationships are discussed in Chapters 5 and 10; packages are discussed in Chapter 12; subsystems are discussed in Chapter 32; instances are discussed in Chapter 13; class diagrams are discussed in Chapter 8; implementation views, in the context of software architecture, are discussed in Chapter 2.

Artifact diagrams commonly contain

- Artifacts
- Dependency, generalization, association, and realization relationships

Like all other diagrams, artifact diagrams may contain notes and constraints.

Common Uses

You use artifact diagrams to model the static implementation view of a system. This view primarily supports the configuration management of a system's parts, made up of artifacts that can be assembled in various ways to produce a running system.

When you model the static implementation view of a system, you'll typically use artifact diagrams in one of four ways.

1. To model source code

With most contemporary object-oriented programming languages, you'll cut code using integrated development environments that store your source code in files. You can use artifact diagrams to model the configuration of these files, which represent work-product artifacts, and to set up your configuration management system.

2. To model executable releases

A release is a relatively complete and consistent set of artifacts delivered to an internal or external user. In the context of artifacts, a release focuses on the parts necessary to deliver a running system. When you model a release using artifact diagrams, you are visualizing, specifying, and documenting the decisions about the physical parts that constitute your software—that is, its deployment artifacts.

Persistence is discussed in Chapter 24; modeling logical database schemas is discussed in Chapter 8.

3. To model physical databases

Think of a physical database as the concrete realization of a schema living in the world of bits. Schemas, in effect, offer an API to persistent information; the model of a physical database represents the storage of that information in the tables of a relational database or the pages of an object-oriented database. You use artifact diagrams to represent these and other kinds of physical databases.

4. To model adaptable systems

Some systems are quite static; their artifacts enter the scene, participate in an execution, and then depart. Other systems are more dynamic, involving mobile agents or artifacts that migrate for purposes of load balancing and failure recovery. You use artifact diagrams in conjunction with some of the UML's diagrams for modeling behavior to represent these kinds of systems.

Common Modeling Techniques

Modeling Source Code

If you develop software in Java, you'll usually save your source code in `.java` files. If you develop software using C++, you'll typically store your source code in header files (`.h` files) and bodies (`.cpp` files). If you use IDL to develop COM+ or CORBA applications, one interface from your design view will often expand into four source code files: the interface itself, the client proxy, the server stub, and a bridge class. As your application grows, no matter which language you use, you'll find yourself organizing these files into larger groups. Furthermore, during the construction phase of development, you'll probably end up creating new versions of some of these files for each new incremental release you produce, and you'll want to place these versions under the control of a configuration management system.

The `file` stereotype for artifacts is discussed in Chapter 26.

Much of the time, you will not need to model this aspect of a system directly. Instead, you'll let your development environment keep track of these files and their relationships. Sometimes, however, it's helpful to visualize these source code files and their relationships using artifact diagrams. Artifact diagrams used in this way typically contain only work-product artifacts stereotyped as files, together with dependency relationships. For example, you might reverse engineer a set of source code files to visualize their web of compilation dependencies. You can go in the other direction by specifying the relationships among your source code files and then using those models as input to compilation tools, such as `make` on Unix. Similarly, you might want to use artifact diagrams to visualize the history of a set of source code files that are under configuration management. By extracting information from your configuration management system, such as the number of times a source code file has been checked out over a period of time, you can use that information to color artifact diagrams, showing "hot spots" of change among your source code files and areas of architectural churn.

To model a system's source code,

- Either by forward or reverse engineering, identify the set of source code files of interest and model them as artifacts stereotyped as files.
- For larger systems, use packages to show groups of source code files.
- Consider exposing a tagged value indicating such information as the version number of the source code file, its author, and the date it was last changed. Use tools to manage the value of this tag.
- Model the compilation dependencies among the source files using dependencies. Again, use tools to help generate and manage these dependencies.

The `trace` dependency stereotype is discussed in Chapter 10.

For example, Figure 30-2 shows five source code files. The file `signal.h` is a header file. Three of its versions are shown, tracing from new versions back to their older ancestors. Each variant of this source code file is rendered with a tagged value exposing its version number.

This header file (`signal.h`) is used by two other files (`interp.cpp` and `.signal.cpp`), both of which are bodies. One of these files (`interp.cpp`) has a compilation dependency to another header (`irq.h`); in turn, `device.cpp` has a compilation dependency to `interp.cpp`. Given this artifact diagram, it's easy to trace the impact of changes. For example, changing the source code file `signal.h` will require the recompilation of three other files: `signal.cpp`, `interp.cpp`, and transitively, `device.cpp`. As this diagram also shows, the file `irq.h` is not affected.

Diagrams such as this can easily be generated by reverse engineering from the information held by your development environment's configuration management tools.

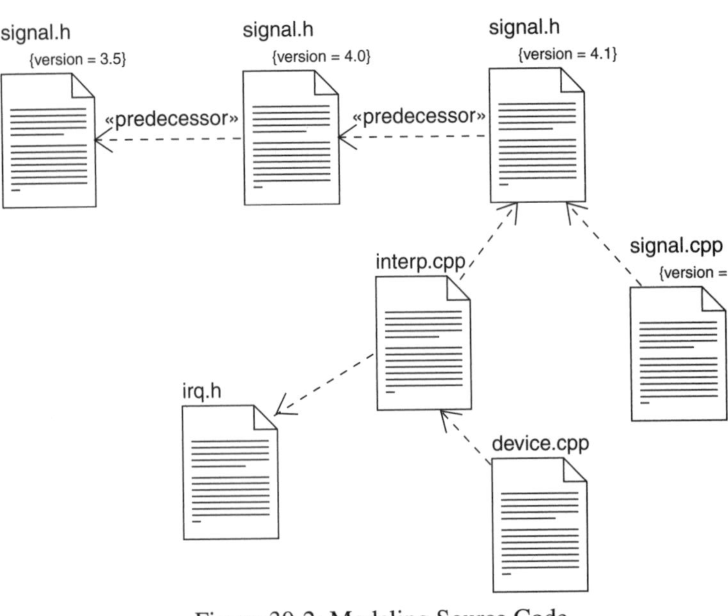

Figure 30-2: Modeling Source Code

Modeling an Executable Release

Releasing a simple application is easy: You throw the bits of a single executable file on a disk and your users just run that executable. For these kinds of applications, you don't need artifact diagrams because there's nothing difficult to visualize, specify, construct, or document.

Releasing anything other than a simple application is not so easy. You need the main executable (usually, a `.exe` file), but you also need all its ancillary parts, such as libraries (commonly `.dll` files if you are working in the context of COM+, or `.class` and `.jar` files if you are working in the context of Java), databases, help files, and resource files. For distributed systems, you'll likely have multiple executables and other parts scattered across various nodes. If you are working with a system of applications, you'll find that some of these artifacts are unique to each application but that many are shared among applications. As you evolve your system, controlling the configuration of these many artifacts becomes an important activity—and a more difficult one because changes in the artifacts associated with one application may affect the operation of other applications.

For this reason, you use artifact diagrams to visualize, specify, construct, and document the configuration of your executable releases, encompassing the deployment artifacts that form each release and the relationships among those artifacts. You can use artifact diagrams to forward engineer a new system and to reverse engineer an existing one.

When you create artifact diagrams such as these, you actually just model a part of the things and relationships that make up your system's implementation view. For this reason, each artifact diagram should focus on one set of artifacts at a time.

To model an executable release,

The UML's extensibility mechanisms are discussed in Chapter 6; interfaces are discussed in Chapter 11.

- Identify the set of artifacts you'd like to model. Typically, this will involve some or all the artifacts that live on one node, or the distribution of these sets of artifacts across all the nodes in the system.
- Consider the stereotype of each artifact in this set. For most systems, you'll find a small number of different kinds of artifacts (such as executables, libraries, tables, files, and documents). You can use the UML's extensibility mechanisms to provide visual cues for these stereotypes.
- For each artifact in this set, consider its relationship to its neighbors. Most often, this will involve interfaces that are exported (realized) by certain artifacts and then imported (used) by others. If you want to expose the seams in your system, model these interfaces explicitly. If you want your model at a higher level of abstraction, elide these relationships by showing only dependencies among the artifacts.

For example, Figure 30-3 models part of the executable release for an autonomous robot. This figure focuses on the deployment artifacts associated with the robot's driving and calculation functions. You'll find one artifact (`driver.dll`) that manifests a component `Driving` that exports an interface (`IDrive`) that is, in turn, used by another component `Path` manifested by another artifact (`path.dll`). The dependency among components `Path` and `Driving` induces a dependency among the artifacts `path.dll` and `driver.dll` that implement them. There's one other artifact shown in this diagram (`collision.dll`), and it, too, manifests a component, although these details are elided: `path.dll` is shown with a dependency directly to `collision.dll`.

There are many more artifacts involved in this system. However, this diagram only focuses on those deployment artifacts that are directly involved in moving the robot. Note that in this component-based architecture, you could replace a specific version of `driver.dll` with another that manifests the same component or one that manifests a different component supporting the same (and perhaps additional) interfaces, and `path.dll` would still function properly.

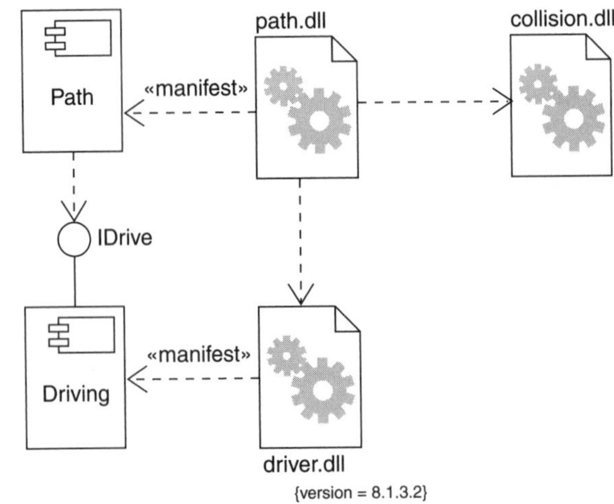

Figure 30-3: Modeling an Executable Release

Modeling a Physical Database

Modeling a logical database schema is discussed in Chapter 8.

A logical database schema captures the vocabulary of a system's persistent data, along with the semantics of their relationships. Physically, these things are stored in a database for later retrieval, either a relational database, an object-oriented one, or a hybrid object/relational database. The UML is well suited to modeling physical databases as well as logical database schemas.

Physical database design is beyond the scope of this book; the focus here is simply to show you how you can model databases and tables using the UML.

Mapping a logical database schema to an object-oriented database is straightforward because even complex inheritance lattices can be made persistent directly. Mapping a logical database schema to a relational database is not so simple, however. In the presence of inheritance, you have to make decisions about how to map classes to tables. Typically, you can apply one or a combination of three strategies.

1. (Push down) Define a separate table for each class. This is a simple but naive approach because it introduces maintenance headaches when you add new child classes or modify your parent classes.
2. (Pull up) Collapse your inheritance lattices so that all instances of any class in a hierarchy has the same state. The downside with this approach is that you end up storing superfluous information for many instances.

3. (Split tables) Separate parent and child states into different tables. This approach best mirrors your inheritance lattice, but the downside is that traversing your data will require many cross-table joins.

When designing a physical database, you also have to make decisions about how to map operations defined in your logical database schema. Object-oriented databases make the mapping fairly transparent. But with relational databases, you have to make some decisions about how these logical operations are implemented. Again, you have some choices.

1. For simple CRUD (create, read, update, delete) operations, implement them with standard SQL or ODBC calls.
2. For more-complex behavior (such as business rules), map them to triggers or stored procedures.

Given these general guidelines, to model a physical database,

- Identify the classes in your model that represent your logical database schema.
- Select a strategy for mapping these classes to tables. You will also want to consider the physical distribution of your databases. Your mapping strategy will be affected by the location in which you want your data to live on your deployed system.
- To visualize, specify, construct, and document your mapping, create an artifact diagram that contains artifacts stereotyped as tables.
- Where possible, use tools to help you transform your logical design into a physical design.

Figure 30-4 shows a set of database tables drawn from an information system for a school. You will find one database (`school.db` with the stereotype `database`) that's composed of five tables: `student`, `class`, `instructor`, `department`, and `course`. In the corresponding logical database schema, there was no inheritance, so mapping to this physical database design is straightforward.

Although not shown in this example, you can specify the contents of each table. Artifacts can have attributes, so a common idiom when modeling physical databases is to use these attributes to specify the columns of each table. Similarly, artifacts can have operations, and these can be used to denote stored procedures.

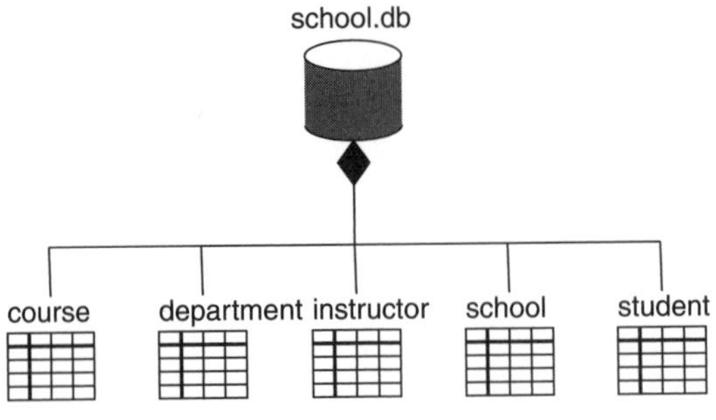

Figure 30-4: Modeling a Physical Database

Modeling Adaptable Systems

All the artifact diagrams shown thus far have been used to model static views. Their artifacts spend their entire lives on one node. This is the most common situation you'll encounter, but especially in the domain of complex, distributed systems, you'll need to model dynamic views. For example, you might have a system that replicates its databases across several nodes, switching the one that is the primary database when a server goes down. Similarly, if you are modeling a globally distributed 24x7 operation (that is, a system that's up 24 hours a day, 7 days a week), you will likely encounter mobile agents, artifacts that migrate from node to node to carry out some transaction. To model these dynamic views, you'll need to use a combination of artifact diagrams, object diagrams, and interaction diagrams.

To model an adaptable system,

The `location` attribute is discussed in Chapter 24; object diagrams are discussed in Chapter 14.

- Consider the physical distribution of the artifacts that may migrate from node to node. You can specify the location of an artifact instance by marking it with a location attribute, which you can then render in an artifact diagram.
- If you want to model the actions that cause an artifact to migrate, create a corresponding interaction diagram that contains artifact instances. You can illustrate a change of location by drawing the same instance more than once, but with different values for its state, which includes its location.

For example, Figure 30-5 models the replication of the database from the previous figure. We show two instances of the artifact `school.db`. Both instances are anonymous, and both have a different value for their location

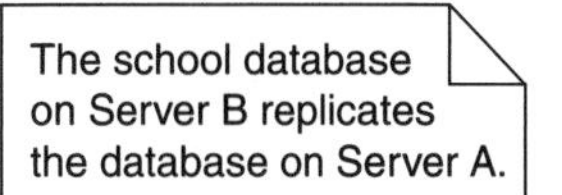

The school database
on Server B replicates
the database on Server A.

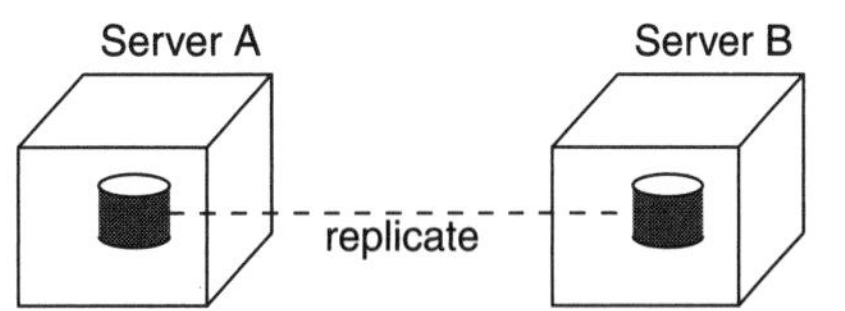

Figure 30-5: Modeling Adaptable Systems

tagged value. There's also a note, which explicitly specifies which instance replicates the other.

If you want to show the details of each database, you can render them in their canonical form—an artifact stereotyped as a `database`.

Interaction diagrams are discussed in Chapter 19.

Although not shown here, you could use an interaction diagram to model the dynamics of switching from one primary database to another.

Forward and Reverse Engineering

Forward engineering and reverse engineering artifacts are pretty direct, because artifacts are themselves physical things (executables, libraries, tables, files, and documents) that are therefore close to the running system. When you forward engineer a class or a collaboration, you really forward engineer to an artifact that represents the source code, binary library, or executable for that class or collaboration. Similarly, when you reverse engineer source code, binary libraries, or executables, you really reverse engineer to an artifact or set of artifacts that, in turn, trace to classes or collaborations.

Choosing to forward engineer (the creation of code from a model) a class or collaboration to source code, a binary library, or an executable is a mapping decision you have to make. You'll want to take your logical models to source code if you are interested in controlling the configuration management of files that are then manipulated by a development environment. You'll want to take your logical models directly to binary libraries or executables if you are interested in managing the artifacts that you'll actually deploy on a running system. In some cases, you'll want to do both. A class or collaboration may be manifested by source code as well as by a binary library or executable.

To forward engineer an artifact diagram,

- For each artifact, identify the classes or collaborations that the artifact implements. Show this with a manifest relationship.
- Choose the form for each artifact. Your choice is basically between source code (a form that can be manipulated by development tools) or a binary library or executable (a form that can be dropped into a running system).
- Use tools to forward engineer your models.

Reverse engineering class diagrams is discussed in Chapter 8.

Reverse engineering (the creation of a model from code) an artifact diagram is straightforward, but obtaining a class model is not a perfect process because there is always a loss of information. From source code, you can reverse engineer back to classes; this is the most common thing you'll do. Reverse engineering source code to artifacts will uncover compilation dependencies among those files. For binary libraries, the best you can hope for is to denote the library as an artifact and then discover its interfaces by reverse engineering. This is the second most common thing you'll do with artifact diagrams. In fact, this is a useful way to approach a set of new libraries that may be otherwise poorly documented. For executables, the best you can hope for is to denote the executable as an artifact and then disassemble its code—something you'll rarely need to do unless you work in assembly language.

To reverse engineer an artifact diagram,

- Choose the target you want to reverse engineer. Source code can be reverse engineered to discover artifacts and then classes. Binary libraries can be reverse engineered to uncover their interfaces. Executables can be reverse engineered the least.
- Using a tool, point to the code you'd like to reverse engineer. Use your tool to generate a new model or to modify an existing one that was previously forward engineered.
- Using your tool, create an artifact diagram by querying the model. For example, you might start with one or more artifacts, then expand the diagram by following relationships or neighboring artifacts. Expose or hide the details of the contents of this artifact diagram as necessary to communicate your intent.

For example, Figure 30-6 provides an artifact diagram that represents the reverse engineering of the ActiveX artifact `vbrun.dll`. As the figure shows, the artifact manifests 11 interfaces. Given this diagram, you can begin to understand the semantics of the artifact by next exploring the details of its interface classes.

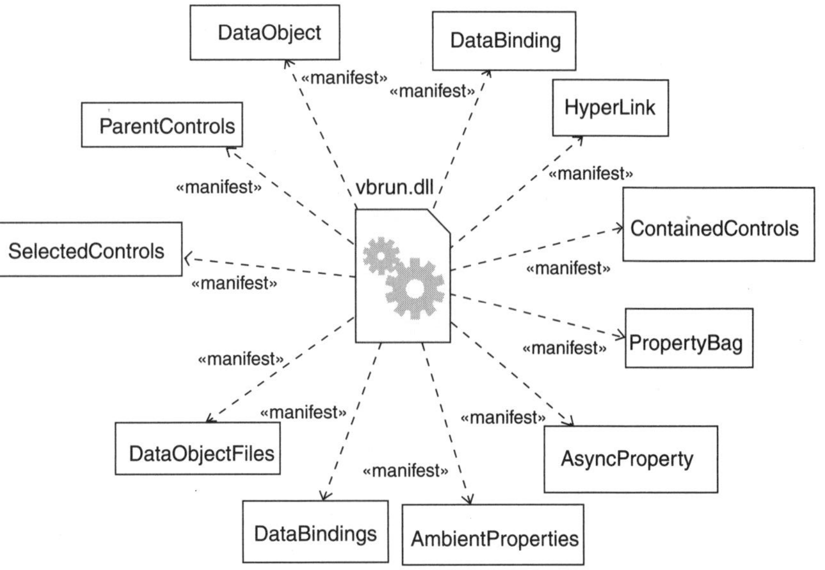

Figure 30-6: Reverse Engineering

Especially when you reverse engineer from source code, and sometimes when you reverse engineer from binary libraries and executables, you'll do so in the context of a configuration management system. This means that you'll often be working with specific versions of files or libraries, with all versions of a configuration compatible with one another. In these cases, you'll want to include a note that represents the artifact version, which you can derive from your configuration management system. In this manner, you can use the UML to visualize the history of an artifact across various releases.

Hints and Tips

When you create artifact diagrams in the UML, remember that every artifact diagram is just a graphical presentation of the static implementation view of a system. This means that no single artifact diagram need capture everything about a system's implementation view. Collectively, all the artifact diagrams of a system represent the system's complete static implementation view; individually, each represents just one aspect.

A well-structured artifact diagram

- Is focused on communicating one aspect of a system's static implementation view.
- Contains only those elements that are essential to understanding that aspect.
- Provides detail consistent with its level of abstraction, with only those adornments that are essential to understanding exposed.
- Is not so minimalist that it misinforms the reader about important semantics.

When you draw an artifact diagram,

- Give it a name that communicates its purpose.
- Lay out its elements to minimize lines that cross.
- Organize its elements spatially so that things that are semantically close are laid out physically close.
- Use notes and color as visual cues to draw attention to important features of your diagram.
- Use stereotyped elements carefully. Choose a small set of common icons for your project or organization and use them consistently.

Chapter 31

DEPLOYMENT DIAGRAMS

In this chapter

- Modeling an embedded system
- Modeling a client/server system
- Modeling a fully distributed system
- Forward and reverse engineering

Artifact diagrams, the second kind of diagram used in modeling the physical aspects of an object-oriented system, are discussed in Chapter 30.

Deployment diagrams are one of the two kinds of diagrams used in modeling the physical aspects of an object-oriented system. A deployment diagram shows the configuration of run time processing nodes and the artifacts that live on them.

You use deployment diagrams to model the static deployment view of a system. For the most part, this involves modeling the topology of the hardware on which your system executes. Deployment diagrams are essentially class diagrams that focus on a system's nodes.

Deployment diagrams are not only important for visualizing, specifying, and documenting embedded, client/server, and distributed systems, but also for managing executable systems through forward and reverse engineering.

Getting Started

When you create a software-intensive system, your main focus as a software developer is on architecting and deploying its software. However, as a systems engineer, your main focus is on the system's hardware *and* software and in managing the trade-offs between the two. Whereas software developers work with somewhat intangible artifacts, such as models and code, system developers work with quite tangible hardware as well.

The UML is primarily focused on facilities for visualizing, specifying, constructing, and documenting software artifacts, but it's also designed to address hardware artifacts. This is not to say that the UML is a general-purpose hardware description language like VHDL. Rather, the UML is designed to model many of the hardware aspects of a system sufficient for a software engineer to specify the platform on which the system's software executes and for a systems engineer to manage the system's hardware/software boundary. In the UML, you use class diagrams and artifact diagrams to reason about the structure of your software. You use sequence diagrams, collaboration diagrams, state diagrams, and activity diagrams to specify the behavior of your software. At the edge of the your system's software and hardware, you use deployment diagrams to reason about the topology of processors and devices on which your software executes.

With the UML, you use deployment diagrams to visualize the static aspect of these physical nodes and their relationships and to specify their details for construction, as in Figure 31-1.

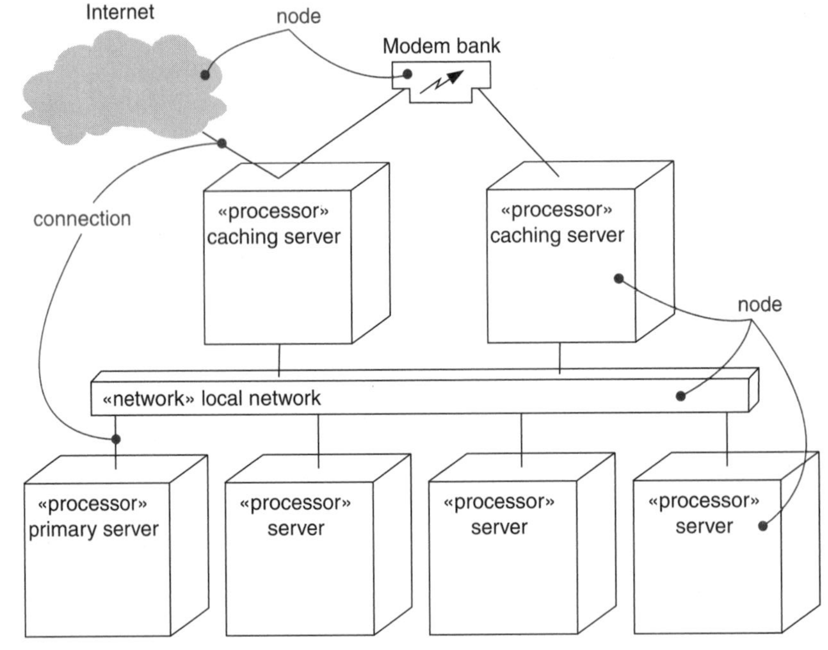

Figure 31-1: A Deployment Diagram

Terms and Concepts

A *deployment diagram* is a diagram that shows the configuration of run time processing nodes and the artifacts that live on them. Graphically, a deployment diagram is a collection of vertices and arcs.

Common Properties

The general properties of diagrams are discussed in Chapter 7.

A deployment diagram is just a special kind of diagram and shares the same common properties as all other diagrams—a name and graphical contents that are a projection into a model. What distinguishes a deployment diagram from all other kinds of diagrams is its particular content.

Contents

Nodes are discussed in Chapter 27; relationships are discussed in Chapters 5 and 10; artifacts are discussed in Chapter 26; packages are discussed in Chapter 12; subsystems are discussed in Chapter 32; instances are discussed in Chapter 13; class diagrams are discussed in Chapter 8.

Deployment diagrams commonly contain

- Nodes
- Dependency and association relationships

Like all other diagrams, deployment diagrams may contain notes and constraints. Deployment diagrams may also contain artifacts, each of which must live on some node. Deployment diagrams may also contain packages or subsystems, both of which are used to group elements of your model into larger chunks. Sometimes, you'll want to place instances in your deployment diagrams, as well, especially when you want to visualize one instance of a family of hardware topologies.

Note: In many ways, a deployment diagram is just a special kind of class diagram, which focuses on a system's nodes.

Common Uses

You use deployment diagrams to model the static deployment view of a system. This view primarily addresses the distribution, delivery, and installation of the parts that make up the physical system.

Deployment views in the context of software architecture are discussed in Chapter 2.

There are some kinds of systems for which deployment diagrams are unnecessary. If you are developing a piece of software that lives on one machine and interfaces only with standard devices on that machine that are already managed by the host operating system (for example, a personal computer's keyboard, display, and modem), you can ignore deployment diagrams. On the other hand, if you are developing a piece of software that interacts with devices that the host operating system does not typically manage or that is physically distributed across multiple processors, then using deployment diagrams will help you reason about your system's software-to-hardware mapping.

When you model the static deployment view of a system, you'll typically use deployment diagrams in one of three ways.

1. To model embedded systems

An embedded system is a software-intensive collection of hardware that interfaces with the physical world. Embedded systems involve software that controls devices such as motors, actuators, and displays and that, in turn, is controlled by external stimuli such as sensor input, movement, and temperature changes. You can use deployment diagrams to model the devices and processors that comprise an embedded system.

2. To model client/server systems

A client/server system is a common architecture focused on making a clear separation of concerns between the system's user interface (which lives on the client) and the system's persistent data (which lives on the server). Client/server systems are one end of the continuum of distributed systems and require you to make decisions about the network connectivity of clients to servers and about the physical distribution of your system's software artifacts across the nodes. You can model the topology of such systems by using deployment diagrams.

3. To model fully distributed systems

At the other end of the continuum of distributed systems are those that are widely, if not globally, distributed, typically encompassing multiple levels of servers. Such systems are often hosts to multiple versions of software artifacts, some of which may even migrate from node to node. Crafting such systems requires you to make decisions that enable the continuous change in the system's topology. You can use deployment diagrams to visualize the system's current topology and distribution of artifacts to reason about the impact of changes on that topology.

Common Modeling Techniques

Modeling an Embedded System

Nodes and devices are discussed in Chapter 27.

Developing an embedded system is far more than a software problem. You have to manage the physical world in which there are moving parts that break and in which signals are noisy and behavior is nonlinear. When you model such a system, you have to take into account its interface with the real world, and that means reasoning about unusual devices as well as nodes.

The UML's extensibility mechanisms are discussed in Chapter 6.

Deployment diagrams are useful in facilitating the communication between your project's hardware engineers and software developers. By using nodes that are stereotyped to look like familiar devices, you can create diagrams that are understandable by both groups. Deployment diagrams are also helpful in reasoning about hardware/software trade-offs. You'll use deployment diagrams to visualize, specify, construct, and document your system engineering decisions.

To model an embedded system,

- Identify the devices and nodes that are unique to your system.
- Provide visual cues, especially for unusual devices, by using the UML's extensibility mechanisms to define system-specific stereotypes with appropriate icons. At the very least, you'll want to distinguish processors (which contain software artifacts) and devices (which, at that level of abstraction, don't contain software that you write).
- Model the relationships among these processors and devices in a deployment diagram. Similarly, specify the relationship between the artifacts in your system's implementation view and the nodes in your system's deployment view.
- As necessary, expand on any intelligent devices by modeling their structure with a more detailed deployment diagram.

For example, Figure 31-2 shows the hardware for a simple autonomous robot. You'll find one node (`Pentium motherboard`) stereotyped as a processor. Surrounding this node are eight devices, each stereotyped as a device and rendered with an icon that offers a clear visual cue to its real-world equivalent.

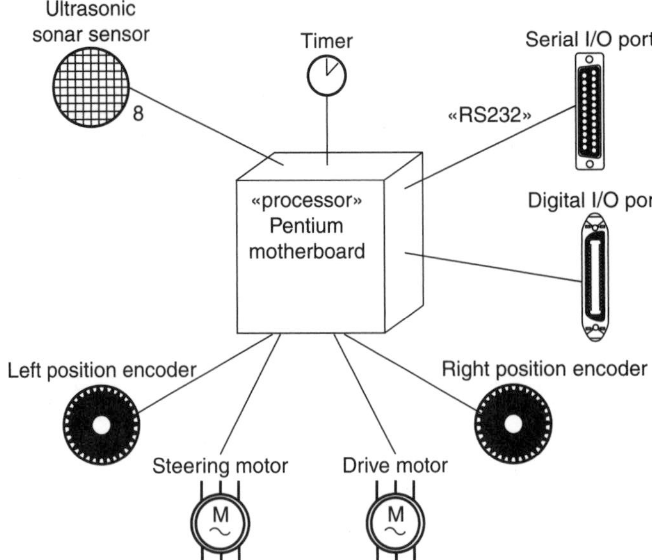

Figure 31-2: Modeling an Embedded System

Modeling a Client/Server System

The moment you start developing a system whose software no longer resides on a single processor, you are faced with a host of decisions: How do you best distribute your software artifacts across these nodes? How do they communicate? How do you deal with failure and noise? At one end of the spectrum of distributed systems, you'll encounter client/server systems in which there's a clear separation of concerns between the system's user interface (typically managed by the client) and its data (typically managed by the server).

There are many variations on this theme. For example, you might choose to have a thin client, meaning that it has a limited amount of computational capacity and does little more than manage the user interface and visualization of information. Thin clients may not even host a lot of artifacts but, rather, may be designed to load artifacts from the server, as needed, as with Enterprise Java Beans. On the other hand, you might chose to have a thick client, meaning that it has a goodly amount of computational capacity and does more than just visualization. A thick client typically carries out some of the system's logic and business rules. The choice between thin and thick clients is an architectural decision that's influenced by a number of technical, economic, and political factors.

Either way, partitioning a system into its client and server parts involves making some hard decisions about where to physically place its software artifacts and how to impose a balanced distribution of responsibilities among those artifacts. For example, most management information systems are essentially three-tier architectures, which means that the system's GUI, business logic, and database are physically distributed. Deciding where to place the system's GUI and database are usually fairly obvious, so the hard part lies in deciding where the business logic lives.

You can use the UML's deployment diagrams to visualize, specify, and document your decisions about the topology of your client/server system and how its software artifacts are distributed across the client and server. Typically, you'll want to create one deployment diagram for the system as a whole, along with other, more detailed diagrams that drill down to individual segments of the system.

To model a client/server system,

- Identify the nodes that represent your system's client and server processors.
- Highlight those devices that are germane to the behavior of your system. For example, you'll want to model special devices, such as credit card readers, badge readers, and display devices other than monitors, because their placement in the system's hardware topology are likely to be architecturally significant.
- Provide visual cues for these processors and devices via stereotyping.
- Model the topology of these nodes in a deployment diagram. Similarly, specify the relationship between the artifacts in your system's implementation view and the nodes in your system's deployment view.

Packages are discussed in Chapter 12; multiplicity is discussed in Chapter 10.

For example, Figure 31-3 shows the topology of a human resources system, which follows a classical client/server architecture. This figure illustrates the client/server split explicitly by using the packages named `client` and `server`. The client package contains two nodes (`console` and `kiosk`), both of which are stereotyped and are visually distinguishable. The server package contains two kinds of nodes (`caching server` and `server`), and both of these have been adorned with some of the artifacts that reside on each. Note also that `caching server` and `server` are marked with explicit multiplicities, specifying how many instances of each are expected in a particular deployed configuration. For example, this diagram indicates that there may be two or more `caching servers` in any deployed instance of the system.

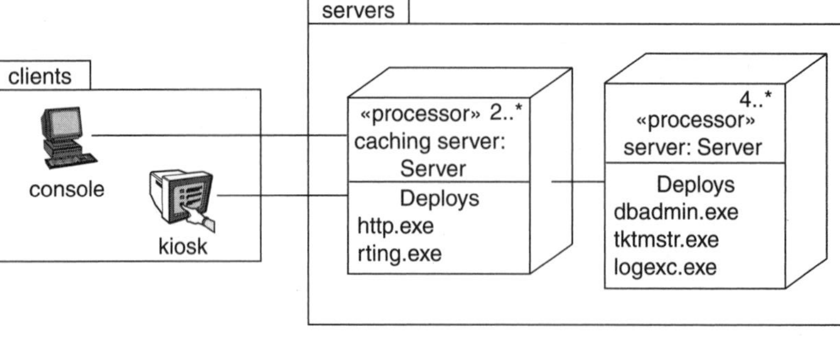

Figure 31-3: Modeling a Client/Server System

Modeling a Fully Distributed System

Distributed systems come in many forms, from simple two-processor systems to those that span many geographically dispersed nodes. The latter are typically never static. Nodes are added and removed as network traffic changes and processors fail; new and faster communication paths may be established in parallel with older, slower channels that are eventually decommissioned. Not only may the topology of these systems change, but the distribution of their software artifacts may change as well. For example, database tables may be replicated across servers, only to be moved as traffic dictates. For some global systems, artifacts may follow the sun, migrating from server to server as the business day begins in one part of the world and ends in another.

Visualizing, specifying, and documenting the topology of fully distributed systems such as these are valuable activities for the systems administrator who must keep tabs on an enterprise's computing assets. You can use the UML's deployment diagrams to reason about the topology of such systems. When you document fully distributed systems using deployment diagrams, you'll want to expand on the details of the system's networking devices, each of which you can represent as a stereotyped node.

To model a fully distributed system,

- Identify the system's devices and processors as for simpler client/server systems.
- If you need to reason about the performance of the system's network or the impact of changes to the network, model these communication devices to a level of detail sufficient to make these assessments.

Packages are discussed in Chapter 12.

- Pay close attention to logical groupings of nodes, which you can specify by using packages.
- Model these devices and processors using deployment diagrams. Where possible, use tools that discover the topology of your system by walking your system's network.

Use cases are discussed in Chapter 17; interaction diagrams are described in Chapter 19; instances are discussed in Chapter 13.

- If you need to focus on the dynamics of your system, introduce use case diagrams to specify the kinds of behavior you are interested in, and expand on these use cases with interaction diagrams.

Note: When modeling a highly distributed system, it's common to reify the network itself as an node. For example, the Internet might be represented as a node (as in Figure 31-1, shown as a stereotyped node). You can also reify a local area network (LAN) or wide-area network (WAN) in the same way (as in Figure 31-1). In each case, you can use the node's attributes and operations to capture properties about the network.

Figure 31-4 shows the topology of a particular configuration of a fully distributed system. This particular deployment diagram is also an object diagram, for it contains only instances. You can see three consoles (anonymous instances of the stereotyped node `console`), which are linked to the `Internet` (clearly a singleton node). In turn, there are three instances of `regional servers`, which serve as front ends of `country servers`, only one of which is shown. As the note indicates, country servers are connected to one another, but their relationships are not shown in this diagram.

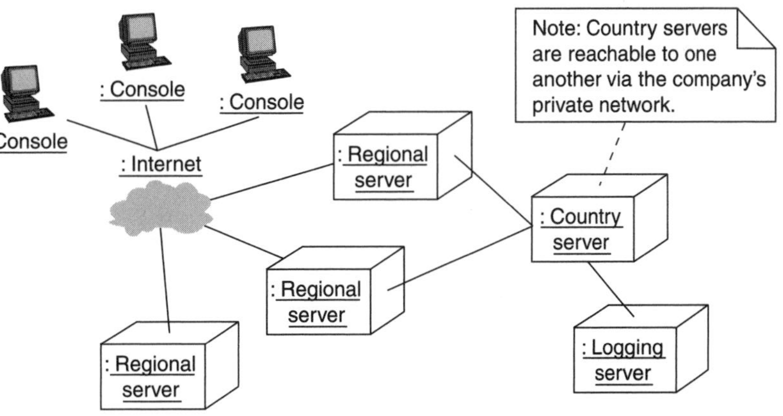

Figure 31-4: Modeling a Fully Distributed System

In this diagram, the Internet has been reified as a stereotyped node.

Forward and Reverse Engineering

There's only a modest amount of forward engineering (the creation of code from models) that you can do with deployment diagrams. For example, after specifying the physical distribution of artifacts across the nodes in a deployment diagram, it is possible to use tools that then push these artifacts out to the real world. For system administrators, using the UML in this way helps you visualize what can be a very complicated task.

Reverse engineering (the creation of models from code) from the real world back to deployment diagrams is of tremendous value, especially for fully distributed systems that are under constant change. You'll want to supply a set of stereotyped nodes that speak the language of your system's network administrators to tailor the UML to their domain. The advantage of using the UML is that it offers a standard language that addresses not only their needs, but the needs of your project's software developers as well.

To reverse engineer a deployment diagram,

- Choose the target that you want to reverse engineer. In some cases, you'll want to sweep across your entire network; in others, you can limit your search.
- Choose also the fidelity of your reverse engineering. In some cases, it's sufficient to reverse engineer just to the level of all the system's processors; in others, you'll want to reverse engineer the system's networking peripherals as well.
- Use a tool that walks across your system, discovering its hardware topology. Record that topology in a deployment model.
- Along the way, you can use similar tools to discover the artifacts that live on each node, which you can also record in a deployment model. You'll want to use an intelligent search, for even a basic personal computer can contain gigabytes of artifacts, many of which may not be relevant to your system.
- Using your modeling tools, create a deployment diagram by querying the model. For example, you might start with visualizing the basic client/server topology, then expand on the diagram by populating certain nodes with artifacts of interest that live on them. Expose or hide the details of the contents of this deployment diagram as necessary to communicate your intent.

Hints and Tips

When you create deployment diagrams in the UML, remember that every deployment diagram is just a graphical presentation of the static deployment view of a system. This means that no single deployment diagram need capture everything about a system's deployment view. Collectively, all the deployment diagrams of a system represent the system's complete static deployment view; individually, each represents just one aspect.

A well-structured deployment diagram

- Focuses on communicating one aspect of a system's static deployment view.
- Contains only those elements that are essential to understanding that aspect.
- Provides detail consistent with its level of abstraction; expose only those adornments that are essential to understanding.
- Is not so minimalist that it misinforms the reader about important semantics.

When you draw a deployment diagram,

- Give it a name that communicates its purpose.
- Lay out its elements to minimize lines that cross.
- Organize its elements spatially so that things that are semantically close are laid out physically close.
- Use notes and color as visual cues to draw attention to important features of your diagram.
- Use stereotyped elements carefully. Choose a small set of common icons for your project or organization, and use them consistently.

Chapter 32
SYSTEMS AND MODELS

In this chapter

- Systems, subsystems, models, and views
- Modeling the architecture of a system
- Modeling systems of systems
- Organizing the artifacts of development

The UML is a graphical language for visualizing, specifying, constructing, and documenting the artifacts of a software-intensive system. You use the UML to model systems. A model is a simplification of reality—an abstraction of a system—created in order to better understand the system. A system, possibly decomposed into a collection of subsystems, is a set of elements organized to accomplish a purpose and described by a set of models, possibly from different viewpoints. Things like classes, interfaces, components, and nodes are important parts of a system's model. In the UML, you use models to organize these and all the other abstractions of a system. As you move to more-complex domains, you'll find that a system at one level of abstraction looks like a subsystem at another, higher, level. In the UML, you can model systems and subsystems as a whole so that you can seamlessly move up to problems of scale.

Well-structured models help you visualize, specify, construct, and document a complex system from different, yet interrelated, aspects. Well-structured systems are functionally, logically, and physically cohesive, formed of loosely coupled subsystems.

Getting Started

Building a dog house doesn't take a lot of thought. The needs of a dog are simple, so to satisfy all but the most demanding dog, you can just do it.

The differences between building a dog house and building a high rise are discussed in Chapter 1.

Building a house or a high rise takes a lot more thought. The needs of a family or a building's tenants are not so simple, so to satisfy even the least demanding client, you can't just do it. Rather, you have to do some modeling. Different stakeholders will look at the problem from different angles and with different concerns. That's why, for complex buildings, you'll end up creating floor plans, elevation plans, heating/cooling plans, electrical plans, plumbing plans, and perhaps even networking plans. There's no one model that can adequately capture all the interesting aspects of a complex building.

Diagrams are discussed in Chapter 7; the five views of a software architecture are discussed in Chapter 2.

In the UML, you organize all the abstractions of a software-intensive system into models, each of which represents some relatively independent, yet important, aspect of the system under development. You then use diagrams to visualize interesting collections of these abstractions. Looking at the five views of an architecture is a particularly useful way to channel the attention of a software system's different stakeholders. Collectively, these models work together to provide a complete statement of a system's structure and behavior.

For larger systems, you'll find that the elements of such systems can be meaningfully decomposed into separate subsystems, each of which looks just like a smaller system when viewed from a lower level of abstraction.

The UML's extensibility mechanisms are discussed in Chapter 6; packages are discussed in Chapter 12.

The UML provides a graphical representation for systems and subsystems, as Figure 32-1 shows. This notation permits you to visualize the decomposition of a system into smaller subsystems. Graphically, a system and a subsystem are rendered as a stereotyped component icon. Models and views have a special graphical representation (other than rendering them as stereotyped packages), but it is rarely used because they are primarily things that are manipulated by tools that you use to organize the different aspects of a system.

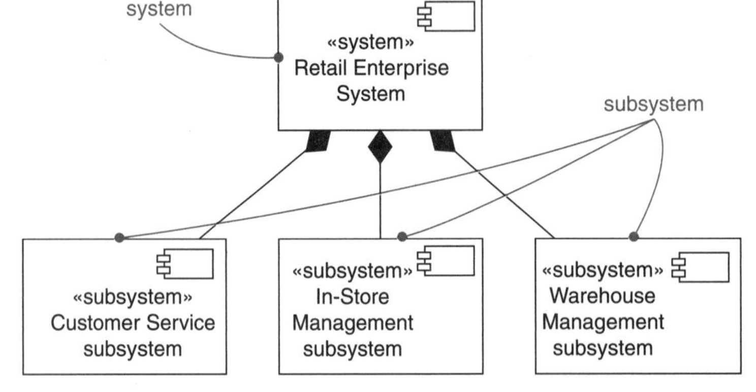

Figure 32-1: Systems and Subsystems

Terms and Concepts

A *system*, possibly decomposed into a collection of subsystems, is a set of elements organized to accomplish a purpose and described by a set of models, possibly from different viewpoints. A *subsystem* is a grouping of elements of which some constitute a specification of the behavior offered by other contained elements. Graphically, a system and a subsystem are rendered as a stereotyped component icon. A *model* is a simplification of reality, an abstraction of a system, created to better understand the system. A *view* is a projection of a model, which is seen from one perspective or vantage point and omits entities that are not relevant to this perspective.

Systems and Subsystems

Stereotypes are discussed in Chapter 6; packages are discussed in Chapter 12; classes are discussed in Chapters 4 and 9; use cases are discussed in Chapter 17; state machines are discussed in Chapter 22; collaborations are discussed in Chapter 28.

A system is the thing that you are developing and for which you build models. A system encompasses all the artifacts that constitute that thing, including all its models and modeling elements, such as classes, interfaces, components, nodes, and their relationships. Everything you need to visualize, specify, construct, and document a system is part of that system, and everything you don't need to visualize, specify, construct, and document a system lies outside that system.

In the UML, a system is rendered as a stereotyped component, as shown in Figure 32-1. As a stereotyped component, a system owns elements. If you zoom inside a system, you'll see all its models and individual modeling elements (including diagrams), perhaps further decomposed into subsystems. As a classifier, a system may have instances (a system may be deployed in multiple instances in the real world), attributes and operations (actors outside the system may act on the system as a whole), use cases, state machines, and collaborations, all of which may specify the behavior of the system. A system may even realize interfaces, which is important when you are constructing systems of systems.

A subsystem is simply a part of a system and is used to decompose a complex system into nearly independent parts. A system at one level of abstraction may be a subsystem of a system at a higher level of abstraction.

Aggregation and generalization are discussed in Chapters 5 and 10.

The primary relationship between a system and its subsystems is composition. A system (the whole) may contain zero or more subsystems (the parts). You can also have generalization relationships among subsystems. Using generalization, you can model families of subsystems, some of which represent general kinds of systems and others of which represent specific tailorings of those systems. The subsystems have various connections among themselves.

Note: A system represents the highest-level thing in a given context; the subsystems that make up a system provide a complete and non-overlapping partitioning of the system as a whole. A system is a top-level subsystem.

Models and Views

A model is a simplification of reality, in which reality is defined in the context of the system being modeled. In short, a model is an abstraction of a system. A subsystem represents a partitioning of the elements of a larger system into independent parts; a model is a partitioning of the abstractions that visualize, specify, construct, and document that system. The difference is subtle but important. You decompose a system into subsystems so that you can develop and deploy these parts somewhat independently; you partition the abstractions of a system or a subsystem into models so that you can better understand the different aspects of the thing you are developing and deploying. Just as a complex system such as an aircraft may have many parts (for example, the airframe, propulsion, avionics, and passenger subsystems), those subsystems and the system as a whole may be modeled from a number of different points of view (such as from the perspective of structural, dynamic, electrical, and heating/cooling models, for example).

Packages are discussed in Chapter 12.

A model contains a set of packages. You'll rarely need to model models explicitly, however. Tools need to manipulate models, however, so a tool will typically use package notation to represent a model as seen by the tool.

The five views of a software architecture are discussed in Chapter 2.

A model owns packages that, in turn, own elements. The models associated with a system or subsystem completely partition the elements of that system or subsystem, meaning that every element is owned by exactly one package. Typically, you'll organize the artifacts of a system or subsystem into a set of non-overlapping models, covered by the five views of software architecture that are described elsewhere.

Diagrams are discussed in Chapter 7.

A model (for example, a process model) may contain so many artifacts (such as active classes, relationships, and interactions) that in systems of scale, you simply cannot embrace all those artifacts at once. Think of a view as a projection into a model. For each model, you'll have a number of diagrams that exist to give you a peek into the things owned by the model. A view encompasses a subset of the things owned by a model; a view typically may not cross model boundaries. As described in the next section, there are no direct relationships among models, although you'll find trace relationships among the elements contained in different models.

Note: The UML does not dictate which models you should use to visualize, specify, construct, and document a system, although the Rational Unified Process does suggest a proven set of models.

Trace

Relationships are discussed in Chapters 5 and 10.

Specifying relationships among elements such as classes, interfaces, components, and nodes is an important structural part of any model. Specifying the relationships among elements such as documents, diagrams, and packages that live in different models is an important part of managing the development artifacts of complex systems, many of which may exist in multiple versions.

Dependencies are discussed in Chapter 5; stereotypes are discussed in Chapter 6.

In the UML, you can model the conceptual relationship among elements that live in different models by using a trace relationship; a trace may not be applied among elements in the same model. A trace is represented as a stereotyped dependency. You can often ignore the direction of this dependency, although you'll typically direct it to the older or more-specific element, as in Figure 32-2. The two most common uses for the trace relationship are to trace from requirements to implementation (and all the artifacts in between) and to trace from version to version.

Note: Most of the time you will not want to render trace relationships explicitly but, rather, will treat them as hyperlinks.

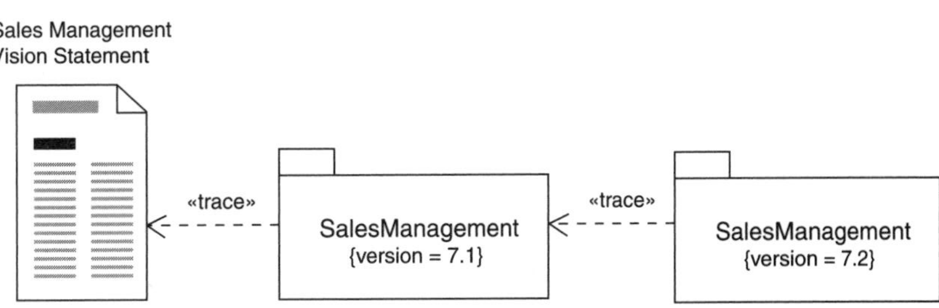

Figure 32-2: Trace Relationships

Common Modeling Techniques

Modeling the Architecture of a System

Architecture and modeling are discussed in Chapter 1.

The most common use for which you'll apply systems and models is to organize the elements you use to visualize, specify, construct, and document a system's architecture. Ultimately, this touches virtually all the artifacts you'll find in a software development project. When you model a system's architecture, you capture decisions about the system's requirements, its logical elements, and its physical elements. You'll also model both structural and behavioral aspects of the systems and the patterns that shape these views. Finally, you'll want to focus on the seams between subsystems and the tracing from requirements to deployment.

To model the architecture of a system,

The five views of a software architecture are discussed in Chapter 2; diagrams are discussed in Chapter 7.

- Identify the views that you'll use to represent your architecture. Most often, you'll want to include a use case view, a design view, an interaction view, a implementation view, and a deployment view, as shown in Figure 32-3.
- Specify the context for this system, including the actors that surround it.

As necessary, decompose the system into its elementary subsystems.

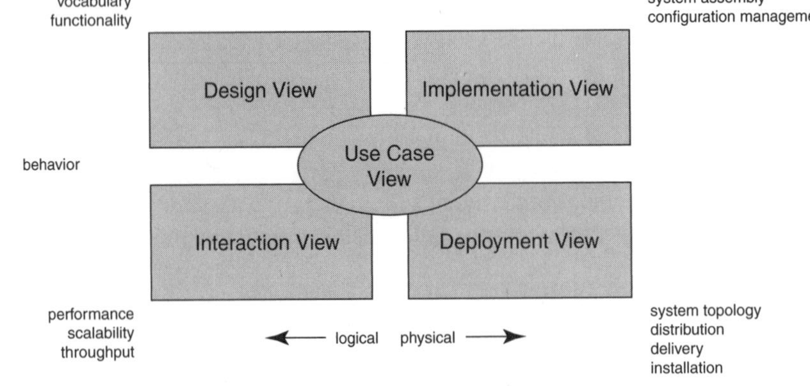

Figure 32-3: Modeling a System's Architecture

The following activities apply to the system, as well as to its subsystems.

- Specify a use case view of the system, encompassing the use cases that describe the behavior of the system as seen by its end users, analysts, and testers. Apply use case diagrams to model static aspects, and interaction diagrams, state diagrams, and activity diagrams to model the dynamic aspects.
- Specify a design view of the system, encompassing the classes, interfaces, and collaborations that form the vocabulary of the problem and its solution. Apply class diagrams and object diagrams to model static aspects, and iteration diagrams, state diagrams, and activity diagrams to model the dynamic aspects.
- Specify an interaction view of the system, encompassing the threads, processes, and messages that form the system's concurrency and synchronization mechanisms. Apply the same diagrams as for the design view, but with a focus on active classes and objects that represent threads and processes as well as on messages and flow of control.
- Specify an implementation view of the system, encompassing the artifacts that are used to assemble and release the physical system. Apply artifact diagrams to model static aspects, and interaction diagrams, state diagrams, and activity diagrams to model the dynamic aspects.
- Specify a deployment view of the system, encompassing the nodes that form the system's hardware topology on which the system executes. Apply deployment diagrams to model static aspects, and interaction diagrams, state diagrams, and activity diagrams to model the dynamic aspects of the system in its execution environment.
- Model the architectural patterns and design patterns that shape each of these models using collaborations.

The Rational Unified Process is discussed in Appendix B.

Understand that you don't ever create a system's architecture in one big-bang event. Rather, a well-structured process for the UML involves the successive refinement of a system's architecture in a manner that is use case–driven, architecture-centric, and iterative and incremental.

The UML's extensibility mechanisms are discussed in Chapter 6.

For all but the most trivial systems, you'll have to manage versions of your system's artifacts. You can use the UML's extensibility mechanisms—and tagged values in particular—to capture your decisions about the version of each element.

Modeling Systems of Systems

A system at one level of abstraction will look like a subsystem of a higher level of abstraction. Similarly, a subsystem at one level of abstraction will look like a full-fledged system from the perspective of the team responsible for creating it.

All complex systems exhibit this kind of hierarchy. As you move to systems of greater and greater complexity, you'll find it necessary to decompose your effort into subsystems, each of which can be developed somewhat separately, and iteratively and incrementally grown into the whole system. The development of a subsystem looks just like the development of a system.

To model a system or a subsystem,

- Identify major functional parts of the system that may be developed, released, and deployed somewhat independently. Technical, political, legacy, and legal issues will often shape how you draw the lines around each subsystem.
- For each subsystem, specify its context, just as you do for the system as a whole; the actors that surround a subsystem encompass all its neighboring subsystems, so they must all be designed to collaborate.
- For each subsystem, model its architecture just as you do for the system as a whole.

Hints and Tips

It's important to choose the right set of models to visualize, specify, construct, and document a system. A well-structured model

- Provides a simplification of reality from a distinct and relatively independent point of view.
- Is self-contained in that it requires no other content to understand its semantics.
- Is loosely coupled to other models via trace relationships.
- Collectively (with other neighboring models) provides a complete statement of a system's artifacts.

Similarly, it's important to decompose complex systems into well-structured subsystems. A well-structured system

- Is functionally, logically, and physically cohesive.
- Can be decomposed into nearly independent subsystems that themselves are systems at a lower level of abstraction.
- Can be visualized, specified, constructed, and documented via a set of interrelated, nonoverlapping models.

UML has a graphical symbol for a model, but it is best to avoid it; model the system and not the model itself. Editing tools will provide facilities for browsing, organizing, and managing sets of models.

When you draw a system or a subsystem in the UML,

- Use each as a starting point for all the artifacts associated with that system or subsystem.
- Show only the basic aggregation among the system and its subsystems; typically, you'll leave the details of their connections to lower-level diagrams.

UNIFIED MODELING LANGUAGE

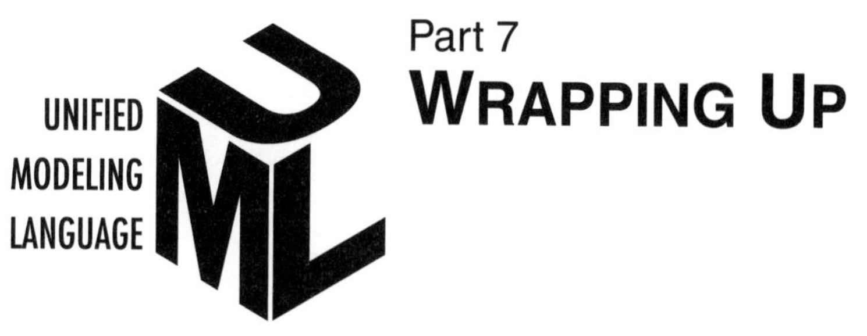

Part 7

Wrapping Up

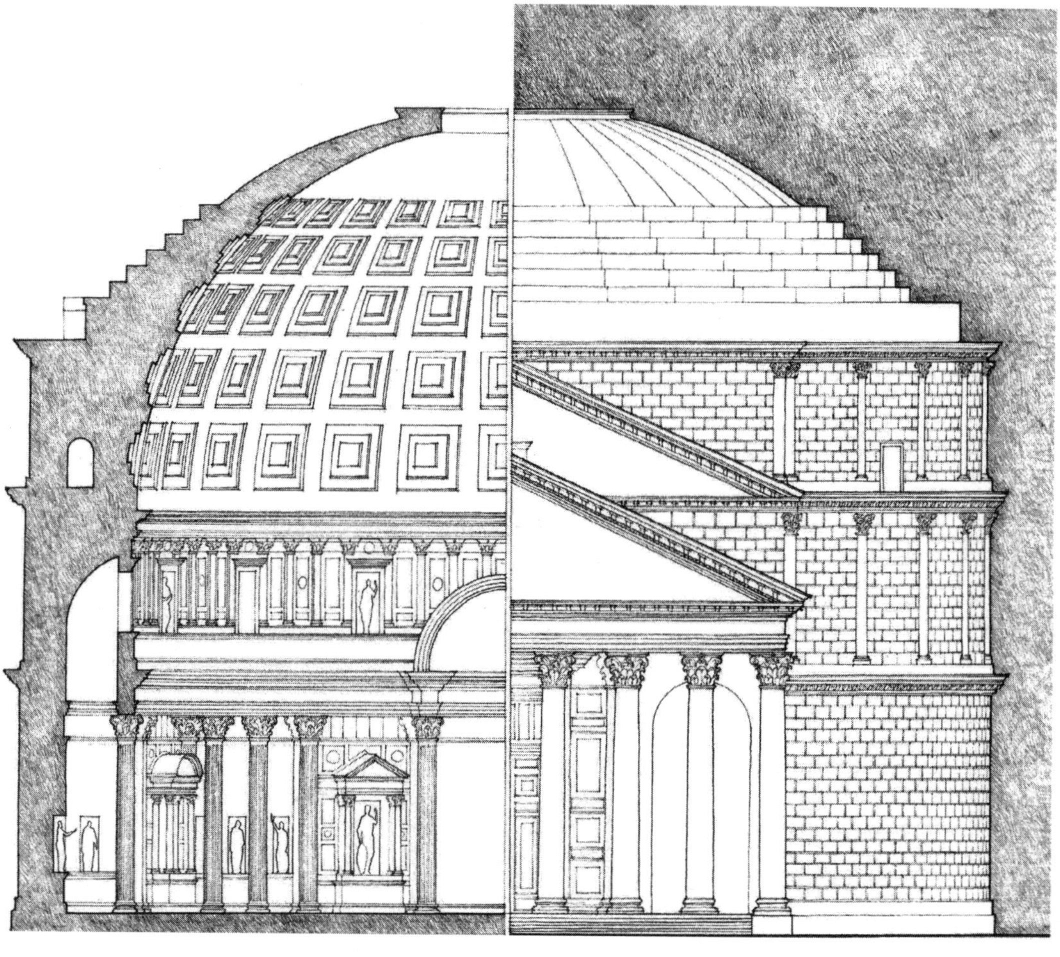

Chapter 33
Applying the UML

In this chapter

- Transitioning to the UML
- Where to go next

Simple problems are easy to model with the UML. Hard problems are easy to model, too, especially after you've become fluent in the language.

Reading about using the UML is one thing, but it's only through *using* the language that you will come to master it. Depending on your background, there are different ways to approach using the UML for the first time. As you gain more experience, you will come to understand and appreciate its more subtle parts.

If you can think it, the UML can model it.

Transitioning to the UML

You can model 80 percent of most problems by using about 20 percent of the UML. Basic structural things, such as classes, attributes, operations, use cases, and packages, together with basic structural relationships, such as dependency, generalization, and association, are sufficient to create static models for many kinds of problem domains. Add to that list basic behavioral things, such as simple state machines and interactions, and you can model many useful aspects of a system's dynamics. You'll need to use only the more advanced features of the UML once you start modeling the things you encounter in more-complex situations, such as modeling concurrency and distribution.

A conceptual model for the UML is discussed in Chapter 2.

A good starting place for using the UML is to model some of the basic abstractions or behavior that already exist in one of your systems. Develop a conceptual model of the UML so that you'll have a framework around which you can grow your understanding of the language. Later on, you'll better understand how the more advanced parts of the UML fit together. As you attack more-complex problems, drill down into specific features of the UML by studying the common modeling techniques in this book.

If you are new to object-orientation,

- Start by getting comfortable with the idea of abstraction. Team exercises with CRC cards and use case analysis are excellent ways to develop your skills of identifying crisp abstractions.
- Model a simple static part of your problem using classes, dependency, generalization, and association to get familiar with visualizing societies of abstractions.
- Use simple sequence or communication diagrams to model a dynamic part of your problem. Building a model of user interaction with the system is a good starting place and will give you an immediate payback by helping you reason through some of the system's more important use cases.

If you are new to modeling,

- Start by taking a part of some system you've already built—preferably implemented in some object-oriented programming language, such as Java or C++—and build a UML model of these classes and their relationships.
- Using the UML, try to capture some details of programming idioms or mechanisms you used in that system, which are in your head but you can't put down directly in the code.
- Especially if you have a nontrivial application, try to reconstruct a model of its architecture by using components (including subsystems) to represent its major structural elements. Use packages to organize the model itself.
- After you become comfortable with the vocabulary of the UML and before you start cutting code on your next project, build a UML model of that part of the system first. Think about the structure or behavior you've specified, and only then, when you are happy with its size, shape, and semantics, use that model as a framework for your implementation.

If you are already experienced with another object-oriented method,

- Take a look at your current modeling language and construct a mapping from its elements to the elements of the UML. In most cases, you'll find a one-to-one mapping and that most of the changes are cosmetic.
- Consider some difficult modeling problem that you found clumsy or impossible to model with your current modeling language. Look at some of the advanced features of the UML that might address that problem with greater clarity or simplicity.

If you are a power user,

- Be sure you first develop a conceptual model of the UML. You may miss its harmony of concepts if you dive into the most sophisticated parts of the language without first understanding its basic vocabulary.
- Pay particular attention to the UML's features for modeling internal structure, collaboration, concurrency, distribution, and patterns—issues that often involve complex and subtle semantics.
- Look also at the UML's extensibility mechanisms and see how you might tailor the UML to directly speak the vocabulary of your domain. Take care to resist the temptation to go to extremes that yield a UML model that no one but other power users will recognize.

Where to Go Next

This user guide is part of a larger set of books that, collectively, can help you learn how to apply the UML. In addition to the user guide, there are:

- James Rumbaugh, Ivar Jacobson, Grady Booch, *The Unified Modeling Language Reference Manual, Second Edition*, Addison-Wesley, 2005. This provides a comprehensive reference to the syntax and semantics of the UML.

- Ivar Jacobson, Grady Booch, James Rumbaugh, *The Unified Software Development Process*, Addison-Wesley, 1999. This presents a recommended development process for use with the UML.

To learn more about modeling from the principal authors of the UML, take a look at the following references:

- Michael Blaha, James Rumbaugh, *Object-Oriented Modeling and Design with UML, Second Edition*. Prentice Hall, 2005.
- Grady Booch, *Object-Oriented Analysis and Design with Applications, Second Edition.* Addison-Wesley, 1993.
- Ivar Jacobson, Magnus Christerson, Patrik Jonsson, Gunnar Overgaard, *Object-Oriented Software Engineering: A Use Case Driven Approach.* Addison-Wesley, 1992.

Information about the Rational Unified Process can be found in:

- Philippe Kruchten, *The Rational Unified Process: An Introduction, Third Edition.* Addison-Wesley, 2004.

The latest information about the UML can be found on the OMG Website at `www.omg.org`, where you can find the latest version of the UML standard.

There are many other books that describe UML and various development methods, in addition to the large number of books that describe software engineering practice in general.

Appendix A
UML NOTATION

A overview of the UML is discussed in Chapter 2.

The UML is a language for visualizing, specifying, constructing, and documenting the artifacts of a software-intensive system. As a language, the UML has a well-defined syntax and semantics. The most visible part of the UML's syntax is its graphical notation.

This appendix summarizes the elements of the UML notation.

Things

Structural Things

Structural things are the nouns of UML models. These include classes, interfaces, collaborations, use cases, active classes, components, and nodes.

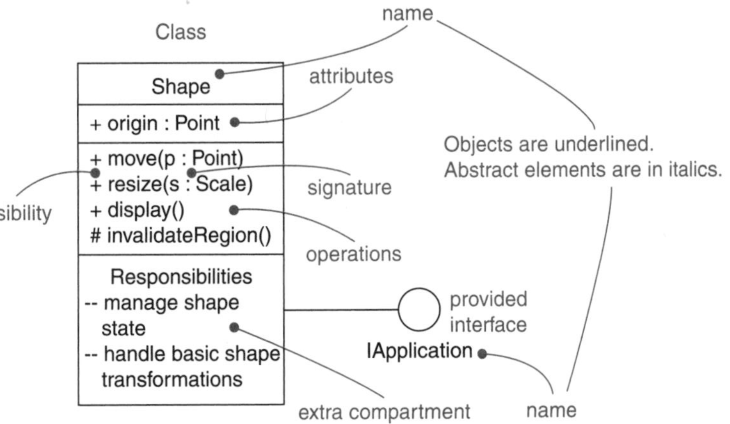

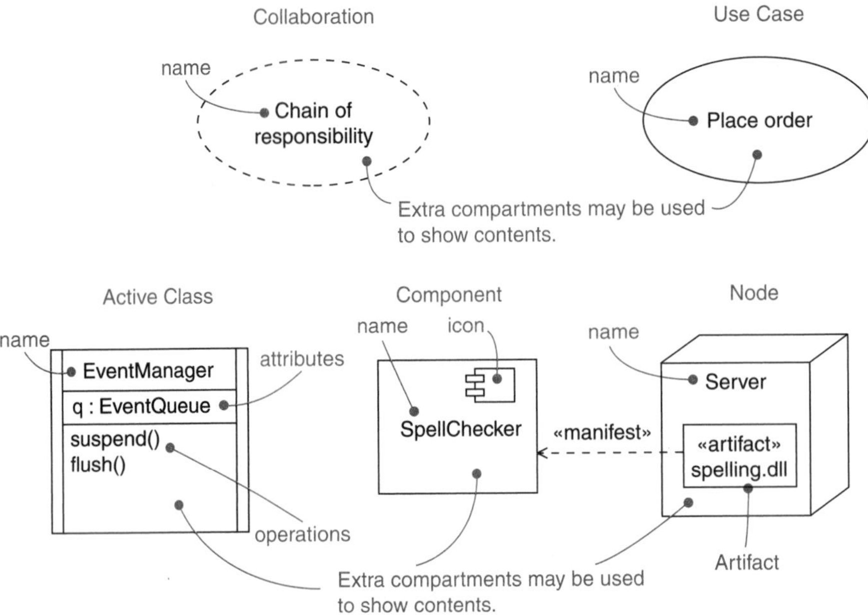

Behavioral Things

Behavioral things are the dynamic parts of UML models. These include interactions and state machines.

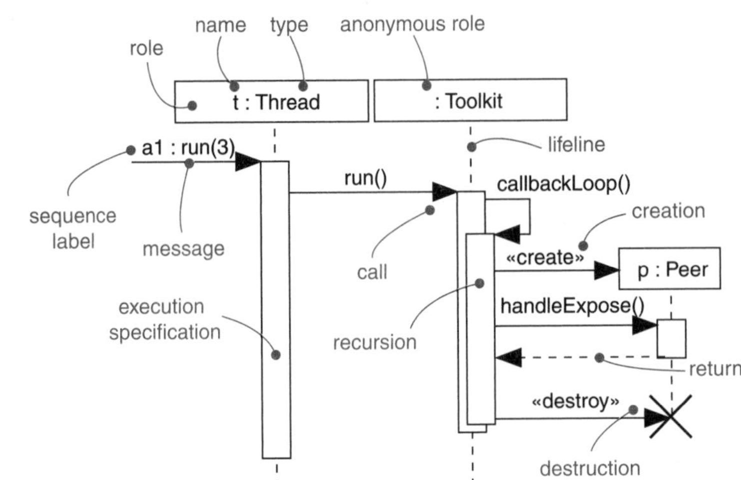

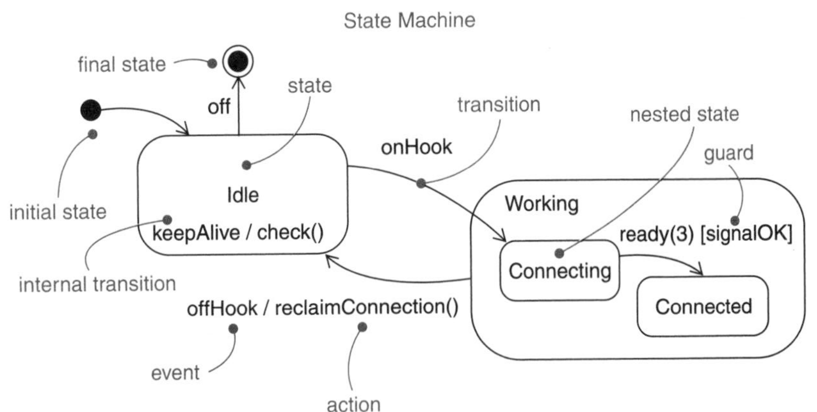

Grouping Things

Grouping things are the organizational parts of UML models. This includes packages.

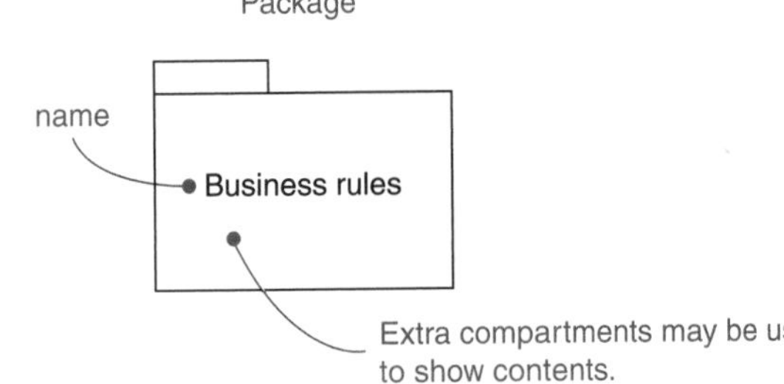

Annotational Things

Annotational things are the explanatory parts of UML models. This includes notes.

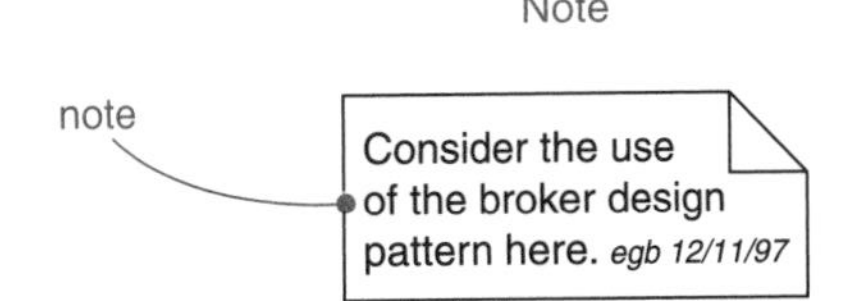

Relationships

Dependency

A dependency is a semantic relationship between two things in which a change to one thing (the independent thing) may affect the semantics of the other thing (the dependent thing).

Dependency

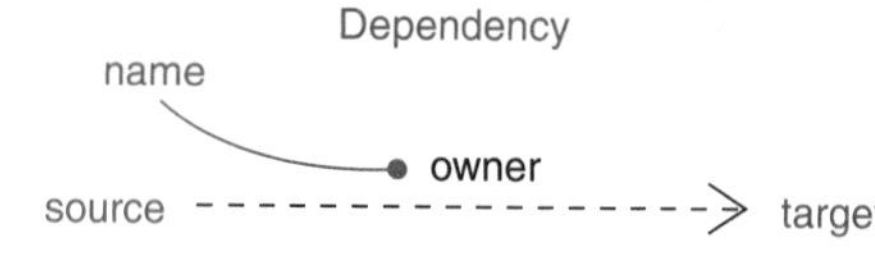

Association

An association is a structural relationship that describes a set of links; a link is a connection among objects.

Association

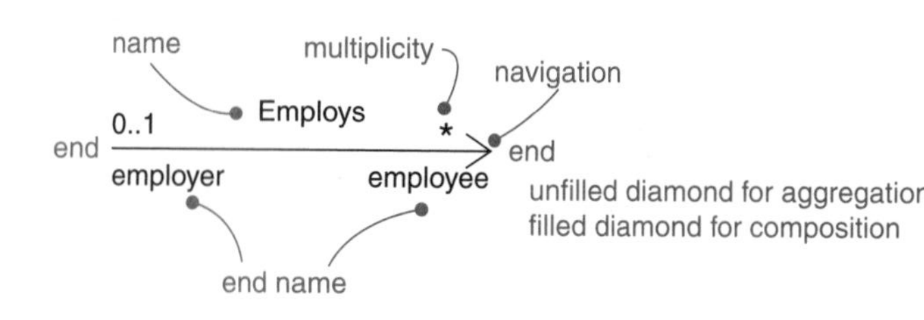

Generalization

Generalization is a specialization/generalization relationship in which objects of the specialized element (the child) are substitutable for objects of the generalized element (the parent).

Generalization

Extensibility

The UML provides three mechanisms for extending the language's syntax and semantics: stereotypes (which represent new modeling elements), tagged values (which represent new modeling attributes), and constraints (which represent new modeling semantics).

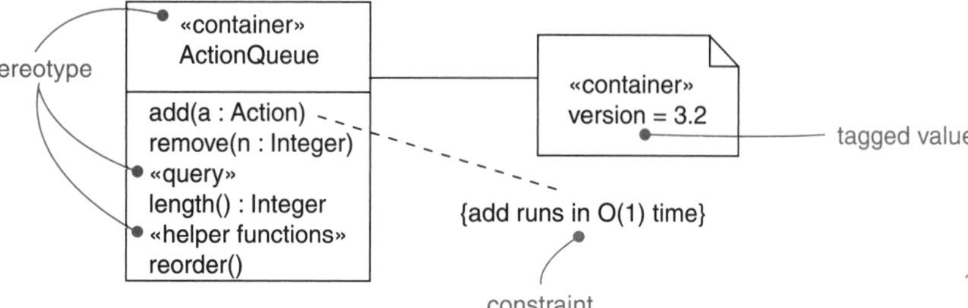

Diagrams

A diagram is the graphical presentation of a set of elements, most often rendered as a connected graph of vertices (things) and arcs (relationships). A diagram is a projection into a system. The UML includes thirteen such diagrams.

1. Class diagram — A structural diagram that shows a set of classes, interfaces, collaborations, and their relationships
2. Object diagram — A structural diagram that shows a set of objects and their relationships
3. Component diagram — A structural diagram that shows the external interfaces, including ports, and internal composition of a component
4. Composite structure diagram — A structural diagram that shows the external interfaces and internal composition of a structured class. In this book, we combine treatment of the composite structure diagram with component diagram.

5. Use case diagram	A behavioral diagram that shows a set of use cases and actors and their relationships
6. Sequence diagram	A behavioral diagram that shows an interaction, emphasizing the time ordering of messages
7. Communication diagram	A behavioral diagram that shows an interaction, emphasizing the structural organization of the objects that send and receive messages
8. State diagram	A behavioral diagram that shows a state machine, emphasizing the event-ordered behavior of an object
9. Activity diagram	A behavioral diagram that shows a computational process, emphasizing the flow from activity to activity
10. Deployment diagram	A structural diagram that shows the relationships among a set of nodes, artifacts, and manifested classes and components. In this book, we also specialize the modeling of artifacts as an artifact diagram.
11. Package diagram	A structural diagram that shows the organization of the model into packages
12. Timing diagram	A behavioral diagram that shows an interaction with messages at specific times. This is not covered in this book.
13. Interaction overview diagram	A behavioral diagram that combines aspects of activity diagrams and sequence diagrams. This is not covered in this book.

Hybrid diagram types are allowed; there is no strict separation among model elements.

Appendix B
RATIONAL UNIFIED PROCESS

A process is a set of partially ordered steps intended to reach a goal. In software engineering, your goal is to efficiently and predictably deliver a software product that meets the needs of your business.

The UML is largely process-independent, meaning that you can use it with a number of software engineering processes. The Rational Unified Process is one such life cycle approach that is especially well-suited to the UML. The goal of the Rational Unified Process is to enable the production of highest quality software that meets end-user needs within predictable schedules and budgets. The Rational Unified Process captures some of the best current software development practices in a form that is tailorable for a wide range of projects and organizations. The Rational Unified Process provides a disciplined approach on how to assign tasks and responsibilities within a software development organization while allowing the team to adapt to the changing needs of a project.

This appendix summarizes the elements of the Rational Unified Process.

Characteristics of the Process

The Rational Unified Process is an *iterative* process. For simple systems, it would seem perfectly feasible to sequentially define the whole problem, design the entire solution, build the software, and then test the end product. However, given the complexity and sophistication demanded of current systems, this linear approach to system development is unrealistic. An iterative approach advocates an increasing understanding of the problem through successive refinements and an incremental growth of an effective solution over multiple cycles. Built into the iterative approach is the flexibility to accommodate new requirements or tactical changes in business objectives. It also allows the project to identify and resolve risks sooner rather than later.

The Rational Unified Process's activities emphasize the creation and maintenance of *models* rather than paper documents. Models—especially those specified using the UML—provide semantically rich representations of the software system under development. They can be viewed in multiple ways, and the information represented can be instantaneously captured and controlled electronically. The rationale behind the Rational Unified Process's focus on models rather than paper documents is to minimize the overhead associated with generating and maintaining documents and to maximize the relevant information content.

Development under the Rational Unified Process is *architecture-centric*. The process focuses on the early development and baselining of a software architecture. Having a robust architecture in place facilitates parallel development, minimizes rework, and increases the probability of component reuse and eventual system maintainability. This architectural blueprint serves as a solid basis against which to plan and manage software component-based development.

Development activities under the Rational Unified Process are *use case–driven*. The Rational Unified Process places strong emphasis on building systems based on a thorough understanding of how the delivered system will be used. The notions of use cases and scenarios are used to align the process flow from requirements capture through testing and to provide traceable threads through development to the delivered system.

The Rational Unified Process supports *object-oriented techniques*. Rational Unified Process models supports the concepts of objects and classes and the relationships among them, and they use the UML as its common notation.

The Rational Unified Process is a *configurable* process. Although no single process is suitable for all software development organizations, the Rational Unified Process is tailorable and can be scaled to fit the needs of projects ranging from small software development teams to large development organizations. The Rational Unified Process is founded on a simple and clear process architecture that provides commonality across a family of processes, and yet can be varied to accommodate various situations. Contained in the Rational Unified Process is guidance about how to configure the process to suit the needs of an organization.

The Rational Unified Process encourages objective ongoing *quality control* and *risk management*. Quality assessment is built into the process, in all activities and involving all participants, using objective measurements and criteria. It is not treated as an afterthought or as a separate activity. Risk management is built into the process, so that risks to the success of the project are identified and attacked early in the development process, when there is time to react.

Phases and Iterations

A *phase* is the span of time between two major milestones of the process in which a well-defined set of objectives are met, artifacts are completed, and decisions are made whether to move into the next phase. As Figure B-1 illustrates, the Rational Unified Process consists of the following four phases:

1. Inception	Establish the vision, scope, and initial plan for the project
2. Elaboration	Design, implement, and test a sound architecture and complete the project plan
3. Construction	Build the first operational system version
4. Transition	Deliver the system to its end users

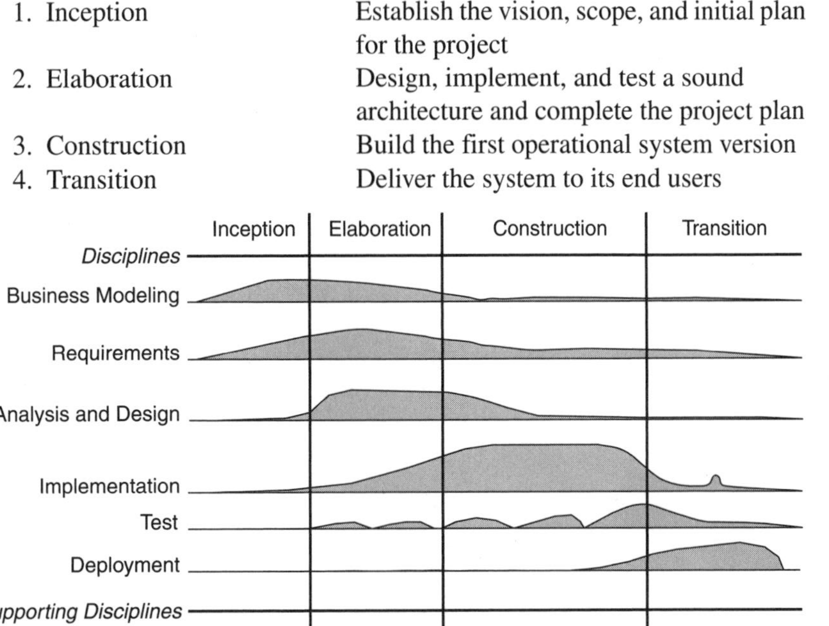

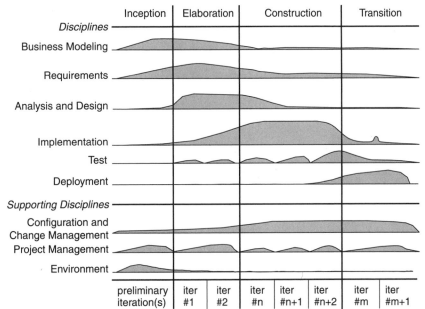

Figure B-1: The Software Development Life Cycle

Inception and elaboration focus more on the creative and engineering activities of the development life cycle, while construction and transition focus more on production activities.

Within each phase are a number of iterations. An *iteration* represents a complete development cycle, from requirements capture in analysis to implementation and testing, that results in an executable release. The release need not include a complete set of features for commercial release. Its purpose is to provide a solid basis for evaluation and testing as well as a uniform baseline for the next development cycle.

Each phase and iteration has some risk mitigation focus and concludes with a well-defined milestone. The milestone review provides a point in time to assess how well key goals have been met and whether the project needs to be restructured in any way to proceed.

Phases

Inception During the inception phase, you establish the vision for the system and delimit the project's scope. This includes the business case, the high-level requirements, and the initial project plan. The project plan includes success criteria, risk assessment, estimates of the resources needed, and a phase plan showing a schedule of major milestones. During inception, it is common to create an executable prototype that serves as a proof of concept.

This phase usually involves a handful of persons.

At the end of the inception phase, you examine the life cycle objectives of the project and decide whether to proceed with full-scale development.

Elaboration The goals of the elaboration phase are to analyze the problem domain, establish a sound architectural foundation, refine the project plan, and eliminate the highest risk elements of the project. Architectural decisions must be made with an understanding of the whole system. This implies that you describe most of the system's requirements. To verify the architecture, you implement a system that demonstrates the architectural choices and executes significant use cases.

This phase involves the system architect and the project manager as key players, as well as analysts, developers, testers, and others. Typically, elaboration involves a larger team than inception and requires more time.

At the end of the elaboration phase, you examine the detailed system objectives and scope, the choice of architecture, and the resolution of major risks, and decide whether to proceed with construction.

Construction During the construction phase, you iteratively and incrementally develop a complete product that is ready to transition to its user community. This implies describing the remaining requirements and acceptance criteria, fleshing out the design, and completing the implementation and test of the software.

This phase involves the system architect, the project manager, and the construction team leaders, as well as the full development and testing staff.

At the end of the construction phase, you decide whether the software, sites, and users are all ready to deploy the first operational version of the system.

Transition During the transition phase, you deploy the software to the user community. Note that you have had involvement with users throughout the project through demonstrations, workshops, and alpha and beta releases. Once the system has been put into the hands of its end users, issues often arise that require additional development to adjust the system, correct some undetected problems, or finish some features that have been postponed. This phase typically starts with a beta release of the system, which is then replaced with the production system.

Key team members for this phase include the project manager, testers, release specialists, marketers, and sales personnel. Note that the work of preparing for external release, marketing, and sales started much earlier in the project.

At the end of the transition phase, you decide whether the life cycle objectives of the project have been met and determine whether you should start another development cycle. This is also a point at which you wrap up the lessons learned on the project to improve your development process, which will be applied to the next project.

Iterations

Each phase in the Rational Unified Process can be further broken down into iterations. An iteration is a complete development loop resulting in a release (internal or external) of an executable product constituting a subset of the final product under development, which then is grown incrementally from iteration to iteration to become the final system. Each iteration goes through the various disciplines, although with a different emphasis on each discipline depending on the phase. During inception, the focus is on requirements capture. During elaboration, the focus turns toward analysis, design, and architecture implementation. In construction, detailed design, implementation, and testing are the central activities, and transition centers on deployment. Testing is important throughout.

Development Cycles

Going through the four major phases is called a development cycle, and it results in one software generation. The first pass through the four phases is called the initial development cycle. Unless the life of the product stops, an existing product will evolve into its next generation by repeating the same sequence of inception, elaboration, construction, and transition phases. This is the evolution of the system, so the development cycles after the initial development cycles are its evolution cycles.

Disciplines

The Rational Unified Process consists of nine disciplines.

1. Business modeling — Describes the structure and dynamics of the customer's organization
2. Requirements — Elicits requirements using a variety of approaches
3. Analysis and design — Describes the multiple architectural views
4. Implementation — Takes into account software development, unit test, and integration
5. Test — Describes scripts, test execution, and defect-tracking metrics
6. Deployment — Includes bill of materials, release notes, training, and other aspects of delivering an application.
7. Configuration management — Controls changes to and maintains the integrity of a project's artifacts and management activities
8. Project Management — Describes various strategies of working with an iterative process
9. Environment — Covers the necessary infrastructure required to develop a system

Captured within each discipline is a set of correlated artifacts and activities. An *artifact* is some document, report, or executable that is produced, manipulated, or consumed. An *activity* describes the tasks—thinking steps, performing steps, and reviewing steps—performed by workers to create or modify artifacts, together with the techniques and guidelines to perform the tasks, possibly including the use of tools to help automate some of the tasks.

Important connections among the artifacts are associated with certain of these disciplines. For example, the use case model generated during requirements capture is *realized by* the design model from the analysis and design discipline, *implemented by* the implementation model from the implementation discipline, and *verified by* the test model from the test discipline.

Artifacts

Each Rational Unified Process activity has associated artifacts, either required as an input or generated as an output. Some artifacts are used to direct input to subsequent activities, kept as reference resources on the project, or generated in a format as contractual deliverables.

Models

Modeling is discussed in Chapter 1.

Models are the most important kind of artifact in the Rational Unified Process. A model is a simplification of reality, created to better understand the system being created. In the Rational Unified Process, there are a number of models that collectively cover all the important decisions that go into visualizing, specifying, constructing, and documenting a software-intensive system.

Model	Description
1. Business use case model	Establishes an abstraction of the organization
2. Business analysis model	Establishes the context of the system
3. Use case model	Establishes the system's functional requirements
4. Analysis model (optional)	Establishes a conceptual design
5. Design model	Establishes the vocabulary of the problem and its solution
6. Data model (optional)	Establishes the representation of data for databases and other repositories
7. Deployment model	Establishes the hardware topology on which the system is executed as well as the system's concurrency and synchronization mechanisms
8. Implementation model	Establishes the parts used to assemble and release the physical system

Architecture is discussed in Chapter 2.

A view is a projection into a model. In the Rational Unified Process, the architecture of a system is captured in five interlocking views: design view, interaction view, deployment view, implementation view, and use case view.

Other Artifacts

The Rational Unified Process's artifacts are categorized as either management artifacts or technical artifacts. The Rational Unified Process's technical artifacts may be divided into four main sets.

1. Requirements set — Describes what the system must do
2. Analysis and design set — Describes how the system is to be constructed
3. Test set — Describes the approach by which the system is validated and verified
4. Implementation set — Describes the assembly of developed software components
5. Deployment set — Provides all the data for the deliverable configuration

Requirements Set This set groups all information describing what the system must do. This may comprise a use case model, a nonfunctional requirements model, a domain model, an analysis model, and other forms of expression of the user's needs, including but not limited to mock-ups, interface prototypes, regulatory constraints, and so on.

Design Set This set groups information describing how the system is to be constructed and captures decisions about how the system is to be built, taking into account all the constraints of time, budget, legacy, reuse, quality objectives, and so forth. This may comprise a design model, a test model, and other forms of expression of the system's nature, including but not limited to prototypes and executable architectures.

Test Set This set groups information about testing the system, including scripts, test cases, defect-tracking metrics, and acceptance criteria.

Implementation Set This set groups all information about the elements of the software that comprises the system, including but not limited to source code in various programming languages, configuration files, data files, software components, and so on, together with the information describing how to assemble the system.

Deployment Set This set groups all information about the way the software is actually packaged, shipped, installed, and run on the target environment.

GLOSSARY

abstract class A class that cannot be directly instantiated.

abstraction The essential characteristics of an entity that distinguish it from all other kinds of entities. An abstraction defines a boundary relative to the perspective of the viewer.

action An executable computation that results in a change in state of the system or the return of a value.

active class A class whose instances are active objects.

active object An object that owns a process or thread and can initiate control activity.

activity Behavior expressed as a set of actions connected by control and data flows.

activity diagram A diagram that shows the flow of control and data from activity to activity. Activity diagrams address the dynamic view of a system.

actor A coherent set of roles that users of use cases play when interacting with the use cases.

actual parameter A function or procedure argument.

adornment Detail from an element's specification added to its basic graphical notation.

aggregate A class that represents the "whole" in an aggregation relationship.

aggregation A special form of association that specifies a whole-part relationship between the aggregate (the whole) and a component (the part).

architecture The set of significant decisions about the organization of a software system, the selection of the structural elements and their interfaces by which the system is composed, together with their behavior as specified in the collaborations among those elements, the composition of these structural and behavioral elements into progressively larger subsystems, and the architectural style that guides this organization—these elements and their interfaces, their collaborations, and their composition. Software architecture is not only concerned with structure and behavior, but also with usage, functionality, performance, resilience, reuse, comprehensibility, economic and technology constraints and trade-offs, and aesthetic concerns.

architecture-centric In the context of the software development life cycle, a process that focuses on the early development and baselining of a software architecture, then uses the system's architecture as a primary artifact for conceptualizing, constructing, managing, and evolving the system under development.

argument A specific value corresponding to a parameter.

artifact A quantized piece of information that is used or produced by a software development process or an existing system.

association A structural relationship that describes a set of links, in which a link is a connection among objects; the semantic relationship between two or more classifiers that involves the connections among their instances.

association class A modeling element that has both association and class properties. An association class can be seen as an association that also has class properties or as a class that also has association properties.

association end The endpoint of an association, which connects that association to a classifier.

asynchronous action A request in which the sending object does not pause to wait for results.

attribute A named property of a classifier that describes a range of values that instances of the property may hold.

behavior A specification of an executable computation.

behavioral feature A dynamic feature of an element such as an operation.

binary association An association between two classes.

binding The creation of an element from a template by supplying arguments for the parameters of the template.

Boolean An enumeration whose values are true and false.

Boolean expression An expression that evaluates to a Boolean value.

cardinality The number of elements in a set.

child A subclass or other specialized element.

class A description of a set of objects that share the same attributes, operations, relationships, and semantics.

class diagram A diagram that shows a set of classes, interfaces, and collaborations and their relationships; class diagrams address the static design view of a system; a diagram that shows a collection of declarative (static) elements.

classifier A mechanism that describes structural and behavioral features. Classifiers include classes, interfaces, datatypes, signals, components, nodes, use cases, and subsystems.

client A classifier that requests service from another classifier.

collaboration A society of roles and other elements that work together to provide some cooperative behavior that's bigger than the sum of all its parts; the specification of how an element, such as a use case or an operation, is realized by a set of classifiers and associations playing specific roles and used in a specific way.

comment An annotation attached to an element or a collection of elements.

communication diagram An interaction diagram that emphasizes the structural organization of the objects that send and receive messages; a diagram that shows interactions organized around instances and their links to each other.

component A physical and replaceable part of a system that conforms to and provides the realization of a set of interfaces.

component diagram A diagram that shows the organization of and dependencies among a set of components; component diagrams address the static implementation view of a system.

composite A class that is related to one or more classes by a composition relationship.

composite state A state that consists of either concurrent substates or disjoint substates.

composition A form of aggregation with strong ownership and coincident lifetime of the parts by the whole; parts with nonfixed multiplicity may be created after the composite itself, but once created they live and die with it; such parts can also be explicitly removed before the death of the composite.

concrete class A class that can be directly instantiated.

concurrency The occurrence of two or more loci of execution during the same time interval. Concurrency can be achieved by interleaving or simultaneously executing two or more threads.

constraint An extension of the semantics of a UML element, allowing you to add new rules or modify existing ones.

container An object that exists to contain other objects and that provides operations to access or iterate over its contents.

containment hierarchy A namespace hierarchy consisting of elements and the aggregation relationships that exist between them.

context A set of related elements for a particular purpose, such as to specify an operation.

construction The third phase of the software development life cycle, in which the software is brought from an executable architectural baseline to the point at which it is ready to be transitioned to the user community.

datatype A type whose values have no identity. Datatypes include primitive built-in types (such as numbers and strings) as well as enumeration types (such as Boolean).

delegation The ability of an object to issue a message to another object in response to a message.

dependency A semantic relationship between two things in which a change to one thing (the independent thing) may affect the semantics of the other thing (the dependent thing).

deployment diagram A diagram that shows the configuration of run time processing nodes and the components that live on them; a deployment diagram addresses the static deployment view of a system.

deployment view The view of a system's architecture that encompasses the nodes that form the system's hardware topology on which the system executes; a deployment view addresses the distribution, delivery, and installation of the parts that make up the physical system.

derived element A model element that can be computed from another element, but that is shown for clarity or that is included for design purposes even though it adds no semantic information.

design view The view of a system's architecture that encompasses the classes, interfaces, and collaborations that form the vocabulary of the problem and its solution; a design view addresses the functional requirements of a system.

diagram The graphical presentation of a set of elements, most often rendered as a connected graph of vertices (things) and arcs (relationships).

domain An area of knowledge or activity characterized by a set of concepts and terminology understood by practitioners in that area.

dynamic classification A semantic variation of generalization in which an object may change type or role.

dynamic view An aspect of a system that emphasizes its behavior.

elaboration The second phase of the software development life cycle, in which the product vision and its architecture are defined.

element An atomic constituent of a model.

elision Modeling an element with certain of its parts hidden to simplify the view.

enumeration A list of named values used as the range of a particular attribute type.

event The specification of a significant occurrence that has a location in time and space; in the context of state machines, the occurrence of an event can trigger a state transition.

execution The running of a dynamic model.

export In the context of packages, to make an element visible outside its enclosing namespace.

expression A string that evaluates to a value of a particular type.

extensibility mechanism One of three mechanisms (stereotypes, tagged values, and constraints) that permit you to extend the UML in controlled ways.

feature A property, such as an operation or an attribute, that is encapsulated within another entity, such as an interface, a class, or a datatype.

fire To execute a state transition.

focus of control A symbol on a sequence diagram that shows the period of time during which an object is performing an action directly or through a subordinate operation.

formal parameter A parameter.

forward engineering The process of transforming a model into code through a mapping to a specific implementation language.

framework An architectural pattern that provides an extensible template for applications within a domain.

generalization A specialization/generalization relationship, in which objects of the specialized element (the child) are substitutable for objects of the generalized element (the parent).

guard condition A condition that must be satisfied to enable an associated transition to fire.

implementation A concrete realization of the contract declared by an interface; a definition of how something is constructed or computed.

implementation inheritance The inheritance of the implementation of a more general element; also includes inheritance of the interface.

implementation view The view of a system's architecture that encompasses the artifacts used to assemble and release the physical system; an implementation view addresses the configuration management of the system's releases, made up of somewhat independent artifacts that can be assembled in various ways to produce a running system.

import In the context of packages, a dependency that shows the package whose classes may be referenced within a given package (including packages recursively embedded within it) without supplying a qualified name.

inception The first phase of the software development life cycle, in which the seed idea for the development is brought to the point of being sufficiently well-founded to warrant entering into the elaboration phase.

incomplete Modeling an element with certain of its parts missing.

inconsistent Modeling an element for which the integrity of the model is not guaranteed.

incremental In the context of the software development life cycle, a process that involves the continuous integration of the system's architecture to produce releases, with each new release embodying incremental improvements over the other.

inheritance The mechanism by which more-specific elements incorporate the structure and behavior of more-general elements.

instance A concrete manifestation of an abstraction; an entity to which a set of operations can be applied and that has a state that stores the effects of the operations.

integrity How things properly and consistently relate to one another.

interaction A behavior that comprises a set of messages that are exchanged among a set of objects within a particular context to accomplish a purpose.

interaction diagram A diagram that shows an interaction, consisting of a set of objects and their relationships, including the messages that may be dispatched among them; interaction diagrams address the dynamic view of a system; a generic term that applies to several types of diagrams that emphasize object interactions, including communication diagrams and sequence diagrams. Activity diagrams are related but semantically distinct.

interaction view The view of a system's architecture that encompasses the objects, threads, and processes that form the system's concurrency and synchronization mechanisms, the set of activities, and the flow of messages, control, and data among them. The interaction view also addresses the performance, scalability, and throughput of the system.

iteration A distinct set of activities with a baseline plan and evaluation criteria that results in a release, either internal or external.

iterative In the context of the software development life cycle, a process that involves managing a stream of executable releases.

interface A collection of operations that are used to specify a service of a class or a component.

interface inheritance The inheritance of the interface of a more specific element; does not include inheritance of the implementation.

level of abstraction A place in a hierarchy of abstractions ranging from high levels of abstraction (very abstract) to low levels of abstraction (very concrete).

link A semantic connection among objects; an instance of an association.

link end An instance of an association end.

location The placement of an artifact on a node.

mechanism A design pattern that applies to a society of classes.

message A specification of a communication between objects that conveys information with the expectation that activity will ensue; the receipt of a message instance is normally considered an instance of an event.

metaclass A class whose instances are classes.

method The implementation of an operation.

model A simplification of reality, created to better understand the system being created; a semantically closed abstraction of a system.

multiple classification A semantic variation of generalization in which an object may belong directly to more than one class.

multiple inheritance A semantic variation of generalization in which a child may have more than one parent.

multiplicity A specification of the range of allowable cardinalities that a set may assume.

n-ary association An association among three or more classes.

name What you call a thing, relationship, or diagram; a string used to identify an element.

namespace A scope in which names may be defined and used; within a namespace, each name denotes a unique element.

node A physical element that exists at run time and that represents a computational resource, generally having at least some memory and often having processing capability.

nonorthogonal substate A substate that cannot be held simultaneously with other substates contained in the same composite state.

note A graphic symbol for rendering constraints or comments attached to an element or a collection of elements.

object A concrete manifestation of an abstraction; an entity with a well-defined boundary and identity that encapsulates state and behavior; an instance of a class.

Object Constraint Language (OCL) A formal language used to express side effect–free constraints.

object diagram A diagram that shows a set of objects and their relationships at a point in time; object diagrams address the static design view or static process view of a system.

object lifeline A line in a sequence diagram that represents the existence of an object over a period of time.

occurrence An instance of an event, including a location in space and time and a context. An occurrence may trigger a state machine transition.

operation The implementation of a service that can be requested from any object of the class in order to affect behavior.

orthogonal substate An orthogonal substate that can be held simultaneously with other substates contained in the same composite state.

package A general-purpose container for organizing elements into groups.

parameter The specification of a variable that can be changed, passed, or returned.

parameterized element The descriptor for an element with one or more unbound parameters.

parent A superclass or other more general element.

persistent object An object that exists after the process or thread that created it has ceased to exist.

pattern A common solution to a common problem in a given context.

phase The span of time between two major milestones of the development process during which a well-defined set of objectives are met, artifacts are completed, and decisions are made whether to move into the next phase.

postcondition A constraint that must be true at the completion of execution of an operation.

precondition A constraint that must be true when an operation is invoked.

primitive type A basic type, such as an integer or a string.

process A heavyweight flow of control that can execute concurrently with other processes.

product The artifacts of development, such as models, code, documentation, and work plans.

projection A mapping from a set to a subset of it.

property A named value denoting a characteristic of an element.

pseudostate A node in a state machine that has the form of a state but doesn't behave as a state; pseudostates include initial, final, and history nodes.

qualifier An association attribute whose values partition the set of objects related to an object across an association.

realization A semantic relationships between classifiers, in which one classifier specifies a contract that another classifier guarantees to carry out.

receive The handling of a message instance passed from a sender object.

receiver The object to which a message is sent.

refinement A relationship that represents a fuller specification of something that has already been specified at a certain level of detail.

relationship A semantic connection among elements.

release A relatively complete and consistent set of artifacts delivered to an internal or external user; the delivery of such a set.

requirement A desired feature, property, or behavior of a system.

responsibility A contract or obligation of a type or class.

reverse engineering The process of transforming code into a model through a mapping from a specific implementation language.

risk-driven In the context of the software development life cycle, a process in which each new release is focused on attacking and reducing the most significant risks to the success of the project.

role A structural participant within a particular context.

scenario A specific sequence of actions that illustrates behavior.

scope The context that gives meaning to a name.

send The passing of a message instance from a sender object to a receiver object.

sender The object from which a message is sent.

sequence diagram An interaction diagram that emphasizes the time ordering of messages.

signal The specification of an asynchronous stimulus communicated between instances.

signature The name and parameters of an operation.

single inheritance A semantic variation of generalization in which a child may have only one parent.

specification A textual statement of the syntax and semantics of a specific building block; a declarative description of what something is or does.

state A condition or situation during the life of an object during which it satisfies some condition, performs some activity, or waits for some event.

state diagram A diagram that shows a state machine; state diagrams address the dynamic view of a system.

state machine A behavior that specifies the sequences of states an object goes through during its lifetime in response to events, together with its responses to those events.

static classification A semantic variation of generalization in which an object may not change type and may not change role.

static view An aspect of a system that emphasizes its structure.

stereotype An extension of the vocabulary of the UML that allows you to create new kinds of building blocks derived from existing ones but that are specific to your problem.

stimulus An operation or a signal.

string A sequence of text characters.

structural feature A static feature of an element.

subclass In a generalization relationship, the child, which is the specialization of another class.

substate A state that is part of a composite state.

subsystem A grouping of elements of which some constitute a specification of the behavior offered by the other contained elements.

superclass In a generalization relationship, the parent, which is the generalization of another class.

supplier A type, class, or component that provides services that can be invoked by others.

swimlane A partition on a sequence diagram for organizing responsibilities for actions.

synchronous call A request in which the sending object pauses to wait for a reply.

system A set of elements organized to accomplish a specific purpose and described by a set of models, possibly from different viewpoints. A system is often decomposed into a set of subsystems.

tagged value An extension of the properties of a UML stereotype, which allows you to create new information in the specification of an element bearing that stereotype.

template A parameterized element.

task A single path of execution through a program, a dynamic model, or some other representation of control flow; a thread or a process.

thread A lightweight flow of control that can execute concurrently with other threads in the same process.

time A value representing an absolute or relative moment.

time event An event that denotes the time elapsed since the current state was entered.

time expression An expression that evaluates to an absolute or relative value of time.

timing constraint A semantic statement about the relative or absolute value of time or duration.

timing mark A denotation for the time at which an event occurs.

trace A dependency that indicates an historical or process relationship between two elements that represent the same concept, without rules for deriving one from the other.

transient object An object that exists only during the execution of the thread or process that created it.

transition The fourth phase of the software development life cycle, in which the software is turned into the hands of the user community; a relationship between two states indicating that an object in the first state will perform certain actions and enter the second state when a specified event occurs and conditions are satisfied.

type The relationship between an element and its classification.

type expression An expression that evaluates to a reference to one or more classifiers.

UML The Unified Modeling Language, a language for visualizing, specifying, constructing, and documenting the artifacts of a software-intensive system.

usage A dependency in which one element (the client) requires the presence of another element (the supplier) for its correct functioning or implementation.

use case A description of a set of sequences of actions, including variants, that a system performs that yields an observable result of value to an actor.

use case diagram A diagram that shows a set of use cases and actors and their relationships; use case diagrams address the static use case view of a system.

use case–driven In the context of the software development life cycle, a process in which use cases are used as a primary artifact for establishing the desired behavior of the system, for verifying and validating the system's architecture, for testing, and for communicating among the stakeholders of the project.

use case view The view of a system's architecture that encompasses the use cases that describe the behavior of the system as seen by its end users, analysts, and testers.

value An element of a type domain.

view A projection into a model, which is seen from a given perspective or vantage point and omits entities that are not relevant to this perspective.

visibility How a name can be seen and used by others.

INDEX

Index

D

N

O

Index

Q

R

S

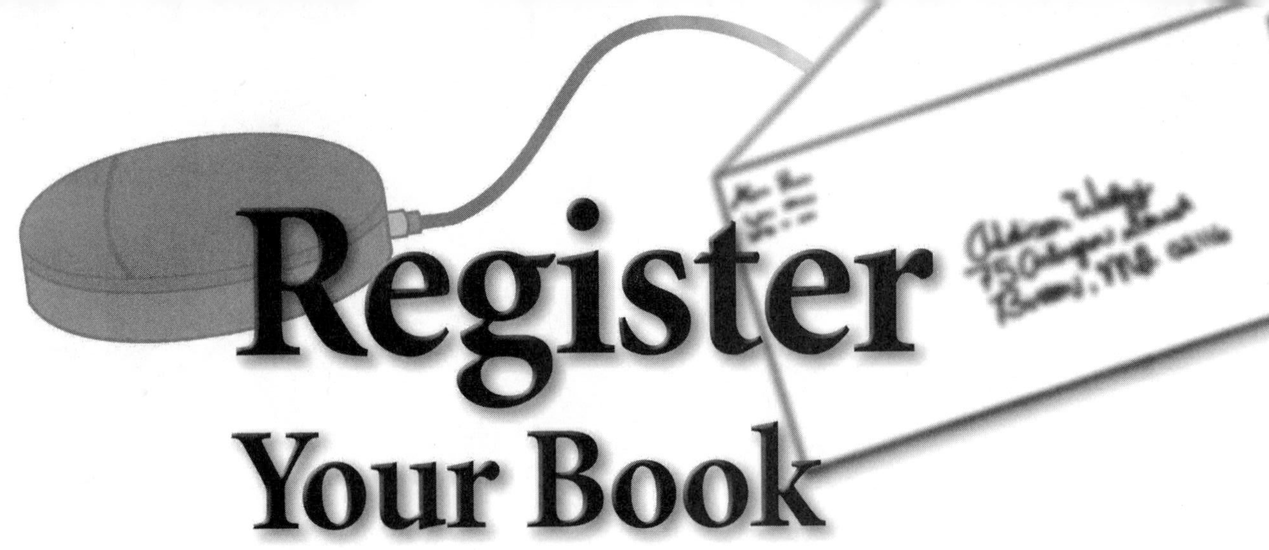

Addison-Wesley